GW00470098

Holocaust and Rescue

Holocaust and Rescue

Impotent or Indifferent?
Anglo-Jewry 1938–1945

Pamela Shatzkes
Department of International History
London School of Economics and Political Science

First published 2002 by
PALGRAVE
Houndmills, Basingstoke, Hampshire RG21 6XS and
175 Fifth Avenue, New York, N.Y. 10010
Companies and representatives throughout the world

PALGRAVE is the new global academic imprint of
St. Martin's Press LLC Scholarly and Reference Division and
Palgrave Publishers Ltd (formerly Macmillan Press Ltd).

ISBN 0–333–96039–4

This book is printed on paper suitable for recycling and made from fully managed and sustained forest sources.

A catalogue record for this book is available from the British Library.

Library of Congress Cataloging-in-Publication Data

Shatzkes, Pamela, 1949–
    Holocaust and rescue: impotent or indifferent? : Anglo-Jewry 1938–1945 / Pamela Shatzkes.
        p. cm.
    Includes bibliographical references (p.) and index.
    ISBN 0-333-96039-4
        1. Jews—Great Britain—Attitudes. 2. Jews—Great Britain—Politics and government—20th century. 3. World War, 1939–1945—Jews—Rescue—Great Britain. 4. Holocaust, Jewish (1939–1945)—Public opinion. 5. Public opinion—Great Britain. I. Title.

DS135.E5 S5 2002
940.53'18—dc21   2001056116

10 9 8 7 6 5 4 3 2
11 10 09 08 07 06 05 04 03 02

Printed and bound in Great Britain by
Antony Rowe Ltd, Chippenham, Wiltshire

For my father
Harry David Greenman (1904–1984)

Contents

List of Figures

Abbreviations

AIWO	Agudat Israel World Organisation
AJA	Anglo-Jewish Association
AJAC	American Jewish Archives, Cincinnati
Board	Board of Deputies of British Jews
CBF	Central British Fund for German Jewry
CBFRR	Central British Fund for Relief and Rehabilitation
CCJR	Central Committee for Jewish Refugees
CGJ	Council for German Jewry
COBSRA	Council of British Societies for Relief Abroad
CRREC	Chief Rabbi's Religious Emergency Council
FAC	Foreign Affairs Committee
GJAC	German Jewish Aid Committee
ICA	Jewish Colonisation Association
ICRC	International Committee of the Red Cross
IGCR	Inter-Governmental Committee on Refugees
JC	Jewish Chronicle
JCRA	Jewish Committee for Relief Abroad
JDC	American Jewish Joint Distribution Committee
JFC	Joint Foreign Committee
JRC	Jewish Refugees Committee
JTA	Jewish Telegraphic Agency
JUS	*Juedische Unterstuetzungsstelle für das Gouvernement General*
RJCC	Refugee Joint Consultative Committee
UNRRA	United Nations Relief and Rehabilitation
WJC	World Jewish Congress
WRB	War Refugee Board

Preface

The idea for this book originated some years ago in a conversation with David Bankier of the Hebrew University, Jerusalem, who made me aware that very little scholarly work had been done on the response of Jews in the free world to the plight of European Jewry in Nazi-occupied Europe and in particular on the role of refugee organisations during the Second World War.

When I began to research this subject, I discovered that the work of Anglo-Jewish refugee organisations in facilitating the arrival of over 50,000 refugees in Britain between 1933 and 1939 had been variously chronicled as a model of charitable endeavour and a half-hearted effort cramped by insecurity and self-interest. More consistently, scholars have argued that Anglo-Jewry failed to respond to the catastrophe of the war years with the resolution and vigour that might have saved more lives. There was hardly any comprehensive study of the Anglo-Jewish organisations; most of the research was focused on government policy towards refugees and its dealings with the organisations. The picture was sweepingly negative. From the start, I have endeavoured to approach this subject with no preconceived opinion regarding the response of Anglo-Jewry to the Holocaust. Unlike much of the literature on Anglo-Jewry during this period, this book tries to eschew both the didactic and speculative approaches to historical interpretation. Instead of attempting to apportion blame or to answer hypothetical questions of responsibility, my intention has been to offer an evaluation based on the evidence available. I have examined the quality and scope of rescue and relief work, both of the organisations and individuals. What was done, rather than what should have been done, has been the main focus of attention. As a result, I have come to a radically different conclusion regarding the role of the Anglo-Jewish leadership and its organisations.

This book is based on my PhD thesis, which was funded by the British Academy, to which I wish to express my sincere gratitude for both a three-year studentship and additional funding for research trips to America and Israel. In addition, the British Academy has recently granted me additional funding for the project of writing this book. Thanks are also due to the Central Research Fund,

London, and to the Memorial Foundation for Jewish Culture, New York, for their generosity, which enabled me to carry out my original research.

I am grateful to the staff of the various libraries and institutions which allowed me to examine their collections and offered me their assistance. In particular, the Central Zionist Archives (Jerusalem), the Wiener Library (Tel Aviv), Yad Vashem (Jerusalem), the Public Record Office (Kew, London), the Board of Deputies of British Jews archives held at the London Metropolitan Archives (London), the Anglo-Jewish Archives held at the Parkes library (Southampton), the Rothschild Archives (London), the Institute of Contemporary History and Wiener Library (London), the Agudat Israel World Organisation (New York), the American Joint Distribution Committee (New York) and the American Jewish Archives (Cincinnati).

A number of private collections were made available to me. Victor, Simon and Joe Goodman generously allowed me to consult material in their private possession, as did Jonathan Schonfeld; they also shared with me recollections of their respective fathers, Harry and Solomon, and of their work for European Jewry. Joseph Munk made some of the Schonfeld paper available to me when they were still housed in the basement of University College London before being transferred to the Parkes Library. David Massell, the Board of Deputies' archivist, granted me access to the papers when they were still at Woburn House. Amy Gottlieb made the Central British Fund files available to me as well as giving of her time and sharing some valuable memories of the period, including her time working with the Jewish Relief Units. I would also like to thank all those whom I was able to interview, for their time and helpfulness. Their names appear in my bibliography at the end of the book.

I wish to express my appreciation for the interest, support and continuous encouragement, as well as the wealth of insight, of my first PhD supervisor at the London School of Economics and Political Science, Donald Cameron Watt; of Michael Burleigh, who guided and inspired me through the next stage of my research; of John Kent, who encouraged me to complete it; and of Anita Prazmowska for her valued help in the final stages prior to completion of my PhD and her encouragement to have this work published. My examiners, Bernard Wasserstein and Richard Overy, gave valuable comments and suggestions, for which I am most grateful. I was also privileged to share my interest in the subject with various scholars, including, among others, Geoffrey Alderman, Richard Bolchover,

David Cesarani, John Fox, David Kranzler, Tony Kushner, Louise London, Bill Rubenstein and Meir Sompolinsky. Although my views often differ from theirs, they all expressed generous interest in my work.

Finally, a personal thanks to my many friends both at the London School of Economics and Political Science and to those abroad and at home, for their constant encouragement and willingness to share my interest. A special thanks goes to Sharon Footerman, who patiently read through the typescript and offered constructive criticism and advice. I am grateful to my family who have provided continuing support for my endeavours over the years. My greatest debt of gratitude is due to my husband Jerry, always enthusiastic and encouraging, who never doubted that one day I would finish.

Introduction

Since the pioneering study by Arthur D. Morse in 1967, many scholars have analysed the response of the 'bystander' nations to the plight of Jews in Nazi Europe. Historians specialising in the United States' response to the Holocaust have largely endorsed Morse's contention that the attitude of the Allied nations was one of indifference and perhaps even of complicity in the 'Final Solution' of the Jewish question. This view is based on what historians see as the Allies' wilful restrictions and apathetic rescue efforts.[1]

An important element in the evaluation of the 'bystander' nations and a partial explanation for their relative inaction has been held to be the failure of their organised Jewish communities to exert pressure on their governments. Some historians maintain that the Jews of the free world must, to some degree, share with the Allied governments the burden of guilt for failing to prevent the destruction of European Jewry. The issue has always been highly sensitive and contentious within Jewish communities themselves. It was first raised during the war, when accusations were levelled by Jewish leaders in Nazi Europe, as well as by fringe Jewish groups in the free world, at 'world' Jewry, for failing to speak out with necessary force.[2] This criticism was based on the premise that 'world' Jewry was capable of such action; little attention was given to the political powerlessness of Jewish communities world-wide during the 1930s and 1940s.[3]

The literature up to the 1970s centred for the most part on American Jewry, for whose negative response disunity, insecurity, misplaced priorities and fear of anti-Semitism have been held largely responsible.[4] Historians hardly addressed the subject of Anglo-Jewry until this point and then only in broadly sympathetic terms. Prior to

1

this, the one study specifically devoted to the work of the Anglo-Jewish refugee organisations was Norman Bentwich's *They Found Refuge* (1956), written for the Tercentenary of Jewish resettlement in England. Bentwich, who was heavily involved in refugee work, generously praised the organisations, in particular the Central British Fund (CBF). He believed that Anglo-Jewry did everything possible, that most refugees who came to Britain were satisfied with their treatment by the refugee organisations and that the conduct of individuals such as Otto Schiff was exemplary.[5]

The pendulum began to swing from almost unqualified praise for Anglo-Jewry's efforts to a more balanced, but still sympathetic view, typified by A.J. Sherman, whose *Island Refuge* (1973), based on then newly released archives, concentrates mainly on the government's pre-war record in assisting refugees from Nazi Germany. He finds it to be 'comparatively compassionate, even generous' compared with that of the United States and other countries.[6] Sherman refers only indirectly to the role of the refugee organisations, but praises their efforts in contrast to those of their American counterparts. He argues that government records show Anglo-Jewry to have demonstrated true concern for the refugees. But Sherman also observes that the socio-economic circumstances of the pre-war period inevitably gave Anglo-Jewry cause for concern about 'anti-Jewish agitation'.[7]

Bernard Wasserstein's *Britain and the Jews of Europe 1939–1945* (1979), which focuses on the response of the British government, finds 'an ocean of bureaucratic indifference and lack of concern', particularly with regard to Britain's Palestine policy. Wasserstein is sympathetic and even positive about the efforts made by the Anglo-Jewish leadership in the context of the political difficulties of the period.[8] Elsewhere, he addresses the issue directly. For the pre-war period, he maintains that without the leadership's formal guarantee of 1933 that no refugee would become a charge on public funds, 'it is very doubtful if the British Government would have admitted such substantial numbers at a time of high unemployment and considerable public anti-semitism'.[9] For the war years, he concludes that 'in its overall results the Jewish campaign to influence the British (and American) governments . . . must be judged a failure – probably an inevitable one'. However, 'the campaign's failure is no reason for forgetting that it was waged'. He rejects the 'myth' that Jews in the free world were silent and maintains that both individuals and organisations 'bombarded Government offices throughout the war with urgent pleas for effective measures to facilitate Jewish rescue and relief'.[10]

The release of these government records stimulated research on British policy towards refugees. Concurrently, the passage of the various Immigration Acts, race relations legislation and the debate surrounding Commonwealth immigration in the 1970s into the 1980s provoked scholarly curiosity about immigration, minorities, racism and Fascism. The waves of Jewish immigration at the turn of the century and in the 1930s became topics of new interest. As a result, in the late 1980s, a new school of British historians began to reappraise the role of the British government as well as that of Anglo-Jewry. The pendulum now swung sharply in the direction of adverse criticism. It has been plausibly suggested that these historians were reacting to the political and economic climate of the day, from a left-wing and anti-establishment stance.[11] It may be added that they seem imbued with a post-Holocaust conception of anti-Semitism as a ubiquitous and homogeneous social phenomenon, the mainspring of historical events and the key to understanding them. For whatever reason, the British revisionists have tended to follow the trend of those American historians who have attacked their Jewish communities for abjectly failing to respond vigorously to the European Jewish catastrophe.

Much of the revisionists' work on Jewish immigration has focused on the earlier period of mass immigration (1880–1914) and explored the Jewish community's negative attitude towards East European Jews. Some historians have shown how communal leaders failed to defend open immigration because they feared that an unregulated influx of alien Jews would endanger their own security.[12] In the course of examining anti-Semitism and British immigration policy in the 1930s, others have drawn similar conclusions about the reaction of Anglo-Jewry to refugees from the Third Reich. They are deeply critical of the leadership's motives and alleged inaction on behalf of European Jewry. In *The Persistence of Prejudice* (1989), Tony Kushner argues that the Board of Deputies of British Jews (Board), the official body representing Anglo-Jewry, failed to offer a serious challenge to government policy on the rescue of European Jewry, due to its own insecurities and fears of anti-Semitism.[13] While Kushner used government documents and the social survey *Mass Observation*, he was unable to consult the archives of the Central British Fund, the main Anglo-Jewish funding agency, these having only recently been opened for research work. Further, he draws only briefly on the Board's files. Kushner saw anti-Semitism as responsible for Britain's restrictive refugee policy. Since then, however, he has modified his position.[14] In *The Holocaust and the Liberal Imagi-nation* (1994), he attempts to explain the failure of the democracies to combat the Holocaust as a 'failure of state and society to solve the contradictions and ambiguities of liberalism'.[15]

Louise London, who has analysed immigration policy, maintains that Jewish communal leaders shared governmental unwillingness to augment the Jewish population, out of anxiety about their own security and believed, like the government, that large-scale immi-gration would exacerbate anti-Semitism. This conviction, coupled with the enormous demands on their charity and, London claims unconvincingly, bolstered by their own social prejudices, made Anglo-Jewish leaders seek controls on both the 'quality and quantity of Jews entering Britain', leading to 'agonised debate about priorities within Britain's Jewish community'. London admits that, despite financial and administrative constraints, the organisations 'played the key role in underwriting and facilitating the pre-war admission of Jews', but declines to explain how unlimited numbers of refugees could have been supported by organisations on the brink of bankruptcy.[16]

Richard Bolchover, in *British Jewry and the Holocaust* (1993), is among the first revisionist historians to have examined Anglo-Jewish responses to the Holocaust and attempted to answer the conten-tious question why the Holocaust, although the supreme crisis facing western Jewry, was marginalised by British Jewry. (This, of course, assumes what has not yet been conclusively established, namely that the Holocaust was indeed marginalised by British Jewry.) Bolchover points to issues that preoccupied the community during the war years, particularly internal friction and fear of increased domestic anti-Semitism, together with contending priorities such as Zionism. He concludes that Jews 'were hamstrung by the political philosophy of emancipation and their belief that they were bound by a contract with British society that determined how they could behave'. In consequence, Anglo-Jewish political strategy was to maintain a low profile and shun any suggestion of Jewish autonomy. Bolchover's highly critical work is narrowly focused on Jewish com-munal attitudes and values and barely considers the practical activities of rescue and relief. Moreover, although providing some insight into the mindset of the established leadership, his work focuses exclusively on public debates, as reported in the *Jewish Chronicle*, on which he relies heavily, as well as on mainly secondary sources, without balancing consideration of events enacted *in camera*.[17]

Geoffrey Alderman, in *Modern British Jewry* (1992), devotes only one chapter to the subject. Nevertheless, he is equally sweeping in his criticism of the Anglo-Jewish leadership, emphasising how 'communal policy resulted and was designed to result in the admission into Britain of a minimum number of Jews . . . from a particular social and economic background and of a particular age'. Alderman accuses Anglo-Jewry of passivity and of seeking to buttress its own precarious security by assertions of loyalty which amounted to a betrayal of European Jewry.[18] Both Alderman and Bolchover argue that in contrast to the pusillanimous response of mainstream Anglo-Jewry, the only really determined efforts to save European Jewry during the war years emanated from the World Jewish Congress, strictly orthodox Jews and certain marginal or 'non-establishment' figures such as Rabbi Dr Solomon Schonfeld. Bolchover adds Revisionist Zionists, socialists, academics and intellectuals to this small list.[19]

This book seeks to overturn the current consensus on both the pre-war and war periods. It is widely held that Anglo-Jewry was suspicious and resentful of the rising tide of immigration from Germany and Austria during the 1930s, partly due to fear of an upsurge in anti-Semitism, and was less than helpful in facilitating the arrival of refugees from Hitler's Europe. A re-examination of the extant evidence and the discovery of new sources provide convincing proof that rather than being insecure and pusillanimous, Anglo-Jewry was a confident, well-integrated community which tackled the escalating problems of refugee immigration in the 1930s with compassion, common sense and an administrative expertise born of a long tradition of communal charity. Its achievement is all the more remarkable measured against the scale of the disaster, the constraints of government immigration policy regulations and the organisations' own chronic lack of funds. A new, clearer and more complex picture is presented, challenging previous writers on the subject.

While some, like Bolchover, believe that the Anglo-Jewish organisations turned a blind eye to the mounting evidence of the plight of European Jewry during the war, there is compelling new material to show that the Anglo-Jewish leadership pressed the government on numerous occasions to act to save lives. Yet Anglo-Jewry was unable to convince the government of this imperative. The annihilation of European Jewry was a central German war aim; preventing it was not an Allied war aim; as a result, Anglo-Jewish efforts were considered a hindrance – an irritant to government officials who consistently refused to divert resources from the primary goal of achieving the speediest possible victory.

Bernard Wasserstein's warning that, despite its failure, we should not forget that the effort was made,[20] receives full consideration in this study. An extraordinary tale of resilience against hopeless odds emerges. Anglo-Jewry (or more accurately, European Jewry) was singularly unfortunate in that the most pressing crises in the European Jewish tragedy coincided with the moments of strongest pressure on the British and Allied governments, so that the greatest importunity of the British Jewish organisations always seemed to occur when it was most unlikely to meet with success. For example, the news of the Final Solution was confirmed in the winter of 1942, coinciding with the Allied invasion of North Africa; the Hungarian deportations were taking place at the time D-day in the summer of 1944. Such unfortunate 'coincidences' illustrate how the outcome of interventions depended not on simple, two-way interactions but on a complex interplay of wide-scale political, military and economic forces.

The official wartime leadership comprised stolid, worthy individuals such as Professor Selig Brodetsky, President of the Board, the representative body of Anglo-Jewry. An academic, Brodetsky failed to grasp the diplomatic arts of shift and stratagem. Misreading the urbane language of his governmental contacts, he doggedly pursued aims such as insisting that the doors of Palestine be opened, which were unrealistic at the time. Brodetsky, and others, lacked the flexibility to manoeuvre in line with the shifting opportunities of the times, preferring to operate within the rigid parameters of his Zionist ideology and blind to the dictum that politics is the art of the possible. Nevertheless, this stolid determination of the Anglo-Jewish organisations, in the face of bureaucratic indifference and buck-passing, is given careful consideration.

Unlike most previous literature on the record of Anglo-Jewry during this period, this book eschews both the didactic and speculative approaches to historical interpretation. Instead of attempting to apportion blame or to answer hypothetical questions about responsibility, it offers an evaluation based on new and original evidence. The book examines the quality and scope of rescue and relief work, both of organisations and individuals. The argument advanced here represents a major qualification of William D. Rubinstein's thesis in his recent work *The Myth of Rescue: Why the Democracies Could Not Have Saved More Jews from the Nazis* (1997), which claims that 'few Jews who perished could have been saved by any action of the Allies'. Yet it was not and could not have been obvious at the time that all efforts were doomed (if indeed they were) and Rubinstein's dismissal of these efforts as 'fatuous and risible', on the grounds that the Jews of Europe were 'prisoners trapped behind Nazi lines', is simplistic. Notwithstanding Hitler's determination to destroy the 'biological basis of Jewry in Europe', exchange and ransom schemes were among various rescue propositions mooted throughout the war; the real stumbling block to even modest rescue schemes was the Allied insistence that no negotiation with the enemy should undermine the principal war aim of unconditional surrender. This principle effectively rendered most of Anglo-Jewry's rescue efforts abortive.

It is further argued that Anglo-Jewry's efforts, both before and during the war, were strenuous and unremitting, but were more successful during the pre-war period. Anglo-Jewry was called upon to play different roles for which it was not equally qualified. In the pre-war years, its roles were primarily fund-raising and administrative, roles for which it was well prepared by a long history of charitable endeavour. Moreover, it had government approval and support. With the outbreak of war, it was no longer required to assist in the selection and admission of refugees. Instead, it was called upon to exert pressure to facilitate rescue on a government engaged in global warfare, an unprecedented role for which it was politically and diplomatically inept.

This book also takes issue with the claim that marginal efforts such as Schonfeld's impugn the integrity and effectiveness of the mainstream organisations, particularly the Board. It shows that Alderman and others distort Schonfeld's genuine achievement by invidiously contrasting it as an 'exception' to the apathy of the Anglo-Jewish mainstream.[21] Schonfeld was a maverick, whose objectives were comparatively modest in scope and his achievements were due largely to superior astuteness in negotiating within and around the parameters of government policy.[22] He also took a more cavalier attitude to official restraints and regulations, something the mainstream organisations could not afford to do.

Besides utilising government records, which provide valuable insight into official responses to Anglo-Jewry's efforts, the book relies heavily on the organisations' and individuals' own documents. These include the files of the Board of Deputies, the Central British Fund, the British Section of the World Jewish Congress, the Agudat Israel and the Schonfeld and Goodman papers. Some of this material has only recently become accessible. The book does not draw on refugee testimony, as it is primarily concerned with the actions of the leadership vis-à-vis the British authorities. The refugees themselves, of course, had no say in these high-level discussions.

The emphasis is on what was actually attempted and whether it was reasonable in principle, in the light of what was known at the time. The book does not debate whether efforts were feasible in the light of what is known today,[23] nor does it aim to establish what 'ought' to have been done. Its purpose is rather to define and analyse the character and calibre of the Anglo-Jewish leadership and community, to consider the efforts made and explain why most of them proved abortive.

The purpose of this book is not to pass moral judgement on the role of the Anglo-Jewish establishment.[24] This has already been undertaken, both by those apologists who have viewed the establishment's actions as exemplary in the circumstances, and by more recent historians who have taken the opposite view and criticised the establishment's conduct as inadequate and insufficient. 'We cannot be the judges of the generation which had to struggle with these issues in the flesh; but we must surely reflect upon these questions'.[25] The moral issue has been and will continue to be debated at the interface of history, politics and ethics.

1

'Englishmen of the Jewish Persuasion'

> Uncertain and afraid
> As the clever hopes expire
> Of a low dishonest decade:
> Waves of anger and fear
> Circulate over the bright
> And darkened lands of the earth,
> Obsessing our private lives...
> W.H. Auden, 'September 1, 1939'

The peculiar political and social ambience of the 1930s, so perfectly captured in Auden's brief lines, had its inevitable influence on Britain's already highly integrated Jewish community. Anxieties about unemployment, fascism, appeasement – all affected the quality and conduct of Jewish communal life, and it is perhaps hardly surprising that in a decade of such timorous leadership at the national level, the Jewish lions abandoned their roaring in favour of the more discreet murmuring which formed the language of political discourse during the period. What is truly surprising is the degree of confidence and determination evinced by the Anglo-Jewish leadership, notwithstanding its cautious demeanour. Its valour was no less real for being cloaked in discretion.

It is against the background of Auden's 'low, dishonest decade' that the complex character of Anglo-Jewry in the 1930s can be most clearly defined. During the inter-war years, Anglo-Jewry enjoyed considerable continuity of leadership, with communal power still vested in descendants of the pre-1881 'grandee' families. The leadership comprised a well-integrated and affluent clique of Sephardic (of Spanish and Portuguese origin) and an almost equally long-established minority of Ashkenazi (Central and East European) origin. Some authority had already begun to pass to first-generation English-born Jews, the progeny of East European immigrant parents. This ensued partly from the depredations suffered by the old leadership as a consequence of the First World War, and partly from the economic success of the new wave of immigrants, among them (Lords) Simon Marks and Marcus Sieff, founders of Marks and Spencer, and Sir Alfred Mond, first Baron Melchett, of ICI.[1] Others of this generation included Neville Laski, KC (1892–1969), elected President of the Board of Deputies in 1930; at 42 years old, he was the youngest person to have been elected to the position, which he held until 1939. Another, Otto Schiff (1879–1975), was a German-born stockbroker and chairman of the Jewish Refugees Committee. In December 1939, the presidency of the Board was assumed by a Russian-born immigrant, Professor Selig Brodetsky (1888–1954). These men, Norman Bentwich notes, quoting his father, 'combined enthusiastically a double loyalty: to the community from which [they] sprang, and to the country which gave civic opportunity to the sons of aliens'.[2]

Anglo-Jewry was never a homogeneous community and has never functioned politically as an ethnic pressure group. Numbering approximately 335,000 by the mid-1930s,[3] Britain's Jews comprised many diverse groups, both socially and religiously, especially following the first wave of immigration from Eastern Europe during the latter part of the nineteenth century. Nevertheless, given its centralised leadership and coordinated institutions, Anglo-Jewry (unlike its American counterpart) may be characterised as a 'community', dominated by a London-based 'establishment'. It is represented by a number of institutions, in particular, the Board of Deputies of British Jews (Board). This body, established in 1760 for the purpose of defending the civil and political rights of Jews in Britain and the Empire, constitutes the lay leadership of Anglo-Jewry. Since 1836 it has enjoyed statutory recognition as the representative organ of the community.[4] In this respect, it is possible to speak of an 'Anglo-Jewish response', notwithstanding differences attributable to class, religious and political ideology, and age.

The Board has always been essentially a political institution. It operates as a parliamentary body whose deputies, elected by synagogue congregations and communal organisations, serve for three years. In 1940 there were some 388 deputies. The deputies meet monthly and elect executive officers, who carry out committee work and official representation. Laski dismissed as misleading a description of the Board as 'the Jewish Parliament', as it is 'not a law-making machine', nor has it any 'sanctions which it could apply'.[5] Although true, this misses the metaphorical aptness of the description; a parliament is, etymologically, a debating chamber and in that sense the Board is indeed the 'Jewish Parliament'.

The Board's Joint Foreign Committee (JFC), the community's *de facto* Cabinet, claimed sole authority to approach the government on matters affecting Jews abroad. The Anglo-Jewish Association (AJA), established in 1871, worked in partnership with the Board, first as the Conjoint Foreign Committee from 1878 until 1917 and then as the JFC until 1943, when following the Zionist takeover, the Board discontinued this association and the JFC became the Foreign Affairs Committee (FAC). The AJA's membership was drawn largely from the old oligarchy. The JFC and the AJA were in effect Anglo-Jewry's central policy-making bodies. To deal with major issues arising out of the war, in late 1939 an Executive Committee began convening on an *ad hoc* basis. Important decision-making was now vested in this small Committee, consisting of the president as chairman, three co-opted members, and former presidents of the Board, including Sir Osmond d'Avigdor Goldsmid and Neville Laski. Many Executive Committee members, including Lionel Cohen, Sir Robert Waley-Cohen, Anthony de Rothschild, Leonard Stein and Lord Swaythling, belonged to the old guard.[6]

Jealously guarding its position and rejecting the concept of 'world Jewry', the Board resented the establishment in 1936 of the World Jewish Congress (WJC), which, in reaction to the rise of Nazism, aimed 'to unite the Jewish communities all over the world in defence of their national and civil rights'. Over seven million Jews worldwide, it claimed, were represented by the Congress, whose British Section acted as its European headquarters. The Board inevitably resented the Congress's encroachment on its own exclusive representative status and refused to accord it official recognition. Members of the British Section included the Revd. Maurice Perlzweig, who, in 1942, became head of the International Affairs Department of the WJC in New York, the political journalist Alex L. Easterman and Noah Barou, a specialist on co-operative finance. The Chairman was Labour MP Sidney Silverman; Eva, Marchioness of Reading, daughter of Alfred Mond, acted as President and her brother Lord Melchett was also involved.

The mainstream religious institution, the United Synagogue,

established in 1870, was and still is headed by the Chief Rabbi. It has always been an orthodox institution by virtue of its strict interpretation of Jewish law, although its membership embraces a wide spectrum of religious practice. A progressive slackening in communal religious observance during the nineteenth century led Chief Rabbi Dr. Nathan Adler to introduce an anglicisation of synagogue buildings and services. This style was in marked contrast to that of the numerous small *chevras* (fraternities) set up by East European Jews in the East End of London, which preserved a more traditional type of orthodoxy. In 1887 Samuel Montagu amalgamated these *chevras* into the 'Federation of Synagogues', in order to provide small, orderly places of worship which would wean the Jewish working classes away from both the *chevras* and the newly forming trade unions and anarchist meeting places. Sixty-nine synagogues and approximately 64,000 Jews were affiliated to the Federation during World War II. At the other end of the religious spectrum were the Reform Congregation, founded in 1845 and the Liberal Movement, started by Claude G. Montefiore in 1902.[8]

The Chief Rabbi's position, like that of the Pope, is primarily one of supreme religious authority but lacks equal sway in secular matters, so that he might at times find himself in conflict with lay leaders. Chief Rabbi Dr. Joseph Hertz (1872–1946) was a staunch Zionist. His zeal was matched by a strong 'loyalty to Britain and . . . belief in British ideals',[9] a loyalty which had signally manifested itself in his defence of the British cause in the Boer War before he came to Britain as Chief Rabbi in 1913. Although head of the United Synagogue, his robust views on Jewish identity and Jewish self-assertion, together with his combative spirit, occasionally placed him at odds with Anglo-Jewry's communal lay leadership. His quarrels with Sir Robert Waley-Cohen, President of the United Synagogue from 1942 to 1952, were legendary. While the two cooperated on many matters, they diverged increasingly in religious direction and orientation.[10]

The majority of mainstream Anglo-Jewry subscribed to the broadly based *Jewish Chronicle*, whose editor, Ivan Greenberg, was a staunch Zionist. Although sectarian interests were served by, for example, the orthodox *Jewish Weekly*, the *Jewish Chronicle*, founded in 1841, never had a serious rival for its position as 'the organ of Anglo-Jewry'. It played an important role in defining the character of Anglo-Jewry, and succeeded in simultaneously forming and reflecting a consensual Anglo-Jewish 'voice', while offering scope for dissent in its letter pages and opinion columns.

Outside the 'establishment', Rabbi Dr. Solomon Schonfeld (1912–1984) represented a small group of strictly orthodox Jews, most of them immigrants, who were members of the Adath Israel Synagogue. This had been established in 1909 with the aim of strengthening the practice of traditional Judaism. His father, Victor, amalgamated the Adath Synagogues and in 1926 formed a Union of Orthodox Hebrew Congregations. By 1943 this comprised 54 affiliated synagogues serving approximately 5,000 families. The Union remained separate from and at loggerheads with the United Synagogue, which it regarded as growing increasingly lax in religious matters. Like the Liberal and Reform branches of Anglo-Jewry, it has never recognised the authority of the Chief Rabbi.[11] Nevertheless, Schonfeld was able to utilise his status of son-in-law to Chief Rabbi Hertz to give the stamp of authority to his own somewhat unorthodox proceedings as head of the Chief Rabbi's Religious Emergency Council. Schonfeld, the British-born son of Hungarian parents, studied from 1930 to 1933 at a religious seminary (*yeshiva*) in Nitra, Slovakia, under Rabbi Michael Ber Weissmandel and then moved to Slobodka, from where he received his rabbinical ordination. Simultaneously, he obtained a doctorate in philosophy from the University of Königsberg. At Nitra, Schonfeld became a sympathiser with, although not an official member of, the ultra-orthodox Agudat Israel and wholeheartedly endorsed the Agudist approach to religious and communal issues. Schonfeld perceived himself first and foremost as a Jew and only secondly as a British subject.

Another prominent figure in the strictly orthodox community was Harry Goodman (1898–1961), a prosperous, English-born clothing manufacturer who was secretary of the Agudat Israel World Organisation (Union of Israel, AIWO), the political wing of the strictly orthodox.[12] He was one of the few English-born Jews to identify with separatist orthodoxy. He served on both the Jewish Refugees' Committee and the Central British Fund, and was a member of the Board. He early developed a provocative and dynamic style, which led even his friends to speak of him as an *'enfant terrible'*, while his lively ripostes 'could invariably be depended upon to brighten up a dull gathering'.[13] Goodman published and edited the *Jewish Weekly*, for a strictly orthodox readership, and during the war he was responsible for weekly broadcasts, via the BBC, on behalf of the Ministry of Information to Jews in Occupied Europe. The war increased his political activities, especially when he became Jewish adviser to the Ministry of Information (where his first task was to read the cablegrams which passed between Jewish organisations deploring his appointment!). In the communal controversy which broke out in 1943, he participated with great zest and by February 1945, before hostilities had ceased, he was visiting France and Switzerland, helping to save the remnants and to restore the Agudist organisation.[14]

Some of Anglo-Jewry's leaders (such as Brodetsky and Hertz) were affiliated to the organised community. Others were co-opted as leaders or patrons because of the prominence they had gained in the non-Jewish world. Examples include Lionel and Anthony de Rothschild and politicians such as Sir Herbert Samuel (later Viscount), High Commissioner in Palestine (1920–25) and Home Secretary in the National Government (1931–32), who was co-opted as Chairman of the Council for German Jewry (CGJ).[15]

Well into the 1930s and even during the war, the old Anglo-Jewish oligarchy still maintained a presence in the major Jewish institutions. As Laski noted in his farewell address to the Board in December 1939, 'The so-called grand dukes have rendered and are still rendering the community yeoman [!] service'.[16] However, by the outbreak of World War II, the personal intercession which had characterised relations between the older leadership and the authorities had largely diminished.[17]

The inter-war period saw the successful absorption and anglicisation of earlier Jewish immigrants and their children into British life. The vast majority of Jewish children were educated in non-Jewish schools. Multiculturalism, in today's sense of the word, was yet to be invoked as an ethos validating alternative lifestyles for minority communities, notwithstanding rare exceptions such as the Society of Friends (Quakers). British Jews followed enthusiastically the principle that 'there is no impediment to Jews as a religious community forming part of the British nation with all that it implies in undivided loyalty, common social and cultural ideas and complete identity of interests'. As Laski observed, the successful integration of twentieth-century Anglo-Jewry into British communal life was made possible by 300 years of harmonious integration.[18] The new generation of mainstream communal leaders was imbued with the anglicised way of life and culture of the older leadership. Laski was born into a prominent and communally active Manchester immigrant family, becoming the son-in-law of the Haham of the Spanish and Portuguese Jewish community, Moses Gaster. The Russian-born Brodetsky, Professor of Applied Mathematics at Leeds University and adviser on aerodynamics to the Ministry of Defence during the war, is widely regarded as representative of the new generation of Anglo-Jewish leadership which assumed prominence during World War II. The rise of the 'prodigy from Fashion Street' to senior Wrangler at Cambridge and thence to Professor at Leeds is the story of a worthy and talented academic who, like many Jewish immigrants of his generation, overcame poverty to achieve a distinguished career in his chosen field. Sharing much of the style of the older leadership, adopting many of its mores and attitudes, he is nevertheless distinguished from it by his ardent Zionism.

During the war years, Brodetsky was assisted by Adolf Brotman (1897–1970), General Secretary of the Board, who functioned both as his personal assistant and as 'senior civil servant of the community'. Educated at the City of London School and King's College, London, graduating in 1919, Brotman began his career as a science teacher. In 1926, he moved to Baghdad, where he was for five years education adviser to the Jewish community, before returning to London and the secretaryship of the Board. A somewhat colourless figure, worthy but unexciting, he nevertheless played an invaluable part during the 1930s and 1940s in dealing with the growing deluge of work inundating the Board, some of it dramatic – negotiating with government officials, refugee work and defence – more often tedious.[19]

Laski is particularly representative of the tendency of British Jews to view themselves as British in all respects except their non-adherence to the Established Church, in parity with Catholics, Quakers, Methodists and other nonconformists. It was comparatively easy for Jews to assign themselves a 'British' identity, which derives from the ethnically composite, political union of four kingdoms, entry to which is acquired through citizenship rather than 'racial' or biological origin. To be 'English' implies (at least in theory) Anglo-Saxon ancestry; but a Scotsman, a Welshman – or a Jew – could be 'British' merely through his legal status. To the integrated sections of the community, Judaism was a wholly private religious bond. Laski, who insisted that 'our duty as citizens must override our sentiments as Jews',[20] typifies those who were concerned to foster the image of a Jewish community visibly loyal to King and country.

This insistence on the duties of loyal citizenship is explicable in the light of the Anglo-Jewish establishment's need to confirm its 'British' credentials: since it could scarcely cite Anglo-Saxon ethnicity as proof of its Englishness, it tried perforce to define itself as British in terms of mindset and loyalty. Laski did precisely this during a conference held in October 1938 to discuss the new refugee crisis following the Munich Agreement: 'Above all [British Jews'] primary obligation is their stern and unswerving allegiance to their citizenship'.[21] Statements such as this could be taken for defensiveness, born of anxiety rooted in a conflict of loyalties – loyalty to the state colliding with the ethical and instinctive imperative to come to the rescue of fellow Jews. However, it would be wrong to interpret Laski's words out of their historical context; the civic virtues of duty, loyalty and service were an active element in public life in the 1930s and formed a natural matrix for Jewish self-definition. Anglo-Jewry's vehement protestations of loyalty were also in great measure defensive; a key component of British anti-Semitism during this period was the perception that Jews were crypto-foreigners. George Orwell, an astute and objective observer of social phenomena, questioned whether 'the Jew is objected to as a Jew or simply as a foreigner. . . . No religious considerations enters. The English Jew, who is often strictly orthodox but entirely anglicised in his habits, is less disliked than the European refugee who has probably not been near a synagogue for thirty years.'[22]

Certainly, there is evidence to show that Anglo-Jewry was not the diffident community it has been portrayed as. Again after Munich, Laski announced that 'we seek no preferential treatment for the Jews, but that status of equality with his non-Jewish fellow-citizens, to which he is by every human law entitled'.[23] Far from seeking civic equality as a privilege for which Jews should render gratitude, Laski demands it as a human right.

During the nineteenth century, the Board had won increasing governmental support not only for Jewish emancipation in Britain and religious freedom for the practice of Judaism, but also in regard to British intervention with foreign powers to ameliorate anti-Semitic persecution abroad.[24] Certain rights were also granted to the Jewish community. In 1836 the Board won statutory recognition through several Acts of Parliament, including rights to the supervision of Jewish marriages. The Board was sensitive to the fact that this and other rights, such as those adumbrated in the Sunday Trading Laws, might be repealed should they be abused and that the authority of the Jewish leadership might easily be undermined should it be misused.[25] Nevertheless, this did not place the Jewish community in any more vulnerable position than any other social or religious sect and it is hard to see how its concern not to abuse its privileges can be read as a symptom of timidity and insecurity. The last serious violence against a religious minority in Britain had been the anti-Catholic Gordon Riots of 1780 – and that rising had been swiftly suppressed. No ulterior motive need be ascribed to the Board's pride in the good name of the community as a whole, or its endeavour to encourage a high standard of behaviour in public life.

Yet the Anglo-Jewish community of the inter-war period has been repeatedly labelled uneasy and timorous. It has been argued that the successful integration of British Jewry into nineteenth-century social and economic life concealed a deeper sense of insecurity nurtured by several factors. During the 1980s, Bill Williams, followed by a group of revisionist historians of Anglo-Jewry, including Tony Kushner and more recently Richard Bolchover, challenged the view that the liberal political culture of early twentieth-century England created a tolerant environment in which Jews could flourish. Williams argued that liberalism bred its own distinctive form of hostility to Jews, which he called the 'Anti-semitism of Tolerance'. Liberalism, he claimed, was hostile to Jewish distinctiveness and supported equal rights for Jews only in so far as they abandoned their distinctive religious and cultural mores: 'Jews were validated not on the grounds of their Jewish identity, but on the basis of their conformity to the values and manners of bourgeois English society.'[26] This 'emancipation contract' theory holds that Jewish acceptance into national life was implicitly conditional upon a high degree of integration and assimilation. The terms of the contract have never been fully explained, and Bolchover himself maintains that there was in reality no such thing, except in the mind of Anglo-Jewry. Thus, Bolchover claims, during the war, British Jews were fearful of an anti-Semitic resurgence caused by Jewish abrogation of the 'contract'. For this reason, 'Anglo-Jewry's understanding of the emancipation as a contract and the inherent threat of antisemitism upon its abrogation led it to maintain a low-profile political strategy'.[27]

In fact the growth of British anti-Semitism during the war was caused by more material factors. Orwell notes that 'the Jews are one people of whom it can be said with complete certainty that they will benefit by an Allied victory. Consequently, the theory that "this is a Jewish war" has a certain plausibility.'[28] He cites various economic and social grounds for anti-Semitic feeling during the war, but seems unaware of the existence of an 'emancipation contract', a concept for which no evidence exists.

Nevertheless, the revisionist historians have rejected the earlier consensus that Britain's liberal political culture, in contrast to the active and extreme Continental style of anti-Semitism in the nineteenth and twentieth centuries, created a tolerant atmosphere in which Jews could flourish socially and economically. The invidious dangers of judgement by contrast, they argue, are exacerbated in this instance by the political and cultural differences which made Britain a 'special case'. The absence of show-trials, pogroms and emigration in the experience of British Jewry does not mean, these historians claim, that less institutionalised forms of anti-Semitism did not flourish at various levels of British society. What is important, Kushner argues, is that the most direct impact of anti-Semitism was on English Jews' sense of identity. It reinforced the perception that Jews were alien and consequently felt compelled to meet the expectation of the host society by maintaining a low profile.[29] The weakness in this circular argument is that it cites an undemonstrated effect as 'proof' of its own hypothetical cause. The existence of anti-Semitism, in whatever form, in early twentieth-century Britain does not, however, support claims for the existence of an 'emancipation contract' – in fact, the opposite is true. Perhaps, the idea that liberalism represented a drive to conformity in the secular sphere is drawn from a false analogy with the potent forces of evangelism which characterised the Church of England in the nineteenth century, leading to repeated campaigns to convert the Jews.

A certain parochialism can also be detected in the work of these historians. Taking the Jewish perspective as central to their analysis, they fail to take account of the wider factors – political, social and cultural – which conditioned nineteenth- and early twentieth-century responses to nonconformism in Britain, of which Judaism was only one example. Their assumptions are predicated on the late twentieth-century premises of a pluralistic society in which minority rights, both ethnic and religious, are enshrined in law. Thus, Kushner complains anachronistically that 'British society, which prides itself on its liberalism, its decency and its humanitarianism, has failed to produce an environment for the healthy existence of a positive Jewish identity',[30] failing to draw a crucial distinction between intrinsic anti-Semitism and general wariness of nonconformism. His conclusion, that British Jews felt pressured to conform to the customs and attitudes of the majority and were thus rendered insecure in their Jewish identity, similarly fails to address the fact that such insecurity is inevitably a psychological function of membership of a minority culture in a host society. Rather than experiencing overtly hostile pressure towards conformity, it seems likely that British Jews were susceptible to a more subtly persuasive phenomenon – the lure of assimilation. At precisely the time when legal and social barriers were being lowered, British Jews began to succumb to the blandishments of a society which offered a model of modern, rational life, through the influence, *inter alia*, of secular education, cultural 'anglicisation' and inter-marriage. Thus, Anglo-Jewry, while necessarily regarding itself as a minority group, was nevertheless also consciously and deliberately well integrated.

An account of the undoubted insecurities and anxieties experienced by Anglo-Jewry in the early twentieth century must therefore consider the broader social pressures which shaped both liberal and intolerant attitudes. Virulently anti-Semitic writers, such as Houston Stewart Chamberlain and, to a lesser extent, T.S. Eliot and H.G. Wells, were active and influential alongside a philo-Semitic culture exemplified (to name only literary figures) by the work of nineteenth- and twentieth-century writers including J.S. Mill, George Eliot, E.M. Forster and James Joyce. The weakness of the 'emancipation-contract' theorists is not only their failure to adduce any evidence for it, or to account for the succession of enabling legislation passed throughout the nineteenth century, but also their simplistic characterisation of a deeply complex society as 'liberal', an epithet which is then used loosely as a term of abuse.

To describe nineteenth-century liberalism as a creed of conformity denies the evidence of the radical social and political reforms brought about through the activities of liberals and nonconformists such as Elizabeth Fry, William Wilberforce and the Anti-Corn Law activists, to name only a few. One of the most important documents of nineteenth-century liberal philosophy, Mill's 'On Liberty', is founded on the 'harm principle' – that the individual must be free to follow his own course unless this interferes with the liberty of another. Reacting against the conformism of contemporary society, Mill insists that 'it is good that there should be differences, even though not for the better, even though . . . some should be for the worse.'[31] Liberalism proper, at least in the cultural sense, is characterised by the creed of E.M. Forster, who described himself as 'an individualist and a liberal who has found liberalism crumbling beneath him': 'Tolerance, good temper, and sympathy – they are what matter really.' Such liberalism is most characteristically associated with Forster's own vigorous philo-Semitism: 'To me, anti-Semitism is now the most shocking thing of all.'[32]

It cannot be denied that there was a powerful strain of anti-Semitism in British social life in the early twentieth century, but its causes cannot be attributed to a putative unwritten emancipation contract or to any comprehensive phenomenon such as 'liberalism'. Other factors played a part, and only in certain cases can it be claimed that an exclusively anti-Jewish, as opposed to anti-alien, form of prejudice operated. Even this is doubtful: the only Christian response to Britain's Jews has for centuries been an evangelical zest for conversion. Racial anti-Semitism was the province of extreme, minority fringe groups. Nevertheless, there was an undoubted culture of latent and sometimes overt hostility which inevitably induced a certain anxiety beneath the solid surface of social and economic success enjoyed by British Jews in the early twentieth century, and which was exacerbated by the wider international spread of Fascism and the rise of the British Union of Fascists (BUF). However, the community's dismissive and 'stiff upper-lip' attitude to anti-Semitism must not be confused with an insecure, 'low-profile' approach. It is in fact another symptom of the community's 'British' response.

Anglo-Jewry's style of leadership has always been indicative of the habit of deference towards authority natural to a culture with an ingrained respect for the 'law' (secular as well as religious). Such deference, which is not in itself defensive, can only have been reinforced by the characteristic respect of the English working classes towards their social superiors, a respect which has been commented on by psephologists and social historians.[33] To a great extent, Anglo-Jewry genuinely shared many of the attitudes and assumptions of the government and ruling classes, to whom it entrusted the protection of its interests. British Jewry took pride in the Empire, which was still a powerful global force in the 1930s. The older leadership had become integrated into middle- and upper-class society; at the highest level, the court circle of the Edwardian period was noted for the number of Jewish bankers and financiers who were personal friends of the King.

What has been viewed as servile echoing of official policy on immigration, anti-Semitism and the conduct of war may more correctly be seen as a reflection of the extent to which the outlook of the host society had genuinely been absorbed by its Jewish community. Laski was exhibiting a peculiarly British fair-mindedness when he urged, 'The Jews must not expect the Jewish problem to be given first consideration when the peace of Europe is at stake. For the statesmen of Europe the peace of the Continent is the paramount consideration. For them, the Jewish question is only one of many problems.'[34] Chaim Weizmann noted of this period in Jewish–Government relations that British Jews were in an awkward predicament: 'their manifest unhappiness at seeing British statesmen on friendly terms with our bitterest persecutors, could give the impression that they wanted the British to fight our war for us; the fact that what they sought was consonant with England's interests was thereby obscured.'[35] Anglo-Jewish leaders were therefore careful to express their views and concerns in a style which could leave no doubt as to where their loyalties really lay. Their attitude is illustrated by the rejection of a proposal, in August 1940, that 'the Board, on behalf of Anglo-Jewry, should raise a fund for the presentation of a squadron of aeroplanes to HMG'. Some urged that such a proposal 'would stand out as a concrete instance of Jewish help in the fight against Hitlerism'. However, the motion was eventually dropped on the grounds that the proposal would have the effect of differentiating Jews from the British citizen body.[36]

The diversity of Anglo-Jewish responses to the question of self-definition is particularly well exemplified by the variety of its attitudes to political Zionism, the movement to create a Jewish state in Palestine. Zionism presented a powerful potential conflict between Jewish and British identities. Early Zionists were an annoying embarrassment to the old Anglo-Jewish oligarchy because they appeared to claim a national, political identity for Jews beyond that which they held as British subjects or citizens. The issue first arose during the negotiations leading to the Balfour Declaration in 1917, which promised a Jewish national home in Palestine. Waley-Cohen declared that British Jews were 'entirely British in thought, aspirations, interests and zeal'. The 'non-Zionists' or 'assimilationists' rejected Zionism not because they feared British hostility, but from a positive and powerful sense of loyalty to Britain and the Empire. Zionism offered a rival national identity to Jews, many of whom had fought in World War I and whose loyalties were already proudly given to Britain.[37] In fact, some of the earlier anti-Zionist British Jews, like the journalist Lucien Wolf, actively supported Zionism once it became clear to them that Zionism offered the government a valuable excuse for annexing a strip of land which would otherwise fall to the French. Others, like Edwin Montague, the wartime Secretary of State for India, feared that support for the establishment of a Jewish national home in Palestine might be 'a thinly cloaked desire to get rid of them' and that the Jews in Britain would inevitably 'be invited to clear out'.[38]

This opposition to Zionism is well illustrated by an acrimonious exchange in late 1940 between Brodetsky and Anthony de Rothschild. Berating Brodetsky for his public statement that Zionists refused to accept 'the policy of assimilation' because it represented 'a capitulation on the part of the Jewish people, an abandonment of its sense of history, its tradition and its national dignity', de Rothschild speaks of the 'civic ideal' of assimilation. He defines this not in the modern sense of biological and cultural absorption into the host community, but in the sense 'that apart from the religious difference our ideal is to assimilate with the rest of the British nation taking our full part as Englishmen without reservation in all the secular activities of the nation'. Rothschild, claiming to speak on behalf of 'a large and vital section of the Community', strongly contested the idea that 'we have nationalistic aspirations which are the reverse of our conception of British citizenship and the traditional position of the Jews in this country'.[39] Brodetsky disagreed: 'I, for one, am not prepared to define Judaism as a system of thought and practice, the aim of which is to place British citizenship before everything else and to ram home the great debt which Jews owe to Britain. Nobody will accuse me of not understanding the world importance of British citizenship and the Jewish debt to Britain but the revelation on Mount Sinai happened before Great Britain existed.'[40] Brodetsky clearly felt some irritation at those who, like de Rothschild, seemed to him obsessed by a compulsion to profess their loyalty *ad nauseam*!

Resistance to Zionism persisted through the 1930s and 1940s, although the Zionist movement attracted greater support following Hitler's rise to power. Until the election of Brodetsky in December 1939, the Anglo-Jewish leadership remained half-hearted about political Zionism although it supported 'practical or constructive Zionism', the economic and cultural development of Jewish Palestine. Opinion was divided as over Lord Peel's Partition Plan of 1937, with Laski and Waley-Cohen (now a vice-president of the Board) opposed to the proposal. Rothschild called for support of government policy against partition, declaring he was 'proud of being British' and that the 'Government will not let us down'.[41] Weizmann bitterly described the terms of the Partition Plan as 'the first steps towards the nullification of the Balfour Declaration'.[42]

Certainly, the White Paper of May 1939, fixing a limit on immigration to Palestine, profoundly disturbed Anglo-Jewish sensibilities. The belief that Britain had reneged on the promises of the Balfour

Declaration, especially at a time of dire need, brought many non-Zionists, like Waley-Cohen and Laski, into greater sympathy with Zionism. The Zionist aspirations of a growing section of the Jewish community found a voice in the leadership of Brodetsky, who used his position as President of the Board to present the Zionist cause to the government on every possible occasion, combining deference for authority with a surprisingly forceful insistence on the Palestine issue when this was evidently at odds with official policy. Yet British Zionists still envisaged a Jewish State in Palestine which would remain 'in one form or another, within the ambit of the British Empire'. In January 1938, the Board called for a solution which would 'provide for the establishment of a Jewish Dominion within the British Commonwealth of Nations'. This was intended to conciliate the non-Zionists, who prided themselves on their patriotism, by offering a means of reconciling a Jewish with a British nationality.[43] By November 1944, the Board was still hoping that Palestine would become a Jewish state or commonwealth and 'find an appropriate and legally secured place within the British Commonwealth of nations'. Such a proposal was deemed practical by most Zionists, since 'a tiny little prosperous state such as Palestine . . . cannot hope to survive in isolation in the midst of a complex Mediterranean zone'.[44]

The Zionist cause gathered momentum as the Nazi threat grew, although Anglo-Jewish responses continued to vary widely. In ideological terms, Jews have always recognised the centrality of persecution in their history. However, by the twentieth century a new optimism had formed under the influence of the comparatively enlightened and tolerant conditions of British society. Anglo-Jewry trusted in liberal democracy and in the philosophy of amelioration, the legacy not only of eighteenth-century Enlightenment rationalism (which saw religious persecution as a form of superstition) but also of nineteenth-century theories of political and social evolution such as Fabianism and social Darwinism.

By extension, the Jews believed they would benefit from this gradual amelioration of the human condition, and as has been argued, it was therefore 'hard for most to accept the reality of irrational facts such as the planned extermination of the Jews'.[45] It would appear that even the widespread acceptance and popularity of eugenic theories of racial purity during the early decades of the century had done nothing to dent this optimism. Anglo-Jewry had not realised that eighteenth-century rationalism expected toleration to lead inevitably to assimilation, nor that religious anti-Semitism had become infused, especially in Europe, with racial anti-Semitism. Conditions in England were profoundly different from those that prevailed on the Continent. Orwell notes: 'anti-Semitism as a fully thought-out racial or religious doctrine has never flourished in England. There has never been much feeling against intermarriage, or against Jews taking a prominent part in public life.'[46] So thoroughly had this tolerance become ingrained into English social and political life, notwithstanding a fair amount of anti-Semitism on a social and cultural level, that it was harder, perhaps, for English Jews to accept the reality of the Nazi plan than it would have perhaps been for other Jewish communities elsewhere in mainland Europe. Hence its initial response to the 'Final Solution' of the European Jewish problem was incredulity compounded with scepticism. The deception and secrecy with which the Nazi policy of extermination was conducted no doubt fuelled this scepticism further.

By contrast, the Agudat Israel (like all strictly orthodox groups), untouched by secular culture, saw the Final Solution within the historical continuum of Jewish persecution, stretching back to the Babylonian and Roman exiles. Hitler was regarded metaphorically as a descendent of Amalek and Haman, the enemies and would-be destroyers of the Jewish people. Untouched by Enlightenment optimism, the orthodox experienced less incredulity at the concept of the Final Solution.[47] Traditional Jewish sources voiced a belief in the inevitability and irrationality of anti-Semitism. In the 1940s, some strictly orthodox authorities controversially saw the unfolding Holocaust as the outcome of 'two idolatries', predicted, like all historical events, by the Torah (Bible). Attributing Jewish suffering in modern times to the forces of assimilation and the twin 'idolatries' of nationalism and socialism, the Agudah was psychologically receptive immediately the news of the Final Solution broke.[48] The early Zionists, for secular and historical reasons, also believed that anti-Semitism was irrational and ineradicable, regarding Jewish statehood as the only solution to the problem.[49]

What is perhaps the greatest irony about the Anglo-Jewish mindset during the pre-war years is that it was precisely its assurance of its own 'Britishness' that rendered it at least partially incapable of internalising the real nature of the Nazi peril until it was too late. A community as timid and insecure as this has been made out to be would surely have reacted differently to a threat that tapped into its own deepest fears.

2

'The Jewish Lions are no longer roaring'

It is still popularly supposed that Anglo-Jewry remained indifferent to the fate of its European brethren. At the operational level, Alderman maintains that 'What is important in the context of Anglo-Jewish reaction to the Holocaust . . . is that no pressure of any significance was ever exerted upon the British Government on this question.' While he concedes that numerous appeals were made, 'there was never a mass lobby, or public demonstrations'. To challenge in these ways the imperative of supporting the war effort was by definition unpatriotic and would 'endanger the good name of the community'. This disparaging view of the community's motives is endorsed by Bolchover, who stresses Anglo-Jewry's overwhelming desire to appear loyal, 'prior to any requests for sympathy or practical help for the Jews of Europe'.[1] The implication is that despite its integration into British society, the Anglo-Jewish community remained insecure. In presenting the issue in this way, however, these historians reduce the community's options to a stark choice between patriotism and Jewishness. Failing to grasp the genuine areas of agreement between the government and the Jewish leadership, they argue fallaciously that the community's patriotism was synonymous with betrayal of its European Jewish brethren and that its concurrence with governmental policy was mere sycophancy.

For the most part the Anglo-Jewish leadership was confident, well-established and highly integrated. This confidence is evidenced by the leadership's immediate and decisive response to the first influx of refugees from central Europe in the two months following Hitler's accession to power in January 1933 and even before the German national boycott of Jewish business and the first anti-Jewish legislation of April 1933. A memorandum, undated but presumably drafted

25

in March 1933, set out proposals of the Jewish community as regards Jewish refugees from Germany. Before the Cabinet Committee on Alien Restrictions discussion of Jewish refugees on 5 April, the Jewish leadership had already taken an 'unprecedented step', which led the Cabinet to modify the rule that immigrants must demonstrate financial independence. Laski and Lionel Cohen of the Board, Leonard Montefiore of the AJA and Schiff undertook, on behalf of the community, that 'all expenses, whether in respect of temporary or permanent accommodation or maintenance will be borne by the community without ultimate charge to the State'. This guarantee was highlighted in the Home Secretary's report to the Cabinet Committee on Alien Restrictions, which also stated that the Jewish leadership estimated the number of refugees entering the country at not more than 3,000–4,000, mostly professionals.[2] The guarantee could be maintained only on the basis of a massive fund-raising effort and the establishment of organisations to deal with the influx. Between 1933 and 1939 the Anglo-Jewish community raised more than £3 million, an impressive sum for a community numbering some 330,000, especially during an economic depression.[3] It was purely because of the commitment of the guarantee, and the subsequent financial support of the Anglo-Jewish community, that the British government allowed the admission of German Jewish refugees throughout the 1930s.

Among the first refugee organisations established was the Jewish Refugees Committee (JRC), founded by Schiff in March 1933 and, to avoid prolonged refugee associations, renamed the German Jewish Aid Committee in January 1938. Schiff was an administrator of extraordinary energy and skill. His work for Belgian refugees during World War I had given him valuable administrative experience as well as close contacts with government officials. The Home Office consequently had 'complete trust in Mr. Schiff and his assistants, and were prepared to accept their word that any particular refugee or group of refugees would be maintained'.[4] Thus, in practice, German Jews were allowed into Britain on Schiff's authority. Emphasis was placed throughout on retraining and resettlement, particularly of younger people, in Palestine. The JRC was the executive body concerned with admission, hospitality, accommodation and financial help. It received its funds from the Central British Fund for German Jewry (CBF), which had been established in 1933.[5] The CBF launched its first appeal in May and raised over £250,000 in the first year. Both organisations were wholly apolitical.

The deteriorating condition of German Jewry following the Nuremberg Laws in 1935, disenfranchising all non-Aryans, convinced Anglo-Jewish leaders of the necessity for a more determined international effort to save German Jewry. In 1936, the CBF became part of a wider structure when the Council for German Jewry (CGJ) was founded to represent American, British and other major Jewish communities. Together with Herbert Samuel, its Chairman, Lord Bearsted, and Simon Marks took a leading part in its work. A major goal of the CGJ was to help fund the settlement of some 100,000 young adults and children, mainly in Palestine, within four years. For that purpose some £3 million was to be raised, two-thirds by American Jewry and one-third by British Jewry, with the help of continental bodies. Zionists and non-Zionists bridged their ideological differences to formulate this plan.[6] The non-denominational Movement for the Care of Children from Germany, better known as the *Kindertransport*, was formed in 1938 and was responsible for bringing 10,000 children to Britain, 90 per cent of whom were Jewish, by September 1939.

Valuable help came from non-Jewish organisations such as the Society of Friends and the Academic Assistance Council (later the Society for the Protection of Science and Learning), which helped to find positions in British universities for refugee scholars, as well as from several outstanding individuals. Prominent among these was Eleanor Rathbone MP (1872–1946), the guiding spirit of the National Committee for Rescue from Nazi Terror, established in March 1943. She had been a suffragist in the reign of Queen Victoria and was elected to Parliament in the first election at which women in Britain could vote. Her lifelong commitment to feminism was rooted in social action and the causes which she espoused reflected this concern to ameliorate the hardships suffered by the oppressed and by persecuted minorities.[7] Dr. George Bell, Bishop of Chichester, Josiah Wedgwood MP, and the Revd. James Parkes were also consistent champions of the refugee cause. Yet, although this would appear to be an impressive list, these people belonged to marginal and uninfluential sectors of society: the Independent MP for the Combined Universities, Eleanor Rathbone, and the Nonconformist Josiah Wedgwood are characteristic in this respect. Similarly, the voice of the Church, though it could not be ignored, was not in the vanguard of decision-making.

At the political level, the Board was reluctant to respond to the Nazi mistreatment of Jews with a 'policy of activism' including protest meetings and a boycott of German goods. One reason cited was that such action was likely to be prejudicial to the interests of German Jewry, as well as likely to jeopardise the *Ha'avara* (Transfer Agreement of 1933) which enabled Germans emigrating to Palestine to retain some of their assets provided it was used to purchase German goods.[8] The boycott also ran counter to the policy of economic appeasement in which the government was engaged. The Board insisted that the boycott was a matter for individual, not collective action. The Anglo-Jewish leadership preferred to discuss with officials the possibility of diplomatic intervention on behalf of German Jews, to solve the problem at source. However, the Foreign Office consistently declined to intervene in Germany's internal affairs. In early 1937 Laski suggested that 'at the appropriate time and within and as part of the Government policy for peace and protection of British interests the adverse effects of the German government's policy to a section of its own population should be drawn in a friendly but firm manner to the attention of that government'. Laski believed, naively from a later perspective but at the time reasonably, that by producing evidence of persecution and showing that Anglo-Jewry had British interests at heart, 'the forces of liberalism and humanitarianism would prevail'.[9] This was by no means a uniquely Jewish attitude. Although fear of war was widespread, belief in the cultured rationality and humanity of Germany as a centre of modern civilisation was still powerful at this stage. There was as yet no understanding of the essential fanaticism of Nazi ideology.

Laski maintained that 'the strongest condemnation of mass hysteria – whether exhibited in meetings or in boycott protests – is its failure to make any impression on Nazi Germany'.[10] However, those in favour maintained that earlier public protests would have mitigated the persecution of Austrian Jewry. In May 1938, following the *Anschluss*, JFC opposition to public protest still prevailed. The first organised Anglo-Jewish protest against Nazism occurred after *Kristallnacht*, on 1 December 1938, at the Royal Albert Hall, when the chair was taken by the former Lord Chancellor, Lord Sankey. Hertz was the only Jewish speaker.[11] The motive behind the Board's favouring public meetings only if prominent non-Jews were involved was pragmatism rather than diffidence. The Board believed that non-Jews would be regarded as more impartial, giving them greater credibility in Nazi eyes, and that eminent men on the right of the political spectrum would wield the most influence with Hitler.[12]

Equally, the Board opposed direct action in response to anti-Semitic

1 Neville Laski, President of the Board of Deputies, 1933–39 (courtesy of the Board of Deputies)

attacks by Fascist groups in Britain. That anti-Semitism existed in Britain during this period is without question, though the term is used indiscriminately by some historians to cover a diverse range of prejudices, from working-class xenophobia and fear about unemployment to the suspicions of the intelligentsia about cultural contamination. Anti-Semitism, which is treated too often as a homogeneous phenomenon, is a more complex compound of socio-psychological factors spawning widely varied responses. Certainly, it would be hard to prove at a political level that a particular climate of opinion had any measurable influence on official government policy.

The crucial event which fanned the flames of anti-Semitism in the early part of the twentieth century was the Russian Revolution; the identification of Jews with revolutionaries (the most prominent being Trotsky) provided fuel for those already hostile to Jews on the grounds that they were a politically destabilising element in a state. The theory of an international Jewish conspiracy was fostered by the circulation in 1919 of the *Protocols of the Elders of Zion*, a lurid account of a Jewish conspiracy to take over the world, which was taken seriously by numerous journalists, politicians and administrators. Although *The Times* eventually exposed the *Protocols* as a forgery in 1921, the period between 1917 and 1921 had been particularly difficult for the Anglo-Jewish community. Subsequently, it became more difficult for respectable opinion to support the charges; additionally, Britain's economic recovery in the 1920s helped to bring about a decline in anti-Semitism. In general, the Board was able to report by the end of 1926, it was 'now rare to find anything to which exception can be taken'.[13]

If explicit anti-Semitism was on the wane in the 1920s, a more insidious resentment of Jews as aliens found discreet expression in numerous ways. Most of the openly anti-Semitic sentiment emanated from marginal groups such as The Britons, an extreme nationalist group (which had ceased to exist by 1928) and the Imperialist Fascist League, founded by Arnold Leese in 1928. Both of these were far less worrying to British Jewry than the British Union of Fascists, founded by Oswald Mosley in October 1932. With the onset of the Depression in the early 1930s, latent prejudice against the Jews resurfaced and became the main weapon of extreme right-wing groups, which prospered throughout the 1930s in the aftermath of a steep rise in unemployment and a prolonged economic slump. *The Jewish Chronicle* reported increased manifestations of anti-Jewish prejudice.

In January 1933, it observed that 'scarcely a week passes without one or more manifestations of Jew-obsession in more or less acute form'. Discriminatory advertisements appearing in respectable newspapers reflected unashamed prejudices, explicitly stating that Jews need not apply.[14]

Such open discrimination represented a significant shift from the informal or covert biases against Jews which proliferated on a minor scale in numerous social milieux. This social discrimination was freely admitted and justified. The fashionable and literary classes routinely expressed openly derogatory remarks about Jews. Harold Nicolson confessed, 'The Jewish capacity for destruction is really illimitable. Although I loathe anti-semitism, I do dislike Jews.'[15] On the other hand, and paradoxically, as anti-Semitic sentiment and discrimination grew during the 1930s and the war years, it also became less 'politically correct', doubtless because the expression of anti-Semitic feeling would imply an affinity with the core ideology of the Nazi regime. George Orwell noted, 'The "Jew joke" has disappeared from the stage, the radio and the comic papers since 1934 [after the rise of Hitler].... there is a great awareness of the prevalence of antisemitism and a conscious effort to struggle against it.' Nevertheless, he is in no doubt that British anti-Semitism remained an ugly phenomenon: 'The milder form of antisemitism prevailing here can be just as cruel in an indirect way, because it causes people to divert their eyes from the whole refugee problem and remain uninterested in the fate of the surviving Jews of Europe.'[16] Clearly, there was no simple homogeneous British attitude to anti-Semitism but a polarisation of attitudes such as we find in contemporary anti-racist sentiment, which is by its very nature reactive. There would have been no need for philo-Semites to come to the defence of the Jews if anti-Semitism had not been a genuine and potent force in British society, notwithstanding the fact that it did not take violent forms.

During the 1930s, taking their lead from the court, the upper classes strongly supported a conciliation with Hitler, notwithstanding German anti-Semitic 'excesses'. The upper classes did not, however, prominently identify with the British anti-Semitic organisations, and only Mosley's BUF to a very small extent succeeded in enlisting their support. Mosley's campaign was concentrated primarily in the East End of London and was addressed mainly to a lower-middle-class audience. Physical violence, the concomitant of Fascist anti-Semitism, had no tradition in mainstream English politics. The particular political culture of Britain, governed by the concepts of legality and compromise, restrained aggressive, violent anti-Semitism. As Orwell noted, English anti-Semitism 'does not take violent forms. English people are almost invariably gentle and law-abiding.'[17]

English Jews recognised and relied on this safeguard. Jewish self-confidence and trust in British institutions and traditions were hardly affected by sporadic exhibitions of hostility. However, this conviction that anti-Semitism would not thrive in England began to waver under the cumulative experience of anti-Semitic incidents. A wave of hooliganism swept the East End of London, notably in October 1936, when a procession of the BUF was effectively stopped by an anti-Fascist front in the Battle of Cable Street. Yet the Board continued to oppose direct action in response to anti-Semitic attacks by Fascist groups in Britain. It expressed appreciation of the Home Secretary's statement that 'Jew-baiting would not be tolerated in England' and expressed gratitude to the Members who had raised the issue. As a result, the working-class Jewish community was forced to deal with the problem itself and in 1936 the Jewish People's Council was created out of a coalition of Communists and Jewish Labour groups. The Board formed the Jewish Defence Committee in 1938; its approach was to negotiate behind the scenes with the police and political leaders to coordinate Jewish defence against anti-Semitism.[18]

With war looming, Fascist propaganda portrayed the Jews as international warmongers, plotting yet again against Britain's interests. The belief that the Jews were dragging Britain into war was not, however, confined to Fascist agitators. On 9 December 1938, Lord Beaverbrook commented on the powerful influence Jews allegedly held in the British press and over public opinion: 'I have been, for years, a prophet of no war. But at last I am shaken. The Jews may drive us into war. I do not mean with any conscious purpose of doing so. They do not mean it. But unconsciously they are driving us into war. Their political influence is moving us in that direction.'[19] There is an ironic contrast between Laski's frustration at the complete lack of Jewish political influence and Beaverbrook's conviction that this 'influence' was driving a reluctant Britain into war.

Even though the Allies were fighting a war against Nazi Germany, whose anti-Semitism was a central plank of its public policy, anti-Semitism did not suddenly disappear from Britain during the war, but persisted and even increased. Orwell's account of anti-Semitism in wartime Britain reflects this. Among the reasons he cites are the tactless insensitivity of German Jewish refugees, the fact that Jews stood to benefit from the defeat of Hitler and heavy Jewish involvement 'in exactly those trades which are bound to incur unpopularity with the civilian public in wartime'. The Jewish war effort, furthermore, 'seldom gets its fair share of recognition'.[20] The Board's non-confrontational attitude remained constant throughout the war. Besides its reliance on governmental help, the Board maintained that 'publicity on Jewish matters . . . often produced an adverse effect and unnecessary publicity should therefore . . . be discouraged'.[21] On the whole the Jewish Defence Council tried to educate the public on the 'internal causes of antisemitism', focusing mainly on the behaviour of Jewish refugees and evacuees, and on Jewish involvement in the black market, which it correctly felt contributed to anti-Semitic sentiment.

The refugees in the pre-war period had sought entry at a particularly inauspicious time. Economic depression had induced restrictionist policies and fears that most refugees would either become a burden on the state or compete for scarce jobs. While public opinion over the apparent lack of concern shown by the British government mounted after *Kristallnacht* in November 1938, anti-alien and anti-Semitic feeling was also increasing. Popular newspapers, notably Beaverbrook's *Daily Express* and *Daily Mail,* frequently expressed anti-alien sentiment and stressed the limited capacity of Britain to absorb foreign Jews. The danger of growing hostility, particularly in view of continued high unemployment, was repeatedly urged by those responsible for relief work and refugee admissions. Groups whose particular interests were affected, such as the medical profession, opposed a sympathetic policy even towards 'desirable' immigrants. Writing in 1942, Orwell noted that 'In the years before the war it was largely trade union opposition that prevented a large influx of German Jewish refugees',[22] an interesting reminder that British governments, in peacetime at least, seldom act in wilful opposition to their electorates.

It has been argued that the Anglo-Jewish response to the plight of European Jewry was equivocal. This view is based on the premise that Anglo-Jewry felt that its own security would be threatened by an influx of Jewish refugees. However, while the evidence suggests that the establishment's attitude was indeed somewhat ambivalent, it can also be shown that in practice Anglo-Jewry, from a position of strength, took a more positive approach to the refugees. Laski countered the argument that refugees were adding to the unemployment problem and dismissed the criticism that they were, like the earlier Russian immigrants, 'ignorant and uncultured, many without a trade and speaking no language save Yiddish. The vast number would be an asset to any country into which they are admitted. They are cultured.'[23] The Board issued a booklet defending and praising them. They were making a substantial contribution to the British economy and, far from taking jobs from the British, they were creating employment. This measure was taken by the Jewish Defence Committee in response to the *Sunday Pictorial* headline 'Refugees get jobs – Britons get dole'.[24]

At the same time, Laski also informed Schiff that 'from my own personal experience, which is confirmed by the experience of a large number of my friends, the refugees are pestilential in the matter of the derogatory remarks about various things in this country'.[25] This concern was behind the decision to produce a booklet entitled *Helpful Information and Guidance for Every Refugee*, listing thirteen 'do's and don'ts'. Refugees were advised to be loyal to Britain, not to criticise British institutions and ways, and to refrain from speaking German in public or making themselves conspicuous in manner or dress. They were warned against telling British Jews that 'it is bound to happen in your country'. The high profile of the German refugees made it even more 'essential to *prevent* the growth of antisemitism than to combat it'.[26]

Such sensitivity on the part of the Anglo-Jewish leadership was due in part to the recurrent manifestations of anti-Semitism at the time, especially the activities of Mosley and the BUF. But there was also a tendency within the Anglo-Jewish establishment to agree that anti-Semitism was in part provoked by Jews themselves. The traditional view is that its 'obsessive nannying [of the refugees] betrays not only insecurity but a very negative perception of what refugees, if unrebuked, might get up to'.[27] Nevertheless, the perception that the alien background, appearance and behaviour of the refugees might generate hostility or fear was hardly irrational. Nor was it unfounded: Orwell describes the tactlessness of some refugees as 'incredible', citing a remark by a German Jewess during the Battle of France: 'These English police are not nearly so smart as our SS men.' Such gross insensitivity was, however, confined to a minority of refugees.[28]

Anglo-Jewish leaders were indisputably concerned at the behaviour of some of the newcomers. However, this was surely due, in part at least, to the community's natural desire to help the refugees settle into their new environment and adapt to British social customs. Its concern was equally motivated by acute awareness of having undertaken responsibility for the entry, maintenance and well being of the refugees. This suggests not insecurity but rather a commitment to help the immigrants to become accepted and integrated in Britain: 'Above all, please do realise that the Jewish community are relying on you – on each and every one of you – to uphold in this country the highest Jewish qualities, to maintain dignity, and to help and serve others'.[29] These values may seem pompous to a modern reader but were much more prevalent throughout British society in the 1930s. It was in any event important to stress them in light of the widespread public perception that 'the Jewish refugees use this country as a temporary asylum but show no loyalty to it'.[30]

There was a communal policy of dispersal of refugees around the country. Helen Bentwich, Hon. Secretary of the Movement for the Care of Children from Germany, advocated the spreading of 'our children as far over the British Isles as possible. We do not want too great numbers of them in any one place.'[31] This measure was designed to avoid placing strain on any one location, which might find difficulty in providing suitable homes for a large number of children. There was certainly a desire that the refugees be settled in and integrated as quickly as possible and not form social and cultural ghettos. Equally, there was concern that refugees should not be isolated in areas with no Jewish community, where 'there would be a certain amount of loneliness'.[32]

It has been suggested that there is a striking contrast between the indifferent response of the mainstream organisations and the inspired, even more heroic efforts of a small number of outstanding individuals. In particular, Schonfeld has been singled out for his 'exceptional' role in rescue and relief.[33] Yet, he was often at odds with the Anglo-Jewish establishment and early acquired a reputation for unconventional and even unscrupulous methods. Bentwich describes him as 'machiavellian', touched with the fanaticism of the religious zealot, whose 'zeal, imagination and energy' commanded respect even though his methods were perhaps less admirable.[34]

In succouring the Jewish victims of Nazi persecution, both religious and lay leaders saw themselves as continuing the age-old Jewish tradition of mutual aid and responsibility, including the ethical imperative of saving life, which had been a distinguishing feature of Jewish communal life since biblical times. According to Jewish law (and indeed English law in certain circumstances), saving life validates the transgression of any other law, Jewish or secular. The Talmud, in discussing a Jew's obligation to the disadvantaged in society, speaks of various categories of need and concludes that 'there is no greater commandment than *"pidyon shevuyim"'*, the obligation to ransom and rescue captives.[35]

For Schonfeld, this justified taking 'short cuts' and 'by-passing the slow-moving wheels of bureaucracy'.[36] More controversially, Schonfeld has been criticised for his 'narrow' concentration on saving religious functionaries, implying a lack of concern for other Jews.[37] Schonfeld, however, was passionately committed to the preservation of Jewish religion, culture and education, as evidenced by his lifelong devotion to the development of Jewish primary and secondary education. In the strictly orthodox view, rescue involved not only saving Jewish lives but also, by extension, saving Judaism as a living religion.[38] For Schonfeld the ideological commitment to the preservation of the practice of Judaism was all the more pressing because the forces of assimilation posed a real threat to the survival of the Jews. It was therefore natural that, without any lack of concern for others, he should have been personally drawn to the rescue of those who would perpetuate these ideals. In addition, according to Jewish law, special consideration should be given to scholars of religious law; in matters of life and death, states Maimonides, 'whoever is greater in wisdom takes precedence over his colleague'.[39] Although the view is alien to modern western sensibilities, this was partly why Schonfeld concentrated on the rescue of rabbis and religious teachers. In marked contrast, the prevailing opinion in Christian Europe and the English-speaking nations has traditionally been that which prevailed on the Titanic: women and children first. Had preference been given to or taken by clergymen and theologians, this would probably have been viewed with outrage and contempt. Nevertheless, while Schonfeld and the Agudah strove to save the orthodox, whether marginalised or not, there is evidence that Schonfeld also helped rescue 'non-orthodox' Jews. His lists of candidates for visas are headed 'orthodox' and 'non-orthodox'. Despite this unconventional taxonomy, it is nevertheless plain that, in the case of List 2, for example, 85 out of a total of 241 names were, by Schonfeld's own criteria, 'non-orthodox'.[40]

Schonfeld believed that orthodox Jews were marginalised in mainstream rescue efforts and that they were often seriously disadvantaged. It has certainly been argued that the refugee committees 'ignored' the rescue of orthodox children and adults because of the consensus of the Anglo-Jewish establishment that child refugees to Britain should ultimately go to Palestine.[41] Presumably orthodox refugees would have objected to this on anti-Zionist grounds. As regards the children's transport of 1938–9, the German Jewish Aid Committee (GJAC) dealt solely with the official Jewish community in Vienna, the *Kultusgemeinde*, which favoured children who could enter training programmes (*hachsharot*) in England for eventual resettlement in Palestine. This passive discrimination in favour of refugees who could be settled in Palestine meant that lower priority was perforce given to rabbis, religious teachers and functionaries, whom the refugee committees considered 'unproductive and largely unassimilable', with little prospect of re-emigrating.[42]

Unlike many in the strictly orthodox camp, Schonfeld remains an inscrutable figure. On the one hand, he atypically averred great loyalty to the British State, as witnessed by the patriotic tone of his *Message to Jewry*. He praised the wartime government in letters to the *Jewish Chronicle* and *The Times* both during and after the war: writing in 1961, he declared: 'My experience in 1942–3 was wholly in favour of British readiness to help, openly, constructively and totally.'[43] He developed important contacts with highly placed individuals such as Colonel Josiah (Lord) Wedgwood and the Archbishop of Canterbury. On the other hand, there is surely something curious about his effusive public professions of loyalty. Although there is a Jewish religious injunction to be loyal to the state in which one lives and indeed to pray for the welfare of the state, this is, according to the Agudist view, necessitated by self-protection rather than inspired by belief in the ideals of the state or by genuine loyalty. Agudists have always seen themselves as sojourners, not immigrants, in the Diaspora and hope ultimately to return to Zion upon the coming of the Messiah. No doubt Schonfeld's extraordinarily fulsome praise of the government was in part motivated by his bitterness and hostility to the Zionists, whom he blamed for stonewalling some of his rescue projects. The Zionists, rather than the government, were in his view the real culprits.[44]

Until the establishment of the CRREC, the Central Executive of the Agudat Israel was the only organisation dealing with the enquiries of strictly orthodox Jews regarding the possibility of emigration. In July 1938, the Agudah opened a special Emigration Advisory Office (EAC) [sic] in London to deal with thousands of individual enquiries about affidavits, search for relatives, finding posts for religious housemaids and apprentices, visas, supplying kosher food on boats, etc. Although the strictly orthodox argued the case for such an organisation, the GJAC opposed it. Schiff was 'heartily sick of Agudat Israel and their machinations',[45] and informed the *Hilfsverein*, the Jewish organisation in Germany dealing with emigration, that 'this committee . . . is absolutely condemned by all the leading organisations'. Schiff regretted that 'such action should be taken by a body which represents only an infinitesimal percentage of the Jewish community', fearing competing appeals and a further drain on the funds of the GJAC.[46] His concern was practical and administrative, rather than anti-orthodox, particularly given the dire financial straits facing the organisations in the late 1930s.

Like other organisations, the Agudah realised during the summer of 1938 that it could no longer handle the burden of emigration work alone. Not only had this work depleted its finances but it was diverting resources from the Agudah's other work in Palestine and Eastern Europe. For this reason Jacob Rosenheim, President of the AIWO, proposed to Hertz the creation of a Fund, to which he offered all the Agudah's experience and cooperation.[47] Schonfeld acted on the idea and work commenced after consultation with Viscount Samuel, who advised the formation of a special fund for these purposes, which the CGJ could not undertake. The result was the founding of the Chief Rabbi's Religious Emergency 'Fund' (changed to 'Council' in November). The chairman was Chief Rabbi Hertz and the driving force was Schonfeld, his future son-in-law. Schonfeld had already been active on behalf of Austrian Jewry, and after *Kristallnacht* in November 1938 the CRREC went into full gear.[48]

The Anglo-Jewish leadership has been criticised for in-fighting and disunity while European Jewry perished: 'The continual arguments between communal organisations and leading personalities damaged their effectiveness in lobbying government, the general public and the grass-roots community'.[49] This implies that had there been a more united front vis-à-vis the government and less time wasted on organisational friction, more could have been done to save European Jewry. There is, however, no evidence to support this view. On the contrary, there is much evidence that the British government's intransigence, conjoined with Germany's obsessive and irrational prioritising of the Final Solution, militated against any possibility of rescue.

In the 1930s, there was in fact remarkably little friction between the various Jewish organisations. In this period, the Anglo-Jewish community was effectively united on fund-raising and refugee issues.

The Board's officers and committees were kept formally notified of the work being carried out by the various refugee organisations. An elaborate network of cross-memberships and co-options linked the Board with the Jewish committees responsible for refugee relief and funds.[50] This close cooperation came under increasing strain after the outbreak of war, as different organisations came to the fore. The three major international Jewish organisations with offices in Britain were the Jewish Agency for Palestine, the British Section of the WJC and the AIWO. As the full extent of the Nazi genocide plan unfolded in the summer of 1942, there was some attempt by these organisations and the Board to consult with each other and coordinate strategies. The idea of a Consultative Committee was first mooted in July by Alex Easterman of the British Section 'in order to eliminate separate approaches to the authorities and to facilitate effective action'. Similar suggestions were made by M.R. Springer, representing the Federation of Czech Jews, and by Goodman.[51] Renewed attempts at cooperation were made in November 1942. In response to a widespread desire to present a united front, the Board approached the various international organisations 'to form an emergency Consultative Committee for collaboration'.[52] The Consultative Committee met every few days throughout December 1942, and weekly thereafter for six months.

In spite of Brodetsky's hope that members would cooperate as smoothly as possible, within a month there was criticism that the Board was acting unilaterally and not consulting the WJC. In its editorial 'Too many Cooks', the *Jewish Chronicle* complained that 'it is no secret that the hoped-for degree of harmony and co-operation has not been achieved. Beneath a superficial appearance of unity, there is still an absence of the willing acceptance of team duty and the ready self-subordination to the general cause'.[53] The Board, the Jewish Agency and the British Section continued to act autonomously, sometimes impeding the efficacy of each others' work. In October 1942, as negotiations were underway for the formation of the Consultative Committee, a Board deputation presented proposals to the Foreign Office which, according to a note of the meeting, 'were (apparently unknown to them) already been actively dealt with by F.O., or H.O. or C.O., on representations from the Jewish bodies – which seems to argue a faulty Jewish liaison [sic]'.[54] Communal disunity, without necessarily influencing government policy or decisions, was evidently perceived as a time-wasting nuisance and a symptom of amateurism, besides undermining the Jewish cause.

The British Section, for example, protested against the Board's arbitrary withdrawal of its agreement to issue a joint statement following the United Nations Declaration of 17 December 1942 on the Nazi persecution of the Jews. Instead, separate statements were issued by the three organisations. Brodetsky disingenuously explained that 'in the rush and urgency of the situation it was often necessary to call meetings at short notice and take quick decisions'.[55] This seems a polite but transparent fiction – there was no good reason why the British Section could not have been invited to attend these 'short-notice' meetings, especially since the purpose of forming 'an emergency Consultative Committee for collaboration' was precisely to involve all agencies at short notice. Brodetsky was adamant that 'the basis of the work of the Consultative Committee is that the other organisations should help, but not control or interfere with the work of the Board'.[56] He was sensitive to any attempt to challenge the Board's 'exclusive' right to deal with the government, apparently unaware that the Board's rights of representation did not preclude the possibility of the Government also dealing with other Jewish groups, such as the Zionists and ultra-orthodox.[57] The *Jewish Chronicle* impatiently described the clash between rival organisations pursuing similar ends in terms of 'reckless and competitive *Koved* [honour]-hunting', pointing to the number of Jewish organisations claiming credit for the December 1942 Declaration. Brodetsky himself claims sole credit for it in his Memoirs.[58]

Much of the difficulty stemmed from the friction between the Board and the WJC. The WJC claimed to represent 'world Jewry', the existence of which the Board denied. Laski had earlier insisted that this concept 'could only add credence to the frequent and unfounded charge against Jews by the anti-Semites that there existed an "international Jewry" and more fundamentally, that the concept of Jewish nationhood posed a danger to the civic rights of Jews in all countries'.[59] The WJC threatened to encroach upon the Board's position in matters such as representation to the government concerning Jewish refugees in Britain. In one sense this was an internal affair for British Jewry and hence the preserve of the Board. But the plight of European Jewry was deemed by the British Section to be equally its own legitimate concern.[60] The WJC and the JFC took up similar issues in similar ways, lobbying the government to intervene to protect Jewish political rights in Europe, and presenting rival petitions to the increasingly moribund League of Nations. Having led the opposition to the formation of the WJC in 1936, Laski tried frequently between 1937 and 1939 to persuade the Foreign Office to have no dealings with the British Section or its Chairman, Perlzweig. The Foreign Office, however, was prepared to accept approaches from the WJC, whose existence it deemed to be predicated on a world-wide Diaspora as distinct from a Jewish state in Palestine.[61] The AJA and the Agudat Israel were also hostile to the British Section. Leonard Stein, president of the AJA, categorically refused to recognise either the WJC or the British Section and the *Jewish Weekly* referred to the 'non-existent World Jewish Congress', dismissing its 'fantastic claim to speak for world Jewry'.[62] In the interest of the 'great task on hand', Hertz appealed to Goodman to tone down his public denunciations.[63]

Nevertheless, there is no evidence that separate approaches had any adverse effect on the government with regard to relief and rescue efforts. Bentwich later observed that the Board and the British Section had presented the Jewish case 'in unhelpful competition' but that this had made no difference: 'We got nowhere; we wasted hours protesting, and composing and criticising memoranda *which had no hope of serious attention by the Governments*'[64] [my emphasis]. Bentwich's point is not that communal disunity resulted in government inertia, but that no effort, however well coordinated, would have influenced government decision-making.

Skirmishes between the Board and the British Section continued throughout the war years. Attempts to reach a *modus vivendi* between the JFC and the British Section were unsuccessful.[65] From October 1941 the British Section tried to ensure close contact and consultation with the JFC. In the event of any foreign policy disagreement, the British Section should be free to act as directed by the WJC, on the understanding that the British Section did not represent British Jewry.[66] However, there was no serious attempt at coordinating policy even though Brodetsky, now President of the Board, had been closely associated with the British Section from its inception in 1936 and, oddly, continued to serve as one of its vice-presidents until 1942.[67] It is therefore curious that Brodetsky did not use his position as President of the Board to foster closer cooperation between the two bodies, particularly in view of his repeated calls for communal unity.

The Consultative Committee lapsed after a period of six months, though efforts were made to revive it. The WJC was reluctant to rejoin, complaining that 'it would be absurd to lend semblance to the pretence of unity, if none in fact exists between important Jewish organisations'.[68] Towards the end of 1943 a draft agreement was published on the maintenance of contact between the Board and the WJC for the exchange of confidential information. This agreement was finalised in March 1944, but the arrangements proved only partly satisfactory.

The most serious clash occurred around the time of the Zionist victory at the Board's July 1943 elections. The Board dissolved the JFC, ending its 65-year-old cooperation with the AJA, and established its own Foreign Affairs Committee. The AJA, under the chairmanship of Leonard Stein, retaliated by setting up its own General Purpose and Foreign Affairs Committee and received assurances that the Foreign Secretary would be willing 'to extend to it the same facilitates for placing its views before him as have been accorded in the past'.[69] Brodetsky was aware that these communal disputes were taking up valuable time. At the end of the third monthly Board meeting devoted to the Zionist dispute, he lamented that 'it was impossible to get on with any job ... [the Board's] time was taken up with irrelevant matters ... [while] something like four million Jews had been exterminated in Europe'.[70] Brodetsky shows an understandable despondency about the annihilation of European Jewry but prefers to blame the Board's preoccupation with 'irrelevant matters' rather than admit that although its President, he lacked vital leadership skills which would have enabled him to focus attention where it belonged.

However, these internal conflicts made little or no difference to the fate of European Jewry. On the contrary, it can be argued that the government was more sympathetic to the organisations precisely because of their lack of unity. While the government may have been disturbed by the Zionist takeover at the Board, it was also reassured by Anglo-Jewry's diversity and disunity: 'the multiplicity of Jewish approaches from the organisations purporting to have Jewish representative status largely neutralised the Board's Zionisation.'[71] One Foreign Office official, Ian Henderson, noted that 'The trend of Jewish organisations in this country appears to be towards the loss of its British character and the assumption of some international one. *The British position vis-à-vis Jewry might be correspondingly weakened, were it not for dissensions among the Jews themselves*' (my emphasis).[72]

This diversity effectively ensured that the government, perhaps subscribing to the strategy of 'divide and rule', could still negotiate with the Anglo-Jewish leadership, not all of which was ardently

Zionist. A.W.G. Randall, head of the Refugee Department at the Foreign Office (1942–44), considered optimistically that British Jewry 'will concentrate for a time on Zionism and gradually lose interest after the war when other countries, now cut off, are once again open to them'.[73] However, he warned 'that Zionist aims will tend to dominate the British Board', adding that Goodman had informed him that Brodetsky, himself a Zionist, had deplored recent developments but had so far been unable 'to withstand his more energetic Zionist colleagues'.[74] The government regarded Brodetsky and Brotman, despite their Zionism, especially compared to more vociferous radical Zionists such as Lewis Namier and Lavy Bakstansky, 'the chief whip' of the Zionists at the Board, as 'moderate' representatives of Anglo-Jewry. Similarly, official attitudes to Schonfeld and Goodman were positive, partly because they did not press the Palestine issue. While this is true, Weizmann, the most formidable of the Zionists, was in touch with ministers – not mere civil servants – throughout the war, and certainly pressed the Zionist cause whenever the opportunity arose.

The Anglo-Jewish community had acquired long experience in charitable and communal administration, which served it well in its handling of the escalating refugee crisis of the immediate pre-war years. After the outbreak of war, however, with the borders sealed and no further influx to deal with and no practical action possible, what was needed was no longer administrative skill but inspired political leadership, forceful and ingenious enough to sway opinion at government level. It was in this realm that the Anglo-Jewish community failed; its leaders lacked the necessary political skills to handle the extraordinary and unique crisis facing European Jewry. It is perhaps unlikely that any difference in leadership style would have influenced government policy; nevertheless, the reputation of the leadership might have been enhanced had it possessed the necessary skills to put up a more forceful, concerted and resourceful challenge to governmental intransigence.

The war years saw a depletion in the ranks of the Anglo-Jewish leadership, with many cases of illness and death, including those involved in the war effort.[75] The lack of cohesion and leadership among the various Jewish factions is remarked on by an anonymous London Jewish journalist: 'The ranks of leaders in Jewry are thinning. The Jewish "platform" that used to be crowded is depleted. The Jewish "lions" are no longer roaring from these platforms . . . we have no Herzl, no Max Nordau, no Zangwill, no

Sokolow or Gaster, not even a Jabotinsky.'[76] It is certainly true that Weizmann attempted throughout the war to use his influence with government ministers to press the case for a Zionist homeland, but by this stage he had become something of an embarrassment to a government that no longer needed a Zionist 'halo' under which to shelter its territorial ambitions in Palestine, as had been the case in 1917. The wartime government's suspicious and negative attitude was in complete contrast to the eagerness with which Asquith's and Lloyd George's governments had embraced Zionism in World War I. By 1939 there had arisen a widespread perception that the Anglo-Jewish leadership was dominated by second-rate, ineffectual figures; nevertheless, it is hard to prove that rescue efforts were impeded by lack of dynamic leadership, nor that any opportunity was lost as a result of disunity or rivalry. Where conscientious administrative effort was required, the Anglo-Jewish community achieved remarkable successes both before and during the war. When political intelligence and imagination were needed, it had little to contribute, trusting naively to what Orwell called 'decency' to touch the conscience of a bureaucratic machine engaged in global warfare.

3
Escalating Crises: Austria and Czechoslovakia 1938–1939

Following the Nazis' rise to power in January 1933, the half million Jews in Germany were increasingly subjected to a series of anti-Jewish laws aimed at excluding them completely from the civic, social and economic life of the country. The first phase began with a decree in April 1933 which barred Jews from employment in the civil service, in schools and universities and the legal profession. Although shocked by the anti-Jewish legislation, most German Jews felt anxiety rather than panic or urgency; their leaders tried to hide their dismay behind a façade of confidence and calm.

The Jewish community had hoped, despite evidence to the contrary, that Nazism was merely a manifestation of restless, right-wing nationalism rather than of deliberate anti-Semitism and that once the Nazis had settled in power, they would become less extreme when faced with the responsibilities of government. Jewish leaders were comforted by the fact that there were only three Nazis in the cabinet and that the aged Hindenburg, a conservative, was still in office. 'Every organized group replied to National Socialism with resounding affirmations of the right of Jews to be German, to live in and love Germany. *Daseinrecht*, the right to maintain a Jewish presence in Germany, was construed as a legal right, a moral necessity, and a religious imperative by all Jewish organizations from Orthodox to reform, right to left, Zionist and non-Zionist.'[1] This attitude was prevalent in the National Representation of German Jews (*Reichvertretung der deutschen Juden*), formally established in 1933, which remained the umbrella organisation of local and national Jewish associations until 1938, headed by Rabbi Leo Baeck and Otto Hirsch. Most German Jews were initially hostile to the idea of mass emigration. In early 1934, Hirsch would still be speaking out against

45

'hasty' emigration: He believed in the possibility of maintaining a dignified Jewish life in the new Germany.[2] Some groups, such as the organisation of independent Orthodox communities, even wrote to Hitler in October 1933, protesting against the persecution and oppression, and stressing their conviction 'that it is not the aim of the German Government to destroy the German Jews'.[3]

Still, in spite of the reluctance of many to leave, some 37,000 of Germany's 525,000 Jews fled in 1933. Only 92,000 more followed in the next four years. Most Germans Jews thought they could 'weather' the crisis and preserve a 'manageable' Jewish life within a segregated society. Even the Zionists anticipated gradual emigration over 20 years or more. In addition, the material difficulty of emigrating was considerable, especially at a time of economic uncertainty. Although emigration was a central goal of the German government's Jewish policy at this point, the Nazis were intent on dispossessing the Jews first by increasingly harsh measures.[4]

The legal assault on the Jews peaked with the Nuremberg Laws in September 1935 which effectively put an end to the 'emancipation' of Jews and their place in German social life. These laws deprived Jews of their German citizenship; they were no longer able to vote in German elections, nor display the German flag. The Laws barred 'interracial' marriages or intercourse between Aryans and Jews and the employment of German maids in Jewish households. No economic discrimination was included in the Nuremberg Laws, which were limited to racial and social anti-Semitic legislation. The economic destruction of the Jews would happen only after *Kristallnacht* in November 1938.

In a curious way, the Nuremberg Laws, loathsome as they were, stabilised the situation by setting clear legal parameters within which the Jewish community could operate. For foreign consumption, Hitler himself declared that the 'National Socialist legislation offered the only possibility of achieving a tolerable relationship with the Jews living in Germany'. 'Such reassuring declarations made it more difficult for the Jewish leadership to understand correctly the gravity of the position and to prepare for a future shrouded in mist.'[5] With a lull in Nazi persecution of the Jews in late 1935 and 1936 (during the Olympic games) many in the Jewish community were misled. Despite the oscillations between intimidation and restraint, the treatment of German Jews stabilised somewhat in the years 1936–37.[6] The number leaving Germany levelled off after the Nuremberg Laws, from 23,000 in 1934, to some 21,000 in 1935; 25,000 in 1936; and

23,000 in 1937. The period 1938–9 saw the greatest impetus to leave German territory and Jewish emigration from Germany escalated sharply following the events of 1938. The *Anschluss* with Austria in March, the acquisition of the Sudetenland in September and the *Kristallnacht* pogrom in November, were followed, in March 1939, by the annexation of the rest of Czechoslovakia (Bohemia and Moravia) as a German 'protectorate'. Following *Kristallnacht* in November 1938, the tactics of the Nazis were aimed at driving Jews out of the country by means of increased economic and physical pressure and had the desired effect. During this period approximately 120,000 Jews left Germany, almost as many as in the entire proceeding five years.[7]

The prospect of huge numbers of Jews fleeing persecution in 1938–39 raised difficult questions for the British government and overwhelmed the private Anglo-Jewish organisations, none of which was prepared for any sudden influx of refugees. Nevertheless, the organisations carried through a programme of fund-raising and constructive assistance, including training, retraining, emigration, employment assistance and relief, such that John Hope Simpson observed, 'There is no parallel in the recent history of British voluntary charitable effort.'[8]

In the face of this overwhelming series of crises, refugee work was still limited by the parameters imposed by immigration law. British policy on refugee immigration was based on legislation dating from the 1905 Aliens Act to the Aliens Restriction Act of 1919 and the ensuing Aliens Order of 1920. In effect, this legislation removed the earlier (unconditional) right of asylum; no alien could now enter the country, other than temporarily, without a Ministry of Labour permit or visible means of support. This legislation, originally renewable annually, was placed on the Statute Book in 1926 and, due to the inter-war depression and post-war austerity, determined Britain's severely restrictive immigration policy until 1951.[9]

The government reacted to the early outrages of the Nazi regime by confirming that Britain was not a country of immigration and that its large population, concern over the state of the economy and high unemployment, and fear of aggravating anti-Semitism by enlarging the Jewish population, precluded any but a carefully restrictive asylum policy. However, this policy did undergo modifications due to the dramatically changing situation.[10] The popular perception is that Britain generously provided a haven for refugees. While this is true, it is important to emphasise the extent to which the

Anglo-Jewish community facilitated Jewish immigration into Britain, as a result of the guarantee it made to the government in 1933 that no refugee would become a charge on public funds. The government imposed no limit on numbers, although in 1933 the estimated numbers were no more than 3,000–4,000. The financial and administrative support of the voluntary bodies was the indispensable condition of entry.

Following the *Anschluss*, visas for Germans and Austrians were reintroduced. The main purpose of the visa was to regulate the flow of refugees to British ports. The Home Office was anxious about the future status of 'undesirable' or impoverished Austrian passport-holders who might seek admission to Britain. The power to secure the removal of an alien by means of a deportation order could be exercised only if that alien were recognised by some other country as one of its nationals. It was now possible that the German government would deprive Austrian Jews of their citizenship and render them stateless.[11] Government fears were compounded by Schiff's indication that the GJAC could no longer honour the 1933 guarantee in respect of any new arrivals, though it would continue financially to support refugees already in Britain and was prepared to make an exception for refugees approved by the Home Office or the Ministry of Labour.[12] It has been suggested that Schiff's letter reinforced the government's decision to impose visa controls.[13] It is doubtful, however, whether Schiff's letter actually affected this decision, given that the sudden surge in applications would inevitably have resulted in some initiative to restrict numbers. The idea of imposing visa restrictions on the entry of Germans had been mooted before the *Anschluss*, in consequence of the recent German law obligating every German living abroad to report to a German consulate. It was anticipated that most German refugees would avoid reporting, thereby forfeiting their German nationality and rendering themselves stateless.[14]

Schiff and the Board certainly shared Home Office concern, not only about the numbers of would-be immigrants but also about what Sir Samuel Hoare, the Home Secretary, termed the 'type of' refugee who could be admitted into Britain. If a flood of the wrong type of immigrants were allowed in there might be serious danger of anti-Semitic feeling being aroused in this country'.[15] The wrong type of immigrant was, according to the Home Office, 'the small Jewish traders and business man [sic] of limited means ... forced out of business and out of his country ... driven by economic and political pressure to seek asylum here'.[16] Such an immigrant presumably would experience difficulty finding work and eventually emigrating. The visa system was meant to facilitate investigation of would-be immigrants before they started their journey, so as 'to obviate the hardships of rejection at the ports, which might have otherwise arisen'.[17] It is difficult to accept that the Anglo-Jewish leadership could have foreseen that it would result in hardship, delays, suicides and, in many cases, failure to escape Nazi-occupied territory.[18]

At the Evian Conference on Refugees in July 1938, the government announced that 'on the grounds of humanity', the Home Office would now adopt 'an even more liberal attitude' in the matter of admissions and employment. While pre-selection remained, certain additions to the categories of admission were outlined, particularly for those to be admitted for training with a view to emigration. Fearing that many of the new arrivals would become a permanent charge on their dwindling funds, the refugee organisations insisted in late July on a formal guarantee of maintenance for any applicant who wished to bring friends or relatives to Britain. By October 1938 the voluntary bodies, overwhelmed by the magnitude of their task and the inadequacy of their resources, threatened to collapse under the strain. The number of casework delays grew and Schiff requested a temporary halt to the admission of refugees until those already admitted had either been assimilated or had emigrated.[19]

In spite of this, following *Kristallnacht*, when other countries were increasing restrictions on refugee admissions, the British government took steps to facilitate immigration into Britain. New categories of refugees, including transmigrants, were admitted. In order to deal more expeditiously with these classes of refugees and to eliminate unnecessary work on the part of the Home Office and Passport Control officers, an arrangement was made towards the end of December with the GJAC for a simplified procedure in regard to these categories of refugees. The Home Office also facilitated the entry of all children and young people whose maintenance could be guaranteed. Domestics and people over sixty whose maintenance was assured were also included. Selection was increasingly delegated to the voluntary bodies, which were now able to submit lists of names.[20] However, in contrast to those who had arrived before 1938, most refugees were not allowed to take up employment and many depended on the refugee organisations for financial support.

Anglo-Jewry's initial response to the *Anschluss* was to take measured

2 Otto Schiff, Chairman of the Jewish Refugees Committee, 1933–49 (courtesy of the *Jewish Chronicle*)

diplomatic action. Until *Kristallnacht*, when it became clear that the only option was immediate emigration, the Anglo-Jewish organisations still believed that the best solution to the refugee crisis was to try somehow to resolve the plight of German and Austrian Jewry. While the JFC recognised that 'in the confusion that followed the *Anschluss* . . . there was little that could be done to help the sufferers', it nevertheless urged HMG to communicate to Berlin the deep anxiety of British Jews for their Austrian co-religionists. However, the Foreign Office insisted that this was a domestic issue and that any representations to Germany would embitter relations between the two countries without helping the persecuted.[21] Perlzweig was similarly advised 'that the treatment of the Jews was an internal matter and no concern of ours'. The Foreign Office did, however, agree that informal enquiries be made through the British Embassy in Berlin about the closing of the Palestine Office in Vienna and saw no objection to the WJC approaching the Italians to use their influence in the matter.[22] The WJC also submitted two strongly worded petitions to the Council of the League of Nations asking it to intervene on behalf of Austrian Jewry under the Minority Rights Treaty (Article 69).[23]

Both the Home Office and the refugee organisations feared that a large influx of Jewish refugees might produce a wave of anti-Semitism in Britain. The Home Office had received a report that 'the Germans were anxious to inundate this country with Jews, with a view to creating a Jewish problem in the United Kingdom'. There was also an increase in British anti-Jewish propaganda, largely foreign-inspired, representing Jewish refugees as potential sources of moral and political contamination.[24] A campaign was therefore launched by the Coordinating Committee (renamed the Jewish Defence Committee in late 1938) of the Board to educate the public about Jews. Leaflets and pamphlets were issued and speakers sent round the country, and Vigilance Committees were established in those trades in which Jews were chiefly concentrated, together with a Trades' Advisory Council and a special Arbitration court.[25]

Laski opposed any protest meeting in response to the *Anschluss*, arguing that 'the Jewish question was one facet of a much larger one which constituted a grave danger to civilisation as a whole'. Rather, it was 'the duty of Jews to act in conformity with their obligations as citizens and at the same time to try to educate those outside the community to the dangers of Nazism'.[26] Laski suggested that an Intercession Service – 'a mass movement of prayer' – would be more beneficial and would provide a high-profile outlet for Jewish sentiment. The *Jewish Chronicle* agreed that a Day of Prayer and an Intercession Service (17 July 1938) would 'arouse the conscience of the world'. The Board considered it a further advantage that the 'Christian churches... have announced their intention of joining this intercession'.[27] The British Section, always more proactive than the Board, held a demonstration on 28 June 1938, attended by Church leaders and other dignitaries. It called on all nations to support the forthcoming conference at Evian by opening new outlets for Jewish immigration and appealed to HMG to ensure that the full economic absorptive capacity of Palestine be made available to Jewish immigration.[28]

These gestures, however, were ineffective; more productively, on an administrative level, the voluntary bodies organised much-needed relief and constructive assistance. The situation of the 180,000 Austrian Jews after the *Anschluss* was considerably worse than that of the Jews in Germany. The system of oppression, humiliation and exclusion of Austrian Jewry from all economic and social activity was ruthlessly applied and accomplished within months, rather than the five years it had taken in Germany.[29] Plundering and violence against Jews were widespread, and mass arrests of Jews and anti-Nazis occurred. In May, the Nuremberg Laws were extended to Austria.[30] Thousands of Jews, now impoverished, besieged foreign consulates seeking immigration permits. A major problem was that, unlike in Germany, the machinery of the Jewish community had been closed down, its small cash reserve (55,000 schillings) confiscated and its communal leaders arrested.[31] It was not until May 1938 that the Viennese Jewish community, after paying 300,000 schillings was able to reopen its offices and resume its activities.

Until the *Anschluss*, the CGJ had been exclusively concerned with the Jews of Germany, mainly in 'constructive' work such as training and resettlement, primarily in Palestine, rather than local relief. Although its burden now included Austrian Jewry, by March 1938 hardly any funds were available to meet the new crisis. During 1933–37 a sum of over £1,000,000 had been collected in Great Britain and the Empire for assistance to German Jewry. The greater part was subscribed under seven-year covenants and had already been spent or allocated for specific purposes of emigration and settlement. The CGJ had to borrow large sums in anticipation of contributions still to be collected.[32]

To a great extent, German-Jewish emigration, comprising some 150,000 refugees since 1933, had been self-financed. Austrian Jews, however, were mostly destitute. After the *Anschluss*, the numbers dependent on Jewish public relief more than doubled to over 60,000. By the summer of 1938, over 60 per cent of Austrian Jewry was partially or entirely dependent on organisational support.[33] The *Kultusgemeinde* (Jewish community) in Vienna was supported by the American Jewish Joint Distribution Committee (JDC) and the CGJ. The two bodies together made a grant for immediate relief in Vienna of about £10,000 for March and April, but this was a mere palliative. The sums required for soup kitchens, as well as for emigration and training schemes, rose considerably. In August, a sum of nearly £20,000 was allocated.[34] Sir Wyndham Deedes, Norman Bentwich and Leo Lauterbach of the Jewish Agency tried unsuccessfully to negotiate with the Nazis the reopening of the Austrian Zionist organisations and the possibility of transferring Jewish capital to Palestine. A member of the GJAC remained in Vienna to assist with emigration.[35]

The CGJ was reluctant to grant funds for relief, maintaining that relief should be provided by the local municipalities. Any such grants would further diminish the reserves available for emigration. Financial support for the *Kultusgemeinde* was largely designed to support training and assist emigration.[36] New funds were needed to meet this emergency, as the funds of the CGJ were fully absorbed and almost exhausted. The CGJ, under the chairmanship of Lord Reading, therefore launched the Austrian Appeal. Attempts to persuade the JDC to launch an international appeal failed. Nevertheless, together with the US contribution, the Austrian Appeal succeeded in raising approximately £170,000.[37] The CGJ was convinced, however, that this figure would not be substantially increased. Even if the whole amount were spent on emigration, it would be sufficient for the emigration of only a minute fraction of those Jews wishing to leave.[38]

One traumatic consequence of the *Anschluss* was the expulsion of Jews from the Burgenland provinces – the so-called 'Seven Communities', home to Jews for centuries – to be 'dumped' over the frontiers of adjacent countries, destitute and threatened with deportation. By early 1939, there were reportedly at least twelve 'no-man's-land' refugee camps along these borders, harbouring thousands of refugees, some confined in appalling conditions.[39] Highlighted by Schonfeld, Goodman and others, the plight of the Burgenland refugees received wide publicity in influential non-Jewish circles and the press, as well as within the Jewish community.[40] By the summer of 1938, efforts were still being made to induce countries overseas to receive the fugitives, most of whom, however, were unable to comply with entry requirements.

The problem of finding homes for European refugees was now assuming international proportions; in consequence of this came the proposal in March 1938, on the initiative of President Roosevelt, that 32 European and Latin American states meet in order to facilitate the emigration of refugees. Yet, as the exodus became evidently enormous, most countries tightened their immigration policies. Thus, Evian offered little hope to the refugee organisations. Cordell Hull, the American Secretary of State, had already confirmed that no country would be expected or asked to receive greater numbers of immigrants than already permitted by existing quota legislation. Any financing of assistance and settlement schemes for refugees would remain the responsibility of the private organisations.[41] Further, as a concession to the British, it was agreed that Palestine would not be discussed at Evian.

Although the Conference purported to 'facilitate the emigration of refugees', it is hard to see what in practice it had in mind if it intended to offload the financial burden onto the private charities and make no changes to existing legislation, especially on Palestine. Lord Bearsted rejected the claim, emanating from Germany, that foreign Jewish communities could raise unlimited sums to support emigration, adding that these communities had 'no intention of impoverishing their mother country by paying ransom to Germany'. Bearsted was aware of the circular nature of the problem, namely, that a willingness to finance emigration would be taken as encouragement to other East European countries to increase persecution, with the dual objects of unloading 'surplus' populations and raising cash. He feared that in default of a practical lead from the United States, the outlook for Evian 'was gloomy' and that 'the meeting would be chiefly occupied with passing the buck'. He predicted that the delegation would be overwhelmed by 'all manner of pressure from private organisations'.[42]

While it is accepted that the Conference was 'convoked without well-defined terms of reference and the Jewish organisations did not know what their status would be in relation to the Conference',[43] the fact remains that the voluntary organisations failed to present a united front. When the Liaison Committee of the High Commissioner of the League of Nations met just before Evian, no unanimous policy could be agreed upon and the various international bodies decided to submit individual proposals.[44] Altogether twelve

Memoranda were submitted to Evian by the various Jewish and non-Jewish voluntary organisations.[45]

However, the Anglo-Jewish organisations did liaise with each other before the Conference. They submitted a Memorandum urging the re-establishment of the principle of economic absorptive capacity for Palestine immigration and stressing that they could not financially support any large-scale emigration schemes – the two issues on which the Conference had already ruled. The Memorandum also suggested that a small executive body be set up by the Conference to supervise emigration and to undertake negotiations with the German authorities to allow refugees to transfer some of their property, in order to facilitate an orderly emigration. The Memorandum shows that the organisations concurred with the government's selection procedures based on economic suitability and re-emigration potential.[46] In practice, they had little option but to acquiesce in the government's criteria especially in view of their own precarious financial position. The consensus was that mass settlement of refugees was neither practicable nor desirable, and that accordingly, 'infiltration' into settled communities was preferable.[47]

The interdenominational Co-ordinating Committee (representing all the voluntary refugee organisations) was concerned about the large number of interested private organisations. The Foreign Office also thought it undesirable that special interest (particularly political) groups should be granted access to the deliberations. Both the Foreign Office and some Anglo-Jewish communal leaders, such as Herbert Samuel, were aware of the danger that Jewish representation at Evian might be taken by the Germans as confirmation that the conference was being engineered by 'international Jewry'.[48] Lord Winterton, head of the British delegation, advised the CGJ 'to be represented only by comparatively subordinate members', and the voluntary organisations themselves opposed 'too much publicity'.[49] In the end, the voluntary organisations were not officially invited to the Conference but sent representatives as observers. The actual work of the Conference was carried out by two sub-committees, one technical, the other established to hear representations from 39 separate refugee organisations.[50]

The organisations knew in advance that it would be impolitic to refer to Palestine[51] but this did not deter them from doing so. They called for a substantial increase in the Palestine immigration quota and assistance for refugee resettlement schemes through an international loan. All speakers stressed that the country of origin must cooperate by relaxing its regulations concerning the conditions attached to emigration and the transfer of refugees' property. On the final point of the status of refugees, several organisations urged that the February 1938 Convention, providing for the juridical position of refugees, be ratified immediately.[52] In the event, attempts to unify the plethora of interested organisations failed and none succeeded in influencing the outcome of Evian. Yet, it must be stressed that the principal failure of Evian was that, with the exception of the Dominican Republic, the governments produced no effective solution to the problem of locating places of settlement for refugees. Most of the discussion focused on German policy rather than on that of potential host countries.

However, several specific requests were met: among these was the establishment of a permanent Inter-Governmental Committee on Refugees (IGCR), under the leadership of the seventy-year-old Washington lawyer George Rublee, whose immediate task was to negotiate with Germany to establish conditions of orderly emigration by allowing refugees to take some of their property with them, which at this stage still appeared a viable proposition. Britain ratified the February 1938 Convention, extending it to Austrian refugees.[53] Yet, these slight achievements did not alleviate the refugee problem. Attempts by the IGCR to engage in dialogue with Germany were deliberately protracted and systematically sabotaged, and negotiations for the transfer of at least part of the prospective emigrants' capital were unsuccessful. One of its secondary duties was to find destinations for refugees. At the insistence of President Roosevelt, the IGCR continued to exist but its role was considerably diminished after the outbreak of war. Its activities were confined to settling refugees who had already left Reich territory and were resident in neutral countries.[54] All the proposed settlement schemes, in remote places such as British Guiana, the Philippines, Madagascar, Angola and Rhodesia, never got beyond the exploratory stage.[55] Ultimately, it was immaterial whether the proposals forwarded by the organisations were practical or not, or whether a united front was presented, since the Conference itself had eliminated at the outset any ideas that might have borne fruit.

Evian was little more than a public relations exercise. A Foreign Office note reveals the hope that the Conference 'would secure sympathy and support of world Jewry for HMG and perhaps make easier a solution of the position of Palestine'. The government was also anxious to respond positively to America's departure from its policy of non-intervention in European affairs. Moreover, if the conference produced concrete results such as the formation of the IGCR, the Evian meeting was likely to 'enhance the prestige of the League in a field of work largely humanitarian in character'.[56] If anything, it was counterproductive, in that the Germans read it as a cynical exercise in empty rhetoric and concluded that the persecution of German Jewry could now proceed with impunity.

The failure of Evian to do anything for European Jewry at this point is all the more striking because the German policy of forced emigration had been gathering momentum throughout 1938. There was, at this stage, no difficulty about extricating Jews from German-occupied territory as there was after the outbreak of war. This did not prevent the Allied Governments at Bermuda (April 1943) lamenting that wartime conditions made it impossible to extricate Jews from enemy-held territory.

Czechoslovakia

The Czech crisis in the summer of 1938 overshadowed the entire question of an approach to Germany about Jewish emigration. Throughout that summer, Hitler dominated European diplomatic activity by his demand, backed by military threats, for the cession of the Sudetenland, the German-speaking region of Czechoslovakia, to Germany. During the Munich negotiations in September, the plight of thousands of refugees in the Sudetenland was raised by neither the British nor French representatives. Anglo-Jewish leaders tried unsuccessfully to introduce this issue onto the international agenda. Of special concern was the anticipated transfer of populations on a linguistic basis. Various appeals were made to the government to safeguard the interests of the Jews. The cession of territory imperilled a large number of people in Sudeten Germany, who were 'obnoxious to the Nazis either on account of their race or their political views'.[57]

The number of refugees from the Sudetenland, now in the newly truncated Czechoslovakia, was approximately 40,000 (of whom 15,000 were in Prague with more arriving at a rate of 1,500 a day). Of these, the 20,000 German Jews and 5,000 Social Democrats from the Sudetenland posed the gravest problem. The latter, most outspoken against the Nationalist Socialist movement and its leader, Konrad Henlein, were considered as enemies of the new regime. Nor could Czechoslovakia risk allowing a new German minority to grow in its midst, serving as a pretext for further German encroachment on the reduced Czech territory. Consequently, these refugees were faced with an order for compulsory return.[58]

The Jewish immigrants from Austria and Germany who had first taken refuge in the Sudetenland, estimated at around 5,000, were also threatened with expulsion. Not only were these refugees aggravating the Czech unemployment problem (totalling 100,000 in October), but they were also competing for scanty relief and resettlement opportunities.[59] While some Sudeten Jews were already residents and hence Czech Jews, these others were being treated by the Czech government as Germans, and expulsion orders had been issued at the request of Berlin. Their fate depended on their being given the right of opting for Czech citizenship; presumably, they could then reclaim the property and possessions they had left behind.[60]

This threat of forcible return of all non-Czech refugees by the Czech authorities to German areas was the most immediate problem. In addition, it was anticipated that when the residents of the newly annexed Sudeten areas began to exercise their 'right of option' under Article 7 of the Munich Agreement, there would be approximately 600,000 who would opt for Czech citizenship and become, in effect, refugees.[61] The British government came under pressure from many quarters to dissuade Germany from enforcing its demands for the return of refugees. British representatives at Berlin and Warsaw were instructed to do everything possible to persuade the German and Czech governments to refrain from such action and to urge an early settlement of the 'right of option' arrangement.[62]

When Laski and Waley-Cohen finally met with Lord Halifax in October, they began by linking the appeasement policy with the wider refugee problem. Intolerance and violence towards Jews and others in Germany was bound 'to create insuperable obstacles to the ultimate success of the policy of appeasement and peace . . . thus, so far from becoming an internal German question this has become an international question of the most far-reaching consequence'. They urged HMG to use its influence to secure for Jews the right of opting for Czech citizenship. Halifax warned that 'sometimes intervention with Germans . . . produced more harm than good', but promised every help that could be given within the limits of international agreements and practice. The 'right of option' was defined in the Agreement between Germany and Czechoslovakia on 23 November 1938. It gave the Czech government the right to demand that persons of 'German nationality' leave the Republic.[63]

Until the establishment of the German Protectorate of Bohemia and Moravia in March 1939, Anglo-Jewish leaders assumed that refugees in Czechoslovakia were better off than those elsewhere.[64] Certainly the Czech government attempted to assist the mass of refugees within its borders, using financial support in the form of an Anglo-French £10 million loan (for the settlement of refugees within Czechoslovakia), of which £4 million was set aside as a free gift, earmarked for migration and settlement of refugees. This agreement (reached on 27 January 1939 and later known as the Czech Refugee Trust) defined as refugees both inhabitants of the ceded areas before 31 May 1938 and Austrians and Germans who had fled to Czechoslovakia before 30 September 1938.[65] However, it did not cover all categories of refugees, including some Jewish inhabitants of the new Protectorate, who could only apply to the Czech Refugee Trust Fund under certain conditions.[66]

Before the Trust was created, several appeals were launched in Britain, indicating strong popular sympathy for the plight of Czech refugees. These included the Lord Mayor's Mansion House Czech Relief Fund (which raised £372,000 within a few weeks) and the News Chronicle Appeal. However, the GJAC, already at the end of its financial and human resources, was unable to help, having informed the government that 'it is very hard pressed and cannot accept responsibility for refugees from Czechoslovakia'.[67] The CGJ advised against the Jewish community making an organised collection on behalf of the Lord Mayor's Appeal as it would 'be detrimental to the collection which the CGJ will be compelled to make'.[68] Consequently, Schiff advised Czech applicants to apply to the voluntary, non-denominational British Committee for Refugees from Czechoslovakia, set up in October to provide temporary hospitality for endangered refugees who could not return to the Third Reich or to any of the ceded territories. Permits had been granted to 350 such persons (Social Democrats) to come to Britain for a limited period and the Committee guaranteed their maintenance. Between October 1938 and March 1939 the British Committee brought 3,500 refugees from Czechoslovakia to Britain, absorbing all the Committee's financial resources.[69]

Emigration was the only solution for these German Social Democrats and Jews, none of whom were wanted in Czechoslovakia. Following *Kristallnacht*, in addition to the problem of the 20,000 Sudeten and Old Reich Jews, the situation of Czech Jews (estimates varied from 150,000 to 250,000) became more precarious. Not only were there reports that the Czech government intended to expel Reich German and Austrian refugees (at the latest by mid-January) but there were indications of the possibility of a 'wholesale expulsion of Jews from Czechoslovakia'. Germany was pressing the Czech government to take action against the Jews, although the latter recognised that 'there must be no pogroms before January or February as nothing must be done to interfere with the possibility of obtaining a further Anglo-French loan'. But it was hoped that before January, 'all the Jews in Czechoslovakia would have decided to emigrate'.[70]

The Liaison Committee, meeting in February, stressed that as the political refugee question would soon be settled (the Social Democrats had obtained temporary visas for England and Canada), 'the problem will then become a problem of Jewish emigration only'. Help from the British loan was available to certain refugees who had the possibility to emigrate. It was feared that Jewish emigration would be subordinated to the political emigration and that the £4 million would be spent without Jewish emigration having derived any benefit from it. There was, additionally, an absolutely destitute mass of 20,000 German Jewish refugees, for whom there would also be no emigration outlets. Sir Herbert Emerson, the High Commissioner for Refugees, pointed out that the Czech Government, while allowing German and Austrian refugees to come to Czechoslovakia, did not acknowledge any responsibility for them. It wanted to confine the benefits of the loan to the Sudeten refugees (by January 1939 numbering 125,000 and continually growing) for whom it felt particular responsibility. Emerson tried, unsuccessfully, to persuade the Czechs to make available some proportion of the loan to the refugees from Austria and Germany. He also stressed the necessity for the Jewish organisations 'not to stand aloof as they have practically done up to now, from the Jews in Czechoslovakia',[71] an unusually forceful criticism of the community's efforts on behalf of Czech Jewry. The comparatively poor response is perhaps accounted for by the community's assumption that Czech Jews were in a less precarious position than those of Germany and that the British Committee would help them.

However, the German invasion of Prague in March 1939 and the extension of Nazi racial laws to Czechoslovakia's large Jewish population seriously worsened the situation. Legal emigration became impossible and even worse, the relief and refugee organisations in Prague and elsewhere in Czechoslovakia, which had run the refugee camps, were immediately disbanded. The refugees dispersed and little could be done to help them leave the country legally.[72] Laski lamented illogically that 'if great democracies could do nothing ... then a body like ourselves ... could only depend on the good offices of the democracies for an amelioration of the position of our brethren' [sic].[73] It now became clear that anti-Jewish legislation in Czechoslovakia would augment the number of refugees. As with holders of German and Austrian passports following the *Anschluss*, the British government imposed visa regulations on Czech nationals in April 1939.[74] After the destruction of Czechoslovakia, the conditions for the proposed loan became inapplicable. The £4 million gift was reaffirmed, but it only provided for 20,000 refugees (£200 per person). This provision proved inadequate for the number of refugees, much larger than contemplated in October 1938, when only those from the Sudetenland were under consideration. Pro-refugee groups vainly tried to ensure that an addition be made to the free gift and that permits be freely given in anticipation of this extra sum.[75]

Not all Czech refugees were maintained by the Czech Refugee Trust Fund after March 1939. According to the White Paper regulations (21 July 1939), the Fund could help only those who had fled Germany and the Sudetenland and found refuge in Czechoslovakia. There was no organisation for refugees unprotected by the Fund. Thus, just after the Germans established the Protectorate, a 'Self-Aid Association for Jews from Bohemia, Moravia and Slovakia' was formed. A separate Jewish group was considered necessary, although the British Committee had on its board a representative of the CGJ. Leo Herrman, its acting chairman, explained that 'while there are Jews who had acted as Social Democrats, Communists, etc. . . . in the former Czechoslovakia, Jews qua Jews were not represented in the framework of the British Committee for Czechoslovakian Refugees . . . who now constituted the main element among refugees'. It now became absolutely imperative that the interests of all Jews 'be co-ordinated, safeguarded and represented vis-à-vis the British Committee'. Goodman had also started a Federation of Czech Jews in March and in November 1939, together with the Self-Aid Association, merged with another two groups to form the Joint Committee of Jews from Czechoslovakia.[76]

The Federation immediately arranged an informal conference to discuss emigration and to cooperate with the British Committee. Its memorandum admits frankly that 'British Jewry has not shown much interest in those people who since 1933 have made great sacrifices

for their unfortunate brethren'.[77] At the outbreak of war it was estimated that 7,000 refugees from Austria and Germany in the
Protectorate of Bohemia and Moravia were still being maintained
and supported by the local Jewish community. Between 1939 and
1945, the Federation alone spent more than £8,500 for the relief of
Czech Jews in exile. It took a special interest in Czech Jewish children
in the UK who had experienced pressure to undergo baptism.[78]

The number of destitute refugee children in Czechoslovakia was
estimated at between 15,000 and 18,000. Many had been removed
to State Recovery Homes, where they were cared for out of the
Lord Mayor's Fund, while others were looked after by the Save the
Children Fund, but apart from the Society of Friends, there was no
organisation to help Czech children to emigrate. Like the CGJ, the
Refugee Children's Movement did not deal with Czech children, its
resources being insufficient to cover the additional responsibility.
In April 1939, the children's section of the British Committee opened.
Those involved were largely unaffiliated to the mainstream refugee
organisations. Eleanor Rathbone visited the refugee camps and drew
constant attention in the Commons to the Czech refugees who were
not covered by the British gift.[79] Nicholas Winton, a young English
stockbroker, visited Prague, arranging for 'child emigration into Sweden
on a big scale'. By May 1939, Winton calculated, there were 5,000
registered cases and an estimated 10,000 needing to register. Winton
appealed, unsuccessfully, to President Roosevelt about the plight of
these refugee children, many of whom were stateless.[80] Only 120
children had so far been brought to Britain, of whom over 85 per
cent were Jewish. The initial 25 children were brought over only
after undertakings had been obtained by the Barbican Mission that
they would be baptised. Goodman drew public attention to this
and attempted to 'rescue' these children.[81] But the missionary bodies
were independent organisations and therefore free from external
interference. In the end, Winton was able to secure the rescue of some
664 children before the war. He lamented that there was a bottleneck:
'if we would have had more families we could have brought out
more – twice the number of families, twice the number of children.'[82]

One result of the Munich Agreement was the escalation of expul-
sions of Jews into no-man's-land. The borders between Slovakia
and Hungary were not yet definitively established. Jews of Hungarian origin were driven from Slovak territory, while Slovak Jews
were expelled by the Hungarian occupation authorities.[83] In October
1938, the Board had expressed the hope that Jews and other minorities

in the affected territories would not suffer loss of security or status. The Foreign Office noted that the issue was 'primarily a matter for the Czech Government . . . but HMG would watch the situation in light of the representations made by the Board and take any opportunity which may present itself for using their good offices in this matter'. In the meantime, the Board attempted to involve leaders of the Catholic Church world-wide in bringing pressure to bear on the Slovak Government and people.[84] Schonfeld and Goodman were particularly concerned about the plight of refugees in Slovakia, many of whom were close friends.[85] However, an appeal to HMG met with the response that 'the Munich Agreement is not applicable' and that it was pointless to protest to the Hungarian Government.[86] Local communities in Bratislava and Budapest supervised the building and maintenance of barracks for the refugees, supported by funds provided by the JDC and the Lord Mayor's Czech Fund. In February 1939, Schonfeld raised the matter with the secretary of the League of Nations Union.[87] By then, however, most of the no-man's-lands on the Czech-Hungarian frontier had been liquidated.

More serious was the expulsion (28–29 October 1938) of 18,000 Polish Jews, long resident in Germany, who had lost their Polish citizenship. The Polish government refused to admit them and they were abandoned in no-man's-land along the Polish–German border between Neu-Bentschen and Zbaszyn. Jewish relief organisations, particularly the JDC, arranged emergency housing and food for them.[88] The CGJ made several insignificant grants to the Warsaw Jewish Refugee Relief Committee. Attitudes towards Polish and German Jews differed, as Polish Jews could always be repatriated to Poland, whereas German Jews had nowhere to return to.[89] Morris Troper, the JDC representative, urged 'greater participation by British Jewry in relief for refugees from the Reich, including those from Czechoslovakia and also those marooned at Zbonszyn [sic] for more than 8 months'.[90]

The Polish Refugee Fund was the first organisation to assist the deportees. It issued a national appeal for funds and a first group of children arrived in Britain in February 1939.[91] A Parliamentary Committee was formed to support the appeal and pledged to use its influence for the purpose of transferring the Zbaszyn deportees. Funds were sent to the Warsaw Committee, but by June 1939 these were almost exhausted. The CRREC launched a Passover Appeal for the refugees.[92] A conference, convened in May 1939, decided to launch a campaign for assistance in the evacuation of further groups of children, estimated at 1,339. Disappointingly, by September, only

160 children had reached Britain from Zbaszyn, by which time the camp had been liquidated.[93]

Up to this point, the Anglo-Jewish community had conscientiously attempted to deal with the deteriorating condition of its central European co-religionists. However, despite the increasing gravity of the situation following the *Anschluss* and the Munich Agreement, there was not the same sense of urgency which was to characterise Anglo-Jewry's response to events after November 1938. It was only after *Kristallnacht* that a marked shift in the community's attitude found expression in a more forthright approach to the emergency in Europe.

4
The Watershed: *Kristallnacht* and After

The *Kristallnacht* pogrom on 9–10 November 1938 struck a savage blow at Jews throughout the Reich. It began with the personal revenge of Herschel Grynspan, whose parents were among the deportees to Zbaszyn, who shot dead Ernst vom Rath, a diplomat at the German Embassy in Paris. This served as a pretext for a state-sponsored orgy of violence against Jews and their property, culminating in a wave of widespread terror and destruction of Jewish property, institutions and places of worship. More disturbing, 91 Jews were killed and more than 30,000 were arrested and sent to concentration camps. On 12 November Goering issued the 'Regulation for the Elimination of Jews from Economic Life in Germany' and the 'Regulation for the Payment of an Expiation Fine by Jews who are German Subjects', of one billion German marks. The declared goal of Germany's Jewish policy was now the complete prohibition of any kind of economic activity by Jews, in order to force them into emigrating more quickly.[1] German Jews were ordered to register their property and the regulations preventing emigrants from taking anything but a fraction of their possessions became more stringent. Previously, many refugees had managed to finance their own emigration; the great bulk were now practically penniless.[2] Further measures were taken that month which excluded Jewish children from state schools; curfews were imposed and Jews were now banned from public places. A major turning point in the Nazi policy towards Jews seemed to have been reached. Goering and Hitler threatened that in the event of 'conflict abroad' (an eventuality which Germany had been preparing for several years), they would 'settle accounts' with the Jews. At this stage, however, German policy was, as Heydrich remarked, 'getting the Jews out of Germany', principally by the application of economic pressure.[3]

Condemnation of *Kristallnacht* came from all sections of the British Government, press and public. Laski condemned both the murder of von Rath and 'the avenge [*sic*] on people devoid of any complicity'.[4] The Anglo-Jewish leadership recognised that the Nazis were now operating the 'Laws of the Jungle' and that the only solution for German Jewry was to leave as quickly as possible.[5] Fearing reports of 'further measures early in 1939 calculated to complete the liquidation of the Jewish population', the CGJ decided that it must 'endeavour to get as many Jews as possible out of Germany immediately'.[6] The first Board meeting following the pogrom, attended by a record 214 deputies, appealed for government intervention and called on the community for financial support to rescue 'those in Germany whom it was still possible to save'.[7]

Laski urged that Jewish defence and anti-defamation activities should be strengthened and enlarged. It may seem curious that the great wave of public sympathy for German Jews was accompanied by resurgent fear of domestic anti-Semitism, as happened after the *Anschluss*. Yet 'the Baldwin appeal for refugees, while revealing on the one hand the open-hearted generosity of the British public, had unfortunately also made manifest a carefully engineered campaign against the refugees as seen in the columns of many newspapers and elsewhere'.[8] Much of the hostility was doubtless inspired by fears about immigrants competing for jobs at a time of high unemployment.

Despite the conviction that protest meetings were futile, one such was now organised. The government, aware of the adverse effects of the pogrom on Anglo-German relations, advised against any intervention or public protest, which it again insisted would only aggravate matters for German Jews and for British Jews with interests in Germany.[9] However, an interdenominational protest meeting was convened at the Albert Hall in December 1938. Hertz also called for a day of 'Prayer and Intercession' to take place in November.[10]

The organisations now concentrated on extricating as many Jews from Germany as possible. The CGJ immediately launched an Appeal, under the chairmanship of Lord Rothschild. This was the first appeal to be extended to the non-Jewish public.[11] At this period, public appeals on behalf of persecuted minorities were rare and the sponsors of this appeal appear to have accepted as justifiable the risk that it might provoke some anti-Semitic response, in view of the urgency of the situation.[12] A deputation from the CGJ met with

Chamberlain. While accepting that diplomatic action was neither feasible nor likely to be effective, and might further damage Anglo-German relations, Viscount Samuel asked that wider facilities be made available for child immigrants, and added that the Jewish organisations would collectively guarantee their maintenance and planned re-emigration. Lord Bearsted added that financial difficulties made Government help essential for any large-scale settlement schemes for German emigrants to places such as British Guiana. Chamberlain gave qualified assurances but ruled out putting pressure on Germany, adding that any state aid or loan scheme to help evacuate Germany's 300,000 remaining Jews was 'premature'. He concluded that 'this was not purely a Jewish problem, but part of a larger question – the refugee problem'[13] – although it is hard to see how he could reconcile this statement with German anti-Jewish legislation since 1933 and the fact that *Kristallnacht* was a specifically Jewish pogrom. This disingenuous reasoning left the organisations in a no-win situation: either the Jews were, legally, 'not Jews, just part of the refugee problem and therefore one could not discriminate in their favour' or they were Jews, and as such could not be favoured ahead of any other category of refugee.

The CGJ urged that the governments of the IGCR cooperate in raising an international loan, guaranteed by the central banks, stressing that the voluntary organisations could not finance the entire rescue operation.[14] Samuel led a further deputation in December to meet with Lord Winterton of the IGCR, to discuss three issues: approaching the German government to facilitate Jewish emigration, setting up refugee camps and government financial assistance. Although there was no objection in principle regarding the first two issues (unofficial talks were already going on with Germany), Winterton raised the familiar objections to using public funds for the benefit of 'one class of refugees.... Not only would it cause anti-semitism but it would only encourage the Germans to banish all Jews once they discovered that other countries were prepared to finance their migration.'[15]

However, Winterton also advised Halifax that the time had perhaps come for a formal protest. He had been impressed by the deputation, which 'represent everything that is best in British Jewry'.[16] Certainly the Government's financial situation had worsened as the threat of war grew and rearmament programmes accelerated. Efforts were made throughout 1939 to change Government policy on financial aid. Finally, in July, Winterton announced that financial

3 Viscount Herbert Samuel, Chairman of the Council for German Jewry
and the Movement for the Care of Children from Germany (courtesy of
World Jewish Relief)

aid for refugee settlement, probably on a basis proportionate to the amount of private subscription, would be forthcoming if other governments were prepared to cooperate.[17]

Three rescue initiatives speedily followed *Kristallnacht*: the Children's Movement, the establishment of transit camps and the opening of training (*hachshara*) centres in Britain.[18] Samuel's request for extended facilities for child immigration marked the beginning of organised Anglo-Jewish activity on behalf of child refugees. Following the government's refusal to allow 10,000 children to go to Palestine, it agreed to facilitate the entry of refugee children by waiving visa restrictions, enabling the Movement for the Care of Children from Germany (Movement), under the joint chairmanship of Sir Wyndham Deedes and Viscount Samuel, to arrange the selection, emigration and temporary settlement of children under seventeen, both Jewish and non-Aryan Christians, provided that guarantees were given regarding their maintenance and eventual re-emigration.[19] The Movement was a merger of the British Inter-Aid Committee for Children from Germany and Austria with other groups interested in child refugees, and worked in cooperation with a proliferation of organisations, including Quaker and Church groups, B'nai Brith and the CRREC, headed by Schonfeld and individuals such as Elaine Laski (Blond) of Wizo, Lola Hahn Warburg and Rebecca Sieff. Children were found places in various locations, including foster homes in London and in the major provincial cities, where local subcommittees of the refugee aid committees were formed. A letter appeared in the principal newspapers, signed by Samuel, and by Lord Selborne on behalf of the Christian organisations, appealing for hospitality for these children.[20]

The Movement itself had no funds. It was subsidised by the CGJ, the Council of the Christian Churches and indirectly but most importantly, by the Lord Baldwin Fund, launched in December 1938.[21] The public was invited to assist in guaranteeing the maintenance of child refugees, who were divided into guaranteed and unguaranteed cases. At first, the Movement gave priority to children whose parents were either dead or interned, or who were themselves in danger of internment. Almost 3,000 children, mostly unguaranteed, arrived between December 1938 and January 1939. However, because of shortage of funds, by February 1939, only guaranteed cases were being considered for selection.[22]

As Hoare had commented, the extent and speed of the arrangements 'depended on the numbers of offers of private homes and

70

4 Refugee children from Vienna, 1938 (courtesy of the Wiener Library).

help'.[23] This became even more difficult following the government's requirement in February that all prospective foster-parents make a cash deposit of £50 to fund the re-emigration of children entering the country from March. This halted the children's transports from February until April, when the stipulation was rescinded. The Movement had a self-imposed limit of 10,000, to comprise children only from Greater Germany.[24]

The Nazis were prepared to release those between 18 and 35 years old, either already in concentration camps or threatened with incarceration, on condition of their immediate emigration. Owing to the difficulty of finding countries of refuge, temporary transit camps were proposed. Winterton saw no objection to Samuel's original proposal, but reported that the government could not finance the scheme. He was, however, willing to grant administrative facilities for admitting persons to camps established and maintained by the Anglo-Jewish organisations.[25] The derelict Kitchener army camp at Richborough was taken over by the CGJ under the chairmanship of Sir Robert Waley-Cohen. By February 1939, the first 100 skilled manual workers had arrived. Regular transports arrived from Germany and Austria until the outbreak of war, by which time it is estimated that it was a place of temporary refuge for over 3,500 men.[26] Reports suggested that the camp functioned well. Following a campaign by the CRREC, the *Jewish Weekly* was able to describe 'a very intensive religious life ... developing in this camp'. It was closed in May 1940, by which time half the inmates had joined the pioneer corps while the rest were temporarily interned on the Isle of Man.[27]

A further initiative was the extension of training facilities outside Germany and Austria, preparatory to eventual settlement in Palestine. *Hachshara* (training) programmes had already begun in the 1920s and became part of the *Auslandshachshara* (*hachshara* outside Germany) created in 1933. By the end of 1938, *hachshara* centres operated in various European countries, now including England. After *Kristallnacht*, the CGJ, with government consent, set up an 'Agricultural Committee for Refugees', under the chairmanship of Col. Charles Waley-Cohen.[28] Most of the Jewish trainees came from the 'Halutz (pioneer) Movement' in Germany. The British 'Halutz Organisation', part of the Zionist Federation, opened an office in London and assigned individuals to specific centres according to their cultural and social needs. The project became a joint undertaking of the Agricultural Committee and the 'Halutz World Movement', which also set up

72

5 *Kindertransport*. Refugee children arriving in England, 1938/9 (courtesy of World Jewish Relief).

offices in London; 'harmonious co-operation lasted throughout the stay of the groups in England'.[29]

While the mainstream organisations were devising strategies for handling large numbers of refugees, Schonfeld was concentrating on small groups, mainly of religious functionaries and orthodox children, the latter of whom were housed in the 'Schonfeld hostels' in North London. Immediately after *Kristallnacht*, he stepped up his operation with the rescue of 47 German rabbis and scholars with their families, enlarging on Anglo-Jewry's 'urgent' need for such functionaries in order to facilitate their immigration. His report claims that 'the list included all Rabbis known to be arrested, and covered all sections from the Liberal to the ultra-orthodox'. These individuals found temporary asylum, their maintenance guaranteed by the CRREC until suitable positions could be found in the UK or abroad. A second list was presented to the Home Office and by February 1939, another 150 teachers and scholars as well as 120 Yeshiva (Talmudic) students had been allowed entry to complete their studies at various rabbinical schools in England. Priority was given to those arrested and interned in Germany.[30]

In some cases Schonfeld found private individuals to undertake the care of refugees but the majority were to be a charge on his Religious Emergency Fund. The CRREC had also commenced a scheme for placing rabbis, teachers and other officials in existing vacancies throughout the English-speaking world.[31] In this way, vacancies in England would become available for more refugee religious functionaries. Schonfeld also persuaded several western European governments to admit families of rabbis and teachers from destroyed German synagogues and schools, totalling 260 people. With calculated enthusiasm, he reported to the Home Office that 'As a direct result of British behaviour many other governments followed her example by granting permits'.[32] Such transparency can hardly have duped the authorities; on the other hand, it cost nothing and could do no harm.

Following direct negotiations with the Home Office, Schonfeld's first transport of children arrived in Britain in December 1938. Altogether he brought over about 300 children before the war. Because Schonfeld's contacts were mainly with orthodox communities, it was natural that most of the children he brought over were from orthodox families.[33] His work was independent of the Movement, but had to follow the same criteria. He established a Refugee Children's Department and a Children's Relief Fund. Children were brought over 'on the understanding that there will be no charge on the Central Funds'.[34] Schonfeld repeatedly requested that representatives of the ecclesiastical authorities be co-opted onto the CGJ to advise on religious matters.[35] After the first children arrived in early December, a Friends of Children's Committee was formed, enabling ministers to care for those placed in their area. In March 1939, every community was urged to form its own local youth hostel in conjunction with the synagogue authorities.[36]

Schonfeld's activities brought him into conflict with the mainstream organisations, especially with regard to children. He invariably insisted that every consideration be given to religious principles, which he considered of equal importance with physical rescue.[37] But for the overburdened and underfunded organisations, physical rescue and placement necessarily preceded matching children with families of similar religious affiliations. This is not to imply that efforts were not made to match children with suitable families. But Schonfeld, whose outlook was conditioned by the long-term implications of placing Jewish children in non-Jewish homes, saw in such 'rescue' a negligent and casual indifference to the survival of Judaism. Unamenable to compromise, he insisted that Jewish families should be made to open their doors to these children.

A contemporary criticism of the Anglo-Jewish community was, as Dr. I. Grunfeld complained, that 'the Jewish community, which had shown such great generosity in donating money for the refugee organisations, were very reluctant to take Jewish children into their homes'. Schonfeld later asserted that placing Jewish children in non-Jewish homes had led to the loss to the Jewish community of many children, and he spoke bitterly of a 'Child-Estranging Movement'.[38] He believed the problem was not a shortage of Jewish homes, but reluctance on the part of Jewish families to take in children. Aryeh Handler agrees: 'they should have ensured that *everyone* was taken into Jewish homes. In the event the bulk went to non-Jewish homes and no one cared.'[39]

The issue became a source of great tension and long-term bitterness between the CRREC and the Anglo-Jewish refugee organisations, continuing throughout and even beyond the war. Most of the 10,000 children who came to Britain between December 1938 and August 1939 were Jewish, of various levels of religious observance.[40] As a general rule, the Movement allocated children to the care of families of their own faith and orientation, although this was not always possible.[41] Appeals for orthodox homes were regularly made at Jewish functions and through the Jewish newspapers.[42] However, insufficient orthodox homes offered hospitality for the numbers of orthodox children. Even for the non-orthodox, more offers came from non-Jewish homes than from Jewish ones. As a result, orthodox children were often placed in non-orthodox homes and non-orthodox children in gentile homes.[43] In order to encourage hospitality within the community, the CGJ agreed to assume responsibility for the re-emigration expenses of all refugee children so that they no longer required a £50 deposit.[44]

Schonfeld would not accept that Jewish homes could not be found. In some cases, he put pressure on members of the orthodox Jewish community to take in children.[45] This stridency was undeniably effective in finding some orthodox homes. However, Schonfeld's forthright approach was not available to the official organisations, which would certainly have laid themselves open to charges of harassment. Schonfeld's criticism of the CGJ as a 'Child-Estranging Movement' is somewhat ill-judged and unreasonable, especially since he himself saw the problem as communal indifference.

Schonfeld and others were always sensitive to the possible dangers of conversionary influence. Consequently, the CRREC worked continuously to remove refugee children from 'conversionist and other unsuitable influences', thereby causing friction with the Movement.[46] While the Movement stood *in loco parentis,* its power to remove a child from an unsuitable foster-home was legally restricted. During the war, the CRREC urged it to take legal action to establish its guardianship over the refugee children.[47] This was finally achieved with the Guardianship Act 1944 and the appointment of Lord Gorell, Chairman of the Refugee Children's Movement, as legal guardian of the hundreds of children. Problems and controversy persisted into the 1950s.[48]

The Anglo-Jewish voluntary organisations, which relied on donations from the community, faced grave shortages of funds in 1939. The CGJ opposed separate fund-raising, which might conflict with the main appeal.[49] Although it made two grants to the CRREC in the pre-war period, it could not stop the latter from launching its own appeals.[50] Like the other organisations, the CRREC was obliged to stipulate that it could only consider guaranteed cases. But Schonfeld included a number of 'particularly urgent' unsubsidised cases in his lists: 'We had a slightly different attitude towards the question of guarantees.'[51] Even with formal guarantees, there were many defaulting guarantors. The GJAC had decided by April 1939 to institute legal proceedings against guarantors who failed to honour their guarantees.[52] In several other cases, refugees brought over by the CRREC applied to the GJAC for support, to be refused on the grounds that 'they received their visas through the guarantee of your [CRREC] Committee'.[53]

When Schonfeld submitted a new list of applications in March 1939, the Home Office consulted the CGJ, which advised that 'extreme caution must be exercised before any further substantial commitments could be undertaken'. Hertz nevertheless convinced the Home Office, in good faith, that his Committee did not rely on the funds of the CGJ for maintenance of the ecclesiastics guaranteed by it, that all 99 teachers and 73 students on its list were fully guaranteed by private individuals and that the CRREC was undertaking their re-emigration.[54] As a result, these refugees were finally admitted. Just how Schonfeld planned to cope financially remains unclear. His approach was in contrast to the more professional attitude of the Anglo-Jewish voluntary organisations, which were understandably apprehensive of Schonfeld's refugees becoming a burden on them and of being tainted with his reputation for unreliability.

The conflict between these approaches is illustrated by the case of a number of students brought over by Schonfeld and placed at a Talmudic college in Manchester, where funds were exhausted. The students, not all *bona fide*, had unofficially applied to the GJAC trainee department for work, unavailable to genuine students. The GJAC notified the authorities.[55] The Home Office now refused to allow any new applications unless the CGJ took responsibility for a further group of 92 students, sponsored by Schonfeld and awaiting visas. The Council would agree only on confirmation from the CRREC that all possessed guarantees and had evidence that they were *bona fide* students.[56] Schiff tried to resolve the situation without impugning any of those involved, but Schonfeld was regarded by the establishment, not unreasonably, as a 'loose cannon'. Joan Stiebel recalls Schiff telling Schonfeld that he did wonderful things but always in the wrong way, so that 'we had to clear up the mess'.[57]

Both at the time and more recently, the Anglo-Jewish organisations have been harshly criticised for their failure to deal effectively with the catastrophe they faced. Contemporary criticism focused on their administrative failure and was often confined to specific complaints about delays and inefficiencies in processing refugee applications and arrivals. Such understandable and no doubt valid criticism is distinct from the critical reappraisal by recent revisionist historians who argue that the organisations not only did not facilitate more rescue but actively sought limitations on both the 'quality' and 'quantity' of those admitted. London maintains that the government made a massive effort to accelerate the entry of those eligible for admission, but that the voluntary bodies moved increasingly to restrict admissions, in order to conserve funds and limit numbers.[58]

Certainly the refugee organisations, facing the prospect of bankruptcy, were obliged to initiate supplementary controls of their own, including formal guarantees and a £50 deposit for children,[59] but London isolates the moral issue and the motives of those involved with insufficient consideration of the financial and administrative crisis which faced them. This indictment of the putative motives of the organisations seems at the very least dangerously speculative. It is difficult to accept London's attempt to blacken the organisations by portraying the government as so extraordinarily anxious to save as many refugees as possible, especially as London elsewhere criticises the government for lack of humanitarianism.[60]

The Anglo-Jewish organisations were under tremendous pressure at this time. The three crises of 1938–39 had created a major financial and administrative problem for them. In 1938 approximately 8,500 were registered with the GJAC. The influx from January to June 1939 amounted to over 22,000 registered cases, more than twice the total for the whole of 1938 and more than the total for the period 1933–38, estimated at 10,500. Re-emigration of registered cases stood at only 1,543 for January–June 1939.[61] The GJAC was registering 500 arrivals per week in January 1939. Many of these immediately became a charge on the Committee, as guarantors had been unable to meet their commitment. Some visas had been issued by the Home Office without reference to the GJAC,[62] which then had to maintain the holders. Schiff warned that the GJAC could not support those brought over under Ministry of Labour permits and the Ministry ceased to issue permits for domestic servants, all of whom now entered through the Domestic Bureau.[63]

The Committee's weekly expenditure during the last months of 1938 had been £5,000, compared to £800 in 1937. The JRC's total expenditure for the six years from 1933 amounted to £233,000. In December 1938, the GJAC's estimated budget for the following twelve months was a minimum of £350,000. The CGJ also had to budget for the agricultural training schemes and the children's scheme.[64] The expenditure of the GJAC alone during the first six months of

1939 was £183,136, while the average number of persons receiving weekly assistance by June 1939 was over 3,000.[65] So fearful was it of the future, that in December 1938 the CGJ, which was subsidising refugees in Shanghai (the one place with an open immigration policy), was obliged to request a halt to further admissions there.[66]

On the administrative level, the *Anschluss* brought a flood of applications to an already overburdened organisation, headed by Schiff with the help of a comparatively small staff, some paid, others voluntary. No competent administration could be organised quickly and efficiently to cope with a pace of work completely transformed after *Kristallnacht*.[67] Towards the end of 1938, the appointment of a full-time director became necessary and in March 1939 the organisations relocated from Woburn House to Bloomsbury House. Even so, numerous complaints continued to be made, often in the national press, about inefficiencies, incompetence, rudeness and delays. Arrears of work piled up and were dealt with by improvised methods, operated for the most part by harassed and inexperienced staff, hurriedly mobilised. The Committee of Investigation, set up in May 1939 to examine the work of the GJAC and make recommendations, expressed admiration for the spirit of service and self-sacrifice displayed by these workers.[68]

Woburn House was receiving 1,500 letters and up to 1,000 personal callers daily by December 1938. By the end of March 1939, the GJAC was receiving 17,000 letters and holding approximately 6,000 interviews a week. By April 1939, over 50,000 letters had still not been dealt with. By July 1939, a staff of over 400 was handling 21,000 letters a week.[69] Nevertheless, the GJAC was pleased that 'the Home Office had so far raised no objection to the increasing influx' and that there was 'a growing realisation on the part of some sections of the public ... that refugees ... need be neither a burden nor a menace'.[70] Clearly, there was no private agenda to restrict immigration, as has been claimed, except for purely practical reasons.

Ironically, the organisations became victims of their own success. Precisely because of the relaxation in government policy, they were now confronted with an impossible avalanche of work. Schiff vigorously defended the GJAC: 'We all have been working here day and night in order to safe [*sic*] human lives ... this Committee can only get back to its previous state of efficiency when the Home Office is able to co-operate'.[71] By the beginning of 1939, substantial staff increases had been made and the Aliens Department was moved to larger premises. Some progress was made in coordinating case-work by attempts at reorganisation in January 1939.[72] To counter the still mounting criticism, the GJAC called a conference in April, at which Schiff admitted there were grounds for criticism, but argued that some of it was unjustified and based on erroneous information. He acknowledged that the Home Secretary had done everything possible to help, but that self-denigration and internal problems were seriously demoralising the Anglo-Jewish establishment.[73] Jewish leaders were conscious that these problems and criticisms had 'alienated and antagonised non-Jewish organisations and people' and a special Committee of Enquiry was appointed to investigate the matter.[74] The Board, through the *Jewish Chronicle,* invited complaints about refugee administration. Schiff protested that this 'placed me in a position of the accused in the dock and the Board of Deputies as the prosecutor'. He added that the expenses of the GJAC were no less than £10,000 per week and wondered where future funds were to come from.[75] Schiff and Simon Marks made various recommendations and by August, Schiff was able to report that the Board was satisfied that everything possible was being done to improve British refugee organisations.[76]

Another target of recent criticism is the selection procedure adopted by the organisations. Alderman claims that 'communal policy towards refugees resulted and was designed to result in the admission into Britain of a limited number of Jews from a particular social and economic background, those easily assimilable and of a particular age'. He accuses Schiff, who had it in his power to accept or reject German Jewish applicants, of complicity with Home Office 'prejudices and preferences'.[77] The extraordinary logic of this argument leads to the 'conclusion' that Schiff's work was designed, not to assist refugee immigration but to prevent it and to prevent anyone else facilitating it. Alderman's case is based on the *a priori* assumption that cooperation with the Home Office was synonymous with treachery to German Jewry, as if hostile relations were more ethically acceptable or could have saved more lives.

The guarantee given by the Jewish organisations in 1933 stated that 'all German Jewish refugees should be admitted without distinction'. It was originally anticipated that the total number would not exceed 3,000–4,000.[78] Only later, when numbers reached unmanageable levels, did choices have to be made. Following *Kristallnacht,* the Home Office was prepared to receive certain categories of German refugees on the recommendation of Jewish organisations, without investigation of individual cases, including children, old persons and persons likely to re-emigrate within 18 months of arrival. Guarantees of maintenance were still required.[79] Since the ultimate liability would fall on the Jewish organisations, they were necessarily circumspect about recommendations. Given the scarcity of resources and the limited employment opportunities, decisions were often reached by singling out those who could be maintained, and therefore guaranteed, by families or friends and those, like the young, who could be retrained prior to re-emigration, thus creating further opportunities for immigration, thereby saving a maximum number of individuals. German Jews over 45 were therefore a lower priority, since, as Bentwich noted regretfully, they were 'not fitted for emigration'.[80]

Interestingly, in spite of this selection procedure and the present perception that only a certain calibre of refugee was admitted, Passport Control Officers abroad expressed 'great concern at the poor type of refugees for whom authorisations for visas were being issued'. In Vienna, candidates for selection were impecunious and in certain cases, visa cards were issued by the committees to individuals who had previously been rejected.[81] The testimony of the Passport Control officials in Central Europe belies arguments that only a certain type of refugee was admitted. The policy of admitting only those whose maintenance was guaranteed and who would not take up employment without special authorisation might also result in some of the 'better' types of refugee, including professionals, being ruled out at the start; only those professing willingness to come, for example, for private domestic service, were admitted.[82]

More crucially, the recent criticism levelled at the refugee organisations should be viewed in the light of the huge discrepancy between the number of visa cards issued and the number of refugees who actually arrived between *Kristallnacht* and June 1939. A disparity was noted as early as November 1938 and at various times during 1939.[83] In November 1938, the total number of refugees entering Britain since March 1933 was 17,000, of whom about 6,000 had re-emigrated. In April 1939, there were 25,136 refugees, an influx of about 14,000 since November 1938. Yet between 1 May 1938 and 31 March 1939, 79,271 visas had been issued.[84] Allowing for a certain number who might have left since November, it seems clear that the great majority of those granted UK visas never arrived. The government wanted to use these figures to 'rebut criticisms of the Government's refugee policy'. However, the voluntary organisations feared 'that they might raise an outcry that far too many visas are being given'.[85]

From January to June 1939, almost 13,000 visas had been issued but only 5,500 refugees had arrived. By the end of July, out of a total of 14,644 visas issued, 7,253 persons had arrived and registered with the GJAC, while 7,391 had not yet registered. It was not known how many of those who had arrived had simply failed to register. This left uncertain how many had remained in Europe, though the report stated that many had probably not yet arrived. Examination of the previous three months of the time-lag between the issue of the visa cards and the arrival of refugees showed that 90 per cent arrived within two months of the issue of the visa.[86] Moreover, during the last months before the outbreak of war, it is now known, British Consular officials in Germany and Austria had issued, without reference to London, huge numbers of visas, which were still unused by the outbreak of war.[87]

The reason why so many visas remained unused is unclear. The Foreign Office suggested that it was 'owing to the difficulties that refugees frequently experienced in winding up their affairs in Germany and securing the necessary permission to leave the Reich'. A GJAC enquiry offered a similar explanation. Passport Control representatives in Europe claimed that the main reason was that these visas were an 'insurance policy', British visas for the United Kingdom being widely regarded abroad as the 'hallmark of perfection', even though holders might have no desire to leave unless absolutely compelled to do so. Again, there were others, a smaller number, who, having obtained UK visas, broke their journey in countries such as Belgium and Holland, stayed with friends and were in no hurry to come to Britain. There was also a larger number who obtained UK visas as a stepping-stone to obtaining a visa for some other country, such as America, to which they genuinely desired to go.[88]

Bentwich commented that 'The refugee organisations were faced with an immense burden. . . . The altogetherness of everything overwhelmed us, and the forced march of time overtook our puny efforts.'[89] Yet it is clear that the overburdened organisations were determined to cope with the mounting difficulties they faced during the final years before the outbreak of war, even though they were ill-equipped for the huge scale of the task. Their efforts, on an administrative level, were vigorous and achieved impressive results. This achievement has, however, been eclipsed by the drama of the war years, during which the role of the organisations changed. Their administrative skills were no longer required, except to some extent during the period of internment. What was now needed was political expertise in devising and negotiating strategies to help European Jewry which the wartime government might find acceptable. This was an area in which the organisations lacked both skill and experience; they were no match in argument for the mandarins of the Foreign Office. Nevertheless, in light of the criticism to which they have recently been subjected by revisionist historians, a reappraisal of their untiring efforts and achievements during the pre-war years seems overdue.

5
Internment and Deportation

The war transformed the work of the voluntary organisations. All visas granted prior to 3 September 1939 to what had now become 'enemy' nationals were automatically invalid. No new immigration applications would be considered. Besides the almost insuperable difficulties of establishing contact, it was necessary to proceed with the utmost caution for fear that enemy agents might infiltrate as 'refugees'. Immigration was restricted to those who had close relatives in Britain and had reached neutral or friendly countries, refugees in neutral countries who had possessed visas prior to the war and refugees proceeding to overseas destinations from neutral territory via Britain.[1] Until 1943, therefore, the work of the GJAC (which reverted to its original title, the Jewish Refugees Committee) and the CGJ, now renamed the Central Council for Jewish Refugees (CCJR), was almost entirely restricted to refugees already in Britain. Among the few exceptions were several hundred refugees, holding United States visas, who escaped to Britain after the fall of the Low Countries and France in May and June 1940.[2] During this period, certainly until late 1941, the Anglo-Jewish community was primarily concerned with internal problems: internment of refugees, growing anti-Semitism and evacuation following the threat of air-raids.

The war exacerbated the already grave financial crisis in the affairs of the refugee organisations. The GJAC had informed the Home Office during the summer that the financial resources of the voluntary organisations did not allow them to accept responsibility for any further refugees.[3] Although immigration into Britain had practically ceased when war broke out, the organisations faced greatly increased expenditure. The CCJR was burdened with the maintenance of numerous refugees, especially some 3,000 domestics, who, on account of the war, had become unemployed and were consequently dependent upon charitable support. In addition, the war put a stop to re-emigration, leaving many transmigrants stranded indefinitely in Britain.[4] The number of refugees being maintained in part or in whole by the voluntary organisations in November 1939 was approximately 15,000. It was estimated, on the basis of current demands, that funds for essential purposes such as maintenance, emigration and administration for six months, would be £375,000, or £15,000 per week.[5]

The CCJR informed the government that if it 'would not help, the refugees would become a charge on local authorities'.[6] Schiff was blamed for bringing refugees to Britain without proper regard to available finances and future liabilities, and had to be dissuaded from resigning.[7] It is rather poignant that Schiff was blamed at the time for carelessly bringing over refugees without regard to expense, and then blamed later for impeding admissions of the 'wrong type of refugee' and conniving in Home Office prejudices.

By December 1939 the crisis was such that the heads of the Anglo-Jewish voluntary organisations informed the Home Office that it would be necessary to close down their organisations and inform all those being maintained to apply to the public assistance authorities for relief. Fearful that the cost of maintaining the refugees would fall on municipal funds, the government finally agreed,[8] after lengthy negotiations, to grant 50 per cent of the expenditure of the voluntary organisations from 1 January 1940, provided that they made a further effort to raise funds. This proved difficult, especially when internment aggravated the situation, and towards the end of 1940, in an unprecedented move, the government agreed to contribute (from 1 October 1940) 100 per cent of the cost of maintenance of the refugees and 75 per cent of the cost of administration, welfare and emigration.[9]

The CRREC was also unable to meet its commitments. It had sole responsibility for maintaining some 985 individuals, many of whom were unsuited, because of age or ill-health, for re-employment.[10] Efforts to secure financial aid from the CCJR meant that the CRREC had to stop its own collection so as not to conflict with the Central Council's fund-raising activities.[11] The CRREC joined the government support scheme under which eventually 100 per cent refugee maintenance under Assistance Board rates and 75 per cent of welfare and administrative expenses were repaid by the Treasury. Its grant from the CCJR thereupon ceased, although the Council continued to contribute to certain causes, such as kosher food. However, the CRREC still had to find the 25 per cent of welfare and administrative costs, as well as undertaking a considerable monthly outlay for its various religious charitable undertakings. Separate appeals, under the heading 'United Jewish Charities', encompassing all the charities administered by the CRREC, were frequently issued.[12]

Internment

The most serious new problem facing the organisations during 1940 was the general internment of enemy aliens, introduced in May, which threw further heavy burdens and responsibilities on all refugee committees, in respect of internees' dependants and the private affairs which refugees were unable to settle before internment.[13]

With the collapse of Norway, the Low Countries and France (April–June), the possibility of invasion created sudden panic in Britain. Lulled into temporary, false security by the 'phoney war', Britain now struggled desperately to prepare for invasion.[14] A wave of anti-alien feeling was exacerbated by reports from Sir Neville Bland, the British Minister at the Hague, and others, of the activities of German 'Fifth Columnists' in Holland and France. Under this stress, aggravated by a press campaign to 'intern the lot' backed by the Chiefs of Staff, the government felt compelled to disregard its previous distinction in favour of most refugees when the Aliens Tribunal had been formed in September 1939. During May and June, over 25,000 aliens, mostly German and Austrian Jewish refugees, under categories 'B' (those hitherto restricted but not interned) and 'C' (those hitherto exempt from internment and restriction) were interned. This was followed in August by the announcement that some 8,000 persons, believed potentially dangerous, had been deported to Australia and Canada.[15]

The government's position on internment, as stated by Sir Herbert Emerson, Director of the IGCR, was that while it was hoped that all German refugees were loyal to Britain, it was impossible to be certain: 'the country faced the gravest crisis in its history, the situation in the battlefields was critical, air-raids on England might be expected at any time, attempts at invasion would almost certainly be made'. In these circumstances, 'considerations of national security had to supersede all other considerations. Internment was not merely intended to allay public uneasiness, but it was also an obvious public safety measure and was based on the known facts of what had

86

6 Women aliens and a child with police escorts leaving for the Isle of Man internment camp, May 1940 (courtesy of the Imperial War Museum)

happened in other countries... of German Fifth Column activities'. This view was shared by the vast majority of the public.[16]

Initially, the voluntary organisations acquiesced in the decision to intern German and Austrian refugees. The interdenominational Refugee Joint Consultative Committee (RJCC), formerly known as the Co-ordinating Committee for Refugees, on which the Anglo-Jewish organisations were represented, agreed that the case-working committees should be apolitical and not comment on general policy. The Council would accept government decisions without question.[17] This support was undoubtedly a product of the intense wave of national solidarity generated by the threat of invasion. The organisations were anxious to be seen to be 'rallying round'. In the same spirit, the *Jewish Chronicle*, referring to 'The Home Front in Peril' and the danger of a Nazi Fifth Column, declared, 'In a life and death struggle for national survival the Government justifiably claims the right to interfere drastically with the freedom of the individual'. This wholehearted support prevailed throughout May.[18]

The Anglo-Jewish leadership accepted that the government had been compelled to adopt a policy involving great individual hardship purely for national security reasons and was not inclined to oppose it while Britain was fighting for survival. Although he had private reservations, Brodetsky agreed 'that in view of the war situation, the Government's policy in regard to internment should not be opposed'.[19] However, acquiescence was not unqualified. Brodetsky questioned whether current procedure was really securing the internment of potentially dangerous persons. Sir Robert Waley-Cohen added that 'there had not been a single case of a person who was supposed to be a refugee, having been found guilty of sabotage or in any way acting in a manner detrimental to the Government of Holland'.[20]

The Board recommended that facilities be provided for access to the internees and for the continuance of welfare, cultural and social work in the internment camps. The CCJR had decided that, for the present, no guarantee as to the bona fides of refugees should be given by any committee.[21] Although it was considered necessary to persuade the War Office to recognise the difference between refugee internees and enemy alien internees, it was decided that, for the moment, individual appeals should not be pressed.[22] The Council was acting on government advice 'that individual applications for release would not be welcomed at present in view of the grave situation'.[23] Indeed, various members of the Council, such as Lady

88

7 An internment camp for aliens, on Huyton housing estate in Liverpool, surrounded by a barbed wire fence, *circa* 1940 (courtesy of Hulton Archives)

Reading, felt that in the circumstances internment was in the interest of the refugees, a view endorsed by the RJCC, which considered it unwise to release internees 'to live in heavily bombed areas'.[24] This attitude was bitterly resented by some internees. Hans Gal, an exiled Austrian composer, recalls a 'shameful event when a prominent Jew . . . came to the camp and . . . told us that they will do everything for us. . . . But we must stay there till the end of the war, it's best for us! . . . they too felt somehow endangered.'[25]

While some elements in British Jewry understandably felt endangered, the crucial consideration, not mentioned by Gal, was the internees' German background. Certainly there was also an acute awareness of increased anti-Semitism at this time. The press campaign against refugees became so fierce during the early stages of internment that the Ministry of Information, in a confidential memorandum dated 27 April 1940, noted that local governments and refugee committees were disturbed by increasingly anti-Semitic attitudes among the general public.[26] While the circumstances of war inevitably meant that it was the German/Austrian background of the refugees, rather than their Jewishness, that attracted suspicion and hostility, nevertheless, the Jewish community became increasingly anxious that the refugees should present as low a profile as possible. Gordon Liverman, chairman of the Jewish Defence Committee, was greatly concerned about 'the thoughtless behaviour of so many [refugees] in areas where they were concentrated, as doing a great deal of harm'.[27] The fear of increased anti-Semitism was reflected in a letter drafted by the Board for circulation to all refugees in England. It was similar to the pamphlet issued before the war, reminding them that it is 'the duty of every refugee to remember that he is a guest in this country. . . . The least he can do is to adapt himself to the customs of this country.' Included was a list of rules of public behaviour, namely not to speak German in public, not to push in queues and not to tell Englishmen that things were done better in Germany.[28]

Internment and deportation remained unopposed until 2 July 1940, when the SS *Arandora Star*, carrying internees to Canada, was torpedoed. The disaster provoked bitter public outrage. Many of the victims had not been Nazi or Fascist sympathisers but refugees mistakenly selected for deportation. By 26 July, the *Jewish Chronicle* was speaking of an 'Internment Scandal' and on 2 August, the *J.C.* was reporting 'Gestapo Methods in Britain' and 'Disgraceful Hounding of Refugees'.[29]

Although public opinion had changed drastically after the *Arandora* tragedy, the RJCC decided not to 'criticise' the principle of internment but to consider how best it could work within the framework of that policy. Nevertheless, it frequently exercised the right 'to indicate to the Government where their policy was felt to be misdirected or needed change'.[30] The Committee evidently drew a fine distinction between 'criticising' and indicating to the government 'where their policy was misdirected'. Whether the government was alive to such delicate semantic nuances is questionable. No doubt the RJCC wished to retain the right to criticise without appearing openly negative.

Schonfeld appears to have been perfectly amenable to internment: 'the whole problem of the refugees from Nazi oppression must be judged in relation to the entire British and international situation.' Unlike Brodetsky, he believed that the refugees were better off interned for their own safety. He praised the authorities' 'sincere determination all round to see as much "fair play" and as many wrongs redressed and improvements carried out as the circumstances permitted'.[31] Schonfeld's surprising complaisance about internment conceals a characteristically pragmatic attitude towards the inevitable. Since there was no question of changing government policy, he concentrated his efforts instead on maintaining good working relations with the authorities. In this way he was able to supervise and improve conditions in the camps.

The British Section did not openly challenge government policy, but pointed out that the 'precautionary measures which the Government are taking have inevitably and unavoidably resulted in grave hardships' and that 'the interests of National Economy would be better served if the labour of aliens whose loyalty is beyond suspicion were made available for the national effort rather than they should become a burden on the public purse in internment camps'. Perlzweig also argued, somewhat naively, for 'the priceless value of our liberal treatment of refugees as an element in securing the sympathetic support of neutrals as well as that of the United States'.[32]

Brodetsky rejected accusations that the Anglo-Jewish leadership had adopted a pusillanimous attitude towards internment, stressing that 'the Board acted through Parliament and other organisations intensely interested in amelioration of the position in regard to internment'.[33] At the Board's two emergency Executive Committee meetings (held on 9 and 17 July), Brodetsky went on the defensive, challenging accusations that he had supinely acquiesced in

government policy from the start. All-inclusive internment had commenced only on 25 June, and he noted that the orders for internment
had originally only affected persons in category 'B', those living in
certain areas, whose numbers were small compared with the total
number of refugees in the country. Brodetsky pointed out that the
situation was now very different: 'when internment had assumed a
general and indiscriminate character and large numbers of people . . .
were being interned at very short notice . . . without knowing what
the Government's intentions were.'[34]

The Board was in constant touch with the Parliamentary Committee for Refugees under Eleanor Rathbone, who brought the plight
of the internees to the attention of the government.[35] Hans Gal
regarded it 'as a great relief to have somebody [Rathbone] open
their mouth for us – very temperamentally she did it'.[36] Brotman
submitted to this Committee various suggestions for consideration,
including, *inter alia*, wrongly interned persons, provisions for welfare work in the internment camps, release of internees who could
be usefully employed in work of national importance and reconsideration of all cases of internment in due course. He recommended
the formation of a joint committee representing the War Office, the
Home Office and the Ministry of Home Security to deal with the
problems of internment.[37] On 24 June 1940, the day before general
internment was to commence, a deputation met Osbert Peake, Parliamentary Under-Secretary at the Home Office, who gave some
reassurances.[38]

Conditions in some of the camps left much to be desired. There was
also a lack of cultural activities and useful employment. Deportations
to Canada had taken place without adequate notice to relatives.
Brodetsky also noted that it was senseless to intern people who had
been, UK-resident for many years, but born in Galicia (or other
territories of the old Austro-Hungarian Empire) and therefore regarded as Austrian nationals. It was pointed out that when Galicia
became part of Poland, its ties with Austria were severed and Galicians
were strongly opposed to Nazism. Brodetsky suggested a review of
policy detail and of internment conditions. He also called for the
centralisation of the government authority supervising internment,
currently administered by several government departments. The general principle of the Committee was that 'persons [of] whose loyalty
to this country the Home Office is satisfied . . . should be released'.
Steps should be taken to expedite those eligible for release and consideration be given to the internees' personal belongings and capital.[39]

At the end of July, the War Cabinet established two Advisory Committees, one to assist the Home Secretary in dealing with applications for the enlargement of the categories of release, and the other to assist the Foreign Office in dealing with the welfare and employment of aliens in internment camps. The Home Office produced its first White Paper at the end of July, detailing 18 categories of internees to be released. The immediate reaction of the voluntary organisations was critical because the White Paper confirmed rather than changed internment policy. It provided for the release of only those internees whose services could be useful to the nation and the war effort.[40] The Central Office of Refugees (now incorporating the RJCC and comprising the principal organisations dealing with refugees from Germany and Austria) presented a memorandum to the Home Office Asquith Advisory Committee on Aliens, urging that 'release from internment should not be restricted by any standard of employability but that consideration should be given to the release of all who . . . give unquestionable proof of their anti-Nazi and anti-Fascist sympathies and their willingness to serve the causes for which this country is fighting and for whose maintenance proper provision has been made'. The Board presented a similar memorandum.[41]

More practically, a sub-committee, formed to deal with the welfare of internees and consisting of Brodetsky, Schiff and Harry Sacher (an executive member of the CCJR), prepared a memorandum on CCJR policy.[42] The ensuing discussions are revealing. Schiff wrote privately to Sacher, 'You might object to the whole approach but I feel simply to go to the Government and say that they must reverse their entire policy would meet with a refusal . . . as we are going to the Government and telling them that we have no funds left and that they must take over the entire maintenance of refugees, we cannot very well dictate to them where to keep them and it is unquestionably cheaper for them to keep large numbers together than have them distributed over the country.'[43] Realism and economics, as ever, conditioned Schiff's attitude. The sub-committee reiterated its commitment to the principle of immediate release for internees of guaranteed loyalty.[44]

The CCJR wanted all approaches to the government to be coordinated with the Christian Council for Refugees; the association of the Jewish and Christian Councils was 'close and harmonious' and 'in all matters they acted together'.[45] But the Bishop of Chichester, George Bell, although maintaining that the government had 'made a great mistake', felt 'that the present time was not one when the

Government should be pressed to reverse its policy regarding internment', as proposed by the Friendly Aliens Committee.[46] This was at
the height of the Battle of Britain and the fear of invasion. The
Bishop therefore suggested that 'they ought to go slow . . . to wait a
month or possibly two to see how things developed, when the
national security problem would not be so acute'.[47]

Brodetsky agreed that the time was not ripe for further representations to the government and that it was best not to send the
sub-committee's memorandum before the House of Commons debate
on 22 August. Rather, the sub-committee should suggest extensions
of the present categories of persons to be released. In October, with
a change in Home Secretary, Brodetsky again felt 'it was not, at
present, advisable to approach the Home Office on the question of
a change of the internment policy'.[48] However, in spite of his reluctance to press for a reversal of internment, he was keen that the
Board should not be seen to be feebly condoning government policy:
'the CGJ fought hard against internment and so of course did the
Board and other bodies.'[49] The fact remains that the Board fought
hard for the internees but not 'against internment' itself. Given the
critical military position during this period, Brodetsky was doubtless
determined at least to win as much humane consideration for internees
as possible. He was also understandably anxious not to antagonise
those whose compliance was essential if the internees were to be
assisted.

Brodetsky's view, with some dissension, prevailed. It was felt that
the Executive was 'wise in not pressing for reconsideration of the
general principles of the policy of internment. Instead they had
rightly tried to obtain new categories of releases', in particular for
aliens of Galician-Polish origin.[50] Again, it was decided that these
suggestions receive Christian Council approval before being submitted to the Advisory Committee.[51] In light of the military emergency
during the summer of 1940, and after, with the imminent prospect
of invasion by a power which had already conquered most of Europe,
any attempt to press for an end to internment would have been
regarded by the Government as, at best, an irritant and at worst,
perversely uncooperative. The practical sense of the organisations'
approach is indisputable.

The organisations' attempts to secure reappraisal and extension of
the categories of interned aliens eligible for release were only partially
successful. Some internees, although apparently perfectly loyal and
reliable, did not fit into any of the categories. The Board continued

its contacts with the Advisory Committee and proposed that the whole basis of internment policy needed reconsideration with a view to making loyalty and reliability the chief criteria of release,[52] rather than economic usefulness. By the end of 1940, when the number of internees had fallen to about 10,000, other issues were dominating the Anglo-Jewish agenda, namely the problems of air-raids and appeals for funds to maintain essential communal services necessary for evacuation.[53] Brodetsky still felt that it was inadvisable to raise the issue of internment with the authorities, even though there were still a number of refugees who should have been released.[54] No concerted effort on the part of the organisations, at a time of national emergency, could have altered government policy. By contrast, in the area of welfare and humanitarian relief, for which they were experienced and well equipped, the organisations, by virtue of not conflicting with government objectives, took a more proactive approach and achieved considerable results.

The White Papers did not deal with the welfare of internees but only with defining categories for release. In view of the fact that 80 per cent of German internees were Jewish, efforts were made to have representatives from the CCJR on the second Advisory Committee. Schiff was particularly concerned that differences between genuine refugees from Nazi oppression and Nazi sympathisers be clarified quickly.[55] Until 5 August, internment camps for both civilians and POWs were controlled by the War Office, which preferred to work with only one voluntary organisation, already known to it, the interdenominational Joint Committee for the Welfare of Civilian Internees and Prisoners of War. This had been formed at the beginning of the war under the chairmanship of the Revd. Dr. D. Paton of the Church Commission and had added a number of Jewish representatives, including Schonfeld. It became known as the Edinburgh House Committee. With general internment, this committee widened its functions and a Central Committee for Internees was set up in Bloomsbury House in mid-June 1940, representing all the major case-working bodies.

Permission to visit the camps was obtained through the Edinburgh House Committee. While the War Office was in charge, there were considerable difficulties in obtaining such permits. Once the Home Office had taken over it became somewhat easier, though permits were issued sparingly.[56] Within a few days of the internment order, however, Schonfeld obtained a War Office 'pass' enabling him to visit all the internment camps both on the Isle of Man and on the mainland.[57] Schonfeld never questioned internment policy itself, but only the conditions he found in the camps, and repeatedly praised the military commandants.[58]

There was close cooperation between the voluntary organisations over ameliorating conditions in the internment camps. At the outset, the CRREC was the only Jewish body dealing with the general welfare of many thousands of internees and remained so until the establishment of the Central Committee for Internees.[59] Apart from official representations on welfare questions and periodic visits by Schonfeld, the CRREC undertook religious welfare work among all refugees. German pastors had been appointed for non-Jewish inmates and Schonfeld tried to secure a parallel arrangement for Jewish internees. Curiously, the United Synagogue Welfare Committee and the JRC initially refused to undertake this work and Schonfeld turned to the Board which agreed to take up the matter. Even the Central Committee for Internees showed an apparent reluctance to advertise its existence, presumably because it would be 'inundated with enquiries'.[60] Eventually, the United Synagogue, as well as other communities and individuals, cooperated in the provision of general welfare and religious requirements.[61]

Within the first few months of internment, Schonfeld carried out five tours of inspection, which proved a source of great moral encouragement by transmitting news to relatives and represented 'the first contact of these unfortunate men and women with Jewry'.[62] Each tour of the camps was followed by a detailed report, together with suggestions for improvements. Schonfeld reported to the Central Council, which praised his report 'for not overstating the facts and for having made practical suggestions'.[63] The Home Office was similarly impressed by Schonfeld's 'constructive' reports. Others also arranged similar visits to the camps.[64]

Most of the issues reported were dealt with effectively. Schonfeld's most pressing demand was for the release of all invalids, many of whom, according to Home Office instructions to the police, should never have been interned. As a result of his first tour and the subsequent White Paper on invalids, he was able to secure the immediate release of sick persons. Schonfeld also secured the closure of the Prees Heath Camp, which he considered unsuitable for internment.[65] Together with others, he made suggestions concerning accommodation, rations, furniture and overcrowding. Educational, religious and social activities for the refugees were of vital importance. Social amenities, such as radios, newspapers and libraries, were arranged.

Censorship delays in correspondence, mixed camps and meetings between husbands, wives and children were issues that required attention. Food supplies and pocket money were given to the destitute. In all these matters, progress was made, although sometimes after long delays.[66] With War Office approval, Schonfeld arranged for the provision of kosher food, religious services and books. A parcel scheme was initiated. Camp rabbis were appointed and Revd. S. Anekstein was sent to the Isle of Man as the Council's representative from September 1940 until May 1942. The CRREC organised the first Jewish plot in the Douglas cemetery on the Isle of Man in November 1940. Both the Isle of Man government and military Headquarters cooperated in this scheme, which received financial assistance from the CCJR and other communities.[67]

Applications for releases were made through the Central Committee at Bloomsbury House. Steps were also taken by the CRREC to obtain the release of refugees classified as *bona fide* by the White Paper regulations. The CRREC participated in Home Office deliberations, Schonfeld representing Hertz at the Asquith Commission. Schonfeld dealt with a different category of internees; besides invalids, he also assisted the aged, ministers of religion, theological students, teachers of religion, Polish and Galician refugees and cases of doubtful nationality. In most cases his suggestions were approved. Close on 1,000 internees were released on the sponsorship of the CRREC alone.[68] The Agudat Israel was also involved in securing the release of certain categories of refugee internees. Releases were obtained in about 75 per cent of cases applied for, including cases that had been previously refused.[69] The recruiting of refugees for the Auxiliary Military Pioneer Corps, which had been stopped in May, was renewed. This was the swiftest way to secure release. During the later part of 1940, with the help of Captain Davidson, the JRC's principal Recruiting Officer, 2,000 more recruits were enrolled, bringing the total number of refugees to 5,000.[70]

The RJCC expressed unease, both that persons for whom the organisations were prepared to vouch were experiencing problems in obtaining release and at what appeared to be over-generosity on the part of the authorities in releasing persons on medical grounds, evidence suggesting that many releases were of doubtful validity. Any evidence of complicity in such releases, as the chairman, Lord Lytton, pointed out, would have seriously impugned the credibility and effectiveness of the RJCC itself.[71] The JRC, however, received praise for its help to the Appeal Tribunal of North-East England, regarding the *bona fides* of the internees: the Committee was assisted in such discoveries as the cases of 2,414 out of a total of 3,760 applicants released under the sickness clause: 'The Government was alarmed at the mistakes made in releasing persons on the grounds of sickness. As a result they tightened up medical examinations and asked the JRC whether any persons have been released without proper reason.'[72] Clearly, there had been sufficient numbers of unauthorised or doubtful releases on medical grounds to provoke this concern, but there was evidently cooperation and trust between the Anglo-Jewish organisations and the government on this point.

The worst consequence of the internment policy was the deportation of approximately 8,000 internees to Canada and Australia in the summer of 1940. The Anglo-Jewish organisations were generally averse to the deportation of refugees, largely due to the manner in which the deportations were conducted and uncertainty about the treatment and fate of deportees once they reached their destination.[73] Deportees were treated by the authorities in these countries as dangerous prisoners-of-war. Even though their treatment complied with the Geneva Convention on POWs, many civilian internees felt distressed and stigmatised. There were complaints that Nazis and non-Nazis were being interned together, creating considerable friction. Saul Hayes, of the United Jewish Refugee and War Relief Agencies in Canada, dealt with the authorities there on these and other related issues. In June 1941 he managed to secure for deportees a change of status from POWs to that of refugee. On the whole, however, all matters of release and policy were referred to the United Kingdom.[74]

The Board, initially unaware that the Central Committee for Internees at Bloomsbury House maintained contact with refugees in Canada and Australia, demanded that regular contact with deportees should be established under its auspices. It then attempted to gain representation on the Central Committee but Leslie Prince, co-chairman of the CCJR, persuaded it that the Committee was 'non-denominational ... and its suggestions for action would be all the more effective, because it would not involve a specifically Jewish aspect'.[75] This impartiality was particularly pertinent in the case of the *Dunera*, the troopship carrying the survivors of the ill-fated *Arandora Star*. The *Dunera*, with the capacity to hold 1,000 people, transported 2,542 German, Austrian and Italian deportees under appalling conditions, on a two-month voyage to Australia, during which the deportees were robbed of their possessions and mistreated by British guards. Among them were many Jews, who were allegedly singled out for harsher treatment.[76] The Board now opposed separate Jewish representation on a government Committee of Enquiry being set up to investigate this.[77]

However, specifically religious concerns could not be subsumed into the interdenominational 'humanitarian' issue and here the attitude of the Board was more forceful. In February 1941, representatives of the Joint Orthodox Jewish Refugee Committee inquired about the religious welfare of internees, citing those in an Australian camp 400 miles from Sydney, whose Jewish community, due to shortages of funds, was unable to help. After some difficulty, religious observance was permitted and kosher food provided, to be paid for by outside organisations or by the internees.[78] Other religious issues included the so-called Sabbath scandal in Camp 'B', an order issued by the office of Internment Operations in Canada penalising Jews who refused to work on the Sabbath. The Board protested strongly and suggested that all such issues be directed to Hayes, via the Central Committee for Internees in London. Within a month the issue was resolved.[79]

The British voluntary organisations approached the Advisory Committee to make overtures to the Dominion governments to arrange for release and integration into the Canadian and Australian war effort of all refugees who wished to stay and whom the Home Office considered eligible for release.[80] They were particularly concerned about deportees who had volunteered for internment in Canada on the mistaken supposition that they would be able to secure visas there for the United States.[81] However, the Home Office refused to approach the Dominion governments; internees eligible for release were either to be returned to Britain or were to emigrate elsewhere.[82]

At the end of 1940, the Home Office appointed two Jewish representatives, Chaim Raphael and Major Julius Layton, to visit Canada and Australia to help in the work of releasing deportees and those who came within the new categories for release as specified in the White Paper.[83] Eventually, in October 1945, the Canadian Immigration Department had agreed to allow all refugees in Canada with non-immigrant status (by then numbering 3,500) to remain permanently.[84] In Australia, where interference from Whitehall was unwelcome, it proved more difficult to obtain release or settlement for deportees, despite the efforts of the Parliamentary Committee for Refugees. By the end of 1942 only some 600 had been released from internment in Australia and permitted to join HM forces, with the prospect of ultimate settlement in Australia after the war.[85]

The Anglo-Jewish establishment's record on internment and deportation effectively refutes the criticism that it weakly condoned government policy. What emerges is its initial philosophical resignation to the policy in view of the wartime emergency and in line with the national mood, and its wholehearted attempts, within the constraints of that policy, to ameliorate the problems and harsh conditions that resulted from it. This amounted to acquiescence rather than endorsement. The leadership here again showed its experience and skill in dealing with matters of a charitable and administrative nature. This is in contrast to its weak and fumbling response – the result of inexperience – to the political and diplomatic challenges of the war years.

Schonfeld appears to have taken an even more supportive view of internment and deportation. Instead of echoing mainstream opinion that these were perhaps necessary evils, he actively sanctioned the internment policy as being in the best short-term interests of those affected, whilst working just as vigorously to improve conditions in the camps. This approach appears at face value to be surprisingly complaisant, though it had the undoubted benefit of placing Schonfeld in a good light with the authorities, whose cooperation was essential for much of his work. This was almost certainly the motive for his resoundingly fulsome and widely publicised praise. Schonfeld's work during this period shows that despite certain ideological and tactical differences, he was able to achieve much through harmonious cooperation with the mainstream organisations. There was certainly a great deal of effort on the part of all concerned in relief work, those whose reputation has perhaps been dimmed over time by their inevitably limited success in terms of influencing government policy. The area of internal relief work, in which the voluntary organisations achieved significant but undramatic results, has been overshadowed by the negative connotations of the whole internment episode and their comparative failure in the sphere of political efforts on the international scene.

6
Anglo-Jewry Mobilises (Summer 1942–Spring 1943)

Recent criticism of Anglo-Jewry's wartime record has focused almost exclusively on the question of whether sufficient effort was made on behalf of European Jewry. However, analysis of the effort itself has been hitherto lacking, the assumption being that what mattered was the will to achieve results rather than the ingenuity or practicality of individual endeavours. Notwithstanding the desperation and good intentions of the organisations, an element of naïveté and short-termism characterised much of their approach. This inevitably doomed their efforts to failure because, understandably, their exclusive focus on the Jewish tragedy, particularly after the summer of 1942, failed to take account of the wider political and military context within which it took place. The Anglo-Jewish leadership appeared unable to understand the dynamics of global war and incapable of comprehending the subtle and complex calculation with which officials treated its requests. The government was committed to a long-term strategy for winning the war whatever the unavoidable human cost; the organisations, by contrast, took the view that immediate rescue must take precedence. The official documents of this period reveal the government's politely concealed impatience at the narrow-minded naïveté of the Jewish organisations, which were sagely offering diplomatically phrased advice on aspects of the conduct of war without regard to logistics or possible consequences.

Until the summer of 1942 Anglo-Jewry still tried to sustain a balanced perspective on the European Jewish problem as both a Jewish and a wider humanitarian issue: 'Anti-semitism and its effects are a world problem . . . aiming at the undermining of decent human relations everywhere and endangering world peace.'[1] By emphasising the malign effects of anti-Semitism on non-Jews as well as Jews, the

Jewish leadership hoped to present the persecution of the Jews as both a Jewish and a non-Jewish issue. Even when the news of the Final Solution broke that summer, Brodetsky still tried to retain the universal perspective on Jewish persecution while at the same time pointing to the special nature of the Final Solution. 'It is thus clear that the Jewish problem cannot be compared with the usual minority problem, and needs special attention.'[2] Soon, however, the leadership's attention turned exclusively to the Jewish nature of the persecution. Contrary to the widely held view of the Anglo-Jewish community as timid and insecure, the documents show that after 1942 it was forceful, if polite, to the point of presumption in virtually instructing the government on its moral responsibilities and the ways in which these might be met. The Board seems at times to have been almost perversely intent on making self-defeating references to Palestine, which it must surely have realised would not be well received, while at the same time deferring perforce to government edict that the only way to help Jews was to win the war.

Certainly in the summer of 1940, the outcome of the war was far from certain. With 'the defeat of the Low Countries and France between April and June, Britain was now on full alert in anticipation of a Nazi invasion. Though 'Operation Sea Lion', the proposed invasion, never materialised, Hitler's bombing campaign against Britain continued for well over a year, killing tens of thousands of civilians and destroying countless homes. Until 1941 the run of spectacular German successes had been uninterrupted; before December 1941, when the US entered the war following Pearl Harbor, Britain faced Nazi Germany alone. With the fall of France in June 1940, the survival of Britain became the pivot on which the outcome of the war would depend. This could by no means be taken for granted, particularly after the disastrous retreat from Dunkirk. The outcome of the German air offensive, the Battle of Britain, was still uncertain at the end of 1941, while the war at sea, the Battle of the Atlantic, continued into mid-1943. The results of this latter campaign were crucial – 'Success for the U-boats would have meant the strangulation of British imports, and perhaps even starvation and surrender.'[3] Even American entry into the war, with its concomitant overwhelming augmentation of resources to the Allies, could not for a long time be perceived as a guarantee of ultimate victory.

It must be borne in mind that the Anglo-Jewish organisations would not have been aware of the true degree of peril facing the country, any more than the population at large, which, for example, was informed via the press that Dunkirk had been a triumph of military strategic skill. The government was engaged in a propaganda campaign designed to keep morale high, and the information distributed to the public was necessarily selective and distorted.[4] The inexperience and impracticality of the organisations was thus compounded by ignorance of the military position, to which civilian groups were of course not privy. This in turn affected the tone and content of the organisations' dealings with the government; their often naïve suggestions were perhaps based on an over-optimistic reading of the situation. Even in the war's later stages, their efforts were hamstrung by a natural assumption that the United States and the Soviet Union, as 'allies', were at the bidding of the British government. The truth was, rather, that the 'anti-Hitler alliance' was united in one purpose only, namely the defeat of Nazi Germany. As this objective came closer to realisation, the allies' conflicting ambitions for post-war Europe led to increasing differences and tensions between them.

From the global military perspective the critical turning points up to 1942 included the fall of France, the German invasion of the Soviet Union (June 1941) and American entry into the war. From the point of view of the Anglo-Jewish organisations, however, the turning point was marked by the breaking of the news of an extermination plan in August 1942. Once evidence of this reached foreign countries, the response of Allied leaders, and to some extent the Anglo-Jewish leadership, was one of cautious restraint. Yet the latter was soon mobilised into action and presented numerous rescue proposals to the government, most of which proved abortive because of the exigencies of Britain's wartime priorities. The government's policy considerations were the crucial factor in all rescue efforts; from the organisations' point of view, their task was not to effect rescue, but to persuade the government to do so. But officials consistently maintained that the only means of helping European Jewry was an Allied victory; the corollary of this was the overriding imperative of subordinating everything else to the war effort. Until mid-1943, while the outcome of the war remained uncertain, there were valid grounds for believing this was in fact the case.

This intractable polarity is exemplified by the issue of shipping where acute shortages presented a persistent grave threat to the viability of Britain's war effort. The authorities invariably dismissed their requests for ships to transport any escapees from occupied Europe, assuming that this was possible, on the grounds of severe shortage. The war effort was undeniably unsustainable without the import of food and raw materials, which included the demands of the British military services fighting a global war. Shortages of fuel and personnel also required for any shipping rescue schemes compounded the difficulties.

The defeat of France in June 1940 resulted in the loss of the French navy for the Allied cause. Italy's entry into the war that month endangered Britain's vital imperial route through the Mediterranean to Suez and India. Moreover, Hitler's attempt to cut off Britain's Atlantic trade route drastically affected the supply of British shipping. Between August 1940 and March 1943, merchant shipping was sunk at a steadily increasing rate and faster than it could be replaced.[5]

Shipping needs were enormous and hard to calculate or plan for. The decision, for example, to launch the North African campaign in the autumn of 1942 imposed a great and unexpected burden on the resources of Allied shipping. Shipping was also a crucial factor in the Allies' postponement of a Second Front until 1944.[6] Escalating demands on British shipping for military purposes had increasingly threatened to curtail imports. Britain imported over half her food (to feed 47 million people) and two-thirds of her raw materials. In early January 1943, the British navy had only two months' supply of oil in reserve.[7] The situation, already worrying in the summer of 1942, had become critical. By spring 1943, stockpile resources had reached their lowest point of the entire war.[8] At the time the Anglo-Jewish organisations were pressing their most urgent requests, a Shipping Committee report (January 1943) estimated that shipping for only two-thirds of required imports for the first half of 1943 could be found from British-controlled sources. It was therefore decided that sailings to the Indian Ocean, which supplied the Middle and Far East theatres of war, be reduced by half (to 40 a month). This was at a time when famine menaced large areas of Asia and Africa.[9] It was hoped that such measures would, together with US help, just about 'keep our heads above water – but it will be a close thing. We cannot afford to forgo a single ton.'[10]

By March 1943, imports were running at less than half their peace-time level, carried by a fleet one third its peace-time size. The monthly requirements of one million tons each of raw materials and food were 'irreducible' and it was feared that by April stocks would be nearly a million tons below minimum safety levels. The prospect arose that 'British ships will have to be withdrawn from their present military service even though our agreed operations are crippled or prejudiced.'[11]

These were the kinds of obstacles that the Anglo-Jewish organisations had to contend with. Requests presented in Parliament to secure Allied or neutral ships for rescue were rejected on the grounds that Britain relied on overseas supplies and 'every ounce of food imported into this country is being brought in by the blood and sweat of British sailors'. With the Battle of the Atlantic still raging in mid-1943, Viscount Cranborne, the Colonial Secretary, warned that there was no margin of safety in the event of any military setback.[12]

Senior officials regarded shipping as the most pressing limit on strategy. The British and US governments thus inevitably dismissed shipping requests at the Bermuda Conference in April 1943. Accepting the principle that winning the war in the shortest possible time was the best service which their respective governments could render prospective refugees, delegates concluded that it would be a grave disadvantage to 'divert shipping from essential war needs'.[13] This view persisted even after mid-1943, when the Battle of the Atlantic had been won and the Mediterranean cleared. By November, the spectre of a shipping shortage had reappeared, partly through the demands of 'Operation Overlord', the projected Allied invasion of north-western Europe. The principal reason, however, was the difficulty in making reliable estimates of requirements. Merchant shipping was apt to fluctuate at short notice and on a considerable scale.[14]

Ironically, in the summer of 1943, just as the situation began to look less bleak from the British perspective, the voluntary organisations appear to have lost momentum and accepted the government's position that little could be done. By the time of the Hungarian crisis in 1944, shipping difficulties had to some extent eased, though it was almost impossible to assemble refugees at ports of embarkation. It was out of the question to keep ships immobilised for long to await their arrival.[15] Even after Britain accepted, following Admiral Horthy's offer in summer 1944 to halt the deportation of Jews from Hungary, that it could draw on neutral shipping and could itself supply ships, Germany refused to grant safe conduct. Hence, for example, the SS *Tari*, the Turkish ship which the War Refugee Board had hoped to charter for the transport of Jews, could not be used, owing to the deterioration of Turkish–German relations.[16]

Furthermore, the difficulties involved in rescue efforts were severely exacerbated by the stringent immigration rules which came into force on the outbreak of war. At this point, for security reasons, all refugees from enemy territory were effectively barred entry to Britain, though a number arrived in 1940 after the German invasion of the Low Countries and France. Allied nationals were admitted only on compassionate grounds in limited categories. In 1943, special consideration was given to parents of persons serving in the army, persons eligible to enlist in the army and parents of children under 16 years already in Britain. However, admission was still conditional on these people already being in neutral countries.[17] In its defence, the government confirmed that between 1940 and 1942, 63,000 refugees had been admitted to Britain and in the first five months of 1943 a further 4,000 had arrived.[18] Most of these, however, were Allied nationals or those useful for the war effort. Immigration policy remained otherwise unchanged, despite increasing pressure on the government from late 1942 to admit Jewish refugees. A token gesture was made by the Home Secretary, Herbert Morrison, when he announced in early 1943 that Britain would accept between 1,000 and 2,000 refugees on condition that the United States and Dominions accepted proportionate numbers. He observed, however, that there were already 100,000 refugees, mainly Jews, in Britain and that accommodation problems were already acute, due to the destruction of some 30 per cent of housing in London during the Blitz of 1940–41, especially in the East End, where most Jews were living. The problem would become critical in the event of renewed air attack. Any substantial increase in the number of Jewish refugees might lead to 'serious trouble'.[19]

The policy of immigration was immeasurably aggravated by a restrictive policy on Palestine. Britain's insistence on rigidly implementing the immigration restrictions of the White Paper of May 1939 effectively closed off Palestine as the main escape route for Jewish refugees fleeing Nazi-occupied Europe. From 1922 immigration into Palestine had been limited by its 'economic absorptive capacity'. Effective limitation began after the outbreak of Arab unrest in 1936, with the introduction of a 'political high level' of immigration of 12,000 per annum, culminating in the White Paper of May 1939, which placed a ceiling of 75,000 Jewish immigrants until 31 March 1944, after which no further Jewish immigration would be permitted without Arab consent.[20] Britain's policy was designed to maintain internal security and stability in the Middle East. Appeasing the Arabs was intended to prevent outbreaks of anti-British feeling at a time when Britain could ill afford to divert large numbers of troops to the region. Immigration into Palestine was sharply reduced during the war, owing partly to the ban on emigration from enemy and enemy-controlled territories, and partly to attempts to stem the tide of illegal immigration. A frequently cited justification for the stringent regulations was fear of Nazi agents infiltrating the refugees entering Palestine. For this reason, when the war began, an overall ban on refugees from Nazi-occupied countries was imposed. As a result, even the restricted Jewish immigration granted by the White Paper was not fully achieved.[21]

Despite Churchill's earlier opposition to the White Paper, the Cabinet consensus was that the status quo in Palestine should be maintained during the war. This was considered even more important after the Biltmore Conference in May 1942 when David Ben Gurion postulated for the first time the foundation of a Jewish state and called for millions of Jews to emigrate to Palestine as soon as the war was over. This was regarded as an overtly hostile proposition. Reports from British representatives in the Middle East endorsed fears that 'the country is heading for the most serious outbreak of disorder and violence which it has yet seen ... Zionism has embarked upon an expansionist programme'.[22]

Illegal immigration rose sharply after the White Paper was announced. In 1939, out of a total of 27,561 Jewish immigrants to Palestine, 11,156 were illegal. The reluctance of the Jewish Agency to deter illegal immigration led the Colonial Office to regard the problem unsympathetically, not as a refugee issue, but as 'an organised political invasion of Palestine which exploited the facts of the refugee problem'.[23] As a deterrent, the government periodically suspended legal immigration and deducted the number of illegal immigrants from the yearly legal quota. The Foreign Office tried to persuade the governments of south-east European states to cooperate by preventing ships from sailing, and requested countries of transit to refuse transit visas. Ships were intercepted and prevented from landing. A dramatic deterrent used by the Colonial Office and the government of Palestine was deportation to the country of embarkation. While only a few suffered this fate, many were deported to Mauritius after the conflict over illegal immigration reached a climax when the *Patria* was blown up in November 1940 with the loss of 252 lives. In this case, as an act of mercy, the government allowed the survivors to remain in Palestine, but excluded survivors of the *Atlantic* about to board the *Patria* at the time of the explosion.[24]

However, the sinking of the *Struma*, carrying 769 passengers, in February 1942 led to a significant modification of policy. The Cabinet, while reaffirming its opposition to illegal immigration, did accede to the Colonial Secretary's proposal that those reaching Palestine should be allowed to remain there in internment camps rather than be deported. Their numbers would still be deducted from the semi-annual immigration quota.[25] This concession was obtained through the pressure brought to bear on the government by British and American Zionists, especially Weizmann, and several MPs, but in effect, it was insignificant since there was no deviation from the White Paper quota.[26]

In order to counter accusations of inactivity and following requests from the Jewish Agency, the ban on immigration from enemy territory was relaxed. In February 1943 the government announced that it would allow some 4,500 Bulgarian Jewish children with 500 accompanying adults, followed by up to 29,000 others from various central and south-eastern European countries, to enter Palestine, still within the White Paper quotas.[27] However, following Bulgaria's decision, under German pressure, to close its border with Turkey to all Jews, there was little prospect of legal immigration into Palestine. Nevertheless, in July, HMG instructed the British Passport Control in Istanbul, in order to encourage Turkey to allow transit of refugees, that all Jews who reached Turkey from enemy-occupied territory would be eligible (after preliminary security checks) to proceed to Palestine.[28] Oliver Stanley, the new Colonial Secretary, accepted the Jewish Agency's case that the problem of immigration was now synonymous with that of rescue and confirmed that these measures reflected the government's desire to help those in Axis-controlled countries. These included the decision, announced in November 1943, to extend the time limit of the White Paper, allowing immigration beyond the March 1944 deadline until all the allotted certificates were used. Nevertheless, the decision to cancel all unused immigration visas issued prior to September 1943 (18,300) for non-enemy countries and give priority to refugees from enemy-occupied countries did not signify any increase in the overall 75,000 quota. Moreover, by 1943, with Europe effectively sealed off by the Nazis, the chances of escaping from enemy territory were remote.[29] Consequently, as of October 1944, there were still 10,300 unused Palestine immigration certificates.[30]

During the Hungarian crisis and at the time of the Horthy offer in the summer of 1944, British officials feared that the 'floodgates of Eastern Europe were going to be opened' and opposed any large-scale immigration into Palestine. R.M.A. Hankey, of the Eastern

108

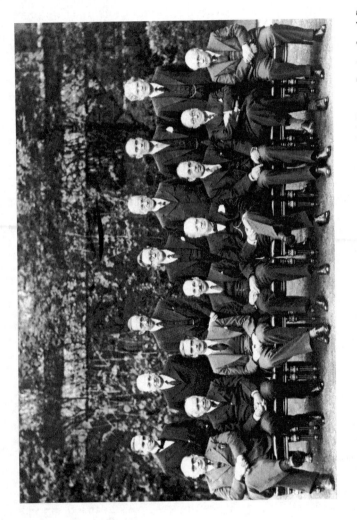

8 Members of the War Cabinet and Ministers, 16 October 1941. Sitting (left to right) Ernest Bevin, Lord Beaverbrook, Sir Anthony Eden, Clement Attlee, Winston Churchill, Sir John Anderson, Arthur Greenwood and Sir Kingsley Wood. Standing (left to right) Sir Archibald Sinclair, A.V. Alexander, Lord Cranborne, Herbert Morrison, Lord Moyne, Captain Margesson, Brendan Bracken (courtesy of Hulton Archives)

Department of the Foreign Office, suggested that camps be established 'somewhere in the Mediterranean area . . . preferably not too
near Palestine', adding that 'the 10,000-odd places *must* be spun
out as long as possible'. A factor was the 'importance of not bur-
dening the army with a new administrative liability at this time'.[31]

In effect, 'the Foreign Office was living in the moral vacuum of
which the White Paper was both a cause and an effect'.[32] The Anglo-
Jewish organisations had little hope of changing Britain's Palestine
policy. Brodetsky, an ardent Zionist, though regarded as a moderate
in official circles, insisted on promoting the importance of Palestine
as a solution to the Jewish refugee problem in all his overtures to the
government. However, political concerns inclined officials to suspect
the motives of Jewish leaders and to reject suggestions considered
contrary to British imperial interests. 'Both the Foreign Office and
Colonial Office feared the radicalisation of Palestine throughout the
war and considerably exaggerated the Jewish political as well as the
military threat.'[33]

The Final Solution

From June 1941, the situation of European Jewry changed dramatically. The cornerstone of Hitler's foreign policy had always been
the long-established ambition to destroy the centre of the 'Jewish-
Bolshevik' world conspiracy and gain *Lebensraum* (living space) in
the east for the 'Aryan' race. 'Operation Barbarossa', the invasion of
the Soviet Union, in June 1941, finally gave Hitler the opportunity
to realise this and provided the cover to expand the killing operation. Special Nazi killing squads, the *Einsatzgruppen*, accompanied
the regular German forces on the Soviet front and began carrying
out systematic mass murder by rounding up and killing hundreds
of thousands of Jews. The Soviet Union, however, was not defeated
in six weeks as had been anticipated, and this failure prompted
Hitler and his henchmen to revise both the method and timetable
for the annihilation of the Jews. Decisions taken in the summer of
1941 onwards accelerated the process. On 31 July 1941, Goering
ordered Heydrich to prepare a plan for the 'Final Solution for the
Jewish Question'. The haphazard killing squads were to be replaced
by a systematic campaign of deportation and extermination which
was to apply modern methods of scientific technology. This decision had been taken well before representatives of the various
German authorities and ministries met under the chairmanship of

Heydrich at Wannsee in January 1942 to discuss the coordination and implementation of the elimination of the Jews of Europe. Towards the end of October 1941, the Nazi regime abruptly reversed its policy of promoting Jewish emigration and forbade Jews to leave German-occupied Europe. At the end of 1941, an extermination camp was put into operation at Chelmno, near Lodz, and by the spring of 1942 the extermination process had been set in motion in other camps in the occupied areas of Poland, namely at Auschwitz, Belzec, Treblinka and Sobibor. Special units of the German police and the SS inspected the ghettos and carried out the deportation of the Jews to the death camps. Those who did not die from disease or starvation either in the ghettos or through forced labour were dispatched *en masse* in gas chambers and crematoria, to which other groups, considered subhuman by the Nazis, such as gypsies, homosexuals and Poles, were also transported.[34]

Recent research has shown that the British had evidence as early as 1941 of Nazi atrocities against Jews and of massacres committed in German-occupied territories in Poland and the Soviet Union. This information was obtained by the British Code and Cypher School at Bletchley Park, which monitored wartime Nazi communications. Various suggestions have been made as to why the British government failed to react to such information; for example, false Allied propaganda during World War I had left a legacy of suspicion about reports of enemy atrocities. One obvious point is that to respond would have alerted the Germans to the success of the code-breaking exercise, thereby jeopardising the Allied war effort.[35] It is hardly surprising that in the interests of expediency it was prepared to suppress the information it was receiving about the Final Solution, which was militarily irrelevant to the war effort. 'In war, morality must often take second place to expediency.'[36]

By June 1942, the Allies had several other sources of information filtering in regarding the Nazis' mass killings of Jews. In May 1942, for example, Jan Karski, a representative of the Polish underground in Warsaw, arrived in London with first-hand details of the systematic liquidation of the Jews. But it was Dr. Gerhart Riegner, Geneva representative of the World Jewish Congress, who spelt out the details of the extermination plan. In August, he passed to the Foreign Office a report stating that 'in the Fuehrer's Headquarters, a plan has been discussed and is under consideration for the extermination after deportation to the East of all Jews in countries occupied or controlled by Germany; action is planned for the autumn; ways

9 Selig Brodetsky, President of the Board of Deputies, 1939–49 (courtesy of the Board of Deputies)

and means are still being discussed including use of prussic acid'.[37] Some of the details in this report, however, later proved to have been out of date. The extermination programme was no longer in the planning stage, but was well under way.

However, the news was received with guarded reserve, not only by the Allied governments, wary of what was considered Jewish hysteria and propaganda, but by the Anglo-Jewish leadership.[38] Brotman had already expressed incredulity at the report that 700,000 Jews had been murdered in Poland: 'The figure seems on the face of it to be an exaggeration, even having regard to the kind of beasts the Germans are, and if it is an exaggeration it is a pity that it is published.'[39] Even when the reports were confirmed later in the year, uncertainty remained about the extent of the extermination of Polish Jewry. Two explanations for the initial incredulity were offered at the time: first, that the information reaching the West from Poland was often fragmentary and incoherent; second, that the concept of genocide in Europe on such a scale was unprecedented. Several historians have since invoked the psychodynamic mechanisms of repression and denial to account for this incomprehension.[40] Not until the end of November did Anglo-Jewry's initial scepticism give way as the news was officially confirmed.[41]

Brotman had always recognised the importance of unremitting publicity. Stimulating neutral, satellite and even German public opinion was one of the few courses available. Brodetsky suggested leaflet drops over Germany and radio broadcasts to the peoples of Romania, Bulgaria and Hungary.[42] The threat of post-war retribution was similarly regarded as an important deterrent, if not for the Nazis, then at least for their satellites. It is dangerously easy, with the benefit of hindsight, to argue that none of this would have impressed the Nazi regime.[43] Certainly the threat of post-war retribution could hardly have acted as a deterrent since most Nazis were convinced until almost the end that Germany would win the war. It must be remembered, however, that the futility of all attempts at persuasion was not, and could not have been, grasped by the Allies, so thoroughly was the essential fanaticism of the Nazi psyche and ideology misunderstood.

The WJC led the publicity campaign with a press conference (sponsored by the British Ministry of Information) in London in June 1942, detailing the systematic destruction of European Jewry. Sidney Silverman, who presided, spoke of 'a conspiracy of silence on the part of the press about this tragic situation' and dismissed

10 Adolf Brotman, General Secretary of the Board of Deputies, 1934–66 (courtesy of the Board of Deputies)

the suggestion that publicity would merely lend credence to Goebbels' claim that 'this is a Jewish war'.[44] Public response was immediate and included forceful denunciations of the Nazis by leading churchmen and parliamentarians. The Board proposed a public protest meeting, to be held in late October.[45]

Nevertheless, the Anglo-Jewish leadership showed some naïveté in its failure to grasp the implications of the Final Solution, as manifested in its emphasis on planning for the post-war period. In August 1942, the JFC convened a two-day conference devoted to Jewish post-war policy. The assumption that there would be large numbers of survivors was reiterated in Brodetsky's public reference to the importance of Palestine as a target for post-war Jewish emigration, which would be 'very much greater than after the last war'. He estimated the number of Jews who would want to emigrate after the war at between four and five million.[46] More realistically (as it turned out), Richard Lichtheim, representing the Jewish Agency in Geneva, warned that estimates of 'seven million dispossessed Jews in Eastern Europe' (cited in the House of Commons in August) were over-optimistic: 'there will not be more than one and a half or two million Jews'. Lichtheim criticised the inactivity of Jewish organisations in Britain and America for failing to alert the public and the authorities and warned of the danger to Europe's remaining Jewish communities. He suggested that a warning, perhaps by the Vatican or some neutral power, might have a deterrent effect.[47]

However, the Board was not entirely inactive, though it felt there was little it could do beyond passing strongly worded resolutions. Its leaders seemed oblivious to the hopelessness of such resolutions reaching an audience wider than the readership of the *Jewish Chronicle*. The Board expressed its gratitude to the Allied governments 'for their expression of sympathy and horror' and to Churchill for his assurance that those responsible would be held to account.[48] Some reserve remained, with Brotman wondering whether the reports from Geneva 'were purposely put about by the Nazis for certain nefarious ends' and stressing that 'we should not necessarily add to the anxieties of the millions of Jews outside Europe who have relatives in it under the Nazis'.[49]

The Anglo-Jewish leadership had appealed several times to the Allied governments to issue warnings to the Nazis and their satellites. However, the Foreign Office invariably opposed emphasising the plight of the Jews. British policy on atrocities had been formulated in October 1941 when Churchill announced that 'retribution for these crimes . . . must henceforth take its place among the major purposes of the war'. This statement, like most that followed, was in line with the government's position that Jews were citizens of their countries of residence rather than a discrete nationality. This was consistent both with Britain's Palestine policy and the principle 'not to single out Jews as that would be a surrender to German racialism'; it would reinforce German claims that the Allies were fighting a 'Jewish war'. The government therefore refused any separate representation of Jewish concerns at international conferences and, until the summer of 1944, the formation of a Jewish army. It also insisted that Jewish organisations should play no specific part in post-war planning or the rehabilitation of European Jewry.[50]

In January 1942 a conference of Allied powers met at St. James's Palace, London, under the presidency of General Sikorski, in order to consider German actions in occupied Europe. The conference issued a declaration regarding Nazi atrocities against civilian populations. At this time, the JFC and the British Section appealed to the Foreign Office and to the signatories of the Nine-Power Declaration to bear in mind 'the suffering of the Jews and the part played by them in the common struggle'. They added, however, that they had 'no desire to differentiate between the sufferings and brutalities inflicted by the Nazis on Jews and non-Jews'.[51] To this, Sikorski reiterated that specific reference to Jews would 'be equivalent to an implicit recognition of the racial theories that we all reject'.[52] Undeterred, Easterman continued to press Eden, unsuccessfully. In August 1942, Brodetsky appealed to the Archbishop of Canterbury to raise the question in the House of Lords debate.[53]

The Board's first official stand against Nazi atrocities was a deputation to the Foreign Office in October 1942, calling for a statement by HMG charging enemy governments with atrocities against Jews and offering refuge to those able to escape. The deputation also mooted the evacuation of Jews to neutral countries and Palestine, and the possibilities of ICRC aid and a separate Jewish council to advise the Allies on post-war relief and rehabilitation. Despite Brotman's urging the exceptional nature of the Jewish persecution, the Memorandum of this meeting reveals considerable official reluctance to draw such a distinction.[54]

Zionists were also calling for a Jewish army and specific mention of the suffering of Jews. The Foreign Office considered this a covert part of Zionist 'propaganda for a Jewish sovereign state in Palestine and it also no doubt aims at securing separate Jewish participation in any Peace settlement'. The more diplomatic approach of the Board, albeit equally unproductive, was received more favourably and it is not surprising that Brotman was considered 'a reasonable person' who was 'unwilling to bother us unreasonably'.[55]

In November 1942, following American confirmation of the genocide reports, Silverman and Easterman handed the Foreign Office the authenticating document received from the Polish government in London. They proposed a Four-Power Declaration by the United Nations, warning of reprisals against the perpetrators, and the broadcasting of messages encouraging gentiles to aid the persecuted Jews. Although doubtful whether much could be achieved, Richard Law noted that 'we would be in an appalling position if these stories should prove to have been true and we have done nothing whatever about them'.[56] One implication of this remark is that the authorities themselves were genuinely sceptical of the authenticity of 'these stories' even as late as November. By December 1942 pressure had mounted on the government from various quarters to secure a joint-government declaration. This was accompanied by suggestions for the relief of Europe's Jews.[57] Confronted with 'reliable and convincing reports' from the Polish government in London, the Foreign Office decided that in view of mounting public concern, a Declaration should be published as soon as possible, though it could be expected to achieve little.[58]

The JFC met in December to consider appropriate action. It resolved to increase pressure on the government to issue a declaration referring specifically to the atrocities committed against Jews. The Board had already approached Law on this issue, but had received no reply. The importance of wide publicity, via the BBC, the Ministry of Information and the Department of Political Warfare, was stressed. Hertz suggested a 'manifestation of a religious character' – a day of mourning and a fast, with services in synagogues. A date, 13 December 1942, was chosen, to be followed by a week of mourning culminating in a public demonstration.[59] The JFC also agreed to send Jewish and non-Jewish delegations to the government, to stimulate debates in Parliament and to seek the mediation of the Pope. Approaches were also to be made to the Protecting Powers, neutral countries and the ICRC; other ideas included broadcasts on the BBC's European Services and leaflet drops over Germany. It was also suggested that Jews in the ghettos be granted the status of prisoners-of-war. How much could be achieved depended, as Brotman observed, on government cooperation, but it was felt that some statement should be published in order 'to demonstrate to the Jewish community that the Board and other Jewish organisations were doing what they considered was *within their power* to meet the situation' [my emphasis]. Shortly after, a resolution of solidarity with the endangered Jews of Europe was unanimously passed.[60]

The Board was in a moral and public relations quandary. It was naturally concerned to be seen to be doing *something* 'within their power' but Brotman's comment implicitly acknowledges that it had no 'power' at all. On the other hand, it needed to justify its 'authority' in the eyes of the Jewish community, so fell back on a resolution of solidarity which, however well intended, can hardly have been expected to impress anyone except the Board's own constituents. Brotman explicitly acknowledged this in a private admission that 'hopeless as is the prospect, there is a strongly expressed desire that something should be attempted. We cannot go to the Government authorities without definite proposals, *for we have none* and it would be purposeless to go simply to depict the situation, of which the Government is fully aware'[61] [my emphasis]. The importance of maintaining communication with the Foreign Office was not so much that it was likely to produce any concrete results as that it reassured the Jewish community that its leaders were acting tirelessly on behalf of European Jewry.

As a result of efforts made by the organisations, a Declaration, sponsored by all the Allied governments, was issued. The sole objective of the December Declaration was to deter further atrocities; it contained no practical proposals for rescue and relief. It was formulated in response to a question by Silverman, in reply to which Eden stated that the Allied governments 'reaffirm their solemn resolution to ensure that those responsible for these crimes shall not escape retribution'.[62] This Allied Declaration was essentially a public commitment to the eventual juridical prosecution of Nazi war crimes against Jews and others. In reality, however, it was also issued in the hope that a rhetorical flourish without direct commitment to action would serve to fob off the pressure groups' agitation. Unfortunately, from Eden's point of view, 'it had a far greater dramatic effect than I expected'.[63] As a result of the mounting pressure and expectations aroused by the Declaration, London and Washington embarked on talks which were to culminate in a further stalling exercise, the Bermuda Conference of April 1943.

In the meantime, Eden referred to the 'immense geographical and other difficulties' preventing the government from taking immediate constructive measures to assist the emigration and relief of Jews in occupied Europe. These self-imposed difficulties included Home Office restrictions on large-scale immigration, constraints on further immigration to the Colonies and the fact that neutral countries 'can hardly be expected to help much'.[64] However, a Cabinet Committee on the Reception and Accommodation of Refugees (hereafter Cabinet Committee on Refugees) was formed at the end of December to consider arrangements for such Jewish refugees who might find their way out of enemy-occupied territory.

Despite some disappointment at the Declaration's lack of constructive measures, it did succeed in stimulating public opinion and encouraging efforts by organisations and by individuals. The Standing Conference of National Voluntary Organisations resolved 'to request HMG to take immediate steps to bring to this country Jewish and non-Aryan refugees now in neutral countries contiguous to Nazi-occupied territory'.[65] Pressure groups were formed in Parliament, most notably around Eleanor Rathbone, while in January 1943, the Archbishops of Canterbury, York and Wales issued an appeal to the government urging immediate measures of rescue and sanctuary within the Empire and elsewhere for those who could be saved.[66] The press joined the campaign and offers of homes and help came from all over Britain. The Declaration also inspired Victor Gollancz's striking and influential pamphlet, 'Let My People Go', which succinctly summarised the various rescue proposals.[67]

Despite initial Jewish expressions of gratitude, exemplified by James de Rothschild and Brodetsky, for the Declaration,[68] members of the Consultative Committee soon voiced their disappointment that the 'perpetrators of these crimes' were not named, that the governments of Hungary, Bulgaria and Romania were not mentioned, and that the question of rescue was not touched upon.[69] The Board added disconsolately that the Declaration seemed merely to have spurred on Nazi propaganda about a 'Jewish war'.[70]

Critics such as Silverman added that the Declaration should have been followed by offers on the part of the United Nations to accommodate Jewish refugees. The Jewish Agency airily urged the government to 'forget legalities and make Palestine into a Jewish sanctuary'.[71] The *Jewish Chronicle* complained of Eden's pusillanimity: 'the occasion was surely there for a splendid offer of sanctuary'. Brushing aside logistical, geographical, political and military difficulties, it appealed for asylum in Britain and encouragement to neutral states.[72] Such solutions are characteristic of the Zionist mindset in

Anglo-Jewry during 1942–43. From the government's perspective Britain's complex role in the Middle East was being reduced to obstructiveness over Palestine and her policy to 'legalities' which she might forget whenever she chose; the rhetoric of a 'splendid offer of sanctuary' suggests a naive belief that 'magic wand' solutions to the Jewish tragedy were feasible. Also typical is the failure to realise that the Declaration was never intended as a public announcement of a grand solution to the refugee problem.

Following the Declaration, the organisations submitted proposals for 'practical' rescue measures. The WJC and the Jewish Agency considered the possibility of removing two million Jews from Europe, a proposal that would have been dismissed as absurd and unworkable even in peacetime. All these measures visualised the admission of refugees into areas controlled by the United Nations, together with (presumably unlimited) financial aid for neutral countries which might be willing to accept refugees. Many proposals had pointed to the suitability of Palestine in the work of rescue and relief.[73] The logistical difficulties of such proposals do not seem to have daunted the organisations any more than the problem of extricating the Jewish population of Europe en masse from enemy territory.

Conflict and rancour arose because each organisation made independent representations to the government, creating in turn a bad impression on the authorities. The British Section, in particular, felt that the Board was not working in collaboration with the Consultative Committee, and had not cooperated during the Week of Mourning.[74] Brodetsky had insisted on sending a delegation to the government, even though Law had advised against it and Churchill refused to meet it. Easterman felt that 'It was absurd, after the announcement of the United Nations Declaration, to send twelve people to see them.'[75] Brodetsky's proposals, of varying practical value, had included supplementing the Declaration by leaflet drops over enemy territories, appeals to neutrals to offer asylum to Jews, the establishment of refugee camps in Spain and an approach to the Pope.[76] A deputation from the Board nevertheless met Eden on 23 December and proposed a number of these immediate rescue measures, including asylum for refugees in areas controlled by the United Nations, particularly Palestine, and substantial concessions in granting visas for Britain to some of the 10,000 refugees then in Spain. Britain was asked to encourage neutral states to continue taking refugees by providing guarantees that other homes would be found for them after the war. Viscount Samuel suggested that the restrictions on entry into Britain be reviewed, stressing the value of refugees in the labour force and war effort. In reply, Eden claimed that the Declaration had been issued earlier than expected and before practical suggestions could be considered. He assured the deputation that full consideration would be given to its points and the Anglo-Jewish leadership felt innocently that it had 'done extraordinarily well'.[77] A week later, the Consultative Committee again discussed with Law its proposals for practical rescue and relief measures. In the event, little was achieved. The 'dilatory attitude of the US Government' was blamed.[78]

Dissatisfied with the government's ambivalence, a group of MPs and Jewish representatives, invited by Rathbone and Professor A.V. Hill, MP, met at Burlington House in January and agreed that a deputation of MPs should see Churchill. Brodetsky summarised the deputation's proposals, which had already been laid before Eden, under two headings: those aimed at preventing the murder of Jews and plans to save those who could escape. The latter involved persuading neutral countries to take a number of refugees, refuge in Palestine and help from the United Nations by way of taking refugees into their own territories. Brodetsky expressed disappointment that despite numerous approaches to the government, 'little had yet been done'.[79] New suggestions included a direct appeal to Hitler, a relaxation of Home Office restrictions on immigration and the setting up of a council to deal with practical and administrative work. Brodetsky compiled a number of 'Suggested Steps for Saving Jews in Nazi Occupied Europe', to be presented by the parliamentary deputation at the end of January. He emphasised the opportunities in Palestine for refugees, who could be readily absorbed in agriculture, industry and war work; 37,000 immigration certificates were still available under the 1939 White Paper. Some consideration was also given to planning for post-war relief.[80]

The mood of the Anglo-Jewish leadership was now one of frustration and impatience, rather than of optimism. Hertz complained of the 'fatal inertia' of governments and proposed that Viscount Samuel act as a liaison officer between the United Nations and Jewry in order 'to ensure an end of Government delay in the work of human salvage.'[81]

While the official organisations were hampered by governmental delays, small-scale individual efforts continued unabated. In early 1943, Schonfeld approached Sir George Jones to form a special Parliamentary Committee to deal with the European Jewish situation.

11 Eleanor Rathbone, 1872–1946, Independent MP for the Combined Universities and guiding spirit of the National Committee for Rescue from Nazi Terror (courtesy of the University of Liverpool)

Although Jones was reluctant, and despite Brodetsky's objection that such a committee already existed (the Parliamentary Refugee Committee), a National Committee for Rescue from Nazi Terror (National Committee) was established in March by Rathbone under the chairmanship of Lord Crewe. Represented on this Committee were prominent political and ecclesiastical figures as well as representatives of the main Jewish and non-Jewish voluntary organisations.[82] It was dedicated to ensuring the closest cooperation between all those engaged in rescue and relief.

Unlike the Anglo-Jewish leadership, which continually pressed the government to relax its restrictive policy on immigration to Palestine, Schonfeld deliberately refrained from including Palestine (or admission into Britain) in his appeals to the government to open up its territories to refugees. This was probably not ideologically but tactically motivated; recognising the hopelessness of trying to change government policy, Schonfeld must have felt it would be more productive to press the suitability of alternative asylum schemes.[83] In consultation with his friend Josiah Wedgwood, Schonfeld decided that the best procedure to obtain government action would be to table a widely supported, non-denominational Motion in both Houses of Parliament. Rathbone thought the idea promising and Schonfeld approached Sir George Jones, who offered cooperation and valuable suggestions. However, when Brodetsky objected, Sir George retracted.[84] Nevertheless, Schonfeld, together with the Archbishop of Canterbury and other leading churchmen and parliamentarians, enlisted the support of 277 MPs for a Motion to be tabled in both Houses of Parliament, asking HMG 'to declare its readiness to find temporary refuge in its own territories or in territories under its control, for endangered persons who are able to leave those countries'. The Motion was worded in such a way as to avoid controversy, leaving matters of detail open to HMG and avoiding direct proposals for admission of refugees into Britain or Palestine. The Motion also suggested that neutral countries might be encouraged to receive refugees and offer transit facilities, an important provision with far-reaching implications since the possession of documents evidencing foreign protection afforded Jews at least temporary protection from deportation.[85]

Brodetsky fiercely opposed Schonfeld's efforts on the grounds that independent initiatives were damaging to Jewish unity and caused 'exasperation on the part of our non-Jewish neighbours'.[86] Defensively but irrelevantly, Brodetsky added that persistent efforts were being made, but that those involved in what he called 'political work' were 'not always free to say what they were doing'. In a private letter to the editor of the *Jewish Chronicle*, Brotman reiterated his own opposition to Schonfeld's initiative as 'an activity with potentialities of great value undertaken in the wrong way. It would have been better that the internal difficulty should have been got over without parading our differences in public.'[87] Understandably, Brotman ignored the fact that the parading of differences which he found so damaging was largely the Board's own doing.

Brodetsky disapproved of the Motion, arguing that 'His original text, in my opinion, was vague, gave little guidance in the way of action and omitted all mention of Palestine'.[88] But Schonfeld knew that any reference to Palestine would lose the Motion valuable support and that, in any case, the term 'territories under the control of the British Empire' implicitly included Palestine.[89] The Motion was opposed on similar grounds by the British Section and the Jewish Agency. The Agudat Israel refrained from outright criticism, but disassociated itself from the Motion, while Hertz made it known that he did not 'accept responsibility for Dr. Schonfeld's action'.[90]

A special meeting of the Emergency Consultative Committee discussed the issue, which was also fought out in the columns of the *Jewish Chronicle*, with Schonfeld accusing Brodetsky of ignoring his invitation to cooperate in the initiative and Brodetsky denying that Schonfeld had made any such overtures. According to Schonfeld, the Motion failed, not because of Government opposition – 'Britain was at her best' – but because of 'the Zionist opposition on the Board of Deputies'.[91] However, Schonfeld's resentment was misplaced. There was never any chance of the Motion being tabled since, as Eden remarked: 'the statement made by Attlee on the 19 January 1943 ... covers the ground more fully than Dr. Schonfeld's draft which now seems therefore superfluous.'[92]

The episode is a striking illustration of the extent to which governmental considerations, rather than the efforts of individuals or organisations, shaped the direction and implementation of policy. It also illustrates the Jewish community's fatal tendency towards disunity and point-scoring. This may have had little bearing on the outcome of events, but is symptomatic of a lack of strong leadership.

However, Schonfeld succeeded in persuading the Archbishop of Canterbury to introduce a Resolution in the House of Lords in March 1943, condemning Nazi atrocities against Jews and demanding government action to 'provide help and temporary asylum to persons in

124 Holocaust and Rescue

danger ... who are able to leave'.[93] During this session, Viscount Samuel complained that 'While Governments prepare memoranda and exchange Notes and hold conferences ... the Nazis go on killing men, women and children.' He enlarged on the Archbishop's proposal, suggesting that a fresh influx of refugees to Palestine would add to the permanent prosperity of that country and denying that immigration into Britain might stir up anti-Semitism, stressing that there would be 'no more than a few thousands at the most who would succeed in making their way here'. This elicited a reassurance from Cranborne of 'the House's fullest support' for immediate and generous measures 'compatible with the requirements of military operations for providing help and temporary asylum to refugees'.[94] As usual, the escape clause of compatibility with military requirements enabled the government to offer the appearance of full support without any commitment to deliver it.

This indifference to the exhortations of such eminent figures as Viscount Samuel and the Archbishop of Canterbury indicates that the government was unlikely to have acted on Schonfeld's Motion even if it had been adopted – again illustrating how unequal the efforts and achievements of the voluntary agencies were in their dealings with the government.

Clement Attlee had reiterated in January 1943 that the only effective remedy for the victims of the Nazis was an Allied victory and that a concerted, rather than a unilaterally British, approach to rescue and relief must be followed. Genuine difficulties presented a convenient pretext for avoiding action, which the government was in any case anxious not to pursue: 'Even were we to obtain permission to withdraw all Jews ... transport alone presents a problem which will be difficult of solution. The lines of escape pass almost entirely through war areas where our requirements are predominately military, and which must therefore in the interests of our final victory receive predominance. These difficulties are very real, and cannot unfortunately be dismissed [quoting Lady Reading] as "fetters of red-tape"; but we shall do what we can.'[95]

Nevertheless, on 28 January, an all-party deputation, led by the Labour MP Arthur Greenwood, met Churchill, Eden, Morrison and Stanley to urge an approach to Germany to release Jews and to suggest that the Allied countries afford transport facilities and sanctuary to Jewish refugees, together with encouragement to neutral countries to assist in this work.[96] The government, however, deemed it 'essential to kill the idea that mass immigration to this country and the British Colonies was possible'.[97] Similarly, Brodetsky and Brotman failed to obtain any assurances from Law, who repeated that the problem could only be dealt with when an appropriate opportunity for international cooperation arose. Law observed that the government was bound to consider Arab sensibilities regarding Palestine, but noted that they 'attached no importance to that'.[98] Notwithstanding the real desperation which can be inferred from this comment, the Anglo-Jewish leadership clearly gave the impression that the government's concerns were immaterial to its own, thereby shutting off the prospect of negotiating some middle course or compromise deal. Brotman shortly afterwards notified Law of his considerable disappointment at the continuing inaction, particularly in view of the escalating urgency of the situation.[99]

Frustrated by the dilatoriness of the British and American governments, the National Committee sent a strongly worded cable to Eden, then in Washington, signed by 206 public figures and 'calling for immediate and boldest measures of rescue. British conscience so deeply stirred that country prepared for any sacrifice consistent with not delaying victory.'[100] In February, the Consultative Committee had considered making another press appeal and suggested that a number of prominent Jewish parliamentarians, such as Lords Samuel, Melchett and Reading, and James de Rothschild, might jointly address the government on the urgency of the situation, followed by a statement from the organisations.[101] On this occasion, Brotman felt, 'the paramount issue of rescue' outweighed even the undesirability of any body (namely the British Section) other than the JFC issuing any public statement.[102]

Further ideas included the suggestion that refugees should be moved from Spain to the Isle of Man or some other territory under British control. Earlier proposals were repeated, and the importance of Palestine reiterated.[103] Brodetsky and others expressed gratitude for the Colonial Secretary's Commons statement in February that the 29,000 Palestine immigration certificates still available would be used to admit Jewish children and some adults from enemy territory, to Palestine. However, they were anxious that this should be done as soon as possible and that the figure of 29,000 should not be treated as immutable. They added suggestions regarding the movement of refugees and a request to bring a substantial number to Britain; they also asked what measures HMG had proposed to the Dominions and Colonies to secure offers of asylum. All these suggestions, which were reasonable in principle, were, from the government's view, untenable in practice. In February, the JFC prepared a six-point programme for providing facilities for immigration, transportation and maintenance of Jewish refugees. Like earlier approaches, this was 'noted for consideration' and reference was made to the imminent Anglo-American preliminary conference on the refugee problem.[104]

British public reaction to reports of the exterminations had led to increased pressure on the government from December 1942. The National Committee's cable to Eden in March typified the mood of urgency and it was hoped that Eden's visit to Washington would lead to speedy and definite rescue measures.[105] However, it soon became clear that the forthcoming Conference would deal not with rescue but solely with the refugee problem. Furthermore, as at Evian, Britain reiterated her opposition to any consideration of Palestine as a haven and America insisted on retaining her current immigration laws.

The refugee crisis had peaked with the Nazi invasion of unoccupied France in November 1942, which resulted in thousands of refugees fleeing into Spain. They were held there in squalid internment camps, notably Miranda del Ebro, designed to accommodate 700 people but holding over 3,000. A few private relief organisations supervised, together with representatives of the British Embassy and a team of Red Cross workers. As the private organisations became increasingly overwhelmed, the British government urged the American State Department in January to call an informal conference of Allied nations to review possible action. Five weeks later, Cordell Hull proposed a meeting at Ottawa for 'preliminary exploration of new ways and means of aiding victims of Nazi oppression'.[106]

Eden's Washington visit exemplified British caution. Referring to the 60,000–70,000 Jews under threat in Bulgaria, he noted that 'we should move very cautiously about offering to take all Jews out of a country like Bulgaria'. He feared that such a move would unleash a torrent of similar requests on behalf of Jews in Poland and Germany and that 'Hitler might well take us up on any offer'. This would result in a open-ended commitment to accept an unquantifiable flood of refugees, a problem which would be further exacerbated by difficulties over transportation and potential security risks.[107] Eden's reservations were designed to show that the logistical difficulties could not be adequately addressed without jeopardising the imperative aim of winning the war as speedily as possible. His implicit conclusion – notable for sophistry rather than logic – was that because little could be done, nothing should be done, a point that was not raised by the Anglo-Jewish leaders.

In view of this continuing official inertia, the National Committee called for a sustained demonstration by all sections of the public in favour of immediate action by HMG and other governments of the United Nations, particularly America.[108] It welcomed the Anglo-American Conference, though the American request for a preliminary meeting at Ottawa was deplored as likely to cause long delays at a time of acute emergency. According to reports, one and a half million Polish citizens, one million of them Jews, had already been killed, along with nearly 750,000 Yugoslavs. (Ironically when the Conference finally met, on 19 April 1943, it coincided with the beginning of the Warsaw Ghetto uprising.) The Committee prepared a 'Twelve-Point Programme' of feasible rescue measures. Rathbone urged that, in the meantime, HMG should take all possible steps, including the relaxation of entry regulations, to rescue endangered refugees.[109]

In order to facilitate cooperation, the JFC and the AJA called a conference in April of representatives of Jewish communities and organisations. Aware that, despite overwhelming public support, little had yet been achieved, the conference endorsed the National Committee's rescue proposals and urged the government to take all possible immediate unilateral action, again citing the suitability of Palestine for the reception of refugees.[110] A Twelve-Point Memorandum with supplementary notes was sent to Bermuda. Its proposals included the issue of visas, the establishment of refugee camps, opportunities in Palestine and the provision of neutral or Allied shipping facilities. The Memorandum reiterated proposals that assurances be offered to neutral countries regarding assistance and speedy transfer and resettlement of refugees. The exchange of refugees for enemy nationals was raised, as was an approach to German and other Axis and satellite Governments to allow Jews – especially Jewish children – to leave enemy-controlled areas.[111]

While Eden was still in Washington, Dr. Nahum Goldmann, President of the WJC, Moshe Shertok, head of the Political Department of the Jewish Agency, and Perlzweig appealed to the Foreign Office for a direct approach to the German government to release Jews or, if this were refused, for facilities to send them food. However, Ian Henderson repeated the objections that Eden had made in Washington.[112] His flat dismissal underlines how there was never any intention of implementing suggestions so totally at variance with government policy on the conduct of the war and the refugee issue, and which, apart from that, given the military and political situation, were impractical to the point of naïveté.

12 British and American delegates to the Bermuda Conference, April 1943. Left to right, George Hall (British), Harold Dodds (USA), Richard Law (Under-Secretary of State at the Foreign Office, head of the British delegation), Sol Bloom (USA) and Osbert Peake (British) (courtesy of Associated Press)

Disturbed that the debate on the refugee question was to follow rather than precede the Bermuda Conference, Rathbone requested that a small deputation present the case for the 'Twelve-Point Programme for Immediate Rescue Measures'. Eden declined to receive the deputation, but, according to Walker, 'As a sop . . . to Miss Rathbone', it was agreed that the Twelve-Point Programme would be communicated to Bermuda. Still dissatisfied, Rathbone continued to press the refugee case: 'What can we all do but go on making ourselves a nuisance to you and everyone else in authority? We recognise the disadvantage of publicity. But nothing here seems to happen without.'[113]

Neither government would countenance facilities for specific Jewish representation at the Bermuda Conference. The US representative, Sol Bloom, a Jew, was considered a concession to Jewish sensibilities, although Bloom himself had never been identified with any recognised Jewish pressure group. The Conference was designed to deal with the refugee issue as a whole, rather than rescue, and its work might be 'embarrassed' or unfairly biased by special consideration for the Jewish interest.[114] Consequently, there was no Jewish representation at Bermuda. Nevertheless, Law, the British delegate, advised Eden that 'We are subjected to extreme pressure from an alliance of Jewish organisations and Archbishops'. Law believed it would be unwise to ignore such pressure, either from the powerful American Jewish lobby or from British Jewry, although he recognised the danger of counter-pressure from those 'afraid of an alien immigration into the country because it will put their livelihood in jeopardy after the war'.[115]

The three principal proposals of the voluntary organisations were dismissed as impractical in the early stages of the Conference. The first was that the United Nations should approach Hitler to release Jews in Nazi-occupied countries: 'It was impossible to negotiate with the enemy – the terms of negotiating with Hitler were unconditional surrender.' It was also 'ridiculous', since the possibility of Hitler releasing 40 million [*sic*] 'useless mouths' would place the Allies in an impossible position. Delegates also rejected the second suggestion, that military prisoners in Allied hands be exchanged for civilians. Finally, the suggestion that food should be sent through the blockade to Jews in Nazi-occupied Europe was also rejected: 'Any modification of the blockade was a matter for the Ministry of Economic Warfare.'[116]

In order to encourage neutral states to grant temporary asylum, the British delegation proposed that members of the United Nations give assurances of immediate financial assistance and guarantees that all exiles would be repatriated when hostilities ended. Although the assurance never materialised, Britain did act unilaterally, providing financial assistance and some easing of blockade restrictions, stimulating a positive response from Switzerland and Sweden.[117] This was an important departure from the principle adopted at the Evian Conference, that refugees were not to be a charge on public funds. Emerson had been pressing the matter for some time and now planned to launch a national appeal to raise public funds for the assistance of European refugees. The Foreign Office approved but felt this ought to wait until after Bermuda.[118] It was also feared that 'some harm [i.e. anti-Semitism] might result because in fact, the funds would be used mainly for Jews'.[119] Here again, 'fear' of potential anti-Semitism became a reason for not trying to save Jews from actual anti-Semitism.

The results of the Bermuda Conference were kept secret, on the grounds that publicity might endanger lives.[120] However, although the final report was not issued until November 1943, it was clear, especially after the Commons debate in May, that the Conference had been a failure. Its few achievements included the reconvening of the IGCR established at Evian, but with a revised mandate enlarging its membership to include all refugees. The other positive outcome was the establishment of two small camps in North Africa, relieving the pressure on Spain and enabling other refugees to enter Spain from France and be extricated in turn. By June, it was noted, some 3,000 French nationals, mainly Jews, had been moved into North Africa.[121]

Many years later, Law frankly described Bermuda as 'a façade for inaction ... there were no results that I can recall'.[122] At the time, however, Law was confident that the IGCR could 'do a great deal for refugees' and offered constructive suggestions for its composition. Interestingly, he did not consider the shipping problem altogether insurmountable: 'If neutral shipping is unobtainable, is it really beyond the bounds of possibility that we should find *one* ship?' His note to Eden concluded with the hope that the inevitably meagre results of the Conference might at least be 'followed up with vigour'.[123]

The Foreign Office acknowledged that 'the conference was able to achieve very little' and expressed thinly disguised irritation at what it saw as the unrealistic and unreasonable demands of Jewish pressure groups. Its report added that the Conference had to dispel the illusion 'that there could be any rescue from enemy territory', in order to concentrate on the tasks 'of removing refugees from countries where it was impossible for them to remain', distributing the refugee problem more widely. Clearly, the existing refugee problem was a sufficient irritant without any need to aggravate it further. It was noted that wartime conditions would hamper the fulfilment of even these modest aims.[124] The Conference was clearly intended as a forum for diffusing the present and post-war refugee crises as widely as possible. Its unspoken and unspeakable agenda was to minimise the refugee burden while appearing to assist refugees. Although the Jewish organisations understandably saw it as a last chance to rescue the endangered Jews of Europe, there was never any realistic possibility of a large-scale rescue operation from Nazi-controlled territory, which it was believed might have seriously undermined the war effort.

The short communiqué issued by the government after the Conference stated encouragingly that 'everything that held out any possibility of a solution was investigated and discussed'.[125] This understandably aroused in the Anglo-Jewish leaders a certain innocent optimism, evidenced in Brotman's naïve proposal that public confidence would be raised if the government were to issue a rough estimate of the numbers it hoped to save. They were also anxious for assurances which would enable them to counter the 'bitter and . . . irresponsible abuse' from within the Jewish community of the Anglo-Jewish leadership itself. Randall noted dryly that the 'the very idea of saving Jews is based on an illusion'.[126] More clear-sighted, the WJC reacted to the Conference's final communiqué with the comment 'that what stands in the way of aid to the Jews in Europe by the United Nations is . . . simply lack of will to go to any trouble on their behalf'.[127] Even while the Bermuda Conference was in session, Colonel Victor Cazalet, chairman of the National Committee Executive, criticised the opening speeches for their pusillanimous insistence on magnifying the difficulties at the expense of practical possibilities. Yet for a short while the National Committee suspended its public activities in the faint hope that the Conference might have some limited results.[128] The Conference's meagre achievements evoked bitter disappointment in the Jewish and national press.[129]

A full-day parliamentary debate on the refugee problem was held on 19 May 1943, opening with a statement on the Bermuda Conference by Osbert Peake, Parliamentary Under-Secretary at the Home Office. The parliamentary members of the National Committee, headed

by Rathbone, pressed the government for evidence of concrete rescue efforts. Several Private Members emphasised the potential problems
of refugee immigration into Britain, while others spoke more sym-
pathetically of the humanitarian need to mitigate the crisis. In response
to the government's critics, Peake observed disingenuously that the
purpose of the Conference had been to consider possible courses of
action 'as a preliminary to wider international collaboration', not
to take executive decisions. He reiterated that 'winning the war
must take priority over all other considerations' and pointed out
that 'the rate of extermination was such that no measure of rescue
or relief on however large a scale could be commensurate with the
problem'.[130] This all-or-nothing logic implied, as Eden had previously,
that it was not worth while trying to save only a very small number
of victims, and that it followed, therefore, that there was no point
trying to rescue anyone. The government's inertia was sharply
criticised by individual Members such as Cazalet and Rathbone,
who condemned Morrison's continued inactivity in the face of strong
public sympathy and complained that their own efforts were apparently perceived as a nuisance.[131]

Continued effort now seemed futile. The day after the debate, the
Board issued a polite statement expressing disappointment at the
limited prospects held out by the United Nations and hinting that
more could surely be done to alleviate the present crisis without
prejudicing the war effort. The Agudat Israel report was equally de-
spondent and noted that even a concerted Jewish approach had
been utterly frustrated by 'considerations of higher politics'. Perlzweig
confided to Easterman: 'We must continue this fight on every front
to which we have access; but it is idle to pretend that the outlook
is . . . encouraging.'[132] Public interest in the fate of European Jewry,
which had been intense from the end of 1942, appears to have
waned by mid-1943, perhaps as a consequence of compassion fatigue.
The National Committee, which was now at the forefront of political
efforts, struggled to sustain public sympathy and continued to press
the authorities on behalf of European Jewry. A year later, Rathbone
expressed deep disappointment that, in spite of initial widespread
public sympathy, since Eden's visit to Washington in March 1943
interest had subsided with official assurances that everything possible
was being done.[133]

The Board passed a resolution in July, expressing concern that
the measures proposed by the Bermuda Conference be implemented
as soon as possible.[134] It is symptomatic of the Board's lack of power

or influence that it could do no more on this occasion than previously: pass resolutions which stated the obvious, show that it was 'doing something' and circulate this information within the Jewish community. The Board accepted that there were no new proposals to make. Brotman had been appealing desperately for shipping, however unseaworthy, to be made available, arguing that 'almost any ordeal would be gladly welcomed . . . rather than the horrors of the sealed railway wagons'.[135] This again illustrates how out of touch the organisations were with the competing demands of rescue and warfare; a complex rescue operation would have to be mounted before the question of shipping could even be broached. Brodetsky observed despondently: 'I cannot say that we have any new proposals to make other than those that were submitted at Bermuda, but that those, if implemented, would go far to rescue the remnants of Jews in Europe.'[136]

The failing of the organisations was not that they did not try hard enough but that the vast majority of their ideas were impractical, unrealistic, even naïve, given their utter incompatibility with government priorities. No amount of mass lobbying or agitation would have made these ideas less so. Communal leaders did not perceive their specific suggestions, such as those relating to shipping and physical rescue, within the overall context of the global war situation. They saw, for example, only a Jewish frame of reference in the government's 'Palestine' policy, failing (either consciously or unconsciously) to realise that Palestine formed only one part of the government's overall policy in the Middle East. The real failure of the Anglo-Jewish organisations in this period was not one of will but of political and diplomatic experience and acumen.

7

Pawns in the Game of War
(Summer 1943–Autumn 1944)

Following Bermuda, the voluntary organisations could only try to ensure that the Conference's few recommendations were implemented and press the Allied Governments to issue further warnings of retribution for war crimes. The focus now shifted to post-war relief and reconstruction.[1] With the invasion of Sicily well advanced, Rome liberated in June and the continued Soviet advance westward, the prospects of an Allied victory were increasing.

It has been argued that divisions within the Board over Zionism, which came to a head in the summer of 1943, distracted its attention from the plight of European Jewry.[2] No doubt these clashes occupied time and energy. But there is no evidence that internal friction within the Board prevented it from accomplishing any useful work it might otherwise have achieved. More importantly, although many of the Anglo-Jewish voluntary organisations and personalities cooperated through the interdenominational National Committee, there was now a pervasive mood of despondency.

Publicity continued to be a vital concern. The National Committee recognised the importance of sustaining public interest in the Jewish catastrophe. Brotman urged that quick action could save hundreds now threatened in the Balkans and called for an intensive publicity campaign. However, in view of public apathy, it was agreed that public meetings should not be held.[3] Rathbone's 'Rescue the Perishing', incorporating the revised Twelve-Point Programme, formed the basis of a renewed publicity campaign. It continued the work begun by Gollancz's pamphlet, 'Let My People Go', already in its sixth edition by March, and now replaced it.[4] The pamphlet strongly criticised government inaction and outlined potential rescue measures. Peake responded for the Government, complaining that these publications, like the title 'National Committee for Rescue from Nazi Terror', were misleading (and by implication sensationalist), since 'Your proposals are in effect limited to those who have already escaped from Nazi territory'.[5]

By June 1943, the National Committee had decided to establish a Press, Research and Information Bureau and was investigating opportunities for collaborating with American organisations and with the Dominions. However, no mass meetings were held during 1943 and the suggestion to hold one in December was rejected on the grounds that it would be difficult to fill the Albert Hall, a reflection of the weakening of public interest.[6] Historians such as Alderman, who have accused the organisations of failing to hold mass demonstrations, seem unaware of the limited effectiveness of rhetoric on empty benches.

Attempts were made during parliamentary debates to keep the issue alive. However, as Rathbone observed, although the National Committee had tried to cooperate with the government by avoiding publicity on sensitive issues, 'Practically every suggestion we have made to them has been rejected'.[7] Rathbone was discouraged from raising in the House of Commons the question of guarantees to neutral states and the failure of the Moscow Conference (November 1943) to refer to atrocities against Jews. The government insisted that it could not publicly support neutrals without embarrassing them and that protest stimulated, rather than deterred, the Nazis. Rathbone finally settled for an assurance, to be given during the debate, that the government was giving the matter close and active attention.[8]

In February 1944, Rathbone issued another pamphlet, entitled 'Continuing Terror', detailing a new 'Ten-Point Programme' devised by the National Committee. It contained nothing new, but called on Britain to take the lead in rescue work. The government complained that this pamphlet gave the misleading and unfair impression that rescue depended solely on its own energy and conviction.[9] The National Committee also arranged a mass meeting in February at Central Hall, Westminster, designed to revive public interest.[10] Speakers continued the growing trend since before Bermuda to denounce Allied inaction as the real impediment to rescue. However, the response to the campaign, throughout 1944, was disappointing. The National Committee received very few contributions and experienced great difficulty in attracting speakers.[11]

Meanwhile, the organisations continued to vest hope in the

neutrals. The most promising avenue of rescue lay in the escape or the permitted departure of threatened victims from enemy-occupied countries to bordering neutral states. To the organisations, the extent to which this might be encouraged or permitted depended partly on how far these states could count on Allied aid for the support and resettlement of such refugees.[12] One of the main influences on the neutrals, however, was the military situation. Hence, after the end of 1942, when Allied victories in North Africa proved that Germany was not invincible, the neutrals became more accommodating towards Jewish refugees and certainly, during 1944, with the end of the war in sight, new refugees were allowed into Switzerland. Despite repeated attempts, however, the voluntary groups failed to secure an Allied Declaration of assurances to the neutrals.

The Board had first proposed such assurances, to be backed with material aid, in February 1943. At that time Schonfeld sought permission to go to Turkey in order to organise assistance for refugees *en route* to Palestine. The government, however, was reluctant, Randall expressing doubts about a 'Rabbi running round in Turkey: the Turks would stiffen and regard him as sent by us'. Such work was in any case regarded as the province of the Jewish Agency and the government decided that a coordinated approach by a single agency would be more effective.[13]

By November, the voluntary groups had become deeply disappointed that no formal declaration of assurances to neutrals had materialised.[14] During the December debate on the war situation, Rathbone urged the government to accept a proportion of the large number of non-repatriable refugees in the neutral states, enabling the latter to take more. Eden replied that he would look into the matter.[15] Non-repatriables comprised Jewish refugees who could not reasonably be expected to return to countries where anti-Semitism was deep-rooted and their families had been massacred. It was considered vital to assure the neutrals, especially Sweden and Switzerland, that the Allied nations would not merely assist in repatriation but assume responsibility for those who could not be repatriated after the war. However, the proposed Declaration, drafted in December, evaded the issue altogether and the National Committee was determined to challenge it.[16]

The government's view on assurances to neutral states was, understandably, more cynical. A few weeks later, Randall observed acidly that 'there was no reason why Switzerland, with her comparatively comfortable economic and financial situation, should be singled out for assurances of relief at the expense of this country and others who had given their all for the purpose of the war'. Britain 'would fully play its proper part' in dealing with non-repatriables, but as part of an international effort, and he advised Brodetsky that it was 'a policy of defeatism' to campaign against the voluntary return of large numbers of German, Austrian and Polish Jews to their countries of origin.[17]

The guarantee to neutrals was again raised in January 1944. In reply, Law reiterated that responsibility for non-repatriable or stateless refugees lay with the IGCR, as agreed at the first session of the Council of the United Nations Relief and Rehabilitation Administration (UNRRA), held in November 1943.[18] He added that Britain and America had approached the Swedish and Swiss governments with proposals regarding financial assurances regarding refugees, which were currently receiving sympathetic consideration. In the circumstances, 'it would be a disservice to the refugees' to force this delicate issue into the open. Rathbone nevertheless urged HMG, together with the Dominions, to take the initiative by offering open assurances to the neutrals. Eden pointed out that a limited Anglo-American guarantee to this effect could not be given, but offered helpful assurances and advice.[19]

Approached again by Brodetsky in February, Randall reiterated that there was no reason to think that the absence of overt assurances had prevented the neutrals from offering asylum. He informed Brodetsky confidentially that Britain and America had given assurances where required and together offered substantial assistance to Sweden in recognition of the extra burden of refugees assumed by that country; negotiations with Switzerland were also underway.[20] It seems that the government believed that negotiations with neutrals on the refugee issue were best conducted in private, as 'the publication of such a statement might well prejudice the escape of refugees' and because any public assurances of help 'would imply that their previous attitude towards refugees had been illiberal and inhospitable'.[21] Brodetsky nevertheless continued to press for a declaration to the neutrals with dogged tenacity, undeterred by repeated and predictable rebuffs. Britain maintained her existing commitments to the neutral states, especially in the summer of 1944,[22] but the official declaration sought by the voluntary organisations never materialised.

The government invariably preferred to avoid unilateral action on refugees in favour of the more cumbersome international approach, which offered enhanced opportunities for buck-passing.

Accordingly, it considered the reconvening of IGCR one of the major accomplishments of the Bermuda Conference. It adopted the Conference's recommendations for reorganising and enlarging the IGCR membership and undertook to cover all except administrative expenses, which were to be shared with other member-states. The Foreign Office welcomed the reconvening of the IGCR as shifting the diplomatic initiative elsewhere, as in the case of the Adler-Rudel scheme for taking 20,000 Jewish children to Sweden, and relieving pressure on Britain. It would now be more difficult for the American State Department to avoid decisions and Law revealingly hoped for American support in steering the IGCR 'free from undue Jewish influence and intrigue in connection with Palestine'.[23]

The IGCR did not meet until August 1943, by which time the Jewish organisations had been given to understand that they would be afforded some representative status. However, because it was a committee of governments, direct representation of specialist and non-governmental bodies was ruled out. Parliament was assured that the IGCR would cooperate with the Jewish and other organisations. However, by June 1944, Brodetsky was complaining of Emerson's failure to involve the organisations effectively.[24]

Before the IGCR's Fourth Plenary Session met in August 1944, the National Committee submitted a range of proposals, including the suggestion that the Allied and neutral powers take advantage of the Horthy Offer and that Jewish refugees be allowed into Palestine.[25] Although thirty-seven states participated, there was no official Jewish representation; observers representing numerous Jewish organisations attended but their role was strictly limited. William Frankel, a Board observer, noted that 'The realities of the Jewish situation in Europe appeared remote from the conference hall'. The IGCR did pass a resolution 'affirming the principle of co-operation with non-Governmental organisations in their humanitarian activities' but the only practical decision of the session concerned travel documents for stateless refugees.[26]

The IGCR did cooperate with other governmental bodies dealing with refugees, in particular UNNRA, which dealt with the vast problem of displaced persons and applied itself particularly to the plight of stateless refugees. It is debatable whether any official representation by the voluntary groups would have made any difference to the IGCR's achievements. It had no relief machinery of its own and no real power to negotiate with neutral or enemy states. One of its functions was to use credit payments to assist Jews, via post-war pledges of repayment. In this way it was able, for example, to provide a secret channel for sending relief to Romania in the summer of 1944. But on the whole it 'failed to acquire sufficient independent authority to play any significant role in the succour of refugees from Nazi Europe'.[27]

Unlike the IGCR, which was engaged in placing refugees temporarily in neutral countries and with affairs in newly liberated countries, the War Refugee Board (WRB), established by an American Presidential Executive order in January 1944, concentrated on rescue from enemy-controlled territories. It later claimed to have facilitated the rescue of 'hundreds of thousands' from the Balkans and western Europe and to have provided relief for those who found refuge in Sweden and Switzerland.[28]

Although the British voluntary organisations were encouraged to maintain regular contact with the WRB, they failed to secure a British equivalent.[29] Hall advised Brodetsky that 'an analogous body already existed in Britain and that the IGCR, the main instrument of rescue and relief, was building up its membership (in the British Dominions and Soviet Union in particular), with the fullest support of HMG'.[30] Brodetsky pointed out that the WRB was engaged in the critical work of rescue, unlike the IGCR, which dealt solely with refugees from occupied territories. He added that rescue measures must 'go outside the ordinary methods, even if "illegally" from the enemy's point of view. We were not bound to consider legal technicalities imposed by the enemy for the very purpose of extermination.' How Brodetsky distinguished 'ordinary' from 'extraordinary' rescue measures remains unclear; nor is it obvious why he considered it necessary to refute the legal niceties of the enemy's extermination programme. Prompted to be more specific, Brodetsky fell back on vague generalisations about 'military measures and instructions to commanders' which went no further once the government confirmed that such an approach would interfere with the war effort.[31] In this, as in many other of Brodetsky's exchanges with the Foreign Office, a surprising lack of argumentative rigour is evident. This was perhaps because Brodetsky himself knew that his proposals were often untenable in principle as well as in practice. He may have hoped that repetition, together with diplomatic rhetoric, would wear down official opposition.

Support for a body similar to the WRB, to replace the ineffectual IGCR came from various quarters.[32] Such pressure was sometimes an irritant to the government, which already viewed the WRB dubiously as the product of the American-Jewish political lobby. Randall objected that 'Miss Rathbone and her friends are going around saying that the War Refugee Board is going really to rescue Jews from Europe by secret means, and that HMG should be urged to do likewise.' He added that 'secret lanes' from France into Spain could only prove effective *'provided there was no publicity'*. This was a reference to the escape routes used by 'our own prisoners, especially the R.A.F. personnel and allied recruits, but refugees have taken advantage of them'.[33] It would have been dangerous to leak the existence of these routes to the Jewish refugee organisations.

The mass meeting called by the National Committee, held in February, resolved to urge the government to speed up the rescue of all those who could still be saved and to set up a British organisation similar to the WRB.[34] The government's refusal to accede to this demand seems to have put an end to any concerted hope of British rescue for the remnant of European Jewry. Later that month, Brodetsky and Hertz tried again. While accepting that a Cabinet Committee already existed to deal with rescue, they proposed that 'a special organisation should be set up which would not in any way be hindered by financial considerations or formalities'. They were politely assured that everything possible was already being done. The naïve proposal that a blank cheque be issued for the use of a committee unrestrained by 'formalities' is characteristic. By March, the issue had finally been dropped.[35]

The organisations fared little better in the realm of propaganda warfare. Allied leaders had promised to place retribution for war crimes among the major objectives of the war. This was first announced by Churchill in October 1941 and was reaffirmed at the Nine-Power Declaration of January 1942, though neither mentioned atrocities specifically against Jews. Sikorsky explained that the omission bore no implication other than that Jews were considered to be victims of crimes committed against nationals of their home-states. The United Nations Commission for the Investigation of War Crimes, established in October 1942, similarly stated that 'The Commission will investigate war crimes committed against nationals of the United Nations'.[36]

Although the Allies did not commit themselves at that time to any formal legal procedure, Jewish bodies feared that some members of the United Nations might disclaim 'national' responsibility for certain Jews who had been dispersed or dispossessed by the Nazis and that these would therefore be excluded from the category of those for whom retribution was promised. Moreover, crimes against Jews of Axis nationality on Axis territory were not included in the retribution which the Allied governments had pledged. In international law, crimes committed by enemy governments against their own nationals were not 'war crimes'; international law dealt only with relations between sovereign states. None of the declarations had gone beyond the general assurance that such 'crimes would not go unpunished.'[37] The organisations therefore lobbied for special mention of Jews in any Allied declaration calling for punishment of Nazi war crimes.

Following the December 1942 Declaration, in which, uniquely, crimes against Jews had been emphasised, the Anglo-Jewish voluntary organisations repeatedly pressed the government for further warnings of retribution, hoping for specific mention of Jews. But the government invariably refused, maintaining that declarations were ineffective and potentially damaging. The Declaration had merely aroused excessive expectation amongst Jewish and other groups and led to 'immense pressure on HMG to undertake measures of rescue which were quite impracticable'.[38] Undeterred, Easterman and others maintained that such action was part of the 'Political Warfare of the Allies' and that any declaration should highlight the plight of Jewish victims. He was told that further declarations would merely 'debase the currency', weakening the effect of those already issued. 'Some quite exceptional incentive would have to arise', as had been the case with the December 1942 Declaration, to justify its reaffirmation.[39] When the December Declaration was reaffirmed in conjunction with the Moscow Conference in November 1943, a general statement was issued to cover future atrocities, but it was not thought necessary to distinguish crimes against Jews, as the December Declaration had already done so.[40] This failed to satisfy the Jewish organisations, which feared that the Jewish issue would be allowed to lapse after the war. On Rathbone's advice, Lord Crewe wrote to Churchill, meeting, in advance, the objection that 'of course, a Polish Jew was a Pole and crimes against him were no different from crimes against Poles in general'. Brodetsky felt that a letter from Crewe on the subject was more effective than a protest from a Jewish organisation.[41]

The demand for a further warning followed the Nazi attempt in early 1944 to 'justify' the extermination of the Jews by declaring all Jews, irrespective of nationality, to be belligerents. This was possibly a protective measure designed to rebut criticism in the event

142

13 Chief Rabbi Dr. Joseph Hertz gives an account of his co-religionists' suffering in Nazi territory at the Council of Christians and Jews held at Bloomsbury House, London, 8 January 1944 (courtesy of Hulton Archives)

of a German defeat. In February 1944 Silverman and Easterman appealed for a new declaration on the grounds that the Germans had aimed 'a fresh blow to international law' by disregarding the legal nationality of the Jews of Greece, many of whom were of Turkish or Spanish origin, and deporting them all. Law's tepid response was that HMG would first need to consult Washington. Easterman also suggested that the satellites be reminded that kindness to Jews would be remembered at the peace conference. Law informed him that both Romania and Hungary were already 'attempting to lay up a treasure of good works against the day of reckoning', though it might be disastrous to draw public attention to this.[42]

Although Eden continued to object to Rathbone's proposal to discuss warnings in the House of Commons, an appalling document, which reached London in February from the Jewish National Committee in Warsaw, revealing that the Germans were butchering the last survivors of Polish Jewry, called for immediate attention. The British Section agitated strenuously for a solemn warning to be issued jointly and simultaneously by Churchill, Roosevelt and Stalin.[43] Eden remained sceptical but the Cabinet Committee 'favoured a declaration addressed to the satellite powers'.[44] Lord Melchett, Vice-President of the British Section, was eventually persuaded that a declaration might make matters worse, though it 'would certainly be a great solace to the Jews condemned to die', and agreed to leave the matter to the government.[45]

Easterman had been negotiating with the Foreign Office since September 1943 for a new declaration, to incorporate the December 1942 one and strengthen it by an appeal to the peoples of Europe for better treatment of Jews.[46] Easterman believed that an Allied statement might encourage some reduction, however minimal, in the atrocities, and observed that the oppressed people themselves, whenever they could communicate with the outside world, called for public condemnation. He pointed out that the government had agreed that failure to condemn the atrocities might be taken by the Germans as a sign of weakness or even complicity. The situation was so desperate that nothing could be lost, even if nothing were gained, by public denunciations.[47]

The Hungarian crisis

Hungary had so far escaped German savagery; although its 800,000 Jews had been subjected to anti-Jewish measures their position was comparatively easier that in any of the Central European and Balkan countries. Jews from Poland and Romania had continually tried to 'escape' to Hungary. The Nazis took control of Hungary on 19 March 1944 under the direction of Adolf Eichmann; provincial Jews were sent to ghettos in larger towns and their mass deportation began on 15 May. The disaster facing Hungarian Jewry, which called for urgent action by the Anglo-Jewish leadership, occurred at the time that the Allied governments were concentrating their energies on preparations for D-Day; moreover, that June the Nazis resumed their air assault against London; the appearance of flying bombs brought about a recurrence of air-raid problems and the disruption of evacuation.

Riegner's telegram of 21 March first alerted the Anglo-Jewish organisations to the fate of Hungarian Jewry. Riegner called for 'a world-wide appeal' to the Hungarian people and for reminders that Hungarian conduct would form 'one of the most important tests of behaviour which allied nations will remember in the peace settlement after the war'. Similar broadcasts should be made every night in Hungarian during the next weeks.[48] The WJC vigorously renewed its campaign for a new declaration, reaffirming previous pledges of retribution for those guilty, addressed to satellites. In late March, with the approval of Churchill and Stalin, Roosevelt condemned the Nazis and their allies and proclaimed the Allied governments' determination to punish the criminals and appealed to the peoples of Nazi Europe to assist the escape of Jews and other persecuted people. Shortly after, prompted by Silverman, Eden called on the satellites 'to join in preventing further persecution and co-operate in protecting and saving the innocent'. These warnings were broadcast to the Hungarians.[49]

An emergency session of the Board's FAC concluded that the only possibility of influence lay with the Soviets, whose armies were now liberating some of the occupied countries and who were therefore in a special position to assist. Support might also come from the Pope, who exerted a strong moral influence over the Hungarian people. Some members argued that warnings might provoke further outrages in the event of a Nazi defeat, others that warnings might have some effect in mitigating the atrocities.[50] Brodetsky, Brotman and Hertz (himself of Hungarian origin) urged that the recent announcements of Roosevelt and Eden be followed by a formal statement to be broadcast to the populations of Germany and the satellites. They mentioned various 'secret' parachute activities which they curiously claimed had saved many Jewish lives in occupied

Europe. More realistically perhaps, they suggested that Marshal Tito be encouraged to facilitate the escape of Jews from Hungary into Yugoslavia, by enlisting those who were fit to serve in his forces and by any other means open to him. Randall assured them that these suggestions would receive careful consideration; approaches to Tito and the Soviets were being made, but he again stressed the necessity of secrecy.[51]

The statements by the Allied leaders in March were welcomed by the organisations, but were also considered vague and ineffectual. A special conference of the leading Jewish organisations, attended by prominent Jewish and non-Jewish figures, was held. Proposals for a mass meeting at the Albert Hall and for a march through London were opposed by government officials. Easterman, on Foreign Office advice, maintained that at the present stage of the crisis 'political action was the important thing and any public action might have a very harmful effect'.[52]

The news from Hungary prompted independent action by the British Section, to the inevitable disapproval of the Board. Like the Board, the WJC maintained that the only possible help lay with the Soviets; the newly affected areas, Hungary, Transnistria and Romania, were now closest to the advancing Russian armies, which would be the first to reach the Jews in the line of retreat. The Soviets were consequently asked to take political and military measures to rescue Jews from those areas and to put on trial captured Germans accused of atrocities against Jews. While the Soviets had already begun such trials in 1943, A. Zinchenko, the Soviet Ambassador, replied that 'there was no distinction between citizens in Russia and the Germans had committed crimes against all sections of the population'. Instead of lamely agreeing, as Brodetsky might have done, Easterman suggested that 'this difficulty could be overcome if the Russians, in their advance into Poland, would put on trial captured Germans who were guilty of terroristic acts specifically against Jews'. Not surprisingly, the Ambassador thought it was 'an excellent idea' and asked for particulars to forward to the proper quarters in Russia.[53]

Czech President (in-exile) Eduard Beneš had been cautiously willing to approach Stalin, while Easterman arranged contact with Tito's representatives to discuss whether his partisans might be employed to secure the protection of refugees. Beneš insisted that these negotiations be conducted in the strictest confidence, as any public agitation on behalf of Hungarian Jewry carried the threat that the Germans might tighten up border controls.[54] Easterman proposed

an exchange of information with the Board but Brodetsky was reluctant to reciprocate.[55]

The BBC's Hungarian service gave full publicity to Roosevelt's
and Eden's warnings to the satellites and their appeals to the Hungarians to protect Jews. Special messages were addressed to the
Hungarians by British church leaders and repeatedly quoted in BBC
Hungarian transmissions. Because Hungary was an important centre
of Roman Catholicism, appeals were also directed by Hertz and the
British Section to the Pope, through Archbishop Godfrey, the Apostolic Delegate in London, to use his influence with the Hungarian
clergy. Archbishop Godfrey had indicated that the Holy See would
be fully supportive.[56] Broadcasts were considered valuable as 'a good
deal depended upon the degree of acquiescence which the Hungarians showed' towards the German occupation and the fate of the
Jews.[57] However, the Refugee Department believed that reiterated
warnings were 'apt merely to intensify German persecution . . . continual exhortations of this kind have convinced the Germans that
the Jewish question is a sore point with us and . . . they prod it
accordingly'.[58]

The Board too felt concern about excessive publicity, although it
was vague about the precise boundary at which publicity became
'excessive'. A few days before the ghettoisation of Hungarian Jewry,
it had received warnings from Riegner and Lichtheim of Nazi plans
for the extermination of Hungary's 800,000 Jews within six months,
beginning by concentrating them in three zones. It was suggested
that the 'Jews should be told to seek refuge, both inside and outside
of Hungary . . . to join the partisans if possible. They should be
warned . . . to destroy in time all relevant lists of communities and
to avoid registration'.[59] Yet inconsistently, the Board also thought it
would be mistaken to broadcast detailed warnings which would
'draw undesirable attention to the Jewish communities who were
in any case well aware of the situation. . . . Warnings . . . should be
couched in general terms only.' The Political Warfare Executive
(PWE) agreed, adding that 'Unless this information is to be regarded
as entirely reliable . . . its release might only cause unnecessary
alarm'.[60] This muddled thinking and vagueness is characteristic. What
sort of warnings could be 'couched in general terms' and still have
the desired effect? No doubt, this further contributed to the fact
that Hungarian Jewry was left ill-informed about the peril. Survivors
remain bitter that Jewish leaders in Hungary and the free world
were part of a 'conspiracy of silence'.[61]

The effectiveness of the broadcasts was hard to gauge. The British Section valued them as among the few positive measures by which Jews might be saved. Easterman wanted appeals to be continuous and varied so as to attract the widest possible attention. He suggested a broadcast appeal by Lord Rothermere, but the PWE declined for political reasons, insisting that current appeals should be maximised before further appeals from distinguished personalities were arranged. Easterman tried unsuccessfully to have this decision reconsidered.[62]

The deportation to Auschwitz had begun in May and by mid-June 1944, detailed accounts reached London of this drastic turn in the fate of Hungarian Jewry. Four escapees from Auschwitz provided eye-witness testimony of the mass killings. They warned that Auschwitz was being enlarged to accommodate Hungarian Jews and compiled a 36-page statistical report on the camp's operations. This report, the 'Auschwitz Protocols', was sent to Jewish organisations in Switzerland, Turkey and Jerusalem, and thence to the Allied governments. Until this point, it has been argued, the immense death factory operated in secrecy.[63] The Polish government in London received the information, dated 14 June, that 'the Germans have gassed in Oswiecim 100,000 Jews deported from Hungary' and that truckloads of Jews were proceeding regularly from Hungary to Poland. The information was passed to the British government and various organisations, together with calls for a renewed warning to the Nazis.[64]

The British Section responded immediately with an appeal that Allied High Command issue a military warning that captured Germans suspected of atrocities against Jews and others would be speedily brought to trial. Easterman again called for a broadcast on behalf of Lord Rothermere and for an appeal by the Pope to the Hungarian people.[65] While the Board passed another resolution, calling on Allied governments to take immediate and urgent action, it deferred making specific proposals until after consultation with the Foreign Office.[66]

The Soviet government and the Vatican, at the instigation of the British Section, were again asked to speak out against the Hungarian atrocities, so that when, some time later, Brodetsky and Lord Bearsted proposed the same action, they were told that their suggestions had either been already received and noted or that action had already been taken.[67] Hall had earlier indicated to the Board the desirability of coordination between the Jewish bodies approaching the Foreign Office and had been assured that such arrangements

14 Delegates to the War Emergency Conference of the World Jewish Congress, including representatives from the British Section, seated from left to right: Rebecca Sieff, Ignacy Schwartzbart, Eva Reading. Standing from left: Sidney Silverman, MP, Norman Jacobs, Noah Barou, Reverend A. Cohen, Jack Cotton, Ben Rubenstein, Alex Easterman. Atlantic City, 1944 (courtesy of Beth Hatefutsoth)

were being made.[68] While this was the case with the AJA, it was evidently not so with the British Section of the WJC, with which a *modus vivendi* was still being negotiated. It must therefore have appeared odd that the Board was unaware of the successful initiative of a 'fellow' organisation. Accusations of petty rivalry seem, in the circumstances, unsurprising, and such episodes can hardly have increased the respect of government officials for the Jewish 'leaders' they were dealing with.

Easterman's suggestion that HMG approach the Vatican received mixed responses from the Foreign Office. Armand Dew, head of the Southern Department, complained, 'Why are we the tools of these people? Why should the Pope condemn murder of Hungarian Jews before he condemns use of flying bombs against this country?' However, Henderson felt that 'There is no harm and may be some good in expressing the interest and sympathy of HMG in a humanitarian cause.' He observed that 'the sympathy of wide Jewish circles' was valued by HMG and that 'concessions when possible, make easier a refusal when essential'. Dew subsequently withdrew his objections.[69] Henderson's comments highlight the degree of calculation involved in every government decision; even a simple, humanitarian expression of sympathy was a trade-off for support from Jewish circles.

Nevertheless, the Foreign Office did approach the Soviets on the subject of German massacres of Hungarian Jewry. Eden explained that 'this action is being taken as the suggestion was pressed on HMG with particular earnestness by high and responsible Jewish circles here'.[70] However, for political reasons, the PWE opposed a broadcast appeal on behalf of Lord Rothermere (he and his father were strong supporters of Hungarian revisionism and a broadcast might imply that HMG regarded revisionism favourably). There was also some reluctance to multiply individual appeals, especially since Eden and the Archbishop of Canterbury, as well as the King of Sweden, had already publicised their condemnation. Eden believed that 'there is no point in "inflating the currency" by continually repeating that we propose to punish the guilty' and proposed that it might even have 'the effect of making the anti-Jewish atrocities worse'.[71]

In July, Lord Melchett asked the Archbishop of Canterbury to join him in drawing Churchill's attention to the situation in Birkenau and Auschwitz. As a result, the Archbishop made a broadcast to the Hungarian people.[72] The British Section also arranged that Silverman should address a Private Notice question to Eden in order to elicit a statement of policy. A German order calling for all lists of deportations to be finalised within twenty days was nearing completion and there seemed no harm in publicising the fact as widely as possible.[73] In response to Silverman, Eden replied that the news from Hungary was almost certainly reliable, but that there was no evidence that repeated declarations and warnings had had any deterrent effect. The best hope 'must remain the speedy victory of the Allied nations'.[74] Although this did not help the Jews of Hungary, the British Section was satisfied that the Hungarian crisis had received 'the fullest possible publicity.'[75]

The British Section submitted further proposals for warnings and appeals, which it considered important in view of the advance of the Allied armies towards territories containing large numbers of Jews. However, following the Horthy Offer, the Foreign Office decided that such measures would be contrary to the interests of the Jews themselves.[76] Nevertheless, the British Section continued its appeals to the Hungarians through the Archbishop of Canterbury and various trade unions. In particular, it arranged that the International Federation of Transport Workers broadcast to Hungarian railway workers an urgent appeal not to operate the trains used to deport Jews. It also sought the support of the Jewish Anti-Fascist Committee in securing the aid of the Soviet government through warnings, appeals to local populations to help Jews and the active aid of the Red Army.[77] Possibly in consequence of Rathbone's appeal to Eden, the Foreign Office approached the Soviets in July, asking that 'given the victorious advance of the Soviet Armies', a declaration of retribution for war crimes committed in Hungary be made. Molotov replied favourably a month later.[78]

A deputation from the National Committee met with Eden in late July, proposing, *inter alia*, a further appeal to Horthy and a broadcast warning of retribution against those guilty of war crimes against Hungarian Jews. Eden, backed by Emanuel Shinwell, Labour MP, expressed concern that such a tone might appear too menacing and that the potency of such warnings might be diminished by constant repetition. Rathbone, however, asserted that only through repetition would such warnings be taken seriously. Eden agreed to consider the matter further. The issue was not whether to have warnings at all, but whether to issue them repeatedly or at carefully chosen intervals. Despite the understandable anxiety of Rathbone and her fellow-workers, the government might have been better placed in this instance to judge the effectiveness and timing of such warnings. In view of the Horthy Offer, Walker noted, an appeal to Hungarian humanitarianism seemed more appropriate.[79] Appeals and warnings by leading statesmen prompted by the organisations were felt to have had a beneficial effect, as evidenced by the Horthy Offer and the suspension of the deportation of Hungarian Jews in mid-July. The Foreign Office believed, more cynically, that the halt might be 'due to difficulties of transport' but acknowledged that protests might have had some beneficial effect.[80]

Various other suggestions were raised during the summer of 1944, among which the best known is the request to bomb Auschwitz and its connecting railway. It coincided with both the Horthy Offer and the notorious Joel Brand Deal to exchange Jews for trucks and certain non-military commodities.[81] The bombing of Auschwitz was not a major issue at the time, and has assumed importance only recently as a symbol of Allied indifference to what could have been done to save lives or at least to lend moral support to those in the camps.

Some Jewish leaders, alerted by the Auschwitz Protocols, made urgent appeals for bombing raids to impede the annihilation of Hungarian Jewry. In mid-May, from Slovakia, Weissmandel made the first of several calls to world Jewry, demanding that the gas chambers and railway lines be bombed. At his request, Schonfeld and Goodman approached the British government.[82] Demands were also presented by the Polish Government-in-Exile and by Chaim Weizmann and Moshe Shertok, on behalf of the Jewish Agency in London. There is no evidence that the Board discussed the issue during the summer months; Brodetsky appears to have taken a subordinate role. He knew of Weizmann's discussion with Eden but 'did not wish to repeat matters' which they had discussed.[83] There were no calls for or comments about the bombing proposal in the *Jewish Chronicle*. At the end of August, Brotman was approached by Schwarzbart, enquiring whether he had any information about the government's intention. He replied that the Board was being kept informed and that he intended to speak to the Foreign Office on the matter.[84]

Other means of destroying the installations at Auschwitz were proposed. Leon Kubowitzki, head of the Rescue Department of the WJC, maintained that the destruction of the death installations should not be accomplished by aerial bombing as 'the first victims would be the Jews' and that it would be a welcome pretext for the Nazis to assert that their Jewish victims had been massacred not by Germans but by Allied bombers. On 1 July, he proposed the (rather unrealistic) idea of Allied paratroopers or underground Polish fighters being sent 'to seize the buildings, to annihilate the squads of murderers and to free the unfortunate inmates'.[85] The Americans rejected this on the grounds that such an operation would entail the 'diversion of considerable air support essential to the success of our forces' and be of 'doubtful efficacy'.[86] Kubowitzki did, however, transmit a request from Ernest Frischer of the Czech Government-in-Exile to the US War Department to bomb the camps. Frischer argued that bombing would prevent the Germans from concealing their crimes and possibly stop further mass exterminations since so little time was left to them.[87]

Some members of the Executive of the Jewish Agency Rescue Committee in Jerusalem opposed the bombing proposal of its chairman, Yitzhak Gruenbaum. But once the Auschwitz Protocols arrived in Jerusalem on 11 June, the Jewish Agency in London promptly launched a concerted lobbying effort to persuade the British government to bomb Auschwitz.[88] Its first request was made in late June, followed by a further appeal on 6 July, which also suggested bombing the railway lines and death camps at Birkenau. Eden was 'in favour of acting on both these suggestions', and sought the Air Ministry's view of their feasibility.[89] Although Weizmann and Shertok pleaded for the bombing, they later acknowledged it would have little practical value, but the 'main-purpose . . . should be its many-sided and far-reaching moral effect'.[90] The Air Minister, Sir Archibald Sinclair, replied that disrupting the railways was 'out of our power' and that 'bombing the plant' was not possible 'because the distance is too great for the attack to be carried out at night'. He suggested that the Americans might do this by daylight. However, he added, 'there is just one possibility, and that is bombing the camps, and possibly dropping weapons at the same time, in the hope that some victims may be able to escape . . . [although] the chances of escape would be small indeed'. Sinclair proposed to put the plan to the Americans. Eden found this 'a characteristically unhelpful letter', and suggested that Weizmann approach Sinclair directly.[91] The Foreign Office did not follow up the suggestion that weapons might be dropped to help Jews escape.

The appeals to bomb Auschwitz coincided with the Horthy Offer (9 July) and the subsequent cessation of the Hungarian deportations (from 20 July). Although the Jewish Agency's priority after the Horthy Offer was securing visas and transport facilities, principally to

Palestine, it still favoured bombing. However, after the deportations stopped, the Foreign Office considered it inadvisable to pursue the bombing proposal. Nevertheless, Sinclair requested photographic cover of the camps and installations in the Birkenau area. Consequently, he was 'perturbed at having heard nothing more from the Foreign Office about the problem of Birkenau' since early August.[92] The Foreign Office then asked whether, in view of Horthy's offer to halt the Hungarian deportations, the Agency still wished the bombing to be carried out. Linton pointed out that 'in the situation that the Germans find themselves to-day, it will be more difficult for them to construct new camps, and this might be the means of saving lives'.[93]

In spite of the Jewish Agency's conviction that the proposal remained worthwhile and Churchill's and Eden's initial support, Foreign Office officials opposed the idea, partly because of technical reasons (which later proved to be of dubious validity), and partly because the deportations had stopped. Henderson cited the Air Minister's view that 'this would cost British lives and aircraft to no purpose'. Roger Allen concluded firmly that 'if . . . we no longer wish on political grounds to proceed with this project, it is for us to tell the Air Ministry'.[94]

The topographical data on Auschwitz and Birkenau supplied by the Jewish Agency were never communicated to the Air Ministry by the Foreign Office and therefore never taken into consideration when the decisions were made.[95] Yet the only reason given to Weizmann was the 'very great technical difficulties'.[96] Walker thought it inadvisable that Weizmann be informed that the other reason was the cessation of the deportations – so as to deny Weizmann and others 'the opportunity of reopening this topic',[97] should the deportations be resumed. Consequently, when the deportations from Hungary resumed on 26 August (and in spite of the fact that deportations had anyway continued from elsewhere), the Jewish Agency, believing that the reasons against bombing were technical, appears to have temporarily dropped the issue.

Goodman was notified immediately the Hungarian deportations were resumed and he was urged to press the government to have the railway lines bombed.[98] It was not until late September that the Jewish Agency, following confirmation that the deportations had resumed, again approached the government.[99] Referring to the previously cited 'technical difficulties', Linton observed that 'Since then, however, we understand that the fuel depots in that area have been bombed on two occasions. If the position has changed, it might be possible to reconsider the question of bombing the Camp'. Even then, officials claimed to be unsure whether the Hungarian deportation policy had been reversed. The Foreign Office was in any event disinclined to pursue requests for a reconsideration of the bombing of Auschwitz.[100] Even the Board's FAC was uncertain of the situation, having received other reports 'that a group of 320 Hungarian Jews had recently arrived in Switzerland'.[101] As late as November, Mason remained sceptical: 'Our evidence suggests that there have in fact been no large scale deportations since about July and indeed the Hungarians themselves, both the Horthy regime and the Szalasi regime, have shown some degree of readiness to let go Hungarian Jews.'[102] Perhaps this was a stalling tactic; operations at Auschwitz were slowing down by this stage, mainly due to shortages of fuel for transportation and extermination. Mason might well have reasoned that the problem would soon go away by itself.

It was also suggested that the Soviets might be persuaded to bomb the camp. Despite fresh allegations, Lady Cheetham maintained that the government had no proof that Hungarian policy had changed again and that Hungary should therefore not be threatened. She agreed that the Soviets might consider bombing the railway lines to Auschwitz,[103] but as the Soviet army was by now so close to Auschwitz, she could hardly have regarded this as a genuine possibility. In October, Brotman inquired whether HMG had considered bombing the camps in association with the Red Air Force. Brotman was doubtless unaware that Churchill was becoming increasingly irritated with Soviet uncooperativeness following the Warsaw Uprising in August. Nevertheless, there is an air of hopelessness about a suggestion which by this late stage Brotman must have realised would be rejected out of hand. Mason, who found Brotman 'as always, entirely reasonable', seems to have had little difficulty persuading him of 'the risk of Germany claiming that *we* had done our best, by bombing the camps, to exterminate the inmates ourselves'.[104] The objection had already been made by Kubowitzki, but this appears to be a unique case of government policy being dictated by the German Ministry of Propaganda. It is interesting that an argument as weak as this was considered adequate to fob off Brotman, whereas more sophisticated 'technical reasons' were felt necessary to put off Weizmann.

The organisations did not pursue the proposal with any force, possibly because they could not argue the technical issue. What matters with regard to their effectiveness is not whether the bombing of Auschwitz was feasible, would have made any significant difference (an issue which remains contentious to this day), or even the issue of morale, but that once again, the organisations lacked the argumentative and negotiating skills to maintain any kind of debate on the issue. Even Brodetsky, an expert in aerodynamics, had nothing to offer, deferring to Weizmann in this matter. Clearly, the reasons for refusing the proposals were not merely technical. It seems that once again, the organisations were victims of unlucky timing – the Horthy offer providing a tempting pretext for inaction and procrastination.

It has been argued that Horthy's decision on 6 July 1944 to halt the deportations was as much in response to the worsening military situation (the Allied forces had landed on the shores of Normandy) as to the intervention of world and Church leaders who had been motivated to speak out by the Auschwitz Protocols and the Swiss press campaign. The threat to bomb Budapest (leaked to Hungarian military intelligence and carried out on 2 July) finally convinced Horthy.[105] On 18 July the Foreign Office received a message from Berne reporting that Horthy had notified the Swiss legation in Budapest that, subject to American and British cooperation, his government was prepared to allow holders of Palestine certificates or foreign visas, together with Jewish children up to the age of ten, to emigrate from Hungary.[106] Unlike Joel Brand's 'Blood for Trucks' deal, the Horthy Offer was unconditional and therefore more likely to be acceptable to the Allied governments; nevertheless, the British were reluctant to accept it because of the sheer scale of the offer and the Palestine issue.[107]

On 19 July, as soon as the offer was made public, Brotman inquired whether, in view of its terms, the Foreign Office would invite the Swedes and Swiss to honour their previous offers to receive Jewish children. He also requested a joint affirmation by the United Nations, or at least by the Great Powers, that they would receive in their territories all those Jews who could leave. Henderson, acknowledging that other Jewish organisations favoured this move, passed the suggestion to the US State Department. Shertok and Linton urged Randall to take 'immediate action to explore and take advantage of the offer'. Their suggestion that the IGCR send a representative to Budapest was rejected on the grounds that the present mandate did not allow such negotiation with enemy governments. This was clearly a stalling device. For Horthy to make the offer at all, some negotiation with an enemy government must already have taken place. However, the IGCR agreed that a swift and clear response was necessary.[108]

On 26 July, a National Committee delegation met Eden. It stressed that the situation called for sacrifices, which the public was prepared to make, in the form of the admission into Britain of considerable numbers of Jewish refugees. Eden disingenuously commented that the difficulty had not been to receive refugees but to assist their escape and added that he had been informed by the ICRC that the deportations had ceased. He observed that a joint Anglo-American request for implementation of the offer was already under way. The deputation took this as an assurance that Hungary had been notified of British readiness to provide transport and accommodation for all Jews who could be evacuated from Hungary. In fact, as Rathbone discovered shortly afterwards, Hungary had not yet been notified because the government was awaiting US cooperation. In effect, the Horthy Offer had not been approved by either government. Rathbone feared that Horthy might revoke it under pressure from the Nazis and she urged the government to take unilateral action.[109]

The government had been obliged to accept the offer in principle, but in practice it was inhibited by fear of a massive influx of Jews into Allied territory, especially Palestine. In early July, Morrison had already expressed anxiety at the prospect of 'the further reception of refugees here' if the Brand deal were accepted.[110] The Foreign Office consequently cabled to Washington its concern that the Jewish Agency would exert strong pressure in favour of increased Jewish immigration to Palestine in the wake of the Horthy Offer. The possibilities of emigration to Palestine were limited to some 14,000 certificates left from the White Paper quota. R.M.A. Hankey feared 'a flood of applications to enter Palestine' and that 'We shall in a very short time have masses of East European Jews on our hands'.[111]

Aware of this, Goodman, in his self-styled capacity as 'representative of the World Movement of orthodox Jewry with a very strong branch-organisation in Hungary', invited all the Dominions, the Colonies and various South American countries to participate in the Horthy scheme. He also appealed to the Red Cross in various countries to assist in issuing block visas, to cooperate in the care of child refugees and to support attempts to persuade the Eire government to accept 500 Hungarian Jewish children. Nothing came of these appeals.[112] Rathbone managed to obtain assurances of visas for children under ten from the Mexican Ambassador, who suggested that she make similar representations to the Cuban and Brazilian representatives in Britain.[113]

The issue of visas was regarded as vitally important in obtaining protected status for Hungary's endangered Jews. The most celebrated example is that of Raoul Wallenberg, the special Swedish diplomat emissary to Hungary, who granted large numbers of Swedish protective papers to Hungarian Jews during the summer and autumn of 1944, often to persons with little or no Swedish connection. On 6 October 1944, the Jewish Agency received news that the Swedish Legation had arranged to issue 5,000 'protective passports' with a further 4,000 to follow in the next few days. Owing to German refusal to allow transit facilities for passport holders, many of these Jews were put into safe houses in Budapest 'under Swedish protection'. Although the majority of them did not leave Hungary, this action probably prevented the deportation of many thousands of Jews.[114]

Similar ideas had been mooted soon after the deportation to Auschwitz began in May, such as Hertz's proposal that Jews in Hungary be accorded British-protected status or Palestinian citizenship.[115] This was rejected on the grounds that such 'protection' would be worthless in Nazi-occupied Europe (as evinced by Germany's wholesale disregard for the Geneva Convention). Even if such protection carried the right of exchange facilities, it was argued, there were insufficient German civilians in British hands to exchange for 'British' civilians. Shipping facilities were anyway limited. Furthermore, Britain's allies would resent preferential treatment accorded to Jews when large numbers of non-Jewish nationals remained in grave danger.[116] In late July, Rathbone unsuccessfully proposed a joint declaration by Britain and other UN member-states to establish a new status for Jews in Europe as persons under special protection for the purposes of retributive justice after the war.[117]

After the Horthy Offer was issued, the Jewish Agency began an intensive campaign to increase immigration to Palestine. On 7 July, Shertok suggested that although Hungary's 350,000 Jews could hardly be declared British-protected persons, those on the Zionist veterans' list, numbering around 5,000, might be issued special certificates purporting to establish that they were already Palestine citizens (thereby freeing more certificates for others). The Jewish Agency was prepared to give a formal undertaking that no claim to full Palestinian citizenship would later be made on the strength of such documents. Christopher Eastwood of the Colonial Office expressed concern, not at the 'dishonesty' of the plan, but at the potential embarrassment of any later claim to genuine Palestinian citizenship. Nevertheless, the Colonial Office appealed to the Palestine

authorities and the Foreign Office to agree to it.[118] Sir Harold
MacMichael dismissed outright the idea of issuing these 'forgeries',
expressing little faith in Jewish Agency undertakings.[119] Nevertheless, special certificates of 'potential Palestine citizenship', intended
purely for protective purposes and numbering around 8,000, were
issued at the end of July.[120]

Since the remaining 14,000 Palestine permits were wholly inadequate in the present crisis, Rathbone proposed that Jews arriving
after the White Paper quota was exhausted should be treated as
temporary immigrants, stressing that 'the mere grant of a Palestine
permit may give the recipient some protection'.[121] The Foreign Office
was more favourably disposed towards a suggestion, not involving
Palestine, from the Council for Rescue of Jews in Poland (established in London in April 1944) that the Polish government should
approach certain neutral countries with a view to their issuing a
number of fictitious passports, to be granted 'to a few selected trust-
worthy persons of the Jewish faith'. The plan depended on British
and American agreement to accept such persons 'in some place
specially reserved for foreign refugees'.[122]

At the Executive Board meeting, however, it was decided not to
approach the Colonial Office to extend the facilities for asylum in
Palestine, nor the Home Secretary for admission into Britain. Rather
'it was felt desirable to get the general scheme of rescue started [the
Horthy Offer] and working before making further approaches'.[123]
Eden, however, was concerned about pressure from the voluntary
organisations 'to accept with the least possible delay the Hungarian
Offer to release Jews'. The Cabinet Committee was faced with a
dilemma. Rejecting the Horthy Offer would inflame public opinion,
while accepting it risked 'civil war in Palestine owing to an inroad
of Jews from Hungary into the Levant'. The United States, without
proposing to relax its own quota regulations, urged that the 'proposal *must* be accepted as quickly as possible'. Undaunted by the
prospect of a vast influx into Palestine of Hungarian refugees for
whom Britain would have to assume responsibility, the Americans
advised a joint undertaking by both governments to 'care for *all*
Jews who are permitted to leave Hungary and who reach neutral or
Allied Nations territory'.[124]

On 8 August the War Cabinet agreed to accept the Horthy Offer in
principle and to warn the Americans not to 'face us with the impossible in the question of providing accommodation'.[125] The
next day a joint declaration by the two governments through the

ICRC accepted the Hungarian offer. Assurances were to be offered to those neutral countries which would be invited to accept refugees.[126] Linton was assured that the necessary instructions for the ICRC had been prepared. However, because of reports of German pressure on Hungary to prevent Jews from departing, he suggested making representations to the Hungarian government through the Vatican; he was told that this had been done via the Apostolic Delegate in London.[127] Nevertheless, there was little endeavour by the Allied governments to implement the offer, and serious reservations remained about depositing unlimited numbers of refugees in Palestine.[128]

Despite the news that the deportations had resumed, Brotman's proposal of fresh warnings to the Hungarians was, as usual, stonewalled. Mason believed that Hungary was likely to follow Romania and Bulgaria in capitulating. Brotman then suggested that given that Romania was now relatively safe for Jewish refugees, the Romanians might be encouraged to help in the rescue of Jews but was told that the armistice terms between Romania and the Allies were still under negotiation. Lastly, he asked whether the Foreign Office might invite the Soviets to deal leniently with refugees found in Romania.[129] Apart from this, Brotman felt it best to await events, as the situation would change rapidly. The National Committee's approaches to the IGCR and the Foreign Office had 'elicited nothing different from the Board's own approaches and the ICRC was doing everything open to it'.[130]

Attitudes within the Foreign Office towards the Jewish organisations varied. Dew stated baldly, 'In my opinion a disproportionate amount of the time of the Office is wasted on dealing with those wailing Jews.' Lady Cheetham, however, responded: 'it is surely not a waste of time to interview a well known representative of a very respectable Jewish society ... The Jews have been given cause to wail by their sufferings under the Nazi regime.' Mason concurred, but agreed with Dew that it would be more appropriate for the Jewish organisations, rather than HMG, to approach the Soviet government, in order to avoid any implied British doubt as to Soviet co-operativeness. He assured Brotman that 'our suggestion is made solely from the standpoint of what we believe to be the most practicable course'. Brotman, as always, understood; he appreciated the 'delicacy of an approach to the Soviets' and hoped that the WRB would be able to help.[131] Indeed, Brotman appears to have been so understanding of the Foreign Office position as to cause some wonder at how he could have thought his proposals viable in the first place.

Despite all efforts, the emigration scheme never materialised, largely because the German government blocked it. Rathbone's concern on this point was justified. Hitler had approved the offer only 'provided the Hungarians allowed the speedy resumption of the deportation of the remaining [i.e. Budapest] Jews'.[132] On 15 October 1944, Horthy was arrested and the Fascist 'Arrow Cross', under German protection, seized power in Budapest. The deportations had indeed resumed at the end of August. Easterman and Silverman urged Churchill and Eden, then at the Moscow Conference, to ensure that Britain and the Soviet Union took all practical measures against the renewed deportations and were informed that Churchill was discussing the issue with the Soviets.[133] Appeals were also addressed to the Pope, and Weizmann cabled Churchill. Brodetsky and Brotman raised the possibility of issuing a joint warning with the Soviets to the new rulers of Hungary. Hall advised that Churchill would do everything possible, but doubted whether a warning would help. The Soviets would be unwilling to cooperate, the present Hungarian regime was only a German puppet and previous warnings had been ineffectual. Hall instanced the most recent British warning, issued in October, concerning the threatened massacre of all internees at Auschwitz, which had merely resulted in a Nazi denial.[134]

Despite comments such as Dew's, it would be simplistically reductionist to assume that the negative attitudes emanating from the Foreign Office were invariably caused by anti-Semitism. In the case of this meeting between Brodetsky, Brotman and Hall, Mason commented wryly, 'As was to be expected, they [Brodetsky and Brotman] had very little in the way of concrete suggestions to make'. Worse even than empty-handedness was the 'general impracticability' of the suggestion that any ex-enemy government suing for an armistice negotiation might be induced to 'take all steps to prevent any action inimical to Jewish welfare within its own territory'. That this did not indicate any anti-Semitism on Mason's part is confirmed by his privately expressed anxiety 'about the situation of Jews in Hungary . . . it is vital that the Russians should get to Budapest at the earliest possible moment: and 48 hours deliberate delay might well make (or may well have made) all the difference by allowing the Arrow Cross time for their *beastly* [my emphasis] work'.[135]

The private opinions of Foreign Office officials, varied as they were, did not seriously impinge on its work. The Foreign Office opposed renewed warnings, which would at this stage carry weight only if issued from Moscow and also because the Hungarians were unlikely to continue the deportations except under pressure from Germany.[136] It had advised that Churchill's reply to the organisations should be non-committal. Brodetsky and Brotman were told that reports of further deportations and massacres of Jews were still un-confirmed. This was despite the fact that information from Stockholm confirmed the resumption of deportations from Budapest. The government believed that rescue would come with the Soviet advance and accordingly decided not to respond to further letters from the WJC.[137]

As long as officials stalled, asserting that a report was 'uncon-firmed', it was impossible to contest the policy of inaction. By this point the Jewish organisations had despaired of moving the authorities to act to save the remnants of European Jewry. With the end of the war in sight, there was a slackening of effort. Ideas had run out. Brodetsky tried in late November to persuade the Foreign Office that the Vatican might be encouraged to protest about the situation in Auschwitz and Birkenau.[138] Another request by the WJC for a broadcast appeal and warning to the Hungarian population elicited a belated response that Hungary was now 'entirely under German domination ... the best hope lay in the speedy liberation of Hungary'.[139]

Once the Nazis had barred all avenues of escape, little could be done for the Jews of Hungary. Nevertheless, the acceptance of the Horthy Offer, following the intercession of various governments and others, delayed mass deportations from Hungary for a crucial period during August 1944.[140] However, by mid-September only a small number had managed to leave. The position of the 1,200 Jews in Budapest, who were to constitute the first convoy of emigrants, was still unclear. Problems arose because of the impossibility of obtaining exit permits from the German authorities.[141]

Those who have argued that the Anglo-Jewish organisations did little and supinely complied with government policy have oversim-plified the record. The consistent and determined efforts of the voluntary organisations on behalf of European Jewry were largely doomed by the government's insistence on the facile but irrefutable argument that military and other wartime priorities must take precedence. No greater success was achieved by the dynamic tactics of the British Section than by the conciliatory Board; neither was able to reconcile the overriding aim of winning the war with saving European Jewry. The latter was not only not a British war aim, but also represented, in British eyes, an impediment to the swiftest possible victory.

The organisations were severely restricted because they had no power to influence government policy. What is striking is the dogged urgency of their activities, however hopeless, in face of the invariable and inevitable frustration confronting them at every turn. Some of their proposals, even had they been accepted, were unrealisable due to Nazi determination to eradicate European Jewry. For example, the proposal in June 1944 by the British Section and the Board that the United Nations fulfil its verbal warnings by immediately putting on trial all captured Germans who could be charged with atrocities against Jewish or non-Jewish populations would probably have had little deterrent effect on the Nazis or their satellite accomplices. Since there is overwhelming evidence that the racial policies of the Nazis were intrinsic to their war aims, concessions to pressure on this point would have been tantamount to moral surrender.

The Anglo-Jewish voluntary organisations, for all their aspirations to political and diplomatic status, were merely pawns in the game of war, and played that game all the less effectively for their failure to realise it. They never understood that – as Harry Goodman observed – 'Amidst all the vital problems of state, the saving of a few individuals is really all we can do.'[142]

8
Rescue Efforts: A Chronicle of Failure?

With Nazi domination over much of Europe from the spring of 1940 and the invasion of the Soviet Union in June 1941, any prospect of immediate rescue of the endangered populations was unrealistic. The Allied governments repeatedly argued that rescue could be accomplished only by an Allied victory. The Jews of the free world lacked military resources and it was not until the summer of 1944 that a Jewish unit within the British army in Palestine was established; it was in any case unable to act independently.

Rescue operations were largely limited to exchanges of Jews either for material compensation (ransom deals) or for German civilians. The goal of 'unconditional surrender', stipulated at the Casablanca Conference in January 1943 and reaffirmed at the Bermuda Conference three months later, precluded any direct negotiation with the enemy for anything other than surrender. It was feared that any such negotiations would create a rift with the Soviets, who constantly suspected the British and Americans of contemplating a separate deal with the Nazis, as argued in the case of Joel Brand's 'trucks for blood' deal in the spring of 1944. Moreover, fundamental mistrust of German intentions meant that most ransom deals were dismissed as Nazi blackmail devices.[1]

Crucially, rescue deals on any large scale were in principle antithetical to the government's concern to avoid an influx of Jewish refugees into Britain or Palestine: it was 'essential that we should do nothing at all which involves the risk that the further reception of refugees here might be the ultimate outcome'.[2] Those who condemn the organisations for 'doing nothing' do not always take into account that the Government was more than merely indifferent to rescue proposals.

Currency restraints were an further obstacle to rescue. Operations involving the transfer of funds or materials directly or indirectly to the Germans conflicted with the principle of economic warfare and thus contravened the Trading with the Enemy Act of 1939. Britain refused to establish a body similar to the American WRB, whose emphasis was on 'rescue', since schemes involving 'the provision of money or goods to persons, principally Jews, in enemy territories, to enable them to bribe Nazi guards etc. . . . is bound to conflict with our economic warfare policy.' The licence recently obtained by the WRB to transfer $100,000 to the ICRC to be spent in enemy territory 'represents a complete breach with joint Anglo-American blockade policy'.[3]

Even the sale of exit permits posed a problem. Since June 1942 there had been a growing organised traffic in the sale of exit permits, costing up to £5,000 per head, from enemy-occupied territories, particularly the Netherlands. Funds were supplied by friends or relatives in neutral countries. The government was well aware that the enemy, using such forms of ransom, was trying to raise foreign currency and thereby evade the effects of the financial blockade. To check this, government strategy was to give wide publicity to the trade and to blacklist anyone acting as an intermediary. Consequently, within a short time 'the traffic had been killed'.[4]

To avoid any transfer of funds to the enemy, the JDC, with US Treasury approval, had created a 'credit system' whereby no hard currency was exchanged in enemy territory, only pledges which could be redeemed in dollars after the war. Against these dollar credits, local funds could then be released to assist Jewish relief and emigration schemes.[5] The Anglo-Jewish organisations were unable to secure a similar arrangement until the summer of 1944, when a credit scheme began operating through the IGCR. A representative of the JDC noted the 'great difference between what the US Government allows us to do with dollars as against the real restrictions which the British Government imposes on pounds'.[6]

In Britain, all transactions with the enemy were dealt with through official channels. Private persons deposited their money with the appropriate government department, which took complete control of such matters as support payments, repatriation and so on. Following the creation of the WRB, the United States had granted private organisations licences enabling them to have financial dealings and communication within enemy territory and asked the British to grant private relief agencies such licences. This raised an important issue for the Treasury and Trading with the Enemy Department, which agreed that if the Americans were permitting this on a large scale, 'genuine propositions' should be approved by HMG.[7]

Emerson had already proposed in March that the IGCR should operate a credit scheme by opening a special banking account into which it would pay sums to provide funds to meet its liabilities and for the JDC to act as its agent in operating the credit scheme. This was accepted in July and Emerson was asked to confirm that 'none of these "credit" funds should be used for schemes of escape, e.g. across the Spanish border which might compete with our own scheme for getting various important people out of occupied Europe'. It was calculated that some part of this fund would be used to transport Jews from Hungary following the Horthy Offer.[8] While private organisations were advised to channel their rescue work through the IGCR and its agent the JDC, it was considered necessary 'to discriminate between one agency and another, not all of whom were equally responsible'. It was feared that the war effort could be harmed, not only financially, by agencies prepared to violate the rules of blockade in order to rescue particular individuals.[9]

Similar restraints operated in the case of private relief organisations striving to support refugees in neutral countries. Following requests in early 1944 from Jewish communal and relief organisations in Sweden to help Jewish refugees who had arrived from Norway, Hertz and Schonfeld proposed a scheme whereby the British organisations would contribute £5,000 to relief activities in Palestine, while the JDC would refund these payments in the form of grants to Sweden. The Foreign Office, however, objected on the grounds that the Swedish government had already undertaken the maintenance of its refugees. Yet it appeared that these refugees were receiving little beyond the bare necessities. Schonfeld was, in effect, trying to get Foreign Office sanction to an arrangement which had already been arrived at between the Federation of Jewish Relief Organisations in Britain, under Hertz, and the JDC. He pressed the Foreign Office to agree, arguing that 'If . . . we are able to carry out activities abroad as well as at home, our experience had shown that the subscriptions to a general appeal enabled activities to be maintained in both spheres.' Otherwise, he warned, it would not be possible to raise funds for local causes and the full burden of provision would therefore fall on the Assistance Board.[10]

The Foreign Office did not disregard this warning outright. The refugee question was impinging on Anglo-American relations and there was no wish to offend Hertz; enquires were accordingly made of the British Minister in Stockholm, who reported that the transfer of further funds was unnecessary and would cause resentment among other refugees there. The Foreign Office accordingly upheld its refusal.[11] Neither the Treasury nor the Foreign Office was moved by Schonfeld's continued rhetoric. The Treasury proposed that 'instead of trying to bully you [the Foreign Office], all requests be co-ordinated through one central Jewish body, namely the Board of Deputies and conducted through the IGC'. The Foreign Office concurred.[12]

Hertz raised the more general question of financial help being extended by British Jews to their representatives in the various neutral countries 'to enable them to carry out any rescue effort that may present itself'. Aware that British currency problems made this more difficult than for the Americans, he suggested that Anglo-Jewish contributions should be put at the disposal of the American Committee in the sterling area in return for repayments in the neutral countries.[13] The Financial and Blockade authorities offered no objection, provided such funds were limited to expenditure in neutral countries, moderate in amount and in no way beneficial to the enemy. However, the MEW preferred the funds to be remitted directly to Jewish representatives in the neutral countries rather than through the American Committee. In this way they could 'make sure that the organisations adhered to the conditions stipulated'.[14] The government had agreed in February 1944 to Schonfeld's request that £2,000 be made available for refugees holding Mauritius visas who were in transit in Turkey. However, Hertz's proposal raised considerations other than the Exchange Control problem of providing the foreign currency required. There would be no problem in assisting refugees who had escaped into neutral territory, but Hertz's proposal did not make clear that the proposed expenditure was limited to this and seemed to suggest that the Jewish relief organisations were contemplating entering, through their representatives in the neutral countries, into financial transactions with, or for the benefit of, persons still in enemy territory. This would then provide the enemy with valuable foreign exchange.[15]

The MEW was still unclear what Hertz intended, but suggested that he coordinate his efforts through the IGCR. Emerson assured Hertz that there was a possibility of financially helping Jews in enemy-occupied territory through the IGCR.[16] Hertz replied that if Jewish relief agencies placed sums at the IGCR's disposal, these could be used for assistance to Jews in occupied countries, by local currency being released to the IGCR agent against promissory notes to pay to the holders sterling sums after the war. However, these concessions were extremely limited and Hertz's use of the regular channels proved unsatisfactory. Similarly, Schonfeld's approach to Emerson in September 1944 for £2,000 to rescue Rabbi Ungar of Nitra and his students was rejected, Slovak currency being unobtainable in Switzerland.[17]

Rescue of children

The impetus for action on behalf of children came in the wake of the round-up and deportation of foreign refugee Jews from unoccupied Vichy France in July and August 1942. Harrowing accounts of the children's fate were widely publicised in the British and American press. For the first time, schemes were improvised for the rescue of Jewish children, by official and private organisations, aiming to persuade the authorities to grant entry permits and thereby enabling the children to leave.[18] The admission of refugee children from unoccupied France was discussed in September by Randall, Emerson and Morrison. Randall remarked that unless most were of Allied origin he would be bound to oppose the idea. However, reports that the American government was about to agree to the admission of 1,000 children and that a substantial number were to be admitted into Santo Domingo,[19] may have changed his mind.

Schiff suggested that children and old people with close relatives in Britain be admitted, a number he calculated at no more than 300–350. Their maintenance would be guaranteed by the Jewish Refugee Committee. The War Cabinet was dubious; allowing children into Britain would only encourage the Vichy government to continue its deportation policy, leaving more children abandoned. Moreover, any increase in Jewish immigration was likely to stir up anti-Semitism, which 'would be bad for the country and the Jewish community'. Nevertheless, Morrison felt that this move would 'make a very strong appeal to the humanitarian feelings' of the public, making it difficult for the government to refuse. He was therefore inclined to accede to Schiff's request provided there were no further concessions.[20]

The initial concession, covering only children with parents in the UK, was considered unrealistic and inadequate. Randall himself minuted that this took 'no account of the much more common hardship' – children left destitute after the deportation of their parents. Hertz urged, as 'an act of charity', that the concession be extended to children with close relatives in the UK.[21] He also enquired whether asylum for Polish Jewish children could be found in any of the colonies. Although sympathetic, Cranborne declined, regretting that the difficulties 'are even greater than I imagined'. Hertz's proposal was rejected not only because of transport difficulties but also on principle: 'the Chief Rabbi's suggestion amounts to discrimination in favour of Jewish children and the segregation of the Jews as a separate nationality.' Cranborne added disingenuously that 'in practice HMG regard the Allied Governments in London as responsible for their own nationals, Jews and non-Jews alike'.[22]

Hertz's appeal was to the moral imperative of saving children, and he was evidently unable to respond to the fallacies in Cranborne's arguments, namely that any refugee, by virtue of being singled out for protection, was in some measure the beneficiary of discrimination, whether he were a Pole, a Czech or a Jew. Furthermore, if the Allied governments in London were capable of assuming responsibility for all their nationals, Jews and non-Jews alike, there would have been no such thing as a refugee problem. Hertz appealed, to no avail, for a reconsideration on the grounds that 'Jews are not being merely maltreated, starved or shot as hostages; a policy of total extermination is pursued'.[23]

Nevertheless, in October, the CCJR obtained permission to bring in from unoccupied France 500 refugee children between the ages of two and sixteen, whose parents were dead or had been deported, provided they had a close relative in Britain. The age limit of sixteen was reduced to fourteen in the case of children of 'enemy nationality'. An undertaking was given on behalf of the Jewish community that the children would not become a charge on public funds. However, these plans came to nothing as a result of the occupation of Vichy France in November. A few children who had been fortunate enough to reach Lisbon and Sweden arrived in Britain. The rest were deported to Auschwitz.[24]

Other proposals were equally unsuccessful. The most ambitious of these was the government's decision in February 1943 to allow 4,500 Jewish children from Bulgaria to enter Palestine.[25] However, owing to Germany's grip on its satellites, the exit was barred. A smaller-scale scheme envisaged by Schonfeld, to evacuate Jewish children to the British colonies, never materialised.[26] The organisations continued their endeavours to rescue children from the Balkans and Hungary, as in the unsuccessful attempt by the CBF, initiated by Salomon Adler-Rudel, to bring 20,000 children to Sweden.[27]

The most dramatic scheme involving children was completed in February 1943. In August 1942 the Soviet government had allowed 5,000 Polish Jews, including more than 800 orphaned children, to leave for Palestine via Teheran, with British permission. The 'Teheran children' constituted the largest contingent (the first group comprising some 856 children) to leave Europe during the war. These children came under the care of Youth Aliyah, an Anglo-Jewish organisation, under the guidance of Henrietta Szold. After political problems with the government of Iraq, which rejected British request for transit facilities, they finally arrived in Palestine.[28] It should be pointed out, however, that these children were not saved from Nazi-occupied Europe but moved from the Soviet Union to Palestine, and in this sense the Teheran children were not technically the object of an 'act of rescue'.

Apart from schemes specifically involving children, one of the commonest rescue devices entailed exchanging Jews holding either Palestine certificates or other 'protective papers' for German civilians held in Allied territory. Holders of such certificates were considered by the Germans potential candidates for exchange. However, Britain feared that German agents might be included in each group and objected to the return of Germans who might contribute to the German war effort. Britain naturally preferred to give priority to British citizens rather than Palestinian Jews in Germany. A small number of Jews had been exchanged for German civilian internees held by the British in Palestine from December 1941, in compliance with Jewish Agency and British government criteria. As a result of representations made by the Jewish Agency, later exchange schemes were broadened to include 'veteran Zionists', rabbis and those with relatives in Palestine.[29]

Throughout 1943 the Jewish organisations struggled to secure further exchanges, but German internees singled out for exchange often 'declined repatriation'. Furthermore, the British authorities objected to ratifying lists of candidates who did not fit their criteria for exchange. For this reason, the organisations tried to broaden the categories of those eligible for exchange. Early in 1943, the Consultative Committee explored the possibilities of an exchange of Axis detainees in Allied lands for similar categories of Jews in Axis countries. Referring to a group of Dutchmen interned in Westerbork, Brotman proposed one such exchange of nationals, but was told that there was a limited number of German internees eligible for exchange and that British subjects, particularly women, must take priority.[30]

The issue was again raised in the memorandum sent by the Jewish organisations to the Bermuda Conference, suggesting that 'all Jews . . . be included in any such schemes of exchange'. However, the Conference dismissed the proposal for reasons similar to those of the Foreign Office.[31] Even within the set categories, there was a disparity in numbers. By the summer of 1943, a second group had already been exchanged. The Foreign Office transmitted approximately 900 names to the Swiss government for inclusion in the next exchange, while only nine Germans in Palestine had opted for repatriation. Germany had objected to the disparity in numbers and the authorities argued that it was not the time to extend the categories of Palestinians eligible for exchange. By the end of 1943, it was clear that there would be no large-scale exchange. Even the established Palestine–German exchange mechanism was beset with difficulties, while the number of Jewish candidates for exchange, following the liquidation of the Polish ghettos, had steadily dwindled.[32]

Nevertheless, attempts to secure exchanges and broaden the categories carried on well into 1944. By March, it had become clear that the British were not prepared to exchange Germans for any but British citizens. With the deportation of Hungarian Jewry, the voluntary organisations tried unsuccessfully to devise ways to broaden the categories of those eligible for exchange by having Jews recognised as British protected persons and as Palestine citizens. This idea, first proposed by Hertz in May, was rejected by Eden who repeated that there 'was a shortage of eligible Germans and priority could not be given to foreign Jews over British subjects'.[33] Other ideas included Shertok's proposal that Hungarian Jews might be issued special certificates purporting to establish that they were already Palestine citizens, an idea initially rejected on the grounds that 'this might prejudice the prospects of future exchanges between Allied and enemy nationals'.[34]

Another scheme involved Polish refugees in Shanghai. After Germany's invasion of the Soviet Union, many Jews who had found refuge in Lithuania fled, via Russia, Siberia and Japan, to Shanghai. The 900 Polish Jews there included a group of over 400 rabbis and theological students. The outbreak of war in the Pacific in December 1941, together with increasing Japanese anti-Semitism, jeopardised the position of these refugees.[35] In the summer of 1942, Schonfeld, Hertz and Goodman decided that they must be evacuated, possibly through an exchange with Japanese civilian prisoners-of-war. They approached the Colonial Office but were told that Allied nationals were primarily the responsibility of their own governments. If the Polish government were persuaded to request the assistance of the Foreign Office, the case of the rabbis would receive full consideration, although they could not be evacuated until further exchanges could be arranged, and they would be low on an already 'congested' list of priorities.[36] In February 1943 Goodman raised the issue again, but was informed that there would be inevitable delays.[37] Everything depended on the number of Japanese available. In March, Japan had proposed an additional exchange of civilian internees up to a total of 1,600 on both sides. The prospects therefore looked bleak. The Jewish refugees were technically Polish nationals and the proportion of Poles included in any exchange was likely to be minimal, as the Polish exchange was only one part of the British quota. Goodman suggested that the US government 'donate' part of its quota for this specific purpose,[38] an unrealistic proposition in view of the American military presence in the Pacific.

In the summer of 1943, a further appeal came from Shanghai for the immediate evacuation of the rabbis and students. Following Goodman's approach, the Polish Foreign Ministry reiterated the point that the only way to procure their evacuation in substantial numbers would be for the Jewish religious bodies to arrange large-scale exchanges via the British and US governments.[39] Although it was clear that the British and Polish authorities were equally intent on fobbing off the organisations, Hertz accordingly approached Eden in October. To justify the rescue of this single category of refugees, Hertz offered the spurious argument that they represented 'the greatest theological College of World Jewry' (namely the Mir Yeshiva). He had already approached Sikorsky in early 1943 to ensure that every effort be made to bring about the evacuation of all Polish nationals from Shanghai, the majority of whom were Jews.[40]

There was also competition between Agudists and non-Agudists among the refugees, the Agudists maintaining that they were discriminated against in terms of numbers (six out of forty-two) in the exchange list. Schwarzbart was accused of favouring his Zionist friends at the expense of the Agudist refugees.[41] Goodman appealed to the Polish authorities in London for full consideration to be given to the orthodox group and that at least proportional representation be afforded these refugees in the present exchange. He was assured that they would receive full consideration and in April 1944 the Polish government gave a written undertaking that in future exchanges of civilians the claims of the orthodox group would be honoured.[42]

The Foreign Office predictably claimed it was not possible to enlarge the Polish quota further because such 'discrimination against other Allies' would cause resentment. Hertz proposed that efforts be made to facilitate the group's emigration to Palestine via the USSR and requested that Australia, as Protecting Power, approach the Soviets with a view to granting transit facilities and ask the Swiss Consul in Shanghai to approach the Japanese to grant exit permits. Law suggested that Hertz approach the Polish authorities, which readily complied.[43]

The Allied governments remained unconvinced that the Polish group deserved priority over thousands of American citizens also waiting for exchange. Negotiations, centring on shipping difficulties, dragged on for over a year between the Allied and Japanese governments.[44] In April 1944, attention shifted towards the establishment of an autonomous Jewish province in Harrar, Ethiopia. Nothing came of this; the group remained stranded in Shanghai until after the war, when 500 were granted exit permits for emigration to Sweden and eventually reached America.[45]

Measures requiring justification for 'queue-jumping' stood little chance of success; more promising were the opportunities afforded by the issue of protective documents which were in reality merely legal fictions. One of the more ingenious though little appreciated rescue ideas was the issuing of so-called protective papers, documents which afforded protection by making their holders citizens of other countries, mainly South American. It was a device intended to effect rescue by rendering holders candidates for exchange with German citizens in those countries and thus avoid deportation; holders were often separated from other detainees and held in special camps, such as Vittel in France and Bergen-Belsen in Germany. In some cases these papers were authentic documents, issued with the approval of the governments concerned. More often the documents were forgeries, issued on the personal initiative of consular representatives in Europe, mostly for monetary reward; in one of a few exceptional cases, George Montello, the Jewish First Secretary-General of San Salvador in Switzerland, acted out of humanitarianism.[46]

As early as May 1942, Emmanuel Ringelblum, the chronicler of the Warsaw ghetto, noted that such documents were widely available and questioned 'whether the newly created citizens, i.e., those who bought their citizenship for a price during the war, will be allowed to benefit from this exchange'.[47] Amongst the first to recognise the value of such papers was Yitzchak Sternbuch, a member of the Agudat

Israel in Switzerland, who noticed in July 1942, a few days before the mass deportation of Jews from Warsaw, that bearers of Latin American papers were afforded special treatment by the Nazis, that is they were detained in prison in Warsaw rather deported to concentration camp. Sternbuch bought from the Paraguayan consul papers which were sent to Jews in the occupied territories. When news reached the West that foreign passports might save Jews, a major effort was undertaken by activists in Geneva, Istanbul and Holland to secure such documents from Latin American consuls in Switzerland.[48]

The initiative to obtain 'protective papers' in Britain was taken by Schonfeld and Goodman, who were among the first few to appreciate their importance. Until the summer of 1943, Brodetsky had heard only vague rumours about the protective value of these papers, but by the summer of 1944 he too was appealing to the Foreign Office to issue such documents, pointing out that some South American governments had saved many Jewish lives by this means. The Foreign Office refused, claiming that the Germans would ignore the visas and that Jewish lives would be further endangered. Brodetsky suggested that the Protecting Power seek out those for whom certificates or visas were available, rather than invite them to come forward, but this too was rejected.[49] Instead of pressing for a small-scale trial, Brodetsky gave up. Here is a further example of Brodetsky's style of dealing with officials; he was determined to make some effort, while at the same time invariably conceding to government arguments, however unconvincing or inconclusive. In this case, the government's argument was especially weak, both in fact and in principle, so that the feebleness of Brodetsky's response is all the more striking.

The illegal trade in Latin American passports grew. By February 1944 it was estimated that over 10,000 had been issued. The figure had grown so high that the Swiss Federal government had to intervene, as its diplomatic position was being compromised. The consuls of Haiti, Paraguay and Peru were dismissed.[50] The German authorities knew what had been going on, but because of their exchange value, at times ignored the dubious validity of these documents. On 26 June 1943, Eichmann wrote to the chief of operations in the Hague, Willi Zopf: 'Though it is undesirable that Jews otherwise designated for deportation should acquire such nationalities by legitimate means, there is nothing we can do about it.' At a later stage, the German Foreign Office intervened in the hope that Latin American countries concerned might be persuaded to release German internees even against these 'pseudo-compatriots'. There was always the fall-back, 'If such exchanges could not be effected, there was time enough to treat them like ordinary Jews.'[51]

Thus, at times, these papers afforded no protection at all, as happened in the winter of 1943 at Vittel. This was an internment camp in eastern France, which held, as well as Allied nationals, some 240 Polish Jews possessing certificates of citizenship of various South-American states issued by consulates of those states, mainly from Berne. In December 1943, Hertz learned that the Germans had confiscated these papers following Paraguay's cancellation of the citizenship of the 'passport-holders', who were now threatened with deportation. The Jewish organisations in Britain lobbied the Latin American governments to 'reaffirm' the citizenship of the 'passport holders'. Schonfeld assured the Foreign Office that the refugees would not attempt to use the 'passports' as a right of entry to Paraguay. Within a few weeks, the Paraguayan government announced that it would continue to recognise the validity of these papers.[52] Several other South American governments followed suit, including the government of Ecuador, which agreed to recognise these passports 'at least for the immediate humanitarian purpose for which they were issued, viz. to afford protection to the holders until they escape to territory outside enemy control.' Unsuccessful efforts were also made to validate the South American papers of a similar group interned at Bergen-Belsen, numbering between 3,000–4,000 refugees, mainly Jews.[53]

From January 1944, certain families in Vittel began to receive certificates from a Zionist organisation in Geneva, and claimed that they were on a repatriation list for Palestine. However, as these had not been ratified by London, they were considered worthless by the German authorities and, as the Anglo-Jewish organisations discovered, the deportation of these detainees began on 18 April. The Board, meanwhile, was assured by the Foreign Office that, contrary to reports, the Latin American governments had recognised the passports issued by their consulates and that all possible steps had been taken to inform the German authorities that some Jewish refugees at Vittel were eligible for admission to Palestine as well as Latin America.[54] Yet coded messages from internees in Vittel urged that only swift exchange for Germans in Allied hands would prevent deportation. In April 1944, Sofka Skipwith, a British civilian internee in Vittel, sent a list of 250 names, microscopically copied onto a flimsy piece of cigarette-paper, together with pleas for help, to friends and officials in various countries. Two such coded messages were smuggled to London, one to Jock Balfour, a British diplomat and family friend, and one to Goodman, containing a similar message from Dr Hillel Seidman, another internee and one of the few survivors, concealed in the coat lining of a British officer freed from Vittel. However, it took until June for Skipwith's letter to reach Balfour. Goodman received the information in April but the cryptic message had so aroused the suspicion of the authorities that Goodman himself was interrogated.[55] Both messages went unheeded, apparently because of bureaucratic confusion. According to Sternbuch, Spain and Switzerland, the Protecting Powers had not yet advised the German authorities to recognise the papers.[56] Conflicting reports stated that deportation had been postponed and that the internees had been returned to Vittel. Goodman heard that they had been transferred to the transit camp at Drancy. The Board and the IGCR again attempted to secure recognition of the 'passports'. Goodman appealed to have the internees included in the next British exchange scheme. He also appealed to the Irish and Polish governments to help ascertain what had happened and to help postpone any deportation order.[57]

The Foreign Office assured Goodman that HMG had made representations to the respective Latin American governments, which had agreed to recognise the documents.[58] However, the Board suspected that recognition of the documents would not satisfy the Germans and that inclusion in an agreed exchange scheme would be required in each individual case. After the second deportation, the commandant of the camp had announced that the papers had been validated but that this was insufficient; the detainees must be exchanged for Germans. A list had been drawn up but would only be accepted by Berlin if ratified by London.[59] Goodman realised that what was required was British confirmation that Palestine certificates had been issued and that the 163 internees would be included in immediate exchange.[60] He and Schonfeld appealed to the Foreign Office to advise the Protecting Power to inform the German government that each internee would be definitely exchanged. They also approached the Spanish and Irish governments directly, urging them to demand the protection and immediate re-internment of the deportees in a camp inspected by the ICRC pending exchange. Walker assured Schonfeld that HMG had cooperated fully in these requests.[61]

No information was received throughout the summer. After the Vittel camp was liberated in mid-September, Schonfeld and Goodman continued their efforts to trace and rescue the group. In November, reports indicated that most of the detainees had been deported and that only some fourteen remained in Vittel. Goodman tried to enlist government support for a joint representation to Berlin by the Vatican and other neutral states. The Foreign Office declined, but Henderson reiterated that the government had asked the Protecting Powers to inform the Germans that persons deported from Vittel were eligible for exchange and should be returned to camps inspected by the ICRC. Schonfeld strove to enlist Government support to ensure that the papers remained valid after their expiry date.[62]

All this proved too late for most of those on Skipwith's list. It has been suggested that while her letters were not exactly ignored, 'it was just the wrong moment because there was D-Day and things were moving'. The German authorities, with defeat impending, proceeded to liquidate the Vittel camp. Only a few benefited from the diplomatic efforts connected with these papers.[63]

By contrast, one of Schonfeld's more successful schemes involved securing visas for the island of Mauritius. He and Hertz were certainly skilful in exploiting the interests of the Colonial Office to facilitate this scheme, but ingenious as it was, its implementation ultimately depended entirely on Government approval. Acceptance of the Mauritius scheme was partly a government concession, but it also served government purposes. The government's strict adherence to the White Paper on immigration into Palestine had resulted in numerous unpleasant incidents during the war which exposed it to fierce criticism both at home and abroad. One example was the deportation to Mauritius of over 900 illegal immigrants, who had tried to break the British blockade of Palestine in November 1940. The appalling conditions under which they were reportedly held prompted ceaseless complaints levelled by the Jewish Agency and other bodies.[64]

In September 1942, Schonfeld and Hertz approached Cranborne with a proposal to transfer thirty rabbis and their families, in all around a hundred, from enemy-occupied countries to any British territories, such as Mauritius or the West Indies, stressing that the 'proposal did not concern Palestine'. Acknowledging that present regulations did not 'permit persons . . . in enemy occupied territory to proceed to countries under British control', Hertz noted that they could sometimes be granted visas once they reached neutral countries and proposed that such an exception be made here. He pointed out that these rabbis could obtain visas to neutral countries only if they succeeded in proving that they would be able to proceed to a final destination. Hertz gave financial assurances regarding their welfare and maintenance.[65]

By deliberately excluding any reference to Palestine, Schonfeld and Hertz hoped that their proposal would be more likely to meet with a positive response. The choice of Mauritius, too, would appeal to the government. The condition of detainees in Mauritius was being criticised constantly not only by Jewish organisations in Britain and America, but also in Parliament. The British Embassy in Washington expressed concern about 'the potential dangers of this problem insofar as it impinges upon British-American relations'. Some 'ammunition' was needed to counter the criticism.[66] Thus, the Mauritius proposal was not unwelcome.

The Colonial Office was more amenable to the scheme than the Foreign Office, which had always maintained that 'no special class or race should be given any preference'.[67] However, in this case, Cranborne wanted, if possible, 'to do what the Chief Rabbi asks', partly on humanitarian grounds, but also out of concern to demonstrate 'that the C.O. are not generally obstructive as regards proposals for assistance to Jews'. He thought the scheme 'not impracticable' and requested the names and numbers of the rabbis in question and their last known addresses, so that they could be vetted by the security authorities.[68] A list of 25 rabbis and their families was submitted at the end of November and the Colonial Office enquired of the governors of the various Colonies about the availability of temporary refuge.

Nevertheless, there was little progress. Oliver Stanley replaced Cranborne as Colonial Secretary in December, but this did not affect the scheme as much as the announcement in February 1943 that the government of Palestine had agreed to admit 4,500 Bulgarian children and 500 accompanying adults, including some doctors, rabbis and 'veteran' Zionists (5 per cent of the total), from enemy-occupied territory.[69] Hertz and Schonfeld were concerned that the Jewish Agency would 'no doubt show preferential treatment for rabbis who are ardent Zionists', thereby excluding 'their' rabbis. This was not quite correct as the Chief Rabbi of Palestine had already appealed to the High Commissioner on behalf of Rabbis Ungar and Schreiber of Nitra and Bratislava respectively and immigration certificates had been granted.[70] Trying to persuade Stanley to pursue 'the plan originally envisaged', Schonfeld explained that 'the proportion of adults to be admitted under the new scheme is rather limited ... [and] will involve considerable delay owing to the unavoidable negotiations with "other parties"', namely the Bulgarian authorities.[71]

Hertz thus had doubts about the new arrangements announced in February. Nor was the Colonial Office prepared to ask the High Commissioner to make additional certificates available for Schonfeld's rabbis and their families. What prompted the Colonial Office to proceed with the original scheme was the requests received from the Czech and Polish governments in April and May and their assurances that the refugees would be repatriated after the war.[72] The Foreign Office had insisted that Schonfeld first approach the national governments of these rabbis 'because it is only from those governments that any guarantees of their removal after the war could be obtained'. The Colonial Office shared the Foreign Office's scepticism about the value of guarantees 'by Agudat Israel or any other body of that kind'. Schonfeld pointed out that the Chief Rabbi had no *locus standi* with the foreign governments located in Britain and requested that Hertz continue to submit cases to the British authorities directly. But the Colonial Office refused. An exception was made for stateless refugees, who had no Allied government to apply on their behalf in Britain.[73]

Most of the Colonial territories refused to accommodate the rabbis. Only the Governor of Mauritius was willing to accept them, on condition that they lived in the same camps as the Jewish refugees already interned there. Hertz not only agreed but added that, contrary to hostile reports, he had heard 'that conditions in the camp are highly satisfactory'.[74] Schonfeld requested that the rabbis' names be sent to the German government, via the Swiss, to facilitate their departure, but the Foreign Office refused to parley thus with the enemy.[75] There were also reports of new regulations stipulating that Jews would be allowed out of enemy-occupied territory only if they had an 'unconditional visa' for a neutral country. Schonfeld enquired whether the neutral governments could be invited to issue an 'ordinary visa', instead of transit visas, on the understanding that the refugees would, as soon as possible, proceed to Mauritius. The Foreign Office complied, its note to the Missions concerned stating: 'We do not wish to modify the terms of this despatch.' However, the Turkish authorities were reluctant to grant unconditional entry visas and the matter was not pursued.[76]

The Foreign Office opposed the extension of the scheme; this 'would create serious difficulties'. However, the political situation again led the government to continue it. The pledge in February that the Bulgarian government would allow 4,500 Jewish children and adults to leave for Palestine had not been fulfilled. In June 1943, under German pressure, Bulgaria closed its frontier to all Jews. There was now little prospect of legal immigration into Palestine from the Balkans, and under pressure from the Jewish Agency, HMG decided in July 1943 that in future all Jews who succeeded in escaping to Turkey would be eligible, after a preliminary security check, for admission to Palestine. Only the Jewish Agency was privy to this new arrangement. The Colonial Office advised keeping it secret, ostensibly 'in the interest of the refugees themselves', but, in effect, so as not to advertise that Palestine was now open for immigration.[77]

Thus, anyone who somehow succeeded in escaping to Turkey or other neutral countries should now have been subject to the new policy, without necessitating special arrangements for admission to Mauritius. The Colonial Office was reluctant to extend the Mauritius scheme beyond the original 32 rabbis and their families. Stanley had fulfilled his predecessor's promises and felt that the new policy rendered further special action unnecessary. In spite of the need for secrecy, it was therefore felt that Hertz should be told of the new Palestine policy, so as to end the pressure to continue the Mauritius scheme.[78] However, it was finally decided that secrecy must be maintained and Hertz was not informed of the new policy. Consequently, in order 'to keep up with him the fiction that these Rabbis may go to Mauritius', the Colonial Office enquired whether Mauritius could accept any more rabbis, pointing out 'that probably not all of them will succeed in reaching neutral countries'. Having secured the agreement of the Governor of Mauritius, Stanley agreed, in September 1943, to extend the scheme to cover 340 persons.[79]

In February 1944, Schonfeld requested the Foreign Office to forward £2,000 to HM authorities in Turkey for the maintenance of refugees holding Mauritius visas, in advance of their arrival. This was to ensure that 'no burdens, however temporary, are placed upon [the Turkish authorities] as a result of the transit facilities they had granted'. Despite exchange control difficulties, the MEW agreed.[80] However, only 28 Turkish visas had so far been granted. Schonfeld offered to go to Istanbul to expedite matters, but the British Ambassador in Turkey rejected this offer, recommending that all work should be coordinated through Chaim Barlas, the Jewish Agency representative, 'otherwise wires would get crossed'.[81]

The news from Turkey continued to worsen. In April 1944, Schonfeld was notified that the 'greatest obstacle to rescue was the limitation of Turkish visas and the suspension of visas granted'. At his instigation, Randall made enquiries which resulted in a report from the British Embassy in Istanbul maintaining that Turkish visas were in fact still available and that facilities had not been withdrawn.[82] In May, Schonfeld proposed that the holders of Mauritius visas be included in some exchange scheme. Since HMG was prepared to accept them in British territory, they might be regarded as 'quasi British-protected subjects'. In this way, 'the enemy would recognise their status and either allow their departure or treat them as protected persons'. However, Randall reiterated that persons to be included in the proposed German–Palestine exchange must be either Palestine residents or relatives of such persons. Nor was it possible to contemplate the inclusion of the rabbis in any exchange of British subjects. This was a similar proposal to Hertz's, made a few days later, that 'all Jews in enemy territories are British-protected persons for whom exchanges would be arranged and places of refuge found'.[83] Not only were the German authorities unlikely to agree to this, but it would almost certainly place genuine 'British-protected' people in greater danger than they were in already, by devaluing the 'protected' status to the point of meaninglessness.

After the German occupation of Hungary in the spring of 1944, Schonfeld tried to extend the Mauritius scheme. In early May, Hertz informed Stanley that in spite of the near-impossibility of transferring the refugees to Mauritius, he had definite evidence that the visas had saved many lives. He added that 'the likelihood of any of these people actually reaching Mauritius was very slight' and therefore appealed for an increase in the number of visas to 1,000. The Colonial Secretary was sympathetic and secured the approval of the Foreign Office, which raised no objection despite wondering how the scheme could save so many lives if none of the rabbis ever reached Mauritius. Schonfeld explained that 'it has been confirmed that the possession of emigration facilities . . . has rescued holders from deportation and all that it implies'.[84] Stanley forwarded Hertz's appeal to the Governor of Mauritius, emphasising the prospects of any refugees reaching the Colony were remote.[85] The Governor accepted the suggestion but demanded in return that Hertz 'influence the Jews in the detainment camp . . . to adopt a more reasonable attitude' (conditions in Mauritius were reportedly worse than ever).[86] Schonfeld persisted with the scheme, submitting three lists of Hungarian, Polish and Czech nationals. Within three months all were granted visas for Mauritius. Following an unsuccessful uprising in Slovakia in October 1944, after which thousands of surviving

Jews were deported to Auschwitz, Schonfeld submitted more lists for Mauritius visas.[87] In his attempt to rescue some of those who had recently been deported from Nitra, Slovakia, among them Chief Rabbi Ungar, Schonfeld requested that the German government be advised that these people held Mauritius visas. The Foreign Office complied.[88]

It is intriguing that the government so readily acceded to Schonfeld's request. However, in December 1944, the Foreign Office was still expressing concern over criticism being voiced in 'liberal quarters' in the United States over its Mauritius policy, which might 'damage our good relations'. In defence, Mason suggested that the Foreign Office should refer to the CRREC's request for visas to Mauritius. Acknowledging that the scheme was primarily a protective measure, Mason added: 'it would be unlikely that the Emergency Council would adopt this line if they felt that conditions in Mauritius were really as bad as some of the complaints make out.' Until the end of the war, the government was still willing to continue the scheme.[89]

Altogether, Schonfeld obtained 340 Mauritius visas (to cover 1,000 people) and the necessary transit visas from Turkey, Spain and Portugal, which, he claimed, saved many lives regardless of whether the holders ever arrived in Mauritius.[90] Schonfeld's comment on the unlikelihood of anyone actually reaching Mauritius implies that no one actually did; what matters, however, is not whether they arrived in Mauritius (this was never the point of the exercise), but whether they were still alive after the war. The value of the scheme was protective, a point not fully appreciated by those who conclude that, 'Unfortunately, due to conditions on the Continent not a single rabbi ever utilised a Mauritius visa'.[91]

In striking contrast, Goodman's attempts to secure Irish visas for Jews trapped in occupied Europe shows that even persistent and relentless efforts, if misdirected, could not necessarily effect rescue. In the final analysis what mattered was the responsiveness of the government concerned, not the actions of individuals or organisations.

Between 1943 and 1945, Goodman continually tried to persuade the Irish government to grant visas for Jewish refugees. This was done with the full consent of the British government, the National Committee and the Joint Consultative Committee, although Goodman acted alone, negotiating directly with the Eire government. He was in regular contact with J.P. Walshe, Secretary of the Department of External Affairs, and made numerous trips to Dublin to talk to him and Robert Briscoe, head of the Irish Jewish community. Nevertheless,

15 Harry Goodman, Political Secretary of the Agudat Israel World Organisation, date unknown (courtesy of Celia Goodman)

the Irish government procrastinated throughout the negotiations.

Irish policy towards refugees generally and Jewish refugees in particular was highly restrictive and ungenerous. However, it would be misleading to depict the policy of Prime Minister Eamon de Valera as anti-Semitic. Policy was motivated by pragmatism and self-interest, and determined by a high level of unemployment. Walshe insisted that 'Small countries like Ireland do not and cannot assume [the] role of defenders of just causes except their own'.[92]

Goodman's proposals included the idea that Ireland grant a limited number of visas (100) to recommended individuals 'whose emigration is of an urgent character' and that Irish consuls in Axis countries approach the German or Italian authorities. Goodman offered guarantees that refugees would not become a charge on the state. In addition, in 1943 the Colonial Office was considering the renewal of Palestine or British visas which had lapsed at the outbreak of hostilities, but was unwilling to commit itself until the refugees reached neutral territory. Goodman asked that Eire grant them visas, pointing out that the likelihood of such visas being used was remote. He also suggested that the Eire government charter a boat, at his own expense, to transport the 4,500 refugee children *en bloc* from Bulgaria to a Turkish or Palestine port. His final request was that the Eire authorities consider the reception of a limited number of child refugees, possibly orphans, into local Jewish homes.[93]

Dr. Paschal Robinson, the Papal Nuncio, agreed to recommend these proposals to De Valera. While in Dublin, Goodman also met representatives of the Irish Red Cross and discussed two more proposals, the sending of Irish food parcels to Poland and the possibility of bringing relief to Polish Jews in Shanghai.[94] In London, Randall saw no difficulty in arranging transit visas for Eire through Britain, subject only to security considerations. Goodman relayed this to J.P. Dulanty, High Commissioner for Ireland in London, adding that Randall was keen to assist the departure of refugees from Spain to enable her to absorb new refugees and was particularly interested in settling the problem of transporting children from Bulgaria.[95] Shortly afterwards, however, Brotman learned that the Bulgarian authorities had retracted their offer. He remarked: 'it was no good chartering a ship, even if that were possible, if there were no children or other refugees to take away'.[96]

The Dublin authorities were apparently prepared to grant a limited number of visas, subject to the approval of the local Jewish community. Hertz and Goodman appealed to the Dublin Jewish community, which, after some reluctance, finally agreed to help.[97] Still there was no progress. Goodman grew impatient: 'It is three months now since the matter was raised in Dublin... I feel sure that a number of cases which might have been saved... have since been lost.'[98] In August, Goodman appealed again to Walshe. There was now a growing fear that territories under Italian occupation might be invaded by German troops.[99] He sent a list of candidates for visas to Dulanty, acknowledging that although the occupying authorities would probably not grant exit permits, the possession of such visas 'tends to ameliorate the treatment which they receive'. Goodman pursued the matter relentlessly, sending in a second list of candidates and emphasising the helpfulness of other neutral countries which had received thousands of refugees.[100] There was no response from Dublin. Goodman's frustration increased: 'All that is asked is that a formal visa be given and even if only one single life is saved the action will not have been without result.' He pointed out that a news agency report had confirmed that persons holding visas were exempt from deportation to the death camps in the East and sent a copy of this letter to the Papal Nuncio in Dublin, who regretted that he could do little to help.[101] Goodman apparently still did not realise that the repeated evasions were more than merely bureaucratic, and that the Irish authorities had no intention of acting.

When the Jewish press, somewhat prematurely, publicised the proposals, Walshe advised Goodman: 'it would be wiser to avoid publicity until something concrete happens... The reports... to say the least, [are] somewhat exaggerated.' When asked to inquire about the death camps at Auschwitz and Birkenau, Walshe replied: 'we have been informed that the rumours in relation thereto are absolutely devoid of foundation.' Still Goodman persisted: '[I] am relieved to hear that the reports about the camps at Oswiecim and Birkenau are unfounded. We can only hope that these statements are correct.'[102] This seems an extraordinary comment to have made in December 1943, though it does reinforce the contention that until June 1944 Auschwitz-Birkenau was not identified as a mass extermination camp.

Certainly, Goodman seems never to have realised that he was wasting his time. Yet there were indications that this was so. Other schemes had been more favourably received. One such was initiated by a Mrs. Patrick Hore-Ruthven, in cooperation with the Irish Red Cross, 'for the reception in Eire of 500 refugee children, preferably Catholic', from France and Belgium. Emerson advised her that the scheme would have a better chance of success if it were taken up directly by the Eire government with the German authorities.[103] Certainly, this scheme would not have posed the cultural and religious problems of assimilation and repatriation after the war that might have arisen from a similar one involving Jewish children.

In early March 1944, Goodman expressed bitter disappointment that nothing had come of the discussions. Many refugees had fled to Hungary and unless they could produce emigration visas for some other country, were threatened with imprisonment or deportation. Visas could be issued only by countries, such as Ireland, which were not at war with Hungary. Goodman reiterated that, apart from the impossibility of transport, there was only the remotest possibility of anybody ever using an Irish visa, and that the main purpose of the visas was to prevent deportation. He pointed to the efforts of other neutral countries and hoped that Eire would not 'refrain from participating in this great endeavour'.[104]

Still undeterred, in July 1944 Goodman appealed to Walshe to intervene with the Hungarian authorities, as King Gustav of Sweden had done. Walshe's diplomatic refusal stated that he would do 'what is possible but no direct contact with Hungarian Government'. Goodman renewed his appeals to the Eire government for reception facilities following the Horthy offer to permit the emigration of all Jewish children aged under ten, in possession of visas.[105] Dulanty discussed the matter with the Dublin authorities, pointing out that other neutral countries had agreed to take some Hungarian Jews and proposing that Eire should offer to take 500 children under ten years of age on the understanding that it would be for the duration of the war and that no maintenance charges would fall on Eire. On his return to London, Dulanty expressed reservations to the Dominion Office about dealing with the representative of 'a body like Agudas Israel ... however responsible it might be'; he preferred to negotiate with the British government, which he presumed 'would make provision for transport to Eire'. In any case, it seems that Dulanty considered these ideas 'not so much on compassionate grounds but from a feeling that it would be useful to Eire if she could say after the war that she had not entirely stood aside from helping as regards the European refugee problem'. The Dominion Office suggested that Dulanty take up with Emerson the possibility of the transport and accommodation in Eire of a certain number of Jewish refugees.[106]

The Irish government was evidently reluctant to deal with the

Agudah. In contrast to its repeated rebuffs to Goodman, it responded positively to the request of the US government in the summer of 1944 to accept 500 Jewish children from the Continent. This agreement originally specified French Jewish children but was later amended to include Hungarian Jewish children. Goodman again intervened, trying, somewhat unrealistically, to have this arrangement extended to include refugees without reservation as to number and age. The Irish government agreed to the amendment in respect of nationality, but insisted that the quota be limited to children, for reasons of security, and to 500 for absorption capacity. Goodman gave way and assured the Irish Red Cross that his organisation would be pleased to assist in any administrative arrangements.[107] Due to the grim developments in Hungary, however, Ireland was unable to proceed.

Goodman's frustrated endeavours might serve as a paradigm for Anglo-Jewish rescue efforts during the war. The organisations made numerous approaches to the government to try to extend the Palestine exchange schemes involving European Jews. Most of these came to nothing. Mainly due to the efforts of the Jewish Agency, the three Palestine exchange schemes between 1941 and 1944 provided some opportunity for rescue, but their scope was limited because Britain lacked exchangeable German citizens. Problems of transport also militated against a further exchange scheme in 1944.[108]

It is impossible to estimate how many people were saved by possession of protective papers. The Anglo-Jewish organisations intervened successfully to secure the validation of documents issued by South American consuls in Europe. However, these papers obtained deferment from deportation only for so long as it suited the Germans to recognise them as valid. While efforts to save the Jews in Vittel were largely unsuccessful, at least many hundreds elsewhere holding South American papers were saved from extermination. A group of holders of South American passports at Bergen-Belsen survived the war.[109]

Schonfeld's Mauritius scheme and Goodman's Irish visa proposal demonstrate that the amount of effort involved was in itself almost entirely irrelevant. However, tactical ingenuity played an important part. Schonfeld and Hertz were able to persuade the government to acquiesce in one of the few attempts during the war to secure protective visas for the British Colonies. This was in part due to their avoidance of the Palestine issue, but more importantly, their scheme served a useful purpose in terms of complementing British objectives. Goodman's equally determined efforts met with failure, largely because his efforts were addressed to a recalcitrant government, which saw them as merely an irritating interference in a matter on which it was only prepared to deal at governmental level. Goodman persisted in directing his energies at the patently unhelpful Irish Government instead of seeking one which might perhaps have been more helpful.

9
Relief Efforts: A Chronicle of Success?

With most rescue schemes doomed, the only possibility of action lay in relieving the suffering of European Jewry. Brodetsky's memoirs frankly admit: 'we could do nothing for them ... except protest, send some food parcels with Government permission and get the BBC European service to speak to them about the freedom for which we were fighting.'[1]

It was well known that systematic mass starvation was one of the weapons of extermination used by the Nazis against the Jewish populations of occupied Europe. To combat this, various organisations, British and American, attempted to initiate food relief schemes.[2] All such schemes, however, were subject to Trading with the Enemy regulations and Ministry of Economic Warfare (MEW) approval. Such efforts inevitably conflicted with British blockade policy, considered an essential weapon of modern warfare and one of the most decisive factors in bringing about the Allied victory in 1918.[3] In August 1940, Churchill announced the government's intention 'to maintain rigorously the blockade of all territories occupied and controlled by the enemy and to lay squarely upon the shoulders of the enemy the responsibility for providing for the needs of the inhabitants'. This policy was reaffirmed in the spring of 1941 and in the autumn of 1942 the British and US governments resolved formally upon a joint policy on these matters.[4]

Until 1942, Germany was little affected by the food blockade owing to its systematic spoliation of the occupied territories. It then faced a mounting crisis and increasing pressure to maintain supplies from the occupied areas. Until late 1944, it was able to maintain a reasonable rationing system, after which time supplies diminished sharply and the food shortage became serious. The Bermuda Conference in

April 1943 dismissed the suggestion that the Allied governments send food through the blockade, on the grounds that such a policy hindered the war effort.[5] Towards the end of 1943, the MEW reaffirmed the importance of the blockade policy, but its justification had changed considerably: 'In 1940 there was a real danger that supplies of foodstuff might be dispatched to enemy Europe under the guise of relief'; it was now 'a question of psychological rather than economic warfare'. There was in fact hardly anything in the way of relief supplies available. It was considered better not to emphasise this, but to continue to base the argument on grounds of blockade rather than supply. The MEW admitted: 'The main reason, nevertheless, for refusing requests ... is that in practice we could not admit the claims of one area while rejecting those of another.'[6]

However, an exception was made for Greece, which was suffering 'absolute famine' and from January 1942 shipments of wheat were permitted to pass through the blockade.[7] The British government had rejected requests throughout 1941 from Allied governments, notably those of Belgium and Norway, to admit relief supplies through the blockade.[8] The concession to Greece had broken the principle of complete blockade and the government anticipated a flood of piecemeal suggestions to convey food through the blockade. It realised that 'it will therefore be invaluable to find a concession which can be extended in varying measures to all the Allied countries ... without the risk of substantial benefit to the enemy'.[9] The government agreed to allow various Allied governments to remit funds and make purchases from neutral countries within the blockade area since the surplus products of such countries might, in any event, be available to the enemy in the ordinary way of trade. These foodstuffs were then sent as relief to various occupied territories. Consignments were limited by the resources of the neutral countries concerned and were 'sharply distinguished' from shipments through the blockade.[10]

Apart from applications by the Allied governments to the MEW, the voluntary Jewish organisations also suggested that Jews in the Polish ghettos be treated as the equivalent of prisoners-of-war in internment camps and receive similar privileges in respect of the blockade. The blockade authorities had categorically refused to allow any consignments from overseas for persons other than prisoners-of-war and civilian internees. They insisted on the formality of the 1929 Geneva Convention relating to POWs, because it seemed to offer the best guarantee that the relief sent actually reached its intended beneficiaries. Although the German government refused to extend POW status to Jewish deportees, claiming that they had been arrested for reasons of 'public security', the organisations, particularly the WJC, tried several times to ensure that Jews in the Polish ghettos and internment camps qualified as beneficiaries of Red Cross parcels by according them POW and civilian internee status.[11]

On the whole the British and US governments cooperated harmoniously on blockade policy. Prior to America's entry into the war, Jewish organisations in the United States had sent almost 100,000 food parcels to the Jews of occupied Poland. The British blockade authorities considered that this would benefit the enemy and both governments therefore tried early in 1941 to stop these schemes. The WJC acquiesced, bringing it into conflict with the Agudat Israel.[12] It was only in deference to the personal request of Lord Halifax, then British Ambassador in Washington, that the Agudah reluctantly complied.[13]

However, the news that Polish Jews were subject to particularly brutal discrimination, and news of dispatch of parcels to Greece and Belgium, made it hard to sustain the case against sending parcels to Poland. As a result of efforts made throughout 1942, and despite British objections, the State Department modified its ban and permitted US relief agencies to send $12,000 worth of food parcels per month to specific addresses in Nazi-occupied Europe.[14] With the creation of the WRB in January 1944, the US position regarding the blockade changed dramatically. On the initiative of several Jewish organisations, the Americans privately took unilateral action over relief, thus threatening the British government with considerable public and parliamentary embarrassment. In February 1944, for example, the WRB approved the proposal of the JDC to make $100,000 immediately available to the ICRC for expenditure including the 'purchase in Romania and Hungary of food and other supplies, and appropriate licences were issued to the JDC by the US Treasury. This represented a complete breach of Anglo-American blockade policy, which had always refused the ICRC permission to buy food in enemy territory.[15]

Food parcels schemes

Britain's blockade policy remained firm, despite public agitation and pressure from Allied governments in Britain during the winter of

1941–42. In the spring of 1942 the Famine Relief Committee was established. Its members, including representatives of the Church and academia, called for a project of child relief to certain occupied countries. Although the scheme was modest in scope, the government was not prepared 'to shift the responsibility for providing for those occupied territories from the shoulders of the enemy Powers on to those of the United Nations . . . they believe that there are grave psychological dangers in accepting any commitment in this respect, however small'. However, the main objection was that 'relief could not be limited in the way they suggest. We could not feed children in Belgium and Southern France, and refuse the others.' Naturally, this argument could not be used publicly, as 'we should be accused of refusing to save any children at all, because we could not save the lot'.[16]

Such was the government's position when in February 1942 the Anglo-Jewish organisations first proposed to instigate a food parcels scheme. However, certain concessions were possible. As mentioned, Allied governments were allowed to buy goods in neutral countries within the blockade area, provided that these goods were not of the kind imported through blockade controls by the supplying country. This activity differed from the sending of small parcels from Portugal to individual addresses in various European countries; however, these contained products imported through the blockade control, and the scheme was consequently frowned on by the MEW.[17]

In the summer of 1941, after pressure from Belgians in Britain, the authorities allowed parcels to be sent on their behalf from Lisbon to their families in Belgium. The total amount requested was four tons weight monthly, and the transfer of funds involved a monthly maximum of £3,000. Since Allied and indeed Axis nationals were freely able to make such arrangements (Portuguese firms had conducted a brisk trade in these parcels since early 1941), the British government agreed. Similar facilities were granted to other Allied governments, such as the Free French and Norwegians, and remained the basis of authorised schemes. The government did not consider that these schemes impinged on the question of blockade and relief policy. It was, however, considered important to keep them within carefully controlled limits on account of the relative shortage of escudo currency and the administrative complications.[18] The authorities, aware that the Portuguese had greatly reduced the range of items which might be included in these parcels, hoped that 'the traffic may therefore die a natural death'.[19]

Thus, when the Anglo-Jewish organisations, prompted by Goodman, presented their request in February 1942, a precedent had been set, which relied on Portuguese postal regulations permitting the dispatch to enemy and most occupied territories of small parcels of foodstuffs weighing one pound apiece. Initially the Board held back, on the grounds that 'To ask for food to be given to one section of the Polish population when all are starving', even allowing for the special hardships suffered by the Jews, seemed inadvisable.[20] Goodman therefore applied directly to the Foreign Office, which passed the request to the MEW.[21] Its main difficulty was how to avoid breaching the blockade of enemy-occupied Europe and prevent food parcels being diverted for German use. While it might be practicable to allow a strictly limited number of parcels to be sent, it was impossible to make arrangements with individual organisations and for this reason W.A. Camps approached the Board directly.[22]

Brodetsky called a meeting of representatives of thirteen Jewish organisations on 23 July at which Camps confirmed the Allied governments' blockade policy. However, Camps pointed out that some neutral countries had a surplus of certain classes of foodstuffs which were available to the enemy and Allies equally, and that Allied governments of the occupied countries were permitted to purchase parcels of these surplus foodstuffs for individuals. The Polish government-in-exile in London had been operating such a scheme during the previous ten months.[23] Permission to transfer money from Britain to Portugal for the purpose of sending food parcels to the Jews of Poland received final approval in September 1942. The concession, like those granted to the Allied governments, was restricted to commodities already in surplus in Portugal. The scheme was to be managed by the Board under the auspices and control of the Polish government in London, so that it 'should not appear to be a specifically Jewish one'.[24] Thus, in agreement with the Trading with the Enemy Department, the scheme provided for the transfer of £3,000 per month to Portugal for the purchase and dispatch of 8,000–10,000 one pound packets of food, mainly fish in oil, produced in Portugal. The dispatch of parcels was handled by Dr. Stanislaw Schimitzek, Polish representative in Lisbon, in cooperation with Dr. Joseph Schwartz, JDC representative there, who agreed to act on the Board's behalf. The Board appointed a small committee for the purpose of, *inter alia*, selecting names and addresses of recipients.[25]

In this case, and under conditions of the strictest privacy, the government was prepared to waive its insistence that Jews were not

entitled to separate or preferential treatment. The scheme was conducted under Polish auspices and kept as secret as possible; the
concession fell well within the limits of the blockade policy and
involved neither political compromise nor material sacrifice on the
part of the government.

The scheme was on a small scale and confined strictly to Britain.
The British authorities insisted on the minimum publicity for the
scheme, which would otherwise attract the attention of the Nazis.
Public fund-raising campaigns were thus undesirable and it was 'considered unwise to allow the general public to form an impression
that the Government had extended facilities to any special class of
persons'.[26] The bulk of the £3,000 monthly requirement was to be
raised privately from Anglo-Jewish sources and from allocations by
the organisations. Brodetsky suggested that the CCJR make a grant
to cover the first three months' supplies. Regarding the scheme's
specifically Jewish character, Sir Robert Waley-Cohen remained
worried that there might be resentment at an arrangement favouring
Jews in preference to other starving peoples. Brodetsky, whose view
on the issue was more favourable, responded that the Jews in the
ghettos were receiving only half the supplies allotted to people outside
the ghettos. The Central Council made available the sum of £6,000,
provided by the Jewish Colonisation Association (ICA), for the first
two months' outlay.[27]

Securing names and addresses presented difficulties, since the
scheme could not be made public. It was accepted that some disclosure
must be made to the Jewish organisations to secure this information.
Although the Board took precautions to keep the matter *sub rosa*,
the secret leaked out in September 1942. The Board was now
inundated with enquires from Jewish organisations abroad, hoping
to arrange similar schemes.[28]

By November 1942, only one month's funds had been transmitted,
via Lisbon, and concern mounted as food shortages in Poland were
becoming desperate.[29] The main concern now was whether the parcels
were arriving. The original arrangement was that parcels were to be
sent to individual recipients whose names and addresses had been
collected in Britain. By December 1942, following the news of
dramatic shifts in population as a result of deportations, it became
necessary to modify the scheme. It was decided that all parcels
should be addressed to Jewish organisations in the ghettos, for distribution as they thought fit.[30]

The scheme was viewed throughout as 'an experiment', the continuance of which would depend on whether the parcels reached their destinations, especially in view of reports that the ghettos were being liquidated.[31] The Board was prepared to run it on a trial basis for six months; according to Brotman, 'a substantial proportion of parcels do get to the intended recipients', although he appears to have had no definite evidence of this. The Germans had placed a complete ban on postal communications and the MEW doubted whether more than a few parcels had reached their destinations. By the end of 1942 it was regarding the scheme more dubiously and Leonard Montefiore requested confirmation before handing over the second £3,000. At the same time, Stanczyk assured the Board that 'postal packets of food were, on the whole, being delivered to their recipients'.[32]

In January 1943, Portugal placed an embargo on sending further postal packets to Poland. The ban was eased in February and by April a number of receipt cards had been returned, indicating that shipments had apparently reached their destination. The Board now looked to the JDC to advise whether to continue the scheme.[33] However, lack of acknowledgement was not proof that goods had not arrived. Conversely, acknowledgement of receipt did not necessarily mean that they had. The difficulties of correspondence with Jews in Poland might easily account for the small number of individual receipts returned or for the fact that receipts were signed by the respective *Judenrat* (Jewish Council).[34] It was not yet realised how far the extermination of Polish Jewry had advanced, even after the Warsaw Ghetto uprising in April 1943. In May, Lisbon announced that collective delivery was no longer possible and that parcels could be sent to individual addresses only. Each change of regulation necessitated a new licence, resulting in more delays.[35] Parcels were thus sent alternately to individuals and to organisations.

The uncertainty about the receipt of packages imperilled the future of the scheme. Until July 1943, out of the first shipment of 12,500 packages, some 7,000 were still unaccounted for, even after making allowances for those reported to have been confiscated, returned or receipted. Of the 925 packages acknowledged, 849 were signed by the *Judenrat*. It was unclear whether the addressee or the *Judenrat* had received it first or whether the latter had passed it on. Only 76 personal acknowledgements were received.[36] It is debatable in any event whether these receipts were genuine.

Thus far, the scheme was not considered a success. Nearly all parcels addressed to Jews in the territories of Upper Silesia had been returned to Lisbon marked 'addressee left to an unknown destination'. It became necessary to revise the plan of action. In July 1943 the German postal authorities decreed that from 31 August food packages addressed to Jews residing in the *Gouvernement General* (GG) would no longer be delivered to addressees; such parcels were to be confiscated without compensation to the sender.[37] It was therefore agreed to interrupt the dispatch of parcels to GG territory. As individuals and *Judenrate* outside the GG seemed to be receiving the parcels, it was decided to continue the scheme for their benefit. Parcels were still to be dispatched during September to the incorporated territories, but would go only to addressees who had previously confirmed receipt.[38]

Power to assist Jews in the GG now lay solely with the *Jüdische Unterstützungsstelle für das Gouvernement General* (JUS), the Jewish Aid Centre in Krakow, the only remaining Jewish organisation in Poland authorised to carry on such work.[39] This organisation, headed by Dr. Michael Weichert, received food parcels and, curiously, continued officially operating even after the liquidation of the ghetto was completed in December 1943. Weichert, who remains a controversial figure, was tried and acquitted after the war on charges of collaboration. His writings nevertheless provide an important source of information about the food parcel programme and although much of it is evidently calculated self-justification, some documents and affidavits produced at the trial remain valuable. Weichert was charged with deliberately misleading Jewish organisations abroad by minimising the extent of the extermination of Polish Jewry. At the trial, evidence was produced that after November 1942 the Germans allowed the JUS to function for propaganda reasons and as a useful tool of deception.[40]

Although the Germans allowed the JUS to function, it was able to operate only intermittently as a receiving and distributing agency for supplies from abroad. The importance of these thousands of small parcels was that Weichert, through the help of the *Rada Glowna Opiekuncza*, the Chief Aid Committee, was able to sell the contents, buying flour and medicines with the proceeds, especially important to Jews in hiding after the liquidation of the ghetto.[41] Weichert claimed that a large quantity of goods did reach the camps, some of it smuggled in. In July 1943, he reported that 'Up to date *all* consignments reached their destination *promptly* and in good condition' [my emphasis]. Weichert explained that each shipment was made in response to an order from the camp, ghetto or factory on the basis of a list furnished by him. Yet a few weeks later, Weichert wrote that since the JUS had resumed its activities, it had not received any parcels from Jewish relief agencies and reserves were almost exhausted.[42] He was evidently anxious to demonstrate that he had done an effective job and that any deficiencies were the fault of the relief organisations. Moreover, it was an effective way to secure further supplies.

By September 1943 only £9,000 had been sent to Lisbon and further transfers of money had been discontinued following reports from Poland that the delivery of parcels was worsening. Nevertheless, as an experiment, a trial shipment of 10–20 parcels to the JUS in Krakow was made.[43] In November 1943, Schwartz told Brotman that the JUS was still functioning, albeit sporadically, and that 30–40 packets a month had been sent and receipts obtained. As a result, the JDC began to send between 1,000 and 1,500 packages to Krakow on a trial basis with the intention of sending further and larger consignments, subject to receipts.[44]

In March 1944, the JDC in Lisbon heard that the JUS had received and distributed these trial packets. By 17 April it was reported that 2,097 parcels sent between February and April had reached their destination and the JDC accordingly contemplated sending larger consignments. In May it was agreed that 2,500 packages a week be sent to the JUS. If this success continued, the parcel scheme would require more funds to carry on. In June the CCJR and the ICA allocated £18,000 for the following three months.[45] Yet Weichert's activities were regarded with increasing suspicion. In May 1944, the Bund notified the Board that 'this organisation was started by the Germans for the purposes of deception' and that 'parcels would never reach the Jewish inmates'. The Bund asked that the dispatch of medicines and gifts from abroad to the JUS be stopped.[46]

The Board was deeply disappointed, yet remained reluctant to abandon the scheme.[47] There may perhaps have been some unconscious compulsion to do (and be seen to be doing) something useful, however small in scale. The reports were in any case conflicting. Donald Hurwitz, the JDC representative in Lisbon, reported that the ICRC and other sources had assured him that 'the scheme has been effective' and urged that it should be continued 'at least at its present level'.[48] Brotman and Stephany felt that 'whilst there was undoubtedly a leakage to the Germans of these food parcels', the

benefit of the scheme outweighed this problem. Stanczyk agreed.[49]
In July, however, Weichert went into hiding. In spite of his claim
that 'help from abroad was invaluable for the survival of Jews', it is
impossible to ascertain how many parcels actually arrived.[50] It must
be remembered that Weichert's remarks were intended to justify
his activities and to defend him from the charge of collaboration.
The claim that food parcels from abroad were instrumental in saving
Jews from death is, on the face of it, absurd. But Weichert's comment
is (no doubt intentionally) so vaguely worded as to be effectively
meaningless.

The Board continued to send parcels to Poland well into September 1944, after the publication of the Auschwitz Protocols and despite
reports of the scheme's ineffectiveness. It also attempted to extend
the parcel scheme to cover Terezin and Hungary, but the MEW
prohibited any increase in the £3,000 monthly allowance for trans-
mission to Portugal. Indirectly, however, the failure of the Polish
scheme helped the other parcel schemes, as funds were eventually
diverted to Terezin and Hungary. It is hard, however, to see what
value can have been placed on the continuation of the Polish scheme
at a time when details of the mass extermination of Polish Jewry
were becoming widely known.

At the end of December 1942, Ernest Frischer, a Jewish member
of the Czech State Council, suggested that the Board extend its Polish
parcel scheme to Terezin.[51] It was believed there was more likelihood of the food parcels reaching Terezin. At this point, however,
the Board could not extend the scheme outside Poland. The Czech
government, after repeated efforts, initiated a scheme for sending
food parcels to Terezin and elsewhere where Czechs and especially
Czech Jews were interned. For this purpose the Czechoslovak Relief
Action Committee was formed. In March 1943, Frischer received
Treasury permission for the Czech government in London to transfer
£3,000 a month to the Czech Embassies in Lisbon and Barcelona to
finance a food parcel scheme for Czech nationals interned in occupied
Europe. The Czech government contributed £6,000 to initiate the
project. The remainder was to be raised from non-governmental
contributions. HMG strictly forbade any publicity for the scheme;
hence there could be no public appeals and the utmost discretion
had to be observed.[52]

These resources could cover only the costs of some 16,000–20,000
parcels monthly, so that each of Terezin's 60,000 internees, for
example, would receive only a single one pound parcel once in

three months. Packages were sent to individuals only. Information had been received by the ICRC that 90 per cent of parcels reached their destination, presumably because the Terezin camp had recently been visited by representatives of the Red Cross.[53] It is now well known that Terezin was set up as an elaborate deception designed to appease international opinion, so it seems questionable whether this information was reliable. So successful was the deception, however, that it can only have encouraged further efforts to provide relief in the form of food parcels. Curiously, recent research has suggested that in the twelve months preceding the end of the war, the ICRC and various voluntary organisations acting with the Red Cross, especially the WRB, were able to dispatch food parcels to increasingly large numbers of concentration camp inmates. This development arose largely out of pressure exerted by the recently formed American WRB. However, Allied blockade policy was so deeply entrenched that there was little chance for these possibilities to be fully exploited.[54] It remains impossible to determine how much, if any, of the food aid actually reached its intended beneficiaries.

Meanwhile the immediate problem with the Czech scheme appeared rather to be shortage of funds. Since little use had been made of the Treasury concession for Poland and the funds had not been fully exhausted, some of the money might be utilised for alternative schemes. Frischer asked Brodetsky to secure a Treasury amendment to this effect. The Board complied and at Frischer's request also tried to obtain Treasury permission for part of the monies to be sent to Switzerland instead of Portugal, as the ICRC in Geneva was better placed to send mass supplies of essential food and medicaments to Terezin. This request met with some success, but efforts to secure an increase in the monthly remittance of £3,000, in order to make up for the period in which it had not been fully used in Poland, were rejected.[55]

Camps agreed to consider a proposal for a single transfer of £9,000 to Portugal, in addition to the current monthly £3,000, to bring relief to Jewish inmates in Terezin. Unaware that Birkenau was a mass extermination camp, Frischer tried to obtain British permission to send large-scale consignments there through Switzerland. The Foreign Office advised that the Czech government should apply to the IGCR to take up the Birkenau proposal. The IGCR would, in turn, seek MEW approval for a remittance to be made to Switzerland to buy supplies to send to Birkenau. It was first necessary to try for an agreement in principle.[56]

The Czech parcel scheme cost £36,000 a year. The Czech government had contributed £10,000 and the Czechoslovak Relief Action Committee collected £6,000 from Czech nationals in Britain. Together with a further £1,000 from the United Relief Appeal, a sum of £17,000 was appropriated for 1944. In April, the ICA was approached for £6,000 but there was still a serious shortfall by the middle of 1944. Frischer now urged British Jewry to contribute to the Czech scheme. The Czech government agreed that any Jewish money contributed in connection with its own parcel scheme could be applied to all Jews, regardless of nationality, in Terezin and other camps.[57]

The Board was unable to ascertain what proportion of funds would be needed for Poland. At the end of May 1944, Frischer informed Brodetsky that the Czech government was able to utilise neither the licence granted by the British government nor the additional licence granted by the MEW for one transfer of £9,000 to Lisbon because the money needed had not been made available. Frischer blamed the apathy of British Jewry, which 'undoubtedly is financially strong enough to support the action [but] has so far contributed very little'.[58]

Brodetsky agreed that the Central Council should make an adequate contribution towards the Czech Government's parcel scheme. Explaining that the ICA grant of £2,000 for the dispatch of parcels through the Czech Relief Action Committee was considered insufficient, Brodetsky asked whether the Central Council would make a vote independently of the ICA. The Council agreed to grant £9,000 for the next three months, to be matched by a similar amount from the ICA. Together with the money available to the Czech government, this resulted for the next three months in the provision of food parcels to the full capacity of the licences for transfer of money to Jews 'wherever they were in the position to receive them'. To the Board, this meant 'Poland, Terezin and Hungary'.[59]

However, the position in Hungary was more problematic. Permission was requested for a proportion of the £3,000 transferred monthly to Lisbon for the Polish scheme to be used for the dispatch of food parcels to Hungarian Jews concentrated in the ghettos. However, political and technical difficulties, especially the problem of sending parcels to enemy territory, prevented this. The IGCR was unable to help. Brotman therefore suggested that as Poland was not at war with Hungary, it might be possible for Stanczyk to enlist Polish support for the scheme.[60] There was no objection to this and in August 1944 the MEW agreed with the Polish Ministry that part of the funds could be diverted to Hungary. The amount to be apportioned to Hungary depended on the extent to which it was still practicable to send parcels to Poland. Brotman explained: 'Our desire is that the Jews in Poland should have first claim on the money available for the dispatch of parcels.'[61]

Despatching parcels was now the main problem, especially across France, as the railways were being sabotaged by French partisans and the bridges bombed by the Allied Air Forces. After 26 July all dispatches from Portugal were interrupted because of these difficulties. By the end of September, transport was so dislocated that there was still no way of conveying parcels across Europe. Nevertheless, the Board made frequent enquires to ascertain whether the Hungarian ghettos continued to exist.[62] This was necessary as the situation of the Jews in Hungary had apparently improved, albeit temporarily, after Horthy's order in July to stop the deportations. According to information sent by the JDC, there had until recently been no food shortage in Hungary. As a result of the Horthy Offer, the ICRC was authorised to provide relief for interned or confined Jews. However, reports indicated that the Red Cross was allowed to visit the ghettos in Budapest only and not elsewhere.[63]

At the end of September, it was still unclear whether there were food shortages in Hungary. In mid-October, due to military developments in south-eastern Europe, the food situation in Hungary seemed likely to deteriorate and worse still, the deportations were resumed. There seemed no possibility of sending parcels either to Poland or Hungary and efforts were now made to divert funds to liberated France.[64]

The food parcel scheme was one of the very few cases of the government authorising a specifically Jewish relief effort, even though this operated under the auspices of the Polish and Czech governments-in-exile. Since precedents had already been set with Allied governments, the scheme was allowed to operate. Nevertheless, it was kept well within the parameters of government regulations. No major concession was involved and the voluntary organisations were hardly able to extend the scheme beyond its original, closely defined limits.

The effectiveness of the food parcel relief schemes is impossible to estimate. Reports conflicted as to the extent to which packages were received.[65] No account was taken of the possibility of systematic deception designed to foster the illusion that *some* parcels were being received, in order to encourage the sending of more. After the war, Brotman wrote defensively that 'considerable risks had to be taken and we felt that even if a large percentage of the parcels sent were lost or purloined by the Nazis, it would still be worth while'. He pointed also to transport difficulties in Europe and the limited facilities of the Portuguese postal arrangements, adding: 'We have not given any particular publicity to the scheme ... The Board has never been an organisation to publicise its activities, and its feeling of restraint in this matter has not entirely gone.'[66] The Board's anxiety, both before and during the war, to be seen to be 'doing something' rather belies the modesty of these remarks. It seems as if Brotman is trying here to defend the Board from charges of engaging in perhaps naïve and futile measures which may have succeeded only in supplying the enemy, also suffering food shortages, with provisions. Certainly, the organisations had valid reasons for their cautious optimism about the relative success of the food parcel projects. Their information came from the JDC, an experienced organisation close to events, on whose authority they quite reasonably relied. In administrative terms they made full use of their limited opportunities to bring whatever relief they could to European Jewry.

Jewish Relief Units

Anglo-Jewish relief work for the post-war period was similarly restricted. All efforts had to be integrated with general British relief work. The guiding principle of British policy remained that European Jews were citizens of their countries of origin and should not be accorded distinctive treatment as Jews.[67] The government had become increasingly worried that any implied recognition of Jewish nationality or any acknowledgement of a Jewish claim to special consideration might give credence to Jewish demands over Palestine. During the liberation, British military commanders refused to accept that Jews had urgent particular needs and insisted that they be classified by their former nationality. Brodetsky's recommendation that the War Office give Allied troops in the liberated countries background guidance on Jewish problems was considered unnecessary.[68]

Anticipating a gigantic post-war relief and rehabilitation problem, in September 1941 the United Nations set up an Inter-Allied Committee on Post-War Requirements Bureau. It had no executive function but was to gather information to plan for the requirements covering the first 18 months of the post-war period. This Bureau was

202 Holocaust and Rescue

eventually absorbed into UNRRA, established in November 1943, which became the major international relief body for distressed populations in Allied-liberated territories.[69] In 1942, at the informal suggestion of the Allied Post-War Requirements Bureau, a number of private relief agencies formed a consultative body known as the Council of British Societies for Relief Abroad (COBSRA). The Jewish organisations represented on the Council were the Board and the CRREC.[70]

The Jewish organisations recognised that this vast problem had to be undertaken by governments, but pointed to distinctively Jewish relief and rehabilitation issues; these included Jewish religious needs and the rebuilding of Jewish communal life. More importantly, at the end of the war, 'the surviving Jewish population will be composed of a mass of homeless, uprooted people . . . Problems of identification, of legal or factual residence, and of nationality are due to arise in respect of every Jewish group.'[71] Beyond the immediate common problems of humanitarian relief, the anomalous status of Jewish refugees posed a greater legal difficulty: stateless Jews, formerly residents of Axis countries, would be particularly difficult to resettle. The organisations therefore wanted Jewish participation in the planning and implementation of post-war relief and reconstruction.

Schonfeld's suggestion that Hertz represent Jewish interests through the agency of the British delegation was rejected on the grounds that HMG 'cannot represent non-British interests' in UNRRA or anywhere else. Furthermore, HMG 'cannot undertake to give more favourable treatment to British subjects who are Jews than to British subjects of other religious denominations'.[72] Despite further appeals for Jewish representation made by various Jewish groups, particularly the WJC, the Council of UNRRA was reluctant to accept representation from private organisations, which it was feared would impede its work. The view that prevailed, as stated in November 1943, was that relief and rehabilitation were to be dealt with 'within each affiliated nation' individually, based on 'the relative needs of the population . . . without discrimination because of race, creed or political belief'. However, UNRRA did add that 'every effort will be made to utilise any additional assistance which could be provided by voluntary organisations to deal with special needs'.[73]

Unlike the American JDC, which already had experience in relief and reconstruction (following World War I), Anglo-Jewry had to create an ad hoc organisation. Prior to the establishment of UNRRA, the JFC proposed in the summer of 1942 the establishment of a central Anglo-American Jewish Advisory Body to advise the Allied Control Commission on problems affecting Jews on the Continent.[74] However, Law and others felt the status of individual Allied governments might thereby be compromised. The Board explained that the proposed organisation would be an entirely non-political relief organisation.[75]

Following the decisive Allied successes in North Africa and at Stalingrad (late 1942–early 1943) and the prospect of victory, the voluntary organisations accelerated their preparations. At the end of 1942 the Board formed an Emergency Committee for European Post-War Relief and in January convened a conference. Brodetsky's renewed attempt to secure Jewish participation in general relief work was unsuccessful. Law advised that although the organisations were free to set up these bodies, relief and reconstruction was 'in each country the responsibility of the particular government'.[76]

There was no official objection to the Jewish Committee for Relief Abroad (JCRA), which was established in January 1943. Under the chairmanship of Dr. Redcliffe Salaman, this body was formed to arrange practical relief and rehabilitation only, and was not concerned with political or legal issues such as the future status of Jews, or emigration and resettlement.[77] Its main activity was to recruit, train and equip teams of volunteer workers to care for Jewish survivors of the Holocaust. The JCRA was financed by the CBF, which since 1940 had restricted its work to refugees in Britain, and now, with liberation imminent, extended its activities abroad, changing its name to the Central British Fund for Jewish Relief and Rehabilitation (CBFRR). In August 1943, the JCRA was officially accepted as a member of COBSRA. All voluntary bodies were required to work within the regulations formulated by COBSRA, which in turn worked under the direction of the Relief Department of the Foreign Office, itself largely bound by the requirements of the military authorities.[78]

A number of factors therefore limited efforts for Jewish relief. As a member of COBSRA, the JCRA, though primarily concerned with Jewish relief, was required to take part in general relief work abroad. The Committee reluctantly accepted that its post-war relief plan must constitute a Jewish contribution to the general effort and that recruits must offer their services unconditionally. The JCRA repeatedly stressed to the authorities the special character of Jewish relief, urging that its volunteers could make their best contribution in work for fellow Jews.[79]

This posed problems for some volunteers: 'Much heart-burning was wasted on an attempt to define the aim of the Jewish Relief Units before they had started to relieve.' Abram Games, chairman of the Volunteers Committee, challenged Leonard Cohen's claim that the object of the JCRA was general relief work, arguing that the Committee had been formed specifically to help Jews. Cohen, Vice-Chairman of the JCRA, considered that to take as a first aim the relief of Jewish suffering was 'too narrow' and insufficiently humanitarian. A consensual statement was finally agreed, accepting that the JCRA had been established by British Jews 'To bring help to their brothers whose spiritual and physical needs they are best qualified to understand, and to all in need.'[80]

The government confirmed that Jewish relief units would be welcomed in the liberated territories, 'provided they went as British units similar to those sent out by other Societies and not as part of an international Jewish organisation'. The Jewish Committee accepted this, but queried the conditions governing eligibility to volunteer. In the pre-Armistice period, the government stipulated that only individuals of British nationality could be enlisted, even though refugees from enemy territories could potentially provide valuable service. The latter were expected to join in the relief efforts of their respective governments. The JCRA, anticipating a relaxation of this rule, nevertheless included 'alien' refugees, numbering well over half of its 400 volunteers, in its training schemes.[81] The Foreign Office feared that Jewish officials appointed to both UNRRA and Palestine Jewish units in Cairo would 'turn out to be actively disposed towards Zionism', and therefore 'will have to be got rid of'. Norman Bentwich, an ardent Zionist, was regarded as an unsuitable candidate for UNRRA because of his 'political views'.[82]

Notwithstanding its integrationist policy, the government did accept that some aspects of relief could only be undertaken by Jewish bodies. Help would certainly be needed in providing religious requisites to the Jewish communities of liberated Europe. This was undertaken by Schonfeld and Hertz, who formed a body in late 1942 for Post-War Religious Reconstruction, later incorporated into the JCRA. The amalgamation 'worked smoothly and satisfactorily', the JCRA acknowledging that it obviated the problem of competing appeals, and that the CRREC was well placed to deal with the specifically religious aspects of Jewish relief.[83]

Schonfeld argued that Jews could not be treated merely as nationals of their country of origin, pointing out that they 'have been persecuted

as a religious group no less than a racial entity, and their rehabilitation should take into account the religious factors as well as the
social aspects'.[84] The government disagreed. Sending Jewish ministers with 'diplomatic privileges' to the ghettos was rejected because
'such a concession would provoke demands for similar favours from
Christian bodies which also suffered'. The military authorities refused
to admit the participation of relief units organised by religious de-
nomination, allowing aid only on the basis of the minimum aid
needed to prevent disease and unrest, without distinction of race or
religion. Moreover, the government was concerned that any individual
relief effort might be construed as 'part of some international Jewish
organisation' – that is, a veiled attempt to bolster the Zionist cause.[85]

However, Schonfeld wanted recognition of the fact that a proportion of the surviving Jewish population regarded the strict observance
of Jewish dietary law as an essential tenet of their faith. Anticipating that it would eventually be allowed to transport kosher food,
the CRREC first arranged to collect stores to supplement official
relief arrangements. Schonfeld issued an appeal inviting British Jews
to save a portion of their kosher foodstuffs for the benefit of co-
religionists. The government had agreed in principle that aid by
religious communities to their co-religionists in connection with
relief stocks (in so far as these were obtainable under rationing
restrictions) be allowed, but this was now regarded as excessive.
The Foreign Office was concerned that the activities of British Jews
should not 'upset Allied national Governments', or provoke
resentment by the allocation to Jews of foodstuffs in excess of that
allowed to their non-Jewish compatriots. It was best left for the
CRREC to approach each of the Allied governments.[86]

Further opposition to voluntary stockpiling of kosher foodstuffs
came from the President of the United Synagogue, Sir Robert Waley-
Cohen, who was also adviser to the Ministry of Food on the Jewish
food question. Consequently, the stockpiling of rationed foods was
disallowed as being likely, according to Lord Woolton, the Minister
of Food, to 'have a bad effect on this nation's war effort'.[87] The
scheme was thus put on hold for several months. After lengthy
discussion, the Ministry of Food unofficially reversed its prohibition and agreed to the voluntary stockpiling of unrationed goods
which the CRREC confirmed would be bought for normal house-
hold consumption and not specially purchased for the purpose of
the appeal. It would lie with individual governments whether or
not they included among their relief requirements articles of food

16 Chief Rabbi's Food Packets Appeal Campaign, 1943 (courtesy of Jonathan Schonfeld)

peculiar to any particular religion. In spite of the delay, which deprived it of much of its initial support, the scheme began operating in September 1943, with the cooperation of the Board's Relief Committee. The community responded generously, with about a hundred collection centres receiving some 150,000 packages, which, when circumstances permitted the resumption of supplies to Europe, were sent abroad and to the liberated concentration camps.[88]

The refusal in 1943 to allow the dispatch of kosher food to liberated Europe was eventually reversed when, in 1945, conditions in the liberated areas revealed an unprecedented scale of disease and starvation. The Ministry of Food consented in February 1945 to the dispatch of 20,000 tins of kosher food to France and Belgium for civilian relief. All further dispatches were to be controlled by the Allied authorities and no dispatch of individual food parcels was allowed during the military period.[89] This was doubtless why Schonfeld was able to obtain permission to implement his food relief and mobile synagogue schemes: the magnitude of the human catastrophe was such that in the confusion which reigned during the early stages of liberation, any help was welcomed, particularly if it contributed to controlling epidemics of disease.

Certainly, during the military period, owing to transport difficulties, it was quite impracticable to deliver certain types of food to specified individuals. However, Schonfeld's Mobile Ambulance-Synagogues scheme provided religious and material relief. These mobile ambulances were to be used initially by chaplains on active service for the welfare of Jewish troops. However, Schonfeld made it clear that they were also to provide relief for Jews in the liberated territories, functioning both as synagogues fully equipped with religious requisites including kosher food and as mobile first aid clinics. Schonfeld persuaded the authorities to grant licences for these vehicles, raised the necessary funds from the community and travelled under the protection of officially recognised agencies. Under the auspices of the War Office, special relief teams of around ten social workers, together with a doctor and nurse, consisting entirely of British and Allied nationals, accompanied the mobile synagogues. The first went abroad in November 1944; by 1945 there were thirteen such vehicles, with a projected total of 50. Some 25 ministers volunteered for service abroad and registered with the CRREC. The Council arranged the mission of four civilian ministers of religion to the liberated concentration camps to facilitate the mental rehabilitation of Jewish sufferers.[90]

208

17 Chief Rabbi's Religious Emergency Council mobile synagogue/ambulance with volunteers including 4 chaplains, right to left, Rabbi J. Vilensky, Rabbi Dr. L. Rabinowitz, Rabbi Shlomo Baumgarten, Rabbi Dr. L. Sanker, *circa* 1944 (courtesy of Jonathan Schonfeld)

The authorities had made it clear that organisations able to provide their own transport would be more welcomed abroad than those without.[91] Schonfeld was also able to undertake this work because the government, and more specifically the Treasury, had come to accept that religious reconstruction was a desirable post-war aim not encompassed by official bodies. He emphasised that his chief concern was the religious side of post-war relief, and that Jewish religious issues were not confined to questions of religious worship but impinged on a number of wider areas: 'The Synagogue is the centre of Jewish communal life, and around it are formed welfare and information centres, as well as educational establishments.'[92]

Schonfeld managed to conduct relief activities within the framework of existing regulations, while operating in a somewhat cavalier manner within these parameters. The Mobile Synagogues were able to 'sail' under the protection of officially recognised agencies. Their officers established personal contact with authorities in local command, both military and civilian. 'Schonfeld went to Europe in British military uniform, as an army chaplain ... People were not too sure about his rank, but he acted as if he were Chief of the Imperial General Staff. He gave orders right and left, set up soup kitchens, synagogues and study rooms and commandeered whole transport fleets.'[93] Schonfeld's roving synagogues later provided a focus for communities attempting to regroup themselves.

In the first year of the JCRA, when its principal task was to prepare volunteers for work abroad, expenditure was moderate, mainly confined to training and maintenance; once liberation began, heavy demands were made for supplies of food, clothing, prayer books and ritual articles. Brodetsky observed that 'our work ought to be mainly of a permanent constructive character rather than a continual pouring of relief with no ultimate end'.[94] Most of the relief work depended on Jewish charity. Both Treasury restrictions and lack of funds constrained the efforts of the organisations. Funds as such could not be sent abroad and efforts were restricted to the reconstruction of communal institutions and synagogues and the establishment of children's homes, as distinct from pure short-term relief.[95]

The JCRA had hitherto made no public appeal for funds, and expenditure for administration and training, which had been kept at a very low figure, had been met by a few individual contributions. The CBFRR was one among some 35 voluntary organisations now attempting to launch appeals and to obtain permission to remit funds abroad for the relief of those in distress following the liberation.

18 Solomon Schonfeld, 1944 (courtesy of Jonathan Schonfeld)

Yet COBSRA had ruled that none of the voluntary organisations should as yet make public appeals.

As these funds would be used outside the sterling area, and thus be subject to exchange control, the Treasury had to draw up a formula that would serve as a guideline for their use. Law announced in February 1945 that monies collected in Britain could not be ordinarily transferred abroad and in most cases would have to be spent on the purchase of goods in Britain. This in turn would interfere with the official programme of supplies through UNRRA and other governmental organisations, as well as create transport difficulties. Instead, the organisations were to place their funds at the disposal of the Allied governments or of UNRRA, to be utilised on their behalf. The Treasury would allow remittances for the support of relatives and dependants abroad and for the reconstruction of religious life in Europe. But relief as such was prohibited. This might be hard to justify, as restoration of Jewish religious life was scarcely separable from the physical relief of Jews. However, officials argued that 'we cannot allow remittances unless we receive some "value" in return. The value may be spiritual, cultural or political, but we cannot be satisfied with the mere satisfaction of a charitable impulse.' It was not explained how the distinction was to be defined. Nevertheless, religious reconstruction was encouraged, as being likely to diminish 'the danger of disintegration in Europe'. The emphasis was on 'spiritual, not material goods'.[96] It was by exploiting the vagueness of this semantic quibble that Schonfeld was able to enlist official support for his activities abroad during this period.

In view of the Treasury's stipulations, the CBFRR now had reservations whether to launch the proposed appeal for £1 million. It had made no appeals to the Jewish community after 1940, since when the greater part of its expenditure on refugees in Britain had been borne by annual grants from the Treasury. The launching of the new appeal was postponed until 1945, when the Jewish Agency's United Palestine Appeal was completed and because of the difficulty in obtaining a Treasury ruling on the transfer of funds abroad.

The committee confirmed that it did not propose to use any of the money for 'relief', but that the money was intended for the equipment and maintenance of the two Jewish voluntary teams working under COBSRA, and for the rehabilitation of Jewish communities, in work such as the rebuilding of synagogues and the establishment of children's homes. Despite the exchange difficulties, it was hoped that the Treasury would allow British Jews to make some contribution to the rehabilitation of their co-religionists on the Continent, particularly as this was something which could not be undertaken by UNRRA since it involved discrimination and was not likely to be undertaken by the governments.[97]

While the Foreign Office sympathised, the CBF was advised not to launch its appeal until Treasury regulations had been finalised. Rothschild accordingly advised the CBF to wait. However, Brodetsky and others felt that it was important to have the money available.[98] After long delays in obtaining a ruling regarding the transfer of money, the One Million Pound Appeal for the assistance of Continental Jewry was finally launched. But Anglo-Jewry's response was disappointing. By the end of 1945, the Appeal had produced only half the hoped-for amount.[99]

Several causes contributed to this inadequate response. The diminution of income as a result of heavy wartime taxation and the loss of earnings of men on military service meant that there was less disposable income available for charitable purposes generally. In addition to the material damage inflicted on Jewish institutions in Britain during the air raids, there were the enormous costs of evacuation and the maintenance of widely scattered Jewish communities. This dispersion resulted in an inevitable loosening of the cultural and religious ties which had formerly bound the Jewish community and encouraged Jewish charitable activity.[100] Perhaps a certain degree of compassion fatigue had set in; survivors were less dramatic than imperilled victims. There was also concern that the appeal might relieve the various governments of their responsibilities and that charitable donations were no longer tax-deductible. Competing appeals were a further drain, especially following the Zionist Conference.[101] Zionist fund-raising had increased during the war, and the United Palestine Appeal fixed its goal at one million pounds for both 1944 and 1945.[102] By contrast, on his return from the Continent in June 1945, Leonard Cohen reported that in terms of religious reconstruction, with only 10–20 per cent of Europe's Jewish population left, there was tragically less need and urgency to rebuild all the synagogues which had existed before the war.[103] Frustration at the difficulty in raising funds led to the resignation of Colonel Fred Samuel, senior Treasurer of the CBF since its inception in 1933.[104] The poor response in 1945 was in marked contrast with the pre-war period, when Anglo-Jewry had raised £3 million.

Jewish volunteers were unable to participate in relief work for over a year after the establishment of the JCRA. After many frus-

19 The first team of the Jewish Relief Units, left to right: Irene Joseph, Israel Kramsky, Phyllis Gerson, Hyman Yantian, William Wolff, Amy Gottleib (Zahl) and Charles Spencer (Zarback). These volunteers, photographed outside Endsleigh Place, London, departed for Egypt in February 1944 (courtesy of the Wiener Library)

trating delays, in February 1944 two relief teams went to Cairo, where they awaited transfer to the Balkans and Italy. The delay in sending more workers to the Continent in 1945 was largely due to official 'red tape'. No relief worker could leave Britain during, and for some time after, the war without the consent of the Foreign Office. Furthermore, Treasury permission had to be obtained to transmit money to support them, so that however keen the volunteers were, there were many hurdles to overcome before help could reach those in need, especially in areas where the war was not yet over.[105]

Writing in 1945, Bentwich observed that the enterprise of organising relief and rehabilitation was more complicated than had been foreseen. The JCRA could send teams abroad only under the auspices of UNRRA. The hopes of the big international teams had been frustrated and the Jewish bodies associated with UNRRA shared this frustration. 'UNRRA had to contend with a certain amount of jealousy on the part of the military, which had its own relief organisation.' The military objected to independent activity by what it regarded as sectional bodies and no relief worker could be dispatched unless specifically asked for by the military. The problem lay in persuading some states liberated from Nazi control to accept expert officers and relief teams. 'Some of them looked askance at the outsiders – "relief busybodies" – bringing help.' Leonard Cohen, the first Director of the teams in the field, made frequent journeys to the Continent to negotiate with officials, military and civil, about opportunities for service. Not until April 1945 were Jewish teams able to go to Belgium and Holland. They were held off in Yugoslavia, Bulgaria and Romania and experienced great difficulties in Greece, where civil strife raged. Only in Italy were they able to work with relative freedom. The Jewish teams were 'a very tiny cog in a very big machine'. While the committees working for relief were committed to help all sufferers, without distinction of religion or nationality, there were opportunities to help fellow Jews. For example, Morris Feinman, the first Jewish volunteer to go abroad, went to the UNRRA refugee centre at Casablanca, where he acted as welfare officer for hundreds of Jewish refugees from southern Europe. He died there from ill health in August 1944.[106]

Relief in Eastern and Central Europe depended on Russian cooperation. Brodetsky and members of the JRCA inquired informally whether the Soviet authorities would accept Jewish volunteers in liberated areas of Eastern Europe under their military control. The Soviets were apparently not 'disposed' to do so and the Jewish relief teams were advised to approach them directly, after the September 1944 meeting of the Montreal Conference of UNRRA.[107] However, by the end of 1944, nothing had been arranged. Brodetsky admitted that 'All one could do was to supply the Soviets with materials for relief purposes, and they do the rest'.[108]

The JCRA was eventually able to send several hundred relief workers to the Continent and provide food, clothing (a joint Relief Clothing Committee was formed in December 1944) and other supplies. Even after the German surrender, there were many delays in bringing help and relief to concentration camps and liberated territories. After years of helpless inactivity, the voluntary organisations were now faced with a situation of unprecedented difficulty, for which they had no previous training or practical experience.

The wartime documents relating to the planning of immediate post-war relief and reconstruction show a remarkable ignorance of what was to confront the relief units entering liberated Europe and especially the concentration and extermination camps. The Board's annual report of 1945 admitted: 'The reports on atrocities which had filtered through during the war were recognised as falling far short of the tragic truth revealed when hostilities ceased.' When the Nazis finally collapsed in May 1945, some six million Jews, according to the indictment at Nuremberg, had been murdered, leaving around one million survivors, most of them in utter destitution facing a bleak future in displaced persons camps.

In hindsight, it seems ironic that so much innocent effort was dedicated to the planned 'reconstruction' of Jewish religious and communal life, when it was assumed that Jewish life in Europe could be restored to its pre-war state. Redcliffe Salaman still felt as late as February 1945, that 'our policy must aim at assisting in the reconstruction of living, self-controlled [*sic*] Jewries . . . our task must be to encourage local self-help, examine local schemes of communal development . . . [in order to] set going once again the machinery of a healthy community working under its own power'.[109] Whatever knowledge they may have had of the Final Solution, nothing could prepare the relief teams for the full horrors that they actually found, or for the scale of the unprecedented disaster they were called on to face.

Conclusion: Lack of Will or Lack of Skill?

> The Record of English Jewry ... is again one of effort rather than achievement, of activity rather than accomplishment.[1]

Shortly after the *Anschluss*, chafing with helpless frustration at the growing German menace, Neville Laski observed 'how difficult the situation was for the British Government and [how] much more difficult it must be for the Board which had none of the resources of a government at its disposal.'[2] What was true in 1938 was even more true during the war.[3] Yet critics have repeatedly attacked Anglo-Jewry for 'doing' little to save the doomed Jews of Europe. What, in practice, they mean by 'doing' is not clear. In effect, Anglo-Jewry was able to 'do' nothing but use negotiation and persuasion to convince the government to change its restrictive policy or to take action the leadership itself could not take.

The Anglo-Jewish leadership pressed the government unremittingly to act to save Jewish lives. Two factors rendered their efforts almost wholly futile: their own lack of the necessary diplomatic and negotiating skills and, more importantly, the government's refusal to divert resources from the critical imperative of achieving the speediest possible victory. The most disastrous periods in the European Jewish tragedy coincided with the greatest pressure on the British and Allied governments, so that the persistent importunity of the Jewish organisations occurred at times when it was least likely to meet a positive response. This is particularly evident in the winter of 1942 when the news of the Final Solution was confirmed while the North

216

African military operation was underway and in the summer of 1944 at the time of the Hungarian deportations and the Allied D-Day landings. The distracting pressure from the Anglo-Jewish leadership would have been a nuisance even in peace time. In wartime, Anglo-Jewish efforts were doubly unwelcome – an irritant to government officials bound by *Realpolitik* rather that 'an ethical politics'. The leadership's lack of political expertise was secondary to the near-insurmountable nature of the task.

The record for the pre-war years is markedly different. Owing to the financial guarantee of 1933, Anglo-Jewry had an important and productive role to play in assisting the admission and maintenance of refugees from Central Europe. The unimpressive wartime record has somewhat overshadowed the pre-war achievement. Indeed, the Anglo-Jewish leadership of the 1940s is currently in danger of being turned into a symbolic scapegoat. Instead of acknowledging the obstacles facing it, recent historians have demonised a 'diffident and insecure' leadership, which put its own selfish interests ahead of its moral responsibilities to European Jewry. Such generalisations about a putative group outlook obscure important individual differences. There was no monolithic leadership. While many were confident and secure in their Anglo-Jewish identity, others were more ambivalent. Certainly, there was a deficiency in the calibre of the Anglo-Jewish leadership during the war; it could boast no inspired, imaginative or charismatic figures. The one exception, Chaim Weizmann, operated on the international stage as a representative of the world Zionist movement, and therefore cannot be regarded as an 'Anglo-Jewish' leader in the communal sense. Nevertheless, he still took an active role in initiating approaches to the government in the summer of 1944 with regard to the Joel Brandt deal and the proposed bombing of Auschwitz.

Anthony de Rothschild, Leonard Montefiore, Waley-Cohen, Laski *et al.* were hardly timid or insecure. It might even be argued that the leadership's failings were exacerbated by a misplaced confidence in its status within what can loosely be described as the English establishment – Anthony de Rothschild had been head boy at Harrow, and many Anglo-Jewish leaders of the period were public school educated. A good public school background during this period certainly provided an *entrée* to society and the professions, but was no guaranteed passport to the inner circles of government and politics.

Brodetsky's predecessor as President, Neville Laski, was by training commercial and practical. He possessed the worldly wisdom of a lawyer, while experience, 'tempered by the caution of the law-yer', convinced him that 'a more activist policy' was liable to do more harm than good: 'We do not loom as large in the eyes of governments as in our own eyes.'[4] Laski was more aware than many other Anglo-Jewish leaders that in a crisis the community defined itself, and was perceived as, more 'Jewish' than 'Anglo'. Yet it was precisely because he was so well integrated into the British Estab-lishment that he understood the limits of integration; in his dealings with the government, he knew perfectly well that he wore the hat of the President of the Board of Deputies, not that of Neville Laski, KC. He was strongly aware of the powerlessness of the Anglo-Jewish community. When asked, 'what can we have done to stay the march of events [sic]', he countered, 'we have not the international political influence or the boundless riches which our enemies so sedulously fasten upon us. . . . Be it remembered that the Powers, great and small, have not been able to stay the forces of evil which now have involved the world'.[5] It was essential to handle negotiations with 'our friends' exceptionally carefully. This is not synonymous with kow-towing to the authorities.

Another sign of Laski's good grasp of the position of Anglo-Jewry lies in his low-key policy of non-aggression in the face of British anti-Semitism in the 1930s. The Board's weak and 'supine' response to Mosley and his ilk is a common theme among revisionist histo-rians. But Laski was astute enough to realise that the British psyche is averse to street violence on a grand scale and that British anti-Semitism was most unlikely to lead to Continental-style pogroms. Provocative counter-displays of strength would only, Laski realised, aggravate a situation that could safely be left to simmer, a view confirmed by George Orwell's observation that British anti-Semitism, though ill-natured, 'does not take violent forms (English people are almost invariably gentle and law-abiding)'.[6]

If Laski's judgement of the anti-Semitic threat was shrewd, his perception of the weakness of the community vis-à-vis the govern-ment was equally astute. Indeed it is possible that he played the loyalty card so strongly because he knew it was the only card he held. If some of his suggestions for polite but firm remonstrances to the pre-war German government seem in retrospect naïve, it should be remembered that Laski was no Machiavellian politician, but a lawyer imbued with the British tradition of justice and the rule of law. Gifted with intelligence, worldly wisdom, urbanity and many other virtues necessary to his position as President and to success at the Bar, Laski lacked only the originality that distinguished his brother and daughter. A review of his career, written in 1960, in which he defined himself with a touch of self-deprecation as 'the brother of Harold and the father of Marghanita', reveals a strong but utterly conventional mind, its prose riddled with clichés: 'palace revolution', 'a legend in his own lifetime', 'a tower of strength', 'last but not least', and so on.[7]

Otto Schiff, a stockbroker, was always conscious of the financial imperative of balancing the books. He felt strongly that his reputation, together with that of the community he served, was at stake. He gave everything to the refugee cause, working day and night at the expense of his own stockbroking business and always maintaining the ethos of the City – 'my word is my bond'. He would not betray the trust that the government had vested in him, and consequently he earned the respect of the authorities. He was able to serve the Jewish community with the administrative skills he had acquired over the years, especially through his dealings with Belgian refugees after World War I. His was a thankless task – he bore the brunt of criticism for all the procedural weaknesses of refugee admissions in the pre-war years, both at the time and later. The task itself was both tedious and difficult, requiring excellent administrative skills, which Schiff possessed in abundance.

It was Schiff's personal achievement to secure the entry to Britain of many thousands of people in peril of their lives at the hands of the Gestapo. His reward at the time was ingratitude on the part of the Jewish community; the British government, more generously, awarded him the OBE after World War I in recognition of his work with Belgian refugees, promoting him to CBE in 1939 for his services as chairman of the Jewish Refugees Committee. More significantly, perhaps, he was a man of wide experience. Wealthy and cultured, with a thriving career in the City, he did not seek glory within the community through playing power politics. He gave instead enormous amounts of time to dealing directly with the victims of persecution, beginning as one of a small band of workers at the Jews' Temporary Shelter, and eventually vetting desperate refugees seeking asylum from Hitler. Yet the carping ingratitude of the wartime Jewish community has swollen into a crescendo of vituperation on the part of 'revisionist' historians on the lookout for scapegoats. Because Schiff could not save all, he is damned for the pragmatic criteria he adopted in order to save as many as possible.

His occasional, privately voiced exasperation with the unhelpful behaviour of some of the refugees has been construed, extraordinarily, as evidence of a secret desire to abandon them to their fate. Even more extraordinarily, his excellent relations with the authorities, whose complete trust he enjoyed, has been read as proof of a conspiracy between Schiff and the government to permit the entry of the fewest possible refugees into Britain.[8] Yet without this relationship of trust, it is uncertain whether the numbers saved by Schiff would have been as large as they were. In fact, Schiff voluntarily assumed a role which by its nature was bound to invite vilification whatever he did. His critics have accused him both of selfishly 'allowing in' the minimum number of refugees and of recklessly encouraging the entry of thousands more than he could reasonably hope to subsidise. Yet, while his staff emerged at the end of a long day 'with tempers frayed and nerves on edge, Otto Schiff was still giving interviews, unruffled, patient and just'.[9]

Selig Brodetsky is the central, representative figure among the Anglo-Jewish leaders of the war years. The outline of his life and work is preserved in his out-of-print *Memoirs* (1960), but except among scholars and at the school in Leeds that bears his name, he is now a largely forgotten name. Brodetsky, wartime President of the Board and therefore the most prominent individual leader, took on the presidency solely out of pique that his nomination had been opposed by Laski and Anthony de Rothschild.[10] In Brodetsky's defence, Israel Finestein claims that 'The Board was an unruly assembly in a turbulent period. It was an unaccustomed role for him.'[11] To blame the Board for Brodetsky's failure to control it and to blame this in turn on inexperience is merely to excuse his inadequacies and to emphasise that Brodetsky was not up to the job. Granted that the presidency of the Board was a much more demanding role during wartime, the fact remains that Brodetsky assumed the position voluntarily. This does not in any way detract from his moral integrity and commitment.

Brodetsky held the chair of Applied Mathematics at Leeds University and was well known for his work in the field of aerodynamics. A dedicated Zionist, he was impractical and idealistic, but obliged to deal in the political game of compromise in the midst of a world war. Brodetsky was especially unqualified for his task. The fact that he was a mathematician rather than a politician or strategist had a lot to do with his failure to grasp the shifting realities of the wartime situation. An abstract theoriser, he was said 'to be the only man in Britain who understood Einstein's theory'.[12] This seems somewhat implausible especially in view of the number of German refugee scientists in Britain in this period; in any case, what mattered for Anglo-Jewry was that he did not understand the arts of shift and stratagem. To some extent, his failings were those of an academic who had been thrust into a political role. Weizmann, an organic chemist, was better able to negotiate and compromise where necessary, and, from the government's point of view, was an altogether more experienced and formidable intellect.

Brodetsky's story is worthy but unremarkable; what sets him apart is his hapless involvement in Anglo-Jewry's wartime political effort on behalf of its European brethren. One suspects that despite his lack of political or diplomatic flair, Brodetsky enjoyed his status as spokesman for the Jewish community; a committee man at heart, he seems to have savoured most of all the role of President. However, unlike Schiff, whose talents were administrative and diplomatic, Brodetsky was ideological, and foundered when he tried to pit his wits against those of the trained diplomats of the British Civil Service.

Brodetsky's memoirs suggest that he failed at times to grasp unspoken ironies or innuendoes; he tended to adopt an over-literal approach to the language of diplomacy, rather than decoding it. A revealing example illustrates this: 'Brotman and I saw Law ... and suggested the possibility of an approach to the German Government to allow Jews to leave. Law said that was possible only if the War were stopped for a period.' Brodetsky's account of this exchange reveals that he completely failed to comprehend Law's sarcasm; on the contrary, he proceeded to make an even more foolishly sweeping suggestion, 'that if the Germans let *all* [my emphasis] the Jews go into neighbouring countries it would create a big problem, but it would not be insuperable.'[13] It is only too easy to imagine what Law must have thought of this idea.

Ultimately, Brodetsky was unable to mount and carry through a rigorous argument: his tendency to assertiveness on the one hand, was coupled with a lack of political ruthlessness on the other: 'It was easier for him to give a qualified yes than an outright no. . . . He had neither the ruthlessness of a politician nor any talent or inclination for political in-fighting. He was an idealist and an optimist.'[14] In short, he was poorly equipped to take on the wartime government. It did not help that the Permanent Under-Secretary at the Colonial Office, when questioning de Rothschild about Brodetsky and his new position as president of the Board, added: 'that he thought it had been a very great mistake that a foreigner like this should be appointed to this post.'[15]

As a lay leader of Anglo-Jewry, Brodetsky was called 'weak' by friends as well as opponents. The kindest construction was the democratic one: his readiness to accede to pressure was 'the mark of the democratic politician', a definition which strangely conflates democracy and pusillanimous pliancy. When strong argument was needed to counter the evasions of the Foreign Office, Brodetsky was both powerless and oddly lacking in insight.

Scholars have had little to say about Brodetsky; he is not a figure of recognisable historic proportions, like Weizmann. Nevertheless, there was a tendency among his admirers to draw parallels between the two. Undoubtedly, they came from similar East European Jewish backgrounds, remained devoted to the Zionist cause throughout their lives, achieved academic distinction, and so on. Yet one gradually realises how superficial the similarities really are – with minor modifications of degree, their career paths and interests could be said to serve as a paradigm for the careers of numerous bright Jewish boys of their generation. Much more significant were the differences. Barnet Litvinoff describes Brodetsky's lectures as reflecting his personality: 'ever matter-of-fact, no artifices, no posturings'.[16] Stolid, uncharismatic, dogmatic, Brodetsky was in personal terms the antithesis of the mercurial, pragmatic, subtle ironist Weizmann. Brodetsky was an academic, Weizmann a scientist, the one trained to apply knowledge, the other to acquire it heuristically.

Weizmann possessed a daring and creative intellect, compounded by a personality which was aloof, ironic, detached and charismatic – the very opposite of the earnest, assertive zeal which characterised the rest of the Anglo-Jewish leadership. Where even Brodetsky's most sympathetic critics speak of his lack of charisma, Weizmann 'cast a spell over those who came in touch with him' – he had already won the respect of Balfour, Smuts, Lloyd George and Harold Nicolson as well as Foreign Office officials such as Sir Mark Sykes. With World War II, Weizmann pressed for the formation of a Jewish Brigade in Palestine, not fully achieving his objective until 1944. Equally frustrating were his attempts to gain admission into Palestine for Jews trapped in occupied Europe; no amount of personal authority, charisma or intellectual strength was able to gain his objective, despite the fierce words he addressed to the Foreign and War Offices. Nevertheless, some of his old contacts in high places, which he assiduously cultivated, remained sympathetic. He saved at least one group of refugees, the *Patria* survivors, from deportation and probable extermination in November 1940, by a vigorous personal intervention to Lord Halifax – a sign that Weizmann still retained his moral authority with important British officials, even though he no longer had any useful bargaining position with them.[17]

Weizmann had already established a formidable reputation within the international Zionist movement and also as the chemist whose research into acetone production had contributed importantly to the British war effort during World War I. With the outbreak of World War II, Weizmann immediately offered his scientific services to the British government, despite his bitter disappointment over the 1939 White Paper. He was appointed honorary chemical adviser to the Ministry of Supply, headed by Herbert Morrison, in 1940; he worked on the production of isoprene in view of the rubber crisis and on ketones and their use in high-octane fuels. He travelled to the United States on several occasions during the war for his scientific work and the Zionist cause; on one such occasion, in 1941, he was encouraged by the British authorities to counter some of the anti-British propaganda then being spread in America, where Jewish opinion was particularly bitter over the delay in forming a Jewish Brigade.

It is ironic that, among the general Jewish public, the name of Chaim Weizmann represents one of the few Anglo-Jewish leaders which remains both familiar and respected. The irony lies in the fact that in the narrative of Anglo-Jewish activity during the war, Weizmann is the most shadowy member of the cast, a figure of enormous potential influence who nevertheless never jockeyed for communal supremacy, never engaged in the factionalist bickering that absorbed his Jewish peers so damagingly.

Brodetsky's faithful assistant, Adolf Brotman, 'the civilest of Jewish civil servants', was Secretary of the Board for 32 years, from 1934 until 1966.[18] It was a cruel misfortune that this eminently reasonable, modest man, with his quiet virtues of intelligence, good will and administrative acumen, should have happened to lack the intellectual aggressiveness and guile that *might* have made some impression, however slight, on officialdom. As it was, Foreign Office records show a barely concealed if indulgent contempt for an 'eminently reasonable' man whose reasonableness was – in the circumstances – construed as weakness.

Brotman's background provides the clue to his character. Educated at the City of London School and King's College, London, he was able to graft onto a strongly rooted Jewish identity the manners and attitudes of an educated Englishman. Like many of his contemporaries, he had imbibed the quintessentially English values of decency and fair play, and he seems to have been unable to grasp that a government at war – even a British government – was obliged to play by less sporting rules. A sense of honour and fair play was if anything a handicap to the rather transparent, slightly naïve Brotman. Perhaps also, immersed as he was in Jewish communal affairs, he lacked the wider perspective and the instinct for second-guessing an opponent that would have stood him in better stead with the government than 'quiet sagacity' and 'English' reserve. Held in great respect and (more unusually) affection by his colleagues, he was the right man in the right job – at the wrong time.

Chief Rabbi Hertz's position, more than anyone else's, remained unchanged on the outbreak of war. As the spiritual leader of Anglo-Jewry, whose commitment to Jewish values presented no problem of divided loyalty, he was entitled to press the humanitarian case for refugee rescue and relief for its own sake, and did so vigorously and unstintingly.[19] His wholehearted support for Zionism was matched by a genuine 'loyalty to Britain and . . . belief in British ideals',[20] a loyalty which had signally manifested itself in his defence of the British cause in the Boer War before he came to England as Chief Rabbi. This loyalty was the product of his faith in the British values of tolerance and liberalism, but Hertz was also deeply committed to the preservation of Judaism and Jewish scholarship. He was able to speak out forcefully on behalf of European Jewry without losing the respect of the government.[21] He was an uncompromising representative of the religious cause; it was said of him 'that Dr. Hertz was always prepared to adopt pacific means when all other means had failed!'[22] Despite this, he passionately deprecated anything that savoured of communal disunity.[23]

Hertz's son-in-law, Solomon Schonfeld, was described admiringly by Bentwich as 'indeed Machiavellian . . . I soon realised that I was no match for him and that I could not follow the twists and turns of his agile if erratic mind.'[24] Schonfeld has been described as 'a loner who cut corners and had no patience with official communal bodies. . . . He did it his way – and succeeded remarkably. If you count the descendants of the people he saved, tens of thousands owe him their lives'.[25] An example of Schonfeld's 'unorthodox' methods was his manner of slipping in extra numbers of children onto the transports leaving Vienna in 1938. One child survivor recalls how 'He used to receive permits for only 100 children at a time, but always took an extra thirty. He disguised the number by splitting them into groups in different coaches of the train, and used to tell the children to move from one coach to another when the passports were inspected.... In order not to upset the British authorities, we were left in a transit camp at the Hook of Holland for about two weeks until we could be absorbed into the next batch of children, and we were then replaced by another 30 children, who were awaiting their entry into England.'[26]

While Schonfeld's methods unquestionably displayed a degree of ingenuity not evident in the pedestrian manoeuvres of Anglo-Jewry's leaders – such as his purchase of Stranger's Key, an island in the Bahamas, to provide protective papers for refugees[27] – he was no more able to influence government policy, and succeeded only in devising creative rescue schemes which worked acceptably within governmental parameters. Critics of the 'timid' Anglo-Jewish leadership who point approvingly to Schonfeld's 'peremptory' dealings with the authorities have not studied his methods closely. Schonfeld had a gift for conciliation which, more than any aggression, achieved his ends.

Harry Goodman, political secretary of the Agudah, was venerated within his own community for his 'selfless vigour', 'outstanding statesmanship' and passionate commitment to the orthodox religious cause.[28] His 'barbed retorts and quick-fire oratory', sarcastic humour and rhetorical passion were in refreshingly sharp contrast to the tedious speechifying of his fellow Deputies and typical of a man who sought a position of independence within the communal framework. His energy and zeal were undoubted assets in his wartime work, which included his role as publisher and editor of the *Jewish Weekly* and his weekly broadcasts to Jews in occupied Europe via the BBC on behalf of the Ministry of Information, providing them with encouragement and faith. Yet Goodman was no blind fanatic, but a shrewd and successful businessman with influence beyond his Orthodox constituency. Despite this, he never suffered from an inflated sense of his own importance and achievements; there is a touching honesty about his own admission that 'all we can do is save a few souls'.

By all accounts a colourful and voluble character, with a great sense of humour, Goodman's strengths – his zeal and idealism – were perhaps also his weakness. His judgement, observed his obituarist, 'was sometimes influenced by his strong emotions and unswerving loyalties'.[29] Goodman's passionate devotion to the cause deserved better success. He was, unfortunately, a contentious man

even within his own organisation, who had difficulty in compro-
mising with others on matters of principle. Certainly, he persevered
doggedly in pursuit of Irish visas for Jewish refugees long after many
others would have accepted the futility of persisting in the face of
Irish indifference and intransigence. Yet Goodman's devotion to
the cause, after many others had despaired, offers proof that no
matter how much effort and determination was put into rescue,
there was no guarantee of success. It also refutes the criticism of
those who complain that Anglo-Jewry did not try hard enough to
save European Jewish lives.

The WJC has also been singled out for special commendation on
account of its forthright approach to relief and rescue. Certainly its
stance was more dynamic than that of the Board. The British Section
was served by a team of devoted and talented leaders. Alex Easterman,
a journalist, who gave up his career to become Chief Political
Officer, was trained and skilled in the art of rhetoric. Dr. Noah
Barou 'was a voluble Russian Jew who drove us to get things done.
"Think hard" was his motto.' Sir Sidney Silverman has been described as 'a somewhat naive man but a born fighter, who intuitively
seems to have understood that European Jewry was facing a disaster
unparalleled in history and that one had to react quickly'.[30] Equally
dedicated were Lord Melchett and his sister Lady Reading, who
observed: 'We were a diverse crew, speaking different languages,
but we managed to get on together.'[31] The British Section, however,
'would have been the first to admit that they were not equipped to
cope with events of such enormity which, of course no one could
have foreseen.'[32]

A number of individuals also worked tirelessly for the refugee
cause. Eleanor Rathbone inspired others and kept the momentum
going within Parliament. For Rathbone, the December 1942 Declaration was 'a challenge to redouble her own efforts and to combine
with others so that nothing should be left undone'.[33] Yet, on her
own admission, Rathbone and her colleagues found it impossible to
impress upon the government either the moral necessity or the
logistical possibility of rescue. Critics of the 'feeble' and 'inactive'
Anglo-Jewish effort might do well to ponder the implications of
Rathbone's self-confessed defeat, especially in view of her confron-
tational style, which proved equally ineffective.

Rathbone might seem at first a powerful political ally of the Anglo-
Jewish refugee organisations, but in reality she was a less influential
figure than they may have assumed. For one thing, the mere fact

that she was a woman MP in an overwhelmingly male-dominated House of Commons counted against her in terms of commanding an interest among her fellow MPs. More seriously, she was an Independent MP (for the Combined Universities), rather than an ideologue for any one political philosophy, rejecting matters of political principle in favour of pragmatism and direct action. She therefore lacked the support of a party machine. Holding a constant belief in the primacy of an ethical politics, she aimed always to awaken the conscience of others, in the perhaps naïve belief that, confronted with the evidence of the suffering of persecuted groups, they would endorse the policies she advocated. Such a belief no doubt appeared especially feasible in the atypical environment of the wartime National Government. Rathbone was in fact ahead of her time, both in her feminist construction of political endeavour and her insistence on an international politics which transcended mere economic and military values to embrace a global ethics which only began to be realised towards the end of the twentieth century.

Lack of will?

Anglo-Jewry's wartime leadership has been accused of a variety of sins, including selfishness, insecurity, jealousy, pettiness and pusillanimity. There is an increasing danger, evident in the writings of revisionist historians, of judging the leadership by its putative motives rather than by what it actually did. Brodetsky's 'main concern at that time was to do something to save Jews from the Nazi hell'.[34] There is no reason to believe that this remark, given the time and zeal he threw into the cause, was insincere. The hostile criticism of a supposedly passive and insecure leadership does not stand up to scrutiny in the light of a documentary record of relentless endeavour. Anglo-Jewry's leaders may well have suffered from inflated self-importance; accusations of 'Koved' (honour)-hunting were possibly grounded in truth, but it is hard to accept that these people would have given up so much time and energy simply for an ego-boost at the expense of their careers.

If the leadership was motivated even in part by egotism, it must certainly have suffered miserably. Its repeated attempts to placate an irate Anglo-Jewish community can hardly have nourished its self-esteem. Laski, Brodetsky and Brotman frequently referred to their wish to be seen to be doing something. This was not vanity. In January 1943, for example, Brodetsky and Brotman complained to

Law of 'having great difficulty in holding their co-religionists at bay',[35] phrasing which smacks more of hunted animals than egomania or exhibitionism.

One explanation suggested for world Jewry's failure to do more to help European Jewry was lack of full knowledge of the horrors of the Holocaust. Certainly this can be inferred from some of the statements made both during and immediately after the war. Brodetsky claimed, somewhat defensively: 'We still did not realise the terrible extent of the annihilation of the Jewish populations of Europe . . . till it all came out at the Nuremberg Trials. . . . The world was shocked by the revelation.'[36] This statement could, of course, be taken literally; Jews and non-Jews alike experienced incredulity at the revelations of Auschwitz and other concentration camps. It may be added that the psychological difficulties of comprehending the unprecedented nature of the Final Solution were exacerbated by the fact that the truth was commingled with a vast amount of rumour, speculation and misinformation. Nazi deception was very effective and in circumstances which made it almost impossible to sift truth from falsehood, scepticism and incredulity were perhaps the inevitable responses of the Anglo-Jewish leadership to the 'information' emanating from Europe.

Lack of skill?

Evaluating the abilities of the Anglo-Jewish leadership is a more objective exercise and involves consideration of two kinds of skill – administrative and political. On an administrative level, following years of philanthropic activity, the Anglo-Jewish organisations drew on their considerable expertise and helped to rescue some 60,000 Jewish refugees before the war, guaranteeing their maintenance and re-emigration. While some of the criticism levelled against them was valid, on balance they did a remarkable job. They raised £3 million (approximately £90 million at today's value[37]), an impressive sum for so small a community, especially at a time of economic depression.

Even for wartime, a good record of administration remains. Internment provides an unusually clear-cut example by which the efforts of the organisations can be evaluated. It was in facilitating humane treatment and conditions for internees that they were most effective. The extent to which the organisations were able to ameliorate conditions for Jews in occupied Europe was necessarily far more limited. Food parcel schemes represented a desperate attempt to do something, notwithstanding their poor probability of success.

One major indictment, however, remains to this day, namely that so many children were lost to the Jewish community by being placed, when they arrived in 1938–39 and during the evacuation period, in non-Jewish foster homes where they were brought up in the faith of their guardians. One critic maintains that 'The Jewish institutions withdrew those children whose relocation presented no particular problem, but did not hurry to exert pressure on those Christian families with whom the children had fully settled in. . . . There was likewise a disinclination to institute legal proceedings for fear of an anti-Semitic backlash.'[38] This was an enormously complex issue, involving many conflicting considerations, which do not necessarily lend themselves to similar conclusions in each individual case. It also raises difficult questions about whether the preservation of a child's religious or Jewish identity was or should have been intrinsic to Jewish rescue and relief. These issues must additionally be set alongside the mounting evidence of appalling physical, sexual and psychological abuse suffered by British child evacuees and no doubt Jewish ones as well.

Politically, the Anglo-Jewish leadership was exceptionally weak during the war. In terms of diplomacy, evaluation of the community's efforts and skills depends largely on the extent to which it was possible to manipulate the levers of power in Britain to effect rescue and relief. Anglo-Jewry was never able to override bureaucratic red tape and intransigence, as demonstrated by its failures in relation to Palestine and British immigration, shipping and relaxation of the blockade rules.

The Anglo-Jewish leadership saw only two extremes – the 'policy of activism' (pressure politics) and conciliation or acquiescence. Communal leaders were unable to channel their desperation in a productive way which might have led to shifts in attitude. Law's note on a 16 December 1942 meeting is revealing: 'the deputation expressed great appreciation of my alleged sympathetic attitude . . . I was very much impressed by their anger against the Home Secretary. . . . It has always seemed to me that the apprehensions of the Home Office have been exaggerated and that it would be very difficult for us to go on confining ourselves to denunciation of the German action while refusing to take any alleviating action ourselves. I did not give the deputation any idea that this was my view.'[39] The Jewish leadership was evidently showing all its cards while Law showed none of his. He read their minds with ease; the leadership, by contrast, assumed he meant exactly what he said. The concept of a 'hidden agenda' does not seem to have struck the stolidly literal-minded deputation. More importantly still, Law's comments suggest that he would have been receptive to persuasive argument. The battle was not necessarily over before it had begun.

Yet the negotiating style of the Anglo-Jewish leadership ensured that in practice it was. Close analysis of a typical document reveals how far the leadership was out of its depth. This document, the record of a meeting between Brodetsky, Brotman and Law in January 1943, betrays a subtext of irritation and contempt beneath an apparently objective surface. Law noted:

'They then attacked me on the general question . . . I spoke to them very strongly. . . . They said that of course the war must come first, but they kept harping back to mass movements running into tens of thousands, which showed clearly enough that they were not really impressed by the difficulties. I repeated that it was an international problem.'[40]

Instead of deploying the fine art of driving a diplomatic bargain, the parties are engaged in a polite war of words ('attacked . . . very strongly'). Whereas bargaining involves a process of adjustment and compromise satisfactory to both parties, Brodetsky and Brotman came in with unrealistically inflated demands for 'mass movements running into tens of thousands', rather than starting low and only gradually raising the stakes. Most damaging of all, there is no negotiation going on, but only repetition of two intractable and incompatible positions, with Brodetsky and Brotman 'harping back' instead of moving on, and Law simply repeating 'that it was an international problem'. Walker's comments on the meeting are equally revealing. 'No reference should be made to the 200,000 lei a head proposal', he writes, concerned that the Foreign Office should show as few of its cards as possible, 'but [Brotman] might be induced to show his hand by asking what he suggests to get the Jews out of Roumania', a comment which attributes more guile to Brotman than was fair. Randall's concluding remark, that the Board proposals amounted to a demand 'to so divert our resources that we might lose the war!', may or may not have been true, but the exclamation mark suggests that he certainly thought it was (the demand can hardly have done Anglo-Jewry's reputation for loyalty much good either). His note ends: 'The Home Office was in favour of putting this point-blank to the enthusiasts with their quite unrealistic proposals.' If anything, bureaucratic indifference and bureaucratic patience were beginning to wear thin as official politeness began to give way (in private) to acid but etymologically precise references to 'enthusiasts' and 'unrealistic proposals'.[41]

It was an unequal contest in which the Board was consistently outwitted. Home and Foreign Office officials were selected and trained, via the Civil Service examinations and years of experience, to handle such negotiations with superlative finesse and adroitness. The Anglo-Jewish leadership lacked both political acumen and training. But it believed it could take on the government on equal terms because its leaders were used to 'playing' Board politics. They knew the language of diplomacy, but could not play the game. For example, in a discussion with Randall in January 1944, Brodetsky failed to capitalise on the government's insistence that European Jews were the responsibility of their home states. On this occasion Brodetsky lost the opportunity to persuade Randall that neutral states should be encouraged to admit refugees on the basis that they would be repatriated to their countries of origin after the war. Instead of using the government's own reasoning to show that such refugees were the responsibility of their home governments and could, if necessary, be deported to their native states, Brodetsky frustrated his own ends by a clumsy, if idealistic, insistence that the refugees would not want to return to their home countries.[42] This was possibly true, and the refugees would no doubt have proved ideal candidates for the Zionist state Brodetsky dreamt of, but it was hardly tactical to press a point whose political and financial implications were so uncongenial to the British government.

Like many of his colleagues, Brodetsky never seemed able to gauge exactly the balance needed between pressing too hard for an unrealistic object and treading too carefully to make any impression at all. Similarly, Anglo-Jewish leaders were unable to challenge specious governmental arguments, stalling tactics such as buck-passing and asserting that reports were 'unconfirmed' or that cooperation with Washington was necessary. Anglo-Jewish leaders tended to repeat their ideas without developing them, in the hope that repetition might do what persuasion could not. The contest and the issues were intellectual rather than ethical; the skills required were argumentative rather than rhetorical. The problem lay not with a 'timid' community but with leaders who were no match for their opponents at the Home, Foreign and Colonial Offices. It was not a matter of persuading the Foreign Office of a humanitarian imperative, as the Board assumed, but of convincing it that action on behalf of Jews was politically expedient (for example, it would deflect American criticism of Britain's Palestine policy). This was clearly a supremely difficult, if not impossible, task, but one that was never properly understood.

Anglo-Jewish leaders were, furthermore, negotiating from a position of weakness. Lack of power and influence led, understandably, to demoralisation, while the argument, continually cited by the authorities, that real rescue could come only with an Allied victory was attractively, if superficially, persuasive and reassuring.[43] However, negotiating from a position of weakness does not invariably entail defeat. In the autumn of 1939, facing financial collapse, the Anglo-Jewish organisations (together with the Quakers and Christian Council for Refugees) told the government that they would have to close their offices and warned that refugees would be thrown onto the National Assistance Board. This moved the government to make an unprecedented huge financial commitment, the first grant-in-aid given but not administered by a government in wartime.[44] While on this occasion financial support was won, the price was a weakening of the organisations' negotiating powers for the future.[45]

The most productive situation occurs when both sides have something to offer. This had been the case during the 1917 negotiations leading to the Balfour Declaration, when the prospect of consolidating its authority over the Suez region was held out to the British government in return for its support for a Zionist state in Palestine. Schonfeld's skill in capitalising on governmental objectives for his own advantage is, on a much smaller scale, somewhat reminiscent of Zionist diplomacy during World War I, which brilliantly exploited British war aims in the Middle East to show how a Zionist homeland in the form of a British protectorate would fend off German and French ambitions in the area and safeguard Britain's vital control over the Suez Canal.[46]

Among the reasons for British support of Zionism was a rather exaggerated belief in the effect that this would have on Jewish opinion in Russia and America at a time when the attitude of both powers was considered of vital importance in deciding the outcome of the war. Britain feared that a disaffected Russian Jewry was pressing for Russian withdrawal for the war. Weizmann, a Russian Jew, was able to provide reassurances that Russian Jews would be more committed to the Entente should Britain make a gesture in favour of Zionism. From Britain's perspective, Russian withdrawal would be disastrous, opening up the grain reserves of the Ukraine to German exploitation, and with it the indefinite prolongation of the war. Threats as well as bargains were deployed: a strong incentive to British support of Zionism was the fact that Germany was wooing its own Zionists with a view to taking control of Palestine. The spectre of a Russian-German peace pact could also not be ignored. Equally, the final outcome of the war could well depend on American financial support. Such support might be more easily won if American Jewish opinion were swayed by a British declaration in favour of Zionism. It was these considerations, rather than Lloyd George's romantic enthusiasm for Zionist aspirations, that finally resulted in the Balfour Declaration.[47]

However, such mutualism was not in question during the Second World War. The Anglo-Jewish community had no bargaining chips. What the Jews had to offer, the government already had. Years of Jewish professions of loyalty culminated in proclamations of support for the war effort. At the outbreak of war, Weizmann wrote to Chamberlain, on behalf of the Jewish Agency, offering the government 'all the Jewish manpower, technical ability and resources at our command', adding that the Jews 'stand by Great Britain and will fight on the side of the democracies'.[48] From the government's point of view, this was a truism, like declaring that British Jews would pay their taxes along with everyone else. Not only were Jews subject to British law, but it would have been extraordinarily self-defeating for British Jews *not* to support the effort to defeat Nazi Germany.

The Anglo-Jewish leadership had only a poor grasp of the dynamics of negotiation. Instead of seeing discussion with government officials as an exercise in diplomatic 'trade-offs', the Board (in particular) tended to make appeals and requests based on absolute ethical imperatives – as if it were dealing with bishops rather than civil servants. The language and values of humanitarianism in which it dealt represented a near-valueless currency from the governmental point of view.

Thus it was unable to grapple with the government's oft-repeated contention that rescue efforts imperilled the war effort and delayed victory. In presenting the issue in simplistic zero-sum terms, the government was able to exploit the fallacy of the excluded middle; its inference, that any action, great or small, was equally capable of delaying victory, was patently untenable, especially after the autumn of 1944, when victory had become a near-certainty. But the organisations, accustomed to think in all-or-nothing moral imperatives, were in-capable of addressing this fallacy and making a case for some form of rescue effort, however modest.[49]

It should be stressed that the inter-war and wartime governments made no secret of their conviction that refugees were an immigration problem rather than a humanitarian disaster. Only in the post-war period has the concept of 'human rights' evolved, since when pressure has increasingly been put on governments to come to the aid of persecuted minorities or disaster victims world-wide.[50] The humanitarian argument, however well pleaded, could hardly have been expected to have any significant influence on the wartime government.

In inventing options for mutual gains or dovetailing differing interests, Schonfeld had the edge over Brodetsky, as exemplified by the Mauritius scheme, which served a governmental purpose in deflecting criticism of British treatment of illegal Jewish immigrants from Palestine held in Mauritius. Schonfeld was skilful at capitalis-ing on chance opportunities and knew that harping on Palestine would subvert his immediate short-term aim of saving lives. The Mauritius scheme also succeeded because Schonfeld started with a modest request, listing only 30 names, gradually increasing the numbers to 100, until finally there were over 1,000.[51] It is unlikely that an initial list of 1,000 names would have been approved. By contrast, Brodetsky thought in all-or-nothing terms, as shown by his impractical suggestion that the whole Jewish population of occupied Europe could be transferred to neutral countries;[52] unfor-tunately, perhaps, Brodetsky's wishful thinking stopped short of an offer to foot the bill.

Both before and during the war, Jews were regarded as the re-sponsibility of their home states, of which they were legally citizens, even though German Jews had been disenfranchised by the 1935 Nuremberg Laws.[53] For reasons of principle as well as of policy, the government was reluctant to recognise a Jewish national identity. This would reinforce German propaganda about the Allies being engaged in a 'Jewish war', complicate Britain's Palestine policy and create problems of repatriation after the war.[54] The result was a specious inference that to discriminate in favour of persecuted Jews was to discriminate against their persecuted compatriots. The prin-ciple was always cited to justify inaction on behalf of Jews by a form of *reductio ad absurdum* which rendered all humanitarian relief and rescue discriminatory. On the one hand, the government argued,

Jews were citizens of their home states and thus the responsibility of their home governments. On the other hand, it was claimed that Jews could not be given priority *because they were Jews* over their fellow Poles, Czechs, etc. Either argument, in any case, was tenable only if the Nazi policy of a Final Solution of the *Jewish* problem in Europe were ignored. That the government chose to do so is not surprising. The Anglo-Jewish leadership was certainly aware that *Sonderbehandlung* required *Sonderpolitik*, but failed to argue and develop this point convincingly.

This was perhaps because the principle that Jews did not constitute a discrete national entity but were nationals of their home states was ingrained in Anglo-Jewish thinking. It had, indeed, formed the principal ground of opposition to Zionism on the part of the Anglo-Jewish 'aristocracy' during the first two decades of the century. Not only was it government policy but it was in Anglo-Jewry's interest that it should be. The last thing it sought was discrimination. The Anglo-Jewish establishment had so enthusiastically imbibed this principle and become so deeply 'anglicised', that it had perhaps become incapable of refuting the governmental sophisms it generated. It would certainly have been difficult to claim that British Jews were British citizens of the Jewish faith while maintaining simultaneously that continental Jews were in any radical sense different from their own compatriots. Certainly the 'minorities treaties' imposed on a number of East European states after World War I did involve some recognition of a Jewish collectivity. Nevertheless, if European Jews comprised ethnic minorities within larger states, as was claimed by the Anglo-Jewish organisations, Anglo-Jewry would necessarily have to acknowledge itself an ethnic minority – hence not 'really' British – an inference it was anxious to avoid.[55]

The official documents of the period give the distinct impression that government officials were irritated by repeated requests on behalf of European Jewry. This view is endorsed by Rathbone's complaint about Morrison during the 19 May 1943 Debate: 'why does he always make us feel . . . as if the whole question of refugees was becoming a bore and an irritation to him and that he was transferring to refugees the dislike which he openly feels for ourselves?'[56]

Foreign Office impatience was perhaps compounded by the frequent naïveté, vagueness and impracticality of the Anglo-Jewish leaders. Following the December 1942 Declaration, Brodetsky recalls suggesting that 'the German Government should be told, through some appropriate channel, that Jews, especially women and children, should be allowed to leave all countries under German control', as though Hitler were likely to be scolded into capitulation. It had been known from the earliest stages of the war that the Germans were treating civilian populations with the utmost brutality and that they had no respect for the Geneva Convention, although until 1941 the Nazis were prepared to allow the Jews to leave occupied Europe. Also, given the Nazi objective of exterminating the Jewish race, children – the future generation – would no doubt have been the last group whose departure would have been endorsed.

The poor quality of some proposals was compounded by the manner of their presentation. Especially amateurish was the way in which ideas about exchange possibilities were presented. Proposals to use limited exchange opportunities to save foreign nationals (Jewish or otherwise) rather than British servicemen and civilians in German hands were vague and naïve. Attempts to grapple with the problem included the suggestion that refugees be accorded the status of British-protected persons. Apart from the unlikelihood that this would impress the Nazis, there was still no reason for the British authorities to give precedence to purported British-protected persons at the expense of real ones.

Neither were shipping proposals well presented. Vagueness did not help; it was much easier to reject in principle a request for 'shipping' than to explain why a thoroughly detailed, properly costed, specific single shipping scheme (what would now be called a feasibility study) imperilled the outcome of the war. The organisations failed to realise that 'selling' a proposition to the government was not helped by leaving the government to do all the preliminary planning itself. Some suggestions were in themselves sound. Rathbone and others pointed to the fact that British vessels returning half-empty from Greece and elsewhere might be used for the carriage of refugees, citing as a precedent a report 'that the U.S.A. was considering importing by this means a quarter of a million Italian labourers for agricultural work'.[57] Yet ideas were not followed through and important points of detail, such as the dangers of sailing without a guarantee of safe-conduct from the German government, were not addressed, leaving it open to the government to use such details to block the idea as a whole.

In any case, the argument against releasing ships was, in principle, well founded. The organisations did not have the detailed knowledge to counter it in practice and the argument itself could not be refuted since it was based on the unverifiable premise that any diversion of resources, however small, was a threat in principle to the swiftest possible victory. Yet the case for shipping was not necessarily hopeless. After Bermuda, Law himself wrote: 'If neutral shipping is unobtainable, is it really beyond the bounds of possibility that we should find *one* ship?'[58] The implication here is that the Foreign Office might have been prepared to make a concession in favour of a single, small-scale plan. It was not, however, Law's job to make the necessary inquiries and the Anglo-Jewish leaders did not seem to think it was theirs.

Attempts to bring pressure to bear on the government by force of public opinion were unsuccessful. There was apparently wide public sympathy – a March 1943 Gallup poll indicated 75 per cent support in favour of Britain helping Jews and Victor Gollancz's pamphlet 'Let My People Go' elicited much public support and offers of help. However, this did not amount to a serious force which could have affected the formation or conduct of policy.[59] Governments are, moreover, more authoritarian during wartime and the National (coalition) Government had no electoral reason to pander to public feeling.

Requests for declarations and warnings were occasionally granted. The December 1942 Declaration, for example, was undoubtedly the result of energetic pressure from Jewish groups. Just how influential these warnings were is another matter. They had little or no effect on the Nazi leadership, but may have acted as a partial deterrent to the satellites and their populations.[60] While the Germans were patently unimpressed, Jewish leaders were convinced that 'many satellites listened; [and] many non-Jews were strengthened in their resolve to assist their hunted fellow men'.[61] The propaganda value of declarations and warnings, like that of radio broadcasts to occupied Europe, was more highly rated by the Jewish organisations than by the government, whose genuine scepticism was compounded by reluctance to lose diplomatic credibility by 'debasing the currency'. But however limited their effectiveness, there can be no doubt that it would have been less still had it not been for the persistent efforts of the organisations.

There is now a tendency to assume that any effort, however far-fetched, was justified by the desperate plight of European Jewry. Some, however, were patently not worth making. The government was right in suspecting that declarations made no difference to the Nazis and considered that they might do harm. It was not simply trying to fob off the organisations, and although a theoretical case might be made for issuing declarations, it was at an early stage evident that repeated threats of retribution were almost completely pointless. The government no doubt also objected to declarations as merely raising unrealistic expectations. Anglo-Jewry was clearly desperate to do something (contrary to what its critics maintain) but was almost always foiled, often because of governmental intransigence but also, at times, because of genuine governmental conviction that the effort itself was futile. This point has been validated more recently when in 1994, an international criminal tribunal was established at the Hague to try war criminals from Rwanda and the former Yugoslavia. This tribunal's existence did not deter continuing atrocities.

The Jewish organisations did not fail for lack of trying; in the final analysis their cause was incompatible with Britain's perceived overall goal. The government saw the Jewish problem as a side-issue of the war. Nazi Germany did not see it thus and nor did the Jews. It has been pointed out that 'None of the pronouncements emanating from the wartime summit meetings made reference to Hitler's war on the Jews; Teheran (November 1943), Yalta (February 1945) and later on Potsdam (July 1945) are eloquent testimony to the low priority enjoyed by the Jewish tragedy'.[62] The refugee problem was consistently slighted by British officials, who were understandably incapable of believing that Hitler 'would devote such a large part of the German war effort to exterminating the Jewish race throughout the whole of Europe'.[63] What was a matter of life-and-death to the organisations hardly features in the memoirs of, for example, Anthony Eden, Herbert Morrison or Frank Roberts.[64]

Opinions about Churchill's role in the fate of European Jewry vary widely. Certainly he seems to have been motivated and concerned to make public statements on its behalf, as he did on numerous occasions. In private too, Churchill was vigorous in his view of the Holocaust, writing to Eden in July 1944: 'There is no doubt that this is probably the greatest and most horrible single crime ever committed in the whole history of the world.'[65] However, Michael Cohen, while conceding that Churchill's 'deepest emotions' were stirred by Nazi persecution of the Jews, argues that he was 'not entirely free of anti-Jewish prejudice'. He maintains that 'humanitarian sentiment... was rarely if ever translated into concrete assistance'.[66] Opinions vary also about the level of anti-Semitism in official circles. Some historians regard anti-Semitism as playing a major role in government decision-making. Bauer contends that 'on the basis of the British documents . . . a good deal of antisemitism, quite openly expressed in internal discussions, entered into the British stand'.[67] Certainly, there was anti-Semitism in the Foreign Office, as evidenced by the openly derogatory comments of individual officials. Certainly also, the rescue of European Jewry was not an Allied war aim. But this is not incontrovertible proof that British wartime policy was actively anti-Semitic. Some officials, such as Paul Mason and Lady Cheetham, expressed private anxiety and were more sympathetic to the Jewish cause.[68] There is no evidence to contradict Wasserstein's contention that 'conscious anti-Semitism should not be regarded as an adequate explanation of official behaviour'.[69] British indifference to the Jewish catastrophe was grounded in the perceptions that the rescue of European Jews posed immigration problems in Britain and Palestine, that anti-Semitism in Britain would be exacerbated by unregulated Jewish immigration and that precious resources could not be diverted from the war effort in order to achieve what was in any case a dangerous and near-hopeless task. It is interesting that neither publicly nor privately did any of the Anglo-Jewish leaders complain of anti-Semitism, whether at the political or the personal level.[70]

The Anglo-Jewish leadership was far from indifferent to the tragedy of European Jewry, but was impotent to act directly. Most of its wartime efforts proved abortive, whether they were the product of polite negotiation, guile or 'activism'. The poor reputation of Anglo-Jewry's wartime leadership is the natural concomitant of its intrinsic inadequacy, but to view this in isolation is to perpetuate a great injustice against a community which lacked nothing in tireless effort or zeal. The only lack of will was on the part of a government inevitably indifferent to the fate of a foreign ethnic minority at a time of national emergency.

Notes

Introduction

1 Arthur D. Morse, *While Six Million Died: A Chronicle of American Apathy* (New York, 1967). See Bibliography for works by Richard Breitman and Alan K. Kraut, Henry Feingold, Saul Friedman, Monty Penkower and David Wyman.

2 Michael Dov Weissmandel, *Min Hameytzar* ('From the Depth of Despair') (Jerusalem, 1960), cited in Abraham Fuchs, *The Unheeded Cry* (New York, 1984), pp. 105–6.

3 Henry L. Feingold, *The Politics of Rescue: The Roosevelt Government and the Holocaust* (New York, 1980). In this edition, Feingold adds an appeal for a more temperate criticism of American Jewry. He maintains that one cannot assign responsibility to a group which has no power.

4 See bibliography for works by Seymour Maxwell Finger (ed.), Saul Friedman, Haskel Lookstein, David Kranzler, Raphael Medoff, Monty Penkower and David S. Wyman.

5 Norman Bentwich, *They Found Refuge, An Account of British Jewry's Work for the Victims of Nazi Oppression* (London, 1956); Bernard Krikler, 'Anglo-Jewish Attitudes to the Rise of Nazism' (unpublished, probably 1960s). For the most recent work on the CBF, see Amy Gottlieb, *Men of Vision, Anglo-Jewry's Aid to the Victims of the Nazi Regime 1933–1945* (London, 1998).

6 A.J. Sherman, *Island Refuge, Britain and Refugees from the Third Reich 1933–1939* (London, 1973, 1994), pp. 264, 267, 269–72. Over 50,000 Jewish refugees from the expanded Reich were admitted to Britain between 1933 and 1939, although Sherman notes that statistics on refugee migration for this period are unreliable. See also Herbert A. Strauss, 'Jewish Emigration from Germany: Nazi Policies and Jewish Responses' (1), *Leo Baeck Institute Year Book* (1980), XXV, Table X, pp. 354–5.

7 Sherman, *Island Refuge*, pp. 175–6.

8 Bernard Wasserstein, *Britain and the Jews of Europe* (Oxford, 1979), p. 351.

9 Bernard Wasserstein, 'Patterns of Jewish Leadership in Great Britain during the Nazi Era', *Jewish Leadership during the Nazi Era*, ed. Randolph L. Braham (New York, 1985), p. 34.

10 Ibid., pp. 29–45, esp. p. 34. B. Wasserstein, 'The Myth of "Jewish Silence"', *Midstream*, vol. 26 (1980), no. 7, pp. 11–12. See also Martin Gilbert, *Auschwitz and the Allies* (London, 1981), p. 341. Gilbert deals mainly with government policy: 'The failures, shared by all the Allies, were those of imagination, of response, of Intelligence . . . of initiative and even at times of sympathy.' He mentions the Jewish Agency and occasionally refers to the Board of Deputies.

11 William D. Rubinstein, *A History of the Jews in the English-Speaking World: Great Britain* (London, 1996), p. 33.
12 For example, see Eugene C. Black, *The Social Politics of Anglo-Jewry 1880–1920* (Oxford, 1988); David Cesarani, 'An Embattled Minority: The Jews in Britain during the First World War', in T. Kushner and K. Lunn, eds., *Politics of Marginality: Race, the Radical Right and Minorities in Twentieth Century Britain* (London, 1990), pp. 61–81.
13 Tony Kushner, *The Persistence of Prejudice: Antisemitism in British Society during the Second World War* (Manchester, 1989), pp. 179–80; Tony Kushner, 'The Impact of British Anti-Semitism', David Cesarini, ed., *The Making of Modern Anglo-Jewry* (MMAJ) (Oxford, 1990), pp. 191–208.
14 Conversation with Tony Kushner, September 1992.
15 Tony Kushner, *The Holocaust and the Liberal Imagination: A Social and Cultural History* (Oxford, 1994).
16 Louise London, 'Jewish Refugees, Anglo-Jewry and British Government Policy, 1930–1940', *MMAJ*, pp. 163–90, esp. 189; Louise London, 'British Immigration Control Procedures and Jewish Refugees 1933–1939', *Second Chance: Two Centuries of German-Speaking Jews in the United Kingdom*, ed., W.E. Mosse (Tubingen, 1991), pp. 515–16. See Louise London, *Whitehall and the Jews 1933–1948: British Immigration Policy and the Holocaust* (Cambridge University Press, 2000).
17 Richard Bolchover, *British Jewry and the Holocaust* (Cambridge, 1993), p. 156.
18 Geoffrey Alderman, *Modern British Jewry* (Oxford, 1992), pp. 295–6, 302.
19 Ibid., pp. 303–5; Bolchover, *British Jewry and the Holocaust*, pp. 146–55. See also Meier Sompolinsky, *Britain and the Holocaust: The Failure of Anglo-Jewish Leadership?* (Brighton, 1999).
20 Wasserstein, 'Myth of Jewish Silence'.
21 David Kranzler and Gertrude Hirschler, eds., *Solomon Schonfeld, His Page in History* (New York, 1982), p. 80. Joseph Elias maintains: 'We can only wonder . . . what could have been accomplished during the war if the Jewish world at large had displayed the same determination.'
22 Ibid. At present, this is the only published work on Schonfeld, a non-scholarly volume commemorating his seventieth birthday. It is a collection of personal reminiscences, both by those who participated in his work and those whom he saved. V.D. Lipman, *A History of the Jews in Britain since 1858* (Leicester, 1990), p. 192; Alderman, *Modern British Jewry*, pp. 303–5.
23 The inevitable speculativeness of such 'reasoning' is demonstrated in Rubinstein's study, *The Myth of Rescue, Why the Democracies Could Not have saved more Jews from the Nazis*.
24 Herbert Butterfield, *History and Human Relations* (London, 1951). Butterfield warns against the pitfalls of writing history as an act of moral judgement.
25 Quotation by Philip Bell, in Paul Hayes, ed., *Themes in European History, 1890–1945* (London, 1992), p. 262.

1 'Englishmen of the Jewish Persuasion'

1 V.D. Lipman, *A History of the Jews in Britain since 1858* (London, 1990), pp. 215–16.

2 Norman Bentwich, *My Seventy-Seven Years* (London, 1962), p. 3.

3 Lipman, *A History of the Jews in Britain*, pp. 204–5.

4 For a fuller description, see A.G. Brotman, 'Jewish Communal Organisations', in Julius Gould and Shaul Esh, eds., *Jewish Life in Modern Britain* (London, 1964), pp. 1–17.

5 Statement by Neville Laski on his retirement from the Presidency (1939), p. 3. (Retirement).

6 Acc 3121 A/30, 13 September 1939, Minute Book, p. 128; Annual Reports 1940, 1943, 1944.

7 CZA C2/319, (n.d., probably 1943), Maurice Orbach, WJC, organising Secretary.

8 Aubrey Newman, *United Synagogue* (London, 1976); Geoffrey Alderman, *Federation of Synagogues* (London, 1987); Acc 3121 E1/43, Federation of Synagogues (n.d., presumably 1942–43). Michael A. Meyer, *Response to Modernity: A History of the Reform Movement in Judaism* (Oxford, 1988). According to Meyer, by 1940, total membership in the two movements reached 6,000.

9 Isidore Epstein, ed., Joseph Herman Hertz, 1872–1946, *In Memoriam* (London, 1947), p. 31.

10 Lipman, *A History of the Jews in Britain*, pp. 217–18.

11 Acc 3121 E2/79, 1 September 1943, Union of Orthodox Hebrew Congregations meeting; Bernard Homa, *Orthodoxy in Anglo-Jewry 1880–1940* (London, 1969) and *A Fortress in Anglo-Jewry: The Story of the Machzike Adath* (London, 1952). The Adath Yisrael was itself a breakaway from the Machzike Adath Synagogue, a strictly orthodox constituency of the Federation.

12 The Agudah movement had been founded in Kattowitz, Germany in 1912, in reaction to the inroads secularism had made into traditional Jewish life. The distinction between 'mainstream orthodoxy' and 'strict orthodoxy' (sometimes referred to as 'ultra-orthodoxy') is a matter of degree rather than of kind and therefore admits an element of overlap at the boundaries. Nevertheless, 'strict orthodoxy' connotes a more conservative attitude towards lifestyle and religious observance, greater aloofness from secular culture, stricter interpretation of Jewish rabbinic law and – frequently but not inevitably – hostility towards Zionism. The Union and the Agudah are particularly noted for their uncompromising stand on the absolute authority of religious law in all aspects of Jewish personal and communal life.

13 *J.C.*, 13 October 1961, Obituary.

14 *J.C.*, 19 December 1958, 'Silhouette'.

15 Jewish Year Books, 1940 and 1945–6, list eleven Jewish Members of the House of Lords. Of these, seven are listed as holding some formal office in the organised community. There were sixteen Jewish MPs. in the House of Commons. Of these, eight are listed as holding communal office. Bentwich, *My Seventy-Seven Years*, pp. 158, 161.

16 Laski, 'Retirement', p. 11.

17 A.M. Hymanson, 'British Jewry in Wartime', *Contemporary Jewish Record*, The American Jewish Committee, New York, vol. V1, no. 1 (February 1943), p. 20.

18 FO 371/20825 E1590/506/31, 4 March 1937, Laski to Sir Robert Vansittart. For the anglicisation process, see Lloyd Gartner, *The Jewish Immigrant in England, 1870–1914* (London, 1973); and Eugene C. Black, *The Social Politics of Anglo-Jewry 1880–1920*.

19 *J.C.*, 20 February 1970, Obituary.

20 Neville Laski, *Jewish Rights and Jewish Wrongs* (London, 1939), p. 132.

21 Acc 3121 B4/CON 22, 15 October 1938, International Conference of Voluntary Organisations.

22 Sonia Orwell and Ian Angus, eds., *The Collected Essays, Journalism and Letters of George Orwell, volume II, My Country Right or Left 1940–1943* (London, 1968), p. 290.

23 Acc 3121 C11/12/15/2, 23 October 1938, Statement by Laski.

24 Moses Montefiore, President of the Board (1835–74), used his connections to enlist support for intervention in Ottoman affairs, beginning with the notorious Damascus Blood Libel case in 1840.

25 David Feldman, *Englishmen and Jews* (London, 1994), p. 299. The Trades Advisory Council demonstrated a continuing concern for ethical practice.

26 Bill Williams, 'Anti-semitism of Tolerance: Middle-Class Manchester and the Jews, 1870–1900', A.J. Kidd and K.W. Roberts, eds., *City, Class and Culture; Studies of Social Policy and Cultural Production in Victorian Manchester* (Manchester, 1985), pp. 74–102. Kushner, *The Persistence of Prejudice*, p. 10.

27 Bolchover, *British Jewry and the Holocaust*, pp. 42, 77–120, 181 n. 2.

28 Sonia Orwell and Ian Angus, eds., *The Collected Essays, Journalism and Letters of George Orwell, volume III, As I Please 1943–1945* (London, 1968), p. 334.

29 Kushner, *The Persistence of Prejudice*, pp. 2, 10.

30 Kushner, 'The Impact of British Anti-semitism', *MMAJ*, p. 208.

31 J.S. Mill, *On Liberty* (London, 1974), p. 140.

32 E.M. Forster, *Two Cheers for Democracy* (London, 1951), pp. 25–6, 75. For a critique of the Emancipation Contract theory, see Todd Endelman, 'English Jewish History', *Modern Judaism*, II (1991), pp. 101–3.

33 On deference and voting, see David Butler and Donald Stokes, *Political Changes in Britain: Forces Shaping Electoral Choice* (London, 1969), p. 120; Robert T. Mackenzie and Alan Silver, *Angels in Marble, Working Class Conservatives in England* (London, 1968). See also Ross McKibbin, *Classes and Cultures: England, 1918–1951* (Oxford, 1998).

34 Laski, *Jewish Rights and Jewish Wrongs*, p. 139.

35 Chaim Weizmann, *Trial and Error* (London, 1949), p. 459.

36 Acc 3121 C10/1/1/, 21 August 1940, Executive Minutes.

37 Gideon Shimoni, 'Non-Zionism in Anglo-Jewry 1937–1948', *Jewish Journal of Sociology* (JJS) (1985–6), vols. 27–28, pp. 89–116. Waley-Cohen's statement is cited in Stephen Aris, *The Jews in Business* (London, 1970), p. 42.

38 Isaiah Friedman, *The Question of Palestine, 1914–18: British–Jewish–Arab*

Relations (London 1973), p. 23. See also, Leonard Stein, *The Balfour Declaration* (London, 1961).

39 Acc 3121 B5/2/2/2, 16 December 1940 and 12 February 1941, Anthony de Rothschild to Brodetsky. Rothschild's understanding of 'assimilation' is essentially synonymous with the modern term 'acculturation'. 'Assimilation' now refers to an irreversible biological absorption into the host community via inter-marriage and loss of one's original religious-cultural identity. 'Acculturation' refers to the acceptance of the values and traditions of the host community without loss of the original religious-cultural identity: in effect a mixed rather than a compounded identity.

40 Ibid., 1 May 1941, Brodetsky to Brotman, General Secretary of the Board. See Laski, 'Retirement', p. 13.

41 *Daily Telegraph*, 28 October 1938.

42 Weizmann, *Trial and Error*, p. 477

43 CZA A/289/65, Harry Sacher, 23 February 1939, 'The Jewish State and the Diaspora'; BOD Annual Report 1938, p. 50; Lipman, *A History of the Jews in Britain*, p. 182.

44 BOD Annual Report 1944, pp. 28–9; *J.C.*, 15 December 1944, p. 10.

45 Kushner, *The Holocaust and the Liberal Imagination*, p. 137.

46 Orwell and Angus, vol. III, p. 337.

47 Gershon Greenberg, 'Sovereignty as Catastrophe: Jakob Rosenheim's *Hurban Weltanschauung*', *Holocaust and Genocide Studies*, vol. 8, no. 2 (Autumn 1994), pp. 202–24.

48 Rabbi Elchonon Wasserman, *Ikveta DeMeshihah*, pp. 11–12, cited in Gershon Greenberg, 'Orthodox Theological Responses to Kristallnacht: Chayyim Ozer Grodzensky ("Achiezer") and Elchonon Wassermann', *Holocaust and Genocide Studies*, vol. 3, no. 4 (1988), pp. 431–41; Menachem Friedman, 'The Haredim and the Holocaust', *The Jerusalem Quarterly*, no. 53 (Winter 1990).

49 Leon Pinsker's Auto-Emancipation (1882) was inspired by the Russian pogroms in 1881. The seeds of Herzl's *Judenstaat* were sown at the Dreyfus trials in Paris and even Jabotinsky was converted to Zionism at the age of 23 only by the Kishinev Pogrom in 1903.

2 'The Jewish Lions are no longer roaring'

1 Alderman, *Modern British Jewry*, pp. 295–302. Bolchover, *British Jewry and the Holocaust*, p. 107.

2 CAB 27/549 A.R. (33) Series, Cabinet Committee on Alien Restrictions, 7 April 1933, Report by Sir John Gilmour, Home Secretary.

3 Joseph L. Cohen, 'Refugees Organisations', in *J.C.*, 10 February 1939, pp. 14–16. Bentwich, *They Found Refuge*, p. 41.

4 Lipman, *A History of the Jews in Britain*, p. 195; Bentwich, *They Found Refuge*, p. 52.

5 Joan Stiebel, 'The Central British Fund for World Relief', *in Transactions of the Jewish Historical Society of England, Sessions 1978–1980*, vol. 27 (London, 1982).

6 David Silberklang, 'Jewish Politics and Rescue: The Founding of the Council for German Jewry', *Holocaust and Genocide Studies*, vol. 7, no. 3 (Winter 1993), pp. 333–71.
7 Johanna Alberti, *Woman of Ideas, Eleanor Rathbone* (London, 1996).
8 *J.C.*, 22 September 1933, p. 11; Laski, *Jewish Rights and Jewish Wrongs*, p. 133; Acc 3121 A/30, 14 June 1933, JFC Minutes, 10 July 1938, Minutes.
9 Acc 3121 C11/6/4, 1 January 1937, interview with O.G. Sargent, Foreign Office.
10 Laski, *Jewish Rights and Jewish Wrongs*, p. 138.
11 *J.C.*, 9 December 1938, pp. 33–4.
12 Lipman, *A History of the Jews in Britain*, p. 194.
13 BOD Annual Report 1926, p. 40.
14 Cited in Gisela C. Lebzelter, *Political Anti-Semitism in England* (1978), pp. 31–2.
15 Ibid., p. 34.
16 Sonia Orwell and Ian Angus, vol. II, p. 291.
17 Lebzelter, *Political Anti-Semitism in England*, p. 34; Sonia Orwell and Ian Angus, vol. III, p. 333.
18 Colin Holmes, *Anti-semitism in British Society 1987–1939* (1979), pp. 200–2.
19 Lebzelter, *Political Anti-Semitism in England*, p. 42.
20 Orwell and Angus, vol. III, p. 334.
21 Acc 3121 BOD C10/1/1/8, 8 April 1941, Executive Minutes.
22 Orwell and Angus, vol. II, p. 178.
23 Laski, *Jewish Rights and Jewish Wrongs*, p. 105.
24 Acc 3121 E3/286/2, 'The Refugees: Plain Facts' (1938).
25 Ibid., E3/532/1, 8 December 1938, Laski to Schiff.
26 Ibid., E3/532/2, 1 December 1938, 'Helpful Information and Guidance for every Refugee', Max Rittenberg to the Chairman of the Anti-Defamation Committee.
27 Lipman, 'Anglo-Jewish Attitudes', Werner E. Mosse, ed., *Second Chance*, p. 528.
28 Orwell and Angus, vol. II, pp. 290–1; Orwell and Angus, vol. III, p. 336.
29 Acc 3121 E3/532/2, 1 December 1938, 'Helpful Information'; E3/280, Guide for Refugee Dentists (n.d.).
30 Orwell and Angus, vol. II, pp. 290–1.
31 *J.C.*, 19 December 1938, p. 32; Lipman, 'Anglo-Jewish Attitudes', pp. 529–31.
32 Acc 3121 E3/525/1, 23 April 1939, meeting between Board and GJAC.
33 Alderman, *Modern British Jewry*, pp. 303–5; Bolchover, *British Jewry and the Holocaust*, pp. 146, 148–9.
34 CZA A255/491, Norman Bentwich Papers, JCRA (n.d.).
35 Ya'akov Blidstein, 'The Redemption of Captives in Halakhic Tradition: Problems and Policy', S.I. Troen and B. Pinkus, eds., *Organizing Rescue: National Jewish Solidarity in the Modern Period* (London, 1992), pp. 20–30.
36 Lord Immanuel Jakobovits, interview, January 1994, London.
37 Bernard Wasserstein, 'Tyranny of Conventional Wisdom: The Jewish

Refugee Issue in Britain 1939–1945', CBF Conference on Jewish Refugees and Refugee Work, 1933–1993 (unpublished, London, 14 March 1993).
38 MS 183 Schonfeld, 668 [EM-EZ]; 655 [FL-FOY]; 640 [MAR-MAZ]; 662 [WA-WAZ]. Israel State Archives, GL 8586/6, Zorach Warhaftig Papers, 'The Jewish Religion in Axis Europe: The War against Religion' (n.d.). Warhaftig documented Nazi attempts to extirpate the institutions of the Jewish religion.
39 Maimonides, *Mishna Torah,* 'Matnot Aryim', 8:18.
40 MS Schonfeld (UCL), n.d. presumably 1939, List no. 2 – 'Orthodox' and 'Non-Orthodox'.
41 Kranzler and Hirschler, eds., *Solomon Schonfeld,* p. 23.
42 Ibid. During the war, the situation was very different, when the Agudat Israel frequently complained to the government about the small number of Palestine certificates (6 per cent) allotted by the Jewish Agency to its members, when numerically, for example in Hungary, they represented a much larger proportion of total applicants. See FO 371/42848 WR1176/21/48, 17 September 1944, Postal and Telegraph Censorship. However, this is not convincing evidence of deliberate marginalisation; the Agudah was militantly anti-Zionist, and had previously shown no interest in obtaining Palestine certificates.
43 Solomon Schonfeld, *Message to Jewry* (London, 1959), *inter alia*, letter to *The Times,* 6 June 1961, p. 13.
44 See p. 123.
45 Acc 3121 E1/1, 8 July 1938, Schiff to Laski.
46 MS Goodman, 6 July 1938, Schiff to *Hilfsverein der Juden in Deutschland.*
47 MS 183 Schonfeld 673 [AG-AL], 21 January 1939, Memorandum, Rosenheim to CRREC. Henry Pels 27 (35), 18 April 1966, Hebrew University, Institute of Contemporary Jewry, Oral History Department. Pels was Secretary of the CRREC.
48 MS 183 Schonfeld, 617/2 (f.1.), Interim Report (n.d. probably January 1939); 290 (f.2.), 19 November 1938, E. Holderness, Home Office to Hertz.
49 Bolchover, *British Jewry and the Holocaust,* p. 56.
50 London, *Whitehall and the Jews,* p. 168; Lipman, 'Anglo-Jewish Attitudes', p. 523. The JFC included members not on the Board, such as Chief Rabbi Hertz, Norman Bentwich, Sir Robert Waley-Cohen, Sir Osmond d'Avigdor Goldsmid, Otto Schiff and Harry Goodman.
51 Central Zionist Archives (CZA), C2/510, 29 July 1942, Easterman to Brodetsky; Acc 3121 E1/1, 8 September 1942, Brodetsky, interview with M.R. Springer. C11/13/16, 23 September 1942, Goodman to JFC.
52 Acc 3121 A/32, 30 November 1942, Board Minutes.
53 *J.C.,* 25 December 1942, p. 8.
54 FO 371/30885 C9844/9844/62, 8 October 1942, A.W.G. Randall, Foreign Office, Minute.
55 Acc 3121 C11/7/1/1, 24 December 1942, Emergency Consultative Committee Meeting, no. 10.
56 Ibid., 30 December 1942, Emergency Consultative Committee Meeting, no. 11.

57 See *inter alia*, Acc 3121 B5/2/1, 25 July 1943, Statement by Brodetsky.
58 *J.C.*, 5 March 1943, p. 10; Selig Brodetsky, *Memoirs: From Ghetto to Israel* (London, 1960), p. 219.
59 Acc 3121 C11/10/2, 6 January 1937, Memorandum, 'WJC'; CZA C2/ 111, 7 September 1943, Lord Nathan's comment at Board Executive Meeting; G. Shimoni, 'Selig Brodetsky and the Ascendancy of Zionism in Anglo-Jewry, 1939–45', *JJS*, vol. 22, no. 2 (December 1980), pp. 128–9.
60 CZA C2/106, 15 October 1941, Brodetsky to Silverman.
61 Acc 3121 C11/10/2, 6 January 1937, Memorandum, 'WJC'; FO 371/ 20825 E1590/506/31, 4 March 1937, Laski to Vansittart; 15 September 1937, W. Strang, Minute.
62 CZA C2/510, 22 November 1943. Easterman to Lavy Bakstansky, general secretary of the Zionist Federation; AIWO, A–37, 19 May 1944, Goodman to Hertz; 26 June 1944, Goodman to Horovitz.
63 Ibid., 18 May 1944, Hertz to Goodman.
64 Bentwich, *My Seventy-Seven Years*, pp. 191–2.
65 The archives of the WJC, British Section, contain much evidence of this conflict. See, *inter alia*, CZA C2/111. Also the file containing the papers of Eva, Marchioness of Reading, CZA C2/61, 11 June 1943, Lord Melchett to Lord Nathan.
66 FO 371/42773 W383/383/48, 7 January 1944, Memo (Beeley), Foreign Office Research Department, 'WJC and Jewish Nationalism'.
67 CZA C2/106, 15 October 1941, Brodetsky to Silverman; (n.d.); January 1942, 'Proposition for Establishment of Collaboration between the British Section and the Board'.
68 CZA C2/279, 13 December 1943, Minutes of the First Meeting of the National Council of the British Section of the WJC.
69 FO 371/36741 W15236/12242/48, 29 October 1943, L. Stein to George H. Hall, Under-Secretary of State, Foreign Office.
70 Acc 3121 E1/111, 12 September 1943, Final Statement by Brodetsky.
71 Shimoni, 'Selig Brodetsky and the Ascendancy of Zionism', p. 150.
72 FO 371/36741 W12242/12242/48, 20 August 1943, Memorandum and Minutes.
73 Ibid.
74 Ibid., W12341/12242/48, 15 July 1943, A.W.G. Randall, Minute.
75 For example, Lord Reading was engaged in military service; Sir Osmond d'Avigdor-Goldsmid, the original chairman of the CBF, died in April 1940; Lionel de Rothschild died in 1942. The Jewish organisations also lost the support of Colonel Victor Cazalet, who was killed in a plane crash in July 1943 and Lord Wedgwood, who died in August 1943.
76 FO 371/32681 W14681/4555/48, 3 November 1942, Postal and Telegraph censorship report on Jewry.

3 Escalating Crises: Austria and Czechoslovakia

1 Lucy Dawidowicz, *The War against the Jews* (London, 1987), p. 220.
2 See S. Friedlander, *Nazi Germany and the Jews: The Years of Persecution, 1933–39* (1997), p. 61.

3   Y. Arad, Y. Gutman and A. Margaliot, eds., *Documents on the Holo-caust* (Yad Vashem, 1987), document no. 22.

4   See S. Friedlander, *Nazi Germany and the Jews*, p. 62. See Herbert Strauss, 'Jewish Emigration from Germany: Nazi Policies and Jewish Responses' (1), *Leo Baeck Institute Year Book*, vol. XXV (1980).

5   *Documents on the Holocaust*, document numbers 36 and 37; see p. 9.

6   Ibid., pp. 9–10. See document no. 38.

7   See Werner Rosenstock, 'Exodus 1933–1939: A Survey of Jewish Emigration from Germany, *LBIY* 1 (London 1956), p. 377 and Strauss, 'Jewish Emigration from Germany', 326.

8   John Hope Simpson, *The Refugee Problem: Report of a Survey* (London, January 1939), p. 342.

9   Bernard Gainer, *The Alien Invasion: The Origins of the Aliens Act of 1905* (London, 1972), pp. 208–9.

10 Sherman, *Island Refuge*, p. 259.

11 HO 213/94, Visas for Holders of German and Austrian passports – General Principle (n.d. presumably March 1938). FO 372/3282, T3517/3272/378, 15 March 1938, Home Office, Memorandum.

12 Ibid. See also Acc 3121 C11/12/1, 14 March 1938, Chairman of the GJAC (presumably Schiff) to Sir Samuel Hoare. Joan Stiebel, Schiff's secretary, maintains that although the guarantee was officially withdrawn after the *Anschluss* except for cases already sponsored by the JRC, In practice it was honoured until after the outbreak of war. Interview with Joan Stiebel, 23 March 1994, London.

13 London, 'Jewish Refugees and British Government Policy', pp. 175–6; London, *Whitehall and the Jews*, pp. 60–1.

14 HO 213/94, 1 March 1938, McAlpine, Memorandum.

15 HO 213/42, 1 April 1938, Minutes of Anglo-Jewish Deputation meeting.

16 FO 372/3282 T3517, 14 March 1938, Home Office, Memorandum.

17 FO 371/22528 W8597/104/98, 29 June 1938, Holderness to R.M. Makins, Foreign Office, Memorandum on UK Immigration Laws.

18 Morse, *While Six Million Died*, pp. 201, 206, 224. For Nazi victimisation of Jews outside the British Consulate in Vienna, see *J.C.*, 29 April 1938, p. 18.

19 Sherman, *Island Refuge*, pp. 108–9, 125, 155–8.

20 *Hansard's Parliamentary Debates* (hereafter HC Debates), Fifth Series, vol. 341, 21 November 1938, cols. 1428–38, esp. 1471–2; FO 371/24074 W1368/45/48, 23 January 1939, Refugee Position in the United Kingdom.

21 BOD Annual Report 1938, p. 57; Acc 3121 C11/6/4/2, 15 March 1938, interview with Vansittart.

22 American Jewish Archives, Cincinnati (AJAC), MS coll. 361 A13/15, 18 March 1938, Perlzweig's correspondence with Foreign Office; FO 371/21748 C2908/2289/18, 21 March 1938, Baxter, Foreign Office, Minute.

23 *J.C.*, 25 March 1938, p. 41; CZA C2/807, WJC, 'Our Fight for Jewish Rights and Jewish Dignity', p. 3.

24 CAB 23/93 14(38), 16 March 1938, Cabinet Conclusions; Acc 3121 A/29, April 1938, Co-ordinating Committee Report; 21 March 1938, 10 April 1938, Minutes.

25 *J.C.*, 15 April 1938, p. 13; BOD Annual Report, 1938, pp. 53–6. Acc 3121 A/29, February 1939, Jewish Defence Committee Report.
26 Acc 3121 A/29, 10 April 1938, Minutes, JFC Report.
27 *J.C.*, 8 July 1938, p. 10; Acc 3121 A/29, 10 July 1938, Minutes, JFC Report.
28 AJAC MS coll. 361 A13/14; CZA C2/342, Press cuttings of 'Mass Meetings against Persecution of Jews in Germany'.
29 Acc 3121 C11/12/2, 27 April 1938, Situation of the Jews in Austria – Jewish Central Information Office; AJJDC AR 3344.445, M. Wischnitzer, 'The Martyrdom of Austrian Jewry, A Year of Trials' (March 1938 to March 1939).
30 Acc 3121 E3/266, 6 May 1938, 'Decree Concerning Registration of Jewish Property'; A/29, 11 May 1938, JFC Report; Karl A. Schleunes, *The Twisted Road To Auschwitz: Nazi Policy Toward German Jews, 1933–1939* (Chicago, 1970), Ch. 7.
31 FO 371/21748 C2908/2289/18, 21 March 1938, Perlzweig, Situation of the Jews in Vienna.
32 CGJ, 15 March 1938, Minutes of Executive Meeting, p. 2.
33 *J.C.*, 25 March 1938, p. 41, 25 August 1938, p. 25.
34 CGJ, 27 July 1938, Norman Bentwich, CGJ, to the IGCR. Special foreign exchange arrangements were made with the consent of the Bank of England. See Joan Stiebel, 'The Central British Fund for World Jewish Relief'. Similar arrangements were worked out with the AJJDC and German financial authorities, so that no dollars were sent into Austria or Germany. See AJJDC AR 3344.541, 12 December 1938, Herbert Katski to J.E. Finn, Dayton, Ohio. The AJJDC expenditure for emigration from Austria, 1938–1941, amounted to $1, 848, 091. See AR 3344.439/440.
35 *J.C.*, 29 April 1938, p. 13; CGJ Annual Report, 1938, p. 9; CGJ, 7 June 1938, Minutes, p. 3; Acc 3121 C11/12/2, 29 April 1938, Report by Leo Lauterbach, 'The Jewish Situation in Austria'; 17 August 1939, Norman Bentwich, 'Report on a Visit to Austria'.
36 CGJ, 13 June 1938, Minutes, p. 2; CGJ, Annual Report, 1938, p. 10. During 1938, it was estimated that 50,000 Jews were enabled to leave Austria with the assistance of foreign organisations.
37 CGJ, 29 March 1938, Minutes, p. 2; AJJDC AR 3344.575, 7 April 1938, Dr. B. Kahn to P. Baerwald; CGJ Annual Report, 1938, p. 20.
38 CGJ, Agenda File, no. 7, June 1938, draft Letter from CGJ to Dr. Loewnhertz, Director, *Kultesgemeinde*.
39 *J.C.*, 6 January 1939, pp. 7, 15, 25.
40 CGJ, 608, Series 5, 9 May 1938, Schonfeld to CGJ; Acc 3121 C11/12/2, 18 May 1938, Goodman to Laski; MS 183 Schonfeld 117/8, 23 May 1938, Minutes of Liaison Conference.
41 Foreign Relations of the United States (FRUS), vol. 1, 23 March 1938, Cordell Hull to Joseph Kennedy, American Ambassador to Britain, pp. 740–1.
42 FO 371/21749 C5681/2289/18, 9 June 1938, Conversation, Bearsted, Strang and Makins.
43 Acc 3121 A/30, 19 June 1938, Minutes, Laski to Goodman.
44 CGJ, Agenda File, no. 7. 12–13 May 1938, 'Note on proposed

International Conference – Norman Bentwich's visit to Geneva', p. 3. The Liaison Committee consisted of the principal organisations, both philanthropic and political, concerned with refugees. *J.C.*, 1 July 1938, p. 29.

45 Acc 3121 E3/282/1, 'Evian Conference – Memorandum of Certain Jewish Organisations' [n.d.]; Memorandum of the Jewish Agency for Palestine (JA) and of the WJC; E3/282/3 First List, Memoranda submitted to the Evian Conference.

46 Acc 3121 E3/282/1, Memorandum of Certain Jewish Organisations.

47 Ibid., 'Inter-Governmental Conference on Refugees Held at Evian', confidential report by Brotman [n.d.]; FO 371/22528 W8435/104/98, 'The Future of Assistance to Refugees', communicated to Vansittart by private organisations, pp. 5–6 [n.d.].

48 FO 371/22528 W8673/104/98, 28 June 1938, Makins, Memorandum, Evian Meeting – Position of Representatives of Private Organisations; CGJ, 27 June 1938, Minutes, p. 2.

49 FO 371/22528 W 8713/104/98, 30 June 1938, inter-departmental meeting at the Foreign Office; W8829/104/98, 2 July 1938, Meeting between James G. McDonald and members of the Anglo-Jewish leadership.

50 S. Adler-Rudel, 'The Evian Conference on the Refugee Question', *Leo Baeck Institute Year Book* vol. XIII (1968), pp. 235–73.

51 CZA S25/9778, 24 June 1938, Interview, Lord Winterton and Chaim Weizmann.

52 AJJDC AR 3344.256, 9 July 1938, 'Report of the Sub-Committee for the Reception of Organisations', Evian.

53 Ibid., 17 August 1938, Digest of the Memorandum for the Evian Conference by the Liaison Committee.

54 Wasserstein, *Britain and the Jews of Europe*, p. 9.

55 Henry L. Feingold, 'Roosevelt and the Settlement Question', M. Marrus ed., *Bystanders to the Holocaust: The Nazi Holocaust*, vol. 8 (London, 1989), pp. 271–329.

56 FO 371/21749 C 5319/2289/18, 23 May 1938, Foreign Office Memorandum, Makins.

57 Acc 3121 C11/6/4/1, 22 September 1938, Laski to Halifax; 23 September 1938, Laski to Butler; C11/12/7, 29 September 1938, Olivier Harvey to Laski; 3 October 1938, Laski to Harvey; AJAC, MS coll. 361 A13/15, 2 June 1938, Perlzweig to Butler; 25 October 1938, Halifax to Perlzweig; BOD Annual Report 1938, p. 63.

58 FO 371/21583 C12266/11896/12, 14 October 1938, Report by Sir Neill Malcolm, pp. 2–3.

59 FO 371/24074 W 1075/45/48, 18 January 1939, Emerson, Report on visit to Prague, p. 4. Victor S. Mamatey and Radomir Luza, *A History of the Czechoslovak Republic, 1918–1948* (Princeton, 1973), p. 261.

60 CGJ, 24 October 1938, Minutes, p. 4.

61 FO 371/21583 C12266/11896/12, 14 October 1938, Report of visit by Sir Neill Malcolm, pp. 2–3; John Hope Simpson, *Refugees: A Review of the Situation since September 1938* (London, August 1939), pp. 35–40.

62 FO 371/21583 C12337/11896/12, 10 October 1938, Deputation from the National Council for Civil Liberties; C12250/11896/12, 13 October

1938, Deputation from the National Council of Labour; C12372/11896/12, Deputation from the League of Nations Union, which included many of the voluntary organisations; C12329/11896/12, 13 October 1938, Telegram, Foreign Office to Sir N. Henderson.

63 Acc 3121 C 11/6/4/1, 26 October 1938, Deputation to Foreign Office; Memorandum, 'An Aspect of Relations between this Country and Germany'; 31 October 1938, 'Memorandum on the Jews in the Sudeten Territories'; 11 November 1938, Strang to Board; Simpson, *Refugees*, p. 36.

64 BOD Annual Report, 1938, p. 63.

65 FO 371/24074 W1368/45/98, 23 January 1939, Refugee Position in UK; A. Tartakower and K.R. Grossman, *The Jewish Refugee* (New York, 1944), p. 38.

66 FO 371/32669 W4693/781/48, 25 March 1942, The Czech Refugee Trust Fund.

67 Ibid., C13325/11896/12, 2 November 1938, Holderness to Mallet.

68 Acc 3121 C11/12/7, 13 October 1938, Stephany to Brotman.

69 Ibid., 'Aim of New British Committee' (unidentified newspaper clipping, n.d.). This Committee was later replaced by the Czech Refugee Trust Fund. See HO 294, Czechoslovak Refugee Trust: Records.

70 Acc 3121 C11/12/7, 2 January 1939, M. Schmolkova, Comite Central Tcheco-Sloavaque [*sic*], to Board; FO 371/21587 C14387/11896/12, 15 November 1938, R.J. Stopford, Prague, to Makins.

71 Acc 3121 E3/286/1, 21 February 1939, Minutes of Liaison Committee meeting, Paris, pp. 10–12.

72 HO 213/268, 31 March 1939, Odo Nansen, Report on the Czecho-Slovakian Refugee Problem.

73 Acc 3121 A/29, 19 March 1939, JFC Report.

74 Tartakower and Grossman, *The Jewish Refugee*, p. 36. Between October 1938 and July 1939, 20, 684 Jews left Czechoslovakia.

75 FO 371/24100 W11762/1873/48, August 1939 [n.d.], Halifax to Lord Balfour.

76 CGJ, 27 March 1939, Minutes of Executive Meeting, p. 4; Acc 3121 C11/12/7, 19 May 1939, Leo Herrman to Stephany; 31 May 1939, Herrman to Stephany.

77 *J.C.*, 24 March 1939, p. 20; AIWO E-31/15R Annual Report of Federation of Czech Jews, 1942; Acc 3121 E3/510, 15 January 1940, 'Memorandum of the Federation'.

78 *J.C.*, 24 March 1939, p. 20; MS 183 Schonfeld 636 [Fau-Feu], Report of the Federation, 1939–45.

79 *J.C.*, 6 January 1939, p. 26; for Rathbone's efforts in the Commons, see *J.C.*, 11 August 1939, p. 20.

80 Nicholas Winton, 'Saving the Children – 1939', A Scrapbook recording the Transportation of 664 Children out of Czechoslovakia, vol. 1; N.Winton, 'Report on the Problem of Refugee Children in Czechoslovakia', [n.d.]; National Archives (Washington D.C.), 840.48 REFUGEES/1635, 16 May 1939, Winton to Roosevelt. However, 'the U.S. Government, in the absence of specific legislation, could not permit immigration in excess of existing laws'.

81 Winton, 'Saving the Children – 1939'; *Jewish Weekly*, 16 June 1939, vol. IV, no. 177, p. 1; MS 183 Schonfeld 658 [Mov-MZ], Hertz to Lord Gorell, [n.d.]; MS 183 Schonfeld, 117/8, 9 May 1939, Meeting of the Committee; *J.C.*, 21 July 1939, p. 29, L. Rabinowitz to Editor; *J.C.*, 11 August 1939, p. 21.
82 Nicolas Winton, 23 July 2000, speech at film preview, 'All my Loved Ones', Institute of Contemporary Arts.
83 AJJDC AR 3344.541, 20 February 1939, Translation, 'No-Man's Lands of the Jews'.
84 Acc 3121 C11/6/4/1, 31 October 1938, Memorandum on Jews in the Sudeten Territory and Elsewhere'; C11/12/7, 24 November 1938, 30 January 1939, Board to Revd. Monsignor Elwes; 12 December 1938, Board to M. Waldman, Secretary of the American Jewish Committee; 6 December 1938, Board to the Alliance Israelite Universelle, Paris.
85 Acc 3121 C11/12/7/1, 9 November 1938, Goodman to Brotman.
86 FO 371/21587 C14581/11896/12, 23 November 1938, Rabbi Weissmandel via Chaplain of Archbishop of Canterbury to Foreign Office.
87 *J.C.*, 3 February 1939, p. 20; Acc 3121 E3/286/1, 3 February 1939, Meeting of the Refugees Committee of the League of Nations Union, Minutes.
88 JTA, 23 January 1939, p. 2; S. Milton, 'The Expulsion of Polish Jews from Germany: October 1938–July 1939: Documentation', *Leo Baeck Institute Year Book*, 29 (1984), pp. 169–99.
89 Acc 3121 C11/7/1/4, 20 April 1939, W.E. Prins, Antwerp, to Schiff.
90 AJJDC AR 3344.541, 9 June 1939, Statement from Paris by Mr. Smolar [n.i.] to JTA.
91 *J.C.*, 17 February 1939, p. 23. Since March 1938 the Polish Refugee Fund was the amalgamation of four bodies concerned with Polish relief. *J.C.*, 25 March 1938, p. 18; CGJ, 27 March 1939, Minutes, p. 4.
92 *J.C.*, 2 December 1938, p. 17; 3 March 1939, p. 27.
93 Ibid., 26 May 1939, p. 20; 1 September 1939, p. 20.

4 The Watershed: *Kristallnacht* and After

1 *Documents on the Holocaust*, pp. 115–17. A. Barkai, *Boycott to Annihilation: The Economic Struggle of German Jews, 1933–1943* (London, 1989), pp. 133–8.
2 FO 371/22536 W15037/104/98, 16 November 1938, Meeting between the CGJ and Chamberlain.
3 Documents on the Holocaust, document 51 and 59.
4 Andrew Sharf, *The British Press and Jews under Nazi Rule* (London, 1964), p. 58; F.R. Gannon, *The British Press and Germany, 1936–1939* (Oxford, 1971), p. 226; *JTA*, 12 December 1938, p. 4.
5 Acc 3121 A/30, 20 November 1938, Minutes of Board Meeting.
6 FO 371/22539 W16166/104/98, 2 December 1938, Sir N. Malcolm to Butler; FO 371/22539 W16205/104/98, 7 December 1938, Sir G. Ogilvie-Forbes, Berlin, shared this prognosis; CGJ, 1 December 1938, Minutes of Executive Meeting, p. 2.

7 Acc 3121 A/30, 20 November 1938, Board Resolution.
8 *J.C.*, 25 November 1938, p. 15; Acc 3121 A/30, 15 January 1939, 19 March 1939, Board Minutes. For fears of anti-Semitism, see *J.C.*, 28 April 1939, pp. 14–16.
9 FO 371/21636 C 13661/1667/62, 10 November 1938, telegram no. 662, Sir G. Ogilvie-Forbes, Berlin. The British government did not follow the American example of recalling its Ambassador from Berlin.
10 *J.C.*, 18 November 1938, p. 32.
11 CGJ Annual Report, p. 21; FO 371/24074 W1368/45/98, 23 January 1939, Refugee Position in UK.
12 *J.C.*, 10 February 1939, p. 15, 'Refugee Organisations – How the Funds and Committees Work'. The Jewish organisations were responsible for raising nine-tenths of all funds in Britain between 1933 and 1938.
13 FO 371/22536 W15037/104/98, 16 November 1938, record of meeting.
14 CGJ, Agenda File, no. 10 (17 November 1938–15 January 1939), 25 November 1938, Confidential Memorandum.
15 FO 371/22539 W16410/104/98, 7 December 1938, H.E. Brooks, Treasury, transmits record of meeting.
16 FO 371/22540 W 16641/104/98, 9 December 1938, Winterton to Halifax.
17 *J.C.*, 24 January 1939, p. 24; 10 February 1939, p. 18; 14 April 1939, p. 15; Acc 3121 A/30, 12 July 1939, JFC Minutes; FO 371/24077 W 10942/45/48, 19 July 1939, Statement by Winterton.
18 J. Stiebel, 'The Central British Fund for World Jewish Relief', pp. 53–4.
19 FO 371/22536 W15037/104/98, 16 November 1938, record of meeting; HC Debates, Fifth Series, vol. 341, 21 November 1938, cols. 1428–83.
20 AJJDC AR 3344.589, 28 November 1938, British Inter-Aid Committee for Children from Germany. In 1940, the Movement became the Refugee Children's Movement.
21 CGJ Annual Report 1938, p. 2. The CGJ undertook a commitment to the Movement of £50,000 for 1939. FO 371/22539 W 16055/104/98, 1 December 1938. 'Lord Baldwin's Broadcast appeal'. By 31 July 1939, £523,000 was raised, half of which was allocated to the Movement.
22 AJJDC AR 3344.589, CGJ, 16 January 1939, 'Note on the Present Position of the Movement'.
23 *J.C.*, 10 February 1939, p. 27.
24 Acc 3121 E3/286/1, 31 March 1939, Dorothy F. Buxton to Laski; FO 371/24100 W6529/3231/48, 6 April 1939, Colonel Wedgwood calls to stop the £50 deposit during Parliamentary Questions. Acc 3121 E3/533/3, July 1939, 2nd Issue, 'Movement – Statistical Analysis', p. 3.
25 FO 371/22539 W16410/104/98, 7 December 1938; FO 371/24074 W1368/45/48, 23 January 1939, Refugee Position in UK.
26 CGJ, Annual Report 1939, p. 15; Bentwich, *They Found Refuge*, pp. 102–7.
27 CGJ, Minutes, 13 April 1939, p. 1; *Jewish Weekly*, 14 July 1939, vol. IV, no. 181, p. 1; 8 September 1939, vol. IV, no. 189, p. 1; interview, Phineas May, Richborough welfare officer, 17 November 1994, London; CGJ, Annual Report, 1933–1943, p. 6.
28 S. Rudel-Adler, (27) 17, p. 12, Oral History Department, Institute of Contemporary Jewry, Hebrew University, Jerusalem.

29 Bentwich, *They Found Refuge*, p. 95; Aryeh Handler, 14 (156), Oral History Department, Institute of Contemporary Jewry, Hebrew University, Jerusalem; Aryeh Handler, interview, 7 May 1994, London.

30 CGJ, Agenda File, no. 10 (17 November 1938–15 January 1939), 24 November 1938, Memorandum from CRREC to CGJ; MS 183 Schonfeld, 290 (f.2), 19 November 1938, Holderness to Hertz. MS 183 Schonfeld 617/2 (f.1), CRREC, Interim Report, (n.d., probably May 1939).

31 MS 183 Schonfeld 652 [SCH-SCHL], 30 November 1938, Hertz to Dr. Schlesinger, Buenos Aires; 665 [WEB-WEIR], 8 June 1939, GJAC Overseas Settlement Department to CRREC, regarding British Honduras; 663/2 [U-Z], 23 June 1939, CRREC to Stephen Wise.

32 MS 183 Schonfeld 290 (f.2), 9 December 1938; 31 January 1939, Hertz to Holderness.

33 MS 183 Schonfeld 117/8, Report year ending 1 October 1941, p. 4; Felice Selton, interview 2 June 1994, London. Selton, a non-orthodox child, was brought over by Schonfeld.

34 MS 183 Schonfeld 676 [SA-SAW], 9 December 1938, Hertz to Samuel. Hertz assured Samuel that this fund would not compete with Lord Rothschild's Appeal and that all monies collected would be handed over to the central organisation. AJJDC AR 3344.589, 28 December 1938, Helen Bentwich, Report on the Movement .

35 MS 183 Schonfeld 617/2 (f.1.), 24 May 1939, CRREC to CGJ

36 *J.C.*, 24 March 1939, p. 22.

37 MS 183 Schonfeld, 384 (f.3), 18 January 1939, CRREC to Stephany, CGJ; 22 March 1939, Schonfeld to CGJ; 28 March 1939, Stephany to Hertz.

38 *J.C.*, 31 December 1943, p. 12; 7 January 1944, p. 6; 14 January 1944, p. 12. 'The Child-Estranging Movement', An Exposé on the Alienation of Jewish Refugee Children in Great Britain from Judaism (The Union of Orthodox Hebrew Congregations, 1944).

39 Aryeh Handler, interview, 7 May 1994, London; *J.C.*, 8 September 1989, p. 29; Acc 3121 E3/533/3, July 1939, 2nd Issue, 'Movement-Statistical Analysis'.

40 Acc 3121 E3/533/3, July 1939, 2nd Issue, 'Movement-Statistical Analysis'. A representative sample of 136 questionnaires found that 24.7 per cent were orthodox, 61 per cent were Liberal and the remaining 14.3 per cent were non-practising [presumably unaffiliated].

41 Ibid. *J.C.*, 10 February 1939, p. 16. For a contrary view, see Barry Turner, '... *And the Policeman Smiled*' (London, 1991), pp. 75–6 and *Marks of Distinction, The Memoirs of Elaine Blond* (London, 1988), p. 86.

42 *J.C.*, 12 May 1939, p. 35; *Jewish Weekly*, 23 June 1939, vol. IV, no. 178, p. 1.

43 MS 183 Schonfeld 617/2 (f.1), Memorandum on Jewish Refugee Children in non-Jewish Homes (n.d., presumably mid-1939). Mention is made of the confusion in Britain with regard to the nomenclature of religious affiliation of German Jews such as Reform Judaism, whose English equivalent is 'Liberal'.

44 *J.C.*, 12 May 1939, p. 35.

45 Mrs. Rosie Goldfield, interview, Jerusalem, July 1994. Mrs. Goldfield

recalls that few Jewish families in Manchester wanted refugee children. Although reluctant, once Schonfeld appealed to them, 'they had no choice but to take them in'. Acc 3121 E3/533/3, July 1939, 'Movement – Statistical Analysis': 'The orthodox Jewish community have as a whole responded better to the appeal for hospitality and ... it has proved that the goodwill is uniformly great but that it only has effect where there is an energetic local committee'.

46 MS 183 Schonfeld 617/2 (f.1), Memorandum on Jewish Refugee Children in Non-Jewish Homes, (n.d.), p. 3a. For another view, see George Bell (Bishop of Chichester) Papers, Lambeth Palace, Volume 29: 'There was no intention of converting children ... They found it difficult to have these children looked after while they were at Church' and therefore took them along.
47 MS 183 Schonfeld 117/8, Report, year ending 1 October 1941, p. 4.
48 MS 183 Schonfeld, 658 [MOV-MZ], 10 September 1943, Maxwell to Hertz; Acc 3121 E1/32, 16 September 1951, Julius Carlebach, Report on the files of children who came to England as refugees.
49 Acc 3121 E1/37, 3 August 1938, Laski to Schonfeld; MS 183 Schonfeld 676 [SA-SAW], 21 November 1938, Hertz to Samuel.
50 MS 183 Schonfeld 384 (f.3), 2 January 1939, Stephany to CRREC; 10 May 1939, Stephany to CRREC.
51 MS 183 Schonfeld 676 [SA-SAW], 27 July 1939, Pels, Secretary of CRREC, to Mr. Salomon, Berlin; Pels, 18 April 1966, 27 (35), Oral History Department, Institute of Contemporary Jewry, Hebrew University, Jerusalem.
52 Acc 3121 E 3/525/1, 23 April 1939, Meeting between Board and GJAC.
53 MS 183 Schonfeld 638 [GA-GE], 15 March 1939, GJAC to CRREC; GJAC, 15 March 1939, Institute of Contemporary History and Wiener Library, Reel 32, no. 175/57, Executive Board Minutes.
54 MS 183 Schonfeld 290 (f.2) 12 May 1939, Hertz to Holderness.
55 *J.C.*, 19 May 1939, p. 40; 2 June 1939, p. 25.
56 MS 183 Schonfeld 652 [SCH-SCHL], 14 July 1939, Schiff to Hertz.
57 Interview, Joan Stiebel, March 1994, London.
58 London, 'Jewish Refugees', pp. 183, 189.
59 Simpson, *Refugees: A Review of the Situation since September 1938*, p. 73.
60 London, 'British Immigration Control Procedures, pp. 485–517.
61 Acc 3121 E3/532/2, May 1939, GJAC Report, p. 1; June 1939, Appendix II.
62 CGJ, 18 January 1939, Minutes, p. 4.
63 Ibid., 1 May 1939, p. 4; 10 August 1939, p. 3; 13 September 1939, p. 5. By September 1939, there were approximately 15,000 German Jewish domestics, of whom 5, 000 had been brought over by the Ministry of Labour.
64 CGJ, Agenda File, no. 10 (17 November 1938–5 January 1939), December 1938, note on GJAC Finances.
65 Acc 3121 BOD E3/532/2, June 1939, GJAC Report, p. 12.
66 FO 371/24074 W405/45/48, 6 January 1939, CGJ to Foreign Office;

256 *Notes to pp. 78–81*

CGJ, 25 January 1939, Minutes, p. 3; Acc 3121 C11/7/1/4, 27 June 1939, report by Laski of meeting in London with M. Speelman, director of the International Saving Society, Shanghai. Nevertheless, the Council was still sending funds to support refugees there. See CGJ, 10 August 1939, Minutes, p. 7.

67 CGJ Annual Report, 1938/1939, p. 7.
68 Acc 3121 E3/532; all three large folders contain numerous complaints.
69 Acc 3121 E3/533/2, 16 December 1938, Schiff to Laski; E3/532/2, March 1939, GJAC Report, p. 8; *J.C.*, 21 July 1939, pp. 15–16.
70 Acc 3121 E 3/532/2, March 1939, GJAC Report, p. 1.
71 Acc 3121 E3/533/2, 16 December 1938, Schiff to Laski.
72 Sherman, *Island Refuge*, pp. 214–16.
73 Acc 3121 E3/525/1, 23 April 1939, Conference of Provincial Jewish Refugee Organisations.
74 Acc 3121 A/30, 21 May 1939, Minutes.
75 Acc 3121 E3/532/3, 23 June 1939, Schiff to Laski.
76 CGJ, 19 June 1939, Minutes, p. 4; 10 August 1939, Minutes, p. 2.
77 Alderman, *Modern British Jewry*, pp. 276–8. See also London, 'Jewish Refugees', pp. 175–6.
78 CAB 27/549, A.R. (33) Series, Cabinet Committee on Aliens Restrictions, 7 April 1933, report by Sir John Gilmour.
79 CGJ, Agenda File, no. 10 (17 November 1938–5 January 1939), 8 December 1938, N. Bentwich, 'Admission of Refugees into England'.
80 Bentwich to Porter Goff, 15 December 1938, cited in London, 'Jewish Refugees', p. 185, ff.119.
81 HO 213/103, 14 February 1939, note on the heavy work thrown on Consuls and Passport Offices abroad.
82 FO 371/24100 W7740/3231/48, 8 May 1939, R.T. Parkins, Passport Control Department, Memorandum.
83 HC Debates, Fifth Series, vol. 341, 1938–1939, col. 1470; FO 371/24100 W10840/3231/48, 20 July 1939, Statement by Winterton to the IGCR. By July 1939, there were approximately 40,000 refugees in the UK, of whom some 29,000 had entered since November 1938.
84 FO 371/24100 W7031/3231/48, 27 April 1939, Jeffes, Passport Control Department, to Randall.
85 HO 213/268, 1 May 1939, Co-ordinating Committee for Refugees, Meeting. E.N. Cooper, Home Office, confirmed that 57,000 visas remained unused.
86 Acc 3121 E3/532/2, May and June 1939, GJAC Report; E3/533/3, July 1939, GJAC Report.
87 FO 371/24074 W1368/45/48, 23 January 1949, Refugee Position in the UK; Acc 3121 E3/532/2, May and June 1939, GJAC Reports. Several British consuls in Europe were extremely lenient in issuing papers to Jews. For example, it is estimated that Frank Foley, British Passport Control Officer in Berlin and head of the MI6 station in Berlin, out of humanitarian concerns, issued over 3,000 emigration visas to Britain. *J.C.*, 3 March 1995, p. 7.
88 FO 371/24100 W7740/3231/48, 8 May 1939, Parkins, Passport Control Department, Memorandum; W10840/3231/48, 20 July 1939, Statement

by Winterton to the IGCR. See also Acc 3121 E3/532/2, May and June 1939, GJAC Reports; E3/533/3, July 1939, GJAC Report.
89 N. Bentwich, *Wanderer between Two Worlds* (London, 1941), p. 283.

5 Internment and Deportation

1 FO 371/24101 W13792/3231/48, 18 September 1939, Cooper to Randall.
2 CCJR Annual Report, 1944, p. 4.
3 FO 371/24100 W13792/3231/48, 18 September 1939, Cooper to Randall.
4 CCJR Annual Report, 1939, p. 17.
5 HO 213/294, 24 November 1940, Central Office for Refugees, Memorandum. Rothschild Archives, XIV/35/19, CCJR Report for the first six months of 1940. The Council had been compelled to borrow nearly £400,000, on the security of instalments from covenants. The money borrowed had already been spent. CCJR Annual Report 1939, pp. 18–19. Expenditure was running at £60,000 a month. The Council maintained its activities by a loan from the Christian Council for Refugees.
6 Rothschild Archives, XI/35/19, 26 October 1939, Memorandum.
7 HO 213/294, 17 November 1940, meeting, Schiff and Sir Alexander Maxwell.
8 HO 213/294, 2 December 1940, Refugee Organisations, Financial Situation.
9 Rothschild Archives, XI/35/19, File (October 1939–March 1940); CCJR Report for 1933–1945, p. 5. As the war progressed and the refugees found employment, expenditure decreased.
10 MS 183 Schonfeld 117/8 Report year ending 1 October 1941, p. 2; CCJR, Agenda File, (19 March–5 June 1940), 4 June 1940, 'The Chief Rabbi's Religious Emergency Fund'.
11 CCJR, 9 May 1940, Executive Meeting, Minutes, p. 1. The CCJR granted on average £400 per month. The CRREC was to rely on private donors to help raise the additional £600 required monthly. See Agenda File (19 March–5 June 1940), CRREC.
12 MS 183 117/8, Report for year ending 1 October 1941, p. 6. The annual budget of the CRREC and its associated organisations amounted to over £20,000, as reported at the end of 1941. MS 183 Schonfeld 297/1, Report for year ending 31 December 1942. MS 183 Schonfeld 665 [WEB-WEIR], Lord Wedgwood Appeal, 1942 and 1943.
13 Schonfeld Papers (UCL), 30 May 1940, Central Office for Refugees, circular no. 50; Rothschild Archives, XIV/35/19, Report of the CCJR for the first six months of 1940.
14 CZA A255/539, 24 May 1940, Herbert Bentwich to Jose [n.i.].
15 For a general review of internment policy see Ronald Stent, *A Bespattered Page?: The Internment of His Majesty's 'Most Loyal Enemy Aliens'* (London, 1980).
16 Schonfeld Papers (UCL), 27 May 1940, Minutes of Refugee Joint Consultative Committee Meeting.
17 Ibid.
18 *J.C.*, 10 May 1940, p. 12; 24 May 1940, p. 1.

19 Acc 3121 C10/1/1, 28 May 1940, Executive Committee, Minutes; C2/3/3/1, 23 May 1940, RJCC, Draft Resolution to the Home Office.
20 CCJR, 22 May 1940, Minutes, p. 2.
21 CCJR, 22 May 1940, Minutes, p. 3; Acc 3121 C10/1/1, 28 May 1940, Executive Committee, Minutes.
22 CCJR, 14 June 1940, Minutes, p. 1.
23 Schonfeld Papers (UCL), 27 May 1940, RJCC, Minutes.
24 Schonfeld Papers, (UCL), 9 October 1940, RJCC, Minutes, p. 3; CCJR, 22 May 1940, Minutes, p. 3.
25 Dr. Hans Gal, Imperial War Museum, Department of Sound Records, no. 004304/4, Reel 03.
26 Stent, *A Bespattered Page?*, pp. 51–2.
27 Acc 3121 C2/3/3/1, 14 May 1940, Gordon Liverman to Brotman.
28 CCJR, Agenda File, 19 March 1940–45 June 1940, 'Draft of Suggested Letter for Refugees'.
29 *J.C.*, 26 July 1940, pp. 1, 10; 2 August 1940.
30 Schonfeld Papers (UCL), 9 October 1940, Minutes, RJCC, p. 2.
31 MS 183 Schonfeld, 593/1, July 1941, 'Great Britain and the Refugees'; *The Times*, 30 July 1940, p. 5, letter to the Editor.
32 Acc 3121 E3/520/1, 27 May 1940, Perlzweig to (presumably) Board; FO 371/24239 A3317/131/45, 20 May 1940, Perlzweig to Halifax.
33 Acc 3121 C 2/3/5/3, 8 August 1940, Nathan Laski to Brotman; 9 August 1940, Laski to Churchill; 15 August 1940, Brodetsky to Laski; 20 August 1940, Laski to Brodetsky.
34 Acc 3121 C10/1/1, 9 July 1940, Executive Committee, Minutes; *J.C.*, 12 July 1940, p. 5. The *J.C.* noted that the Board had foregone its usual two months vacation. Acc 3121 A/31, 25 July 1940, Executive Report.
35 The Parliamentary Committee for Refugees' dual function was to influence Government policy and public opinion in favour of generous treatment of refugees and to assist individual refugees in presenting their cases for release from internment. By February 1942 it had a membership of nearly 200 MPs of all parties, with 25 members on its executive. See Acc 3121 C2/3/4/2, Refugee Conference February 1942, Parliamentary Committee, statement by Rathbone, pp. 22–3.
36 Dr. Hans Gal, Imperial War Museum, Department of Sound Archives, Tape no. 004304/04; Dr. Fritz Hallgarten, Tape no. 003967/06, 'Civilian Internment in Britain 1939–1945'.
37 Acc 3121 C2/3/5, 4 June 1940, note of 'Meeting of Parliamentary Committee on Refugees', signed by Brotman; Acc 3121 C2/3/5/3, 11 June 1940, Brotman to Rathbone; CCJR, Executive Minutes, 14 June 1940, pp. 2–3.
38 Stent, *A Bespattered Page?*, pp. 81–2.
39 Ibid; *J.C.*, 2 August 1940, p. 1.
40 CMD 6217, July 1940, copy in Schonfeld papers (UCL); *JTA*, 27 July 1940, p. 3.
41 Schonfeld Papers (UCL), 6 August 1940, Memorandum, p. 2; CCJR, 8 August 1940, Executive Minutes, p. 4.
42 Ibid., pp. 3–4.
43 Acc 3121 C2/3/5/1, 13 August 1940, Schiff to Harry Sacher.

44 CCJR, 16 August 1940, Executive Committee, Minutes, p. 1; 21 August 1940, Executive Committee, Minutes, p. 2. See *J.C.*, 31 May 1940, p. 10, with reference to the Duke of Devonshire's criticism of internment as a 'gross waste of effort and man-power which we can ill afford in this grave emergency'.

45 CCJR, Agenda File (14 June–13 November 1940), 14 August 1940, 'Policy Regarding Internment of German and Austrian Refugees'; CCJR, Annual Report, 1941, p. 5.

46 Stent, *A Bespattered Page?*, pp. 80–1; Ronald Jasper, *George Bell, Bishop of Chichester* (London 1967), p. 152; CCJR, 28 August 1940, Executive Committee, Minutes, p. 2.

47 *J.T.A.*, 27 August 1940, p. 3.

48 Acc 3121 C10/1/1, 28 August 1940; 9 October 1940, Executive Committee, Minutes; *J.C.*, 18 October 1940, p. 14.

49 Brodetsky, *Memoirs*, pp. 200–1.

50 Acc 3121 A/31, 18 December 1940, Minutes; *JTA*, 20 December 1940, p. 3; CCJR, Agenda File (14 June–13 November 1940), 6 September 1940, Brodetsky to Justice Asquith, Advisory Committee on the Internment of Aliens; 1 October 1940, Schiff to Brotman.

51 CCJR, 18 September 1940, Executive Committee, Minutes, p. 3.

52 Acc 3121 A/31, 17 November 1940, Minutes; Board Annual Report 1940, p. 18.

53 *J.C.*, 18 October 1940, p. 1; 18 October 1940, p. 14.

54 Acc 3121 A/31, 25 February 1941, Minutes.

55 CCJR, 24 July 1940, Executive Committee, Minutes, p. 3.

56 Schonfeld Papers (UCL), 9 October 1940, Minutes, RJCC.

57 Acc 3121 C2/3/5, 17 July 1940, Brotman to Julius Jung, Secretary of the Federation of Synagogues; 26 July 1940, Brotman to Norman Bentwich.

58 *The Times*, 30 July 1940, p. 5, Schonfeld's Letter to the Editor; MS 183 Schonfeld 117/8, Report for the year ending 1 October 1941, Internees.

59 Ibid., p. 4.

60 MS 183 Schonfeld 673 [AG-AL], 31 March 1940, Pels to Rosenheim; Acc 3121 C2/3/5/3, 27 December 1939, Schonfeld to Brotman; Acc 3121 B5/2/2, 24 July 1940, Brotman to Brodetsky.

61 MS 183 Schonfeld 117/8, Report for the year ending 1 October 1941, Internees-Ministrations and Religious Services; Acc 3121 C2/3/5/3, 17 June 1940, Report of visit to internment camp on Isle of Man.

62 MS 183 Schonfeld 117/8, Report for the year ending 1 October 1941, p. 4; D. Kranzler and G. Hirschler, eds., *Solomon Schonfeld, His Page in History*, pp. 93–4.

63 MS 183 Schonfeld, 593/1, Reports on visit to Internment camps (16–23 July; 23–28 August; 5–7 September; 4–6 November 1940); 228/1, 12 August 1940, Schiff to Schonfeld; 297/1, Report for the year ending 31 December 1942, p. 3; CZA A173/63, 1 August 1940, Schiff to Simon Marks.

64 Schonfeld Papers (UCL), 24 August 1940, Home Office to Dame Joanna Cruickshank; MS 183 Schonfeld 228/1, 10–17 July 1940, Report by

W.R. Hughes, Society of Friends, visit to Huyton Internment Camp; Rathbone and Major Victor Cazalet visited Huyton Camp; Acc 3121 C2/3/5/2, 26 July 1940, Brotman to Bentwich; 5 August 1940, Wilfred Israel, Overseas Department, JRC, visit to Isle of Man Camp. For Israel's role, see Naomi Shephard, *Wilfred Israel, Germany's Secret Ambassador* (London, 1984), pp. 173–6.

65 MS 183 Schonfeld 117/8, Report for year ending 1 October 1940, Internees; *The Times*, 30 July 1940, p. 5, Schonfeld's letter to the Editor; MS 183 Schonfeld, 228/1, 16–23 July 1940, Report on Schonfeld's visit to Internment Camps.

66 MS 183 Schonfeld 117/8, Report for year ending 1 October 1941, Internees; CCJR, Annual Report, 1940, p. 8.

67 MS 183 Schonfeld 673 [AG-AL], May 1941, Report on Activities of Agudat Israel, p. 8; MS 183 Schonfeld 297/1, Report for year ending 31 December 1942, p. 3.

68 MS 183 Schonfeld 117/8, Report for year ending 1 October 1941, p. 4; 297/1, Report for year ending 31 December 1941, p. 4. and Internees – releases.

69 MS 183 Schonfeld 673 [AG-AL], 30 July 1940, Rosenheim, London, to Joint Orthodox Refugees Committee; May 1941, Agudat Israel, Report p. 8.

70 CCJR, Annual Report, 1940, p. 8.

71 Schonfeld Papers (UCL), 9 October 1940, RJCC, Minutes, p. 3.

72 Acc 3121 C2/3/5/4, 3 October 1940, R. Clare Martin, Secretary of the RJCC, to Board.

73 CZA A173/63 17 July 1940, Sacher, Note on Deportation.

74 MS 183 Schonfeld 673 [AG-AL], August 1940, Report by United Jewish Refugee and War Relief Agencies, p. 2. According to this report, 6, 735 people were interned in Canada, of whom 2,290 were considered non-dangerous. Included in this latter category were 1,746 Jews. *J.C.*, 22 November 1940, p. 13, 28 February 1941, pp. 5, 19; Acc 3121 C2/3/5/5, 30 July 1941, Saul Hayes, Central Committee for Interned Refugees, Montreal, to Stephany.

75 Acc 3121 B5/2/2, 14 February 1941, Brotman to Brodetsky; C2/3/5/5, 23 February 1941, Brotman to L. Prince.

76 Major Julius Layton, Imperial War Museum, Department of Sound Archives, no. 004382/03, 'Jewish Refugee Question'; Michael Blakeney, *Australia and the Jewish Refugees 1933–1948* (Sydney, 1985), pp. 167–8; Benzion Patkin, *The Dunera Internees* (Sydney, 1979), p. 51; Acc 3121 C2/3/5/5, 2 February 1941, David Brotmacher to Brotman.

77 Ibid.; 18 February 1941, Brotman to Prince; 6 February 1941, Lady Reading to Brotman.

78 Ibid., 15 February 1941, Brotman to Schildenkraut; 29 January 1941, extract of letter from the Australian Jewish Welfare Society, Sydney; CCJR, 13 November 1940, p. 5 and 15 May 1941, p. 5, Executive Committee, Minutes. The CCJR authorised £1,000 out of the £2,000 landing money granted by it for destitute refugees. MS 183 Schonfeld 673 [AG-AL], Canada – August 1940, Report by United Jewish Refugee and War Relief Agencies, p. 4.

79 Acc 3121 C2/3/5/5, 13 March 1941, R.W. Oppenheimer, Joint Ortho-
    dox Jewish Refugees Committee, to Brotman; 18 March 1941, Brotman
    to Oppenheimer.
80 Ibid., 8 October 1940, Internment of Aliens: Suggestions.
81 Chaim Raphael, Imperial War Museum, Department of Sound Ar-
    chives, no. 004289/2, 'Civilian Internment in Britain 1939–1945'; Acc
    3121 C2/3/5/5, 30 July 1941, Hayes to Stephany; CCJR, Annual Re-
    port, 1941, pp. 4–5.
82 Stent, *A Bespattered Page?*, p. 226.
83 CCJR, Annual Report 1940, p. 8.
84 Acc 3121 E3/520, 26 October 1945, Government House, Ottawa; 14
    November 1945, Hayes to Brotman.
85 Acc 3121 C2/3/5/5, 21 November 1941, Brodetsky to Anthony de
    Rothschild; 28 November, Schiff to Brodetsky; 20 July 1942, Schiff to
    Brotman; Board Annual Report, 1943, p. 27.

6 Anglo-Jewry Mobilises (Summer 1942–Spring 1943)

1 CZA A82/6, 31 August 1942, Brodetsky, 'The Jewish Problem', p. 1.
2 Ibid.
3 Philip Bell, 'Europe in the Second World War', in Paul Hayes, ed.,
   Themes in European History (London, 1992), p. 258.
4 Martin Gilbert, *Second World War* (London, 1999), p. 98.
5 J.R.M. Butler, *History of the Second World War: Grand Strategy*, vol.
   III, part II (London, 1964), p. 541; Richard J. Overy, *Why the Allies
   Won* (London, 1995), pp. 25–62.
6 M. Howard, *History of the Second World War Grand Strategy*, vol. IV
   (London, 1972), p. 289.
7 Ibid., p. 10.
8 C.B.A. Behrens, *Merchant Shipping and the Demands of War* (London,
   1955), pp. 305–6.
9 Howard, *History of the Second World War Grand Strategy*, pp. 291–2.
10 W.P. (43) 46, cited in ibid., p. 635.
11 W.P. (43) 100, cited in ibid., pp. 632–6.
12 HL Debate, 23 March 1943, vol. 26, cols. 849–50.
13 FO 371/36734 W7542/7542/48, 4 May 1943, Foreign Office to Washington; 19 May 1943, Draft Speech for Refugee Debate.
14 J. Ehrman, *Grand Strategy*, vol. V (London, 1956), p. 32.
15 Acc 3121 BOD C11/7/3a/2, 28 March 1944, interview with Major
   Arthur Henderson.
16 FO 371/42812 WR 500/3/48, 27 July 1944, Foreign Office Memorandum.
17 FO 371/36648 W121/49/48, 29 December 1942, Randall, Minute; HC
   Debates, Fifth Series, 1942–43, vol. 389, col. 1127.
18 Ibid., col. 1123.
19 CAB 95/15, 31 December 1942 and 19 February 1943, Cabinet Committee on Refugees, Minutes.
20 Statement of Policy, May 1939, Cmd. 6019, cited in Sherman, *Island
   Refuge*, p. 232, ff.32; Wasserstein, *Britain and the Jews of Europe*, p. 13.

21   Malcolm J. Proudfoot, *European Refugees 1939–1952* (London, 1957), p. 68. During 1940–44, a total of 58,296 Jews entered Palestine.

22   CAB 66/37 W.P. (43) 246, 17 June 1943, Memorandum, Minister of State to War Cabinet.

23   CO 733/396/75113/38 (40), December 1939–January 1940, Foreign Office Memorandum, cited in Ronald Zweig, *Britain and Palestine during the Second World War* (London, 1986), p. 56; Wasserstein, *Britain and the Jews of Europe*, pp. 21–6.

24   Ibid., pp. 40–80.

25   CO 733/445 (76021/41), 18 May 1942, Cabinet Conclusions, cited in Wasserstein, *Britain and the Jews of Europe*, p. 161.

26   See Norman Rose, *Chaim Weizmann; A Biography* (London, 1986), pp. 386–7; Weizmann, *Trial and Error*, pp. 495–6; Nathaniel Katzburg, 'British Policy on Immigration to Palestine During World War Two', *Rescue Attempts during the Holocaust, Proceedings of the Second Yad Vashem International Historical Conference, Jerusalem 1977* (April 1974), pp. 185–6.

27   FO 371/36711 W4070/1315/48, 9 March 1943, E. Boyd, Colonial Office, to Randall.

28   CO 323/1846/2, July 1943 [n.d.], Colonial Office to Foreign Office.

29   Ibid., 29 July 1943, Minutes. While these arrangements were in force, 7,739 Jews reached Palestine during 1943–44. See Katzburg, 'British Policy on Immigration', p. 186; FO 371/42724 W5424/15/18, 5 April 1944, G.H. Gater, Permanent Under-Secretary at the Colonial Office, to Jewish Agency for Palestine (JA).

30   *J.C.*, 3 November 1944, p. 6.

31   FO 371/42810 WR 315/3/48, 20 July 1944, Hankey to Randall; FO 371/42816 WR 890/3/48, 30 August 1944, Hankey, Minutes; 25 August 1944, Lord Moyne, Cairo, to Foreign Office.

32   Abba Eban, 'Tragedy and Triumph', in *Chaim Weizmann, A Biography by Several Hands* (London, 1962), p. 273.

33   Michael Marrus, *The Holocaust in History* (London, 1987), p. 166.

34   For the historical debates surrounding the Final Solution, see Marrus, *The Holocaust in History.*

35   See Richard Breitman, *Official Secrets: What the Nazis Planned, What the British and Americans Knew* (London, 1999).

36   Bell, 'Europe in the Second World War', p. 266.

37   FO 371/30917 C7853/61/18, 10 August 1942, C. Norton, Berne, to Foreign Office, containing message from G. Riegner to S. Silverman. See Yehuda Bauer, 'When Did They Know?', *Midstream*, vol. 14 (April 1968), pp. 51–8.

38   FO 371/30917 C7853/61/18, 10 September 1942, D. Allen, Minutes; FO 371/30885 C9844/9844/62, 1 October 1942, Frank Roberts, Minute; Walter Laqueur, *The Terrible Secret* (London, 1980), pp. 65–84.

39   Acc 3121 B5/2/2/1, 25 June 1942, Brotman to Brodetsky.

40   CZA C2/279, 13 December 1942, First Meeting of National Council of WJC, Minutes, Dr. Ignacy Schwarzbart, member of the executive of the British Section and of the Polish National Council. See also A. Leon Kubowitzki, *Unity in Dispersion, A History of the World Jewish*

Congress (New York, 1948), p. 194; Walter Laqueur, 'Jewish Denial and the Holocaust', *Commentary* (December 1977), pp. 44–55; Yehuda Bauer, *Jewish Reactions to the Holocaust* (Jerusalem, 1989), pp. 110–14. Bauer drew a crucial distinction between information and knowledge.

41 *J.C.*, 11 December 1942, p. 8.
42 FO 371/30917, C7839/61/18, 14 July 1942, Brotman to M. Stanczyk, Polish Minister of Social Welfare; Acc 3121 A/32, 19 July 1942, BOD Minutes; *J.C.*, 24 July 1942, p. 5.
43 Rubenstein, *The Myth of Rescue*.
44 CZA C2/409, 29 June 1942, Press Conference, Minutes.
45 Acc 3121 A/32, 15 July 1942, JFC Minutes; BOD Annual Report 1942, p. 31.
46 Acc 3121 B5/2/2, 3–4 August 1943, JFC Meeting; CZA A82/6, 31 August 1942, Brodetsky, 'The Jewish Problem'; Acc 3121 C2/2/5/1, Aide-Mémoire on Post-War Emigration (February 1943). By February 1943, Brodetsky modified this to 'perhaps two million' admitting that this figure 'in light of later developments, may be subject to radical revision'.
47 CZA L22/177, 27 August 1942, Lichtheim to Joseph Linton, JA representative, London; CZA L22/149, 15 September 1942, Lichtheim to Linton.
48 Acc 3121 A/32, 9 September 1942, BOD, Minutes.
49 Acc 3121 BOD B5/2/2/3, 7 October 1942, Brotman to Brodetsky.
50 FO 371/30917 C8055/61/18, Statement on War Criminals [n.d., presumably August 1942]; C7839/61/18, 19 August 1942, Randall, Minute.
51 ACC 3121 C11/7/2/8, 12 January 1942, Brodetsky and Stein, to Sikorski; FO 371/30914 C487/61/18, 12 January 1942, JFC and AJA to Foreign Office.
52 CZA C2/295, 9 May 1942, Report, translation of letter by Sikorski to WJC, p. 8.
53 FO 371/30914 C2009/61/18, 18 February 1942, Easterman to Eden; 9 May 1942, Sikorski to WJC; CZA C2/295, WJC (British Section) October 1942 reports, no. 2, St. James's Conference; Acc 3121 C11/13/16, 20 September 1942, Brodetsky to Archbishop of Canterbury; CZA Z4/302/25, 17 September 1942, JA, Minutes.
54 FO 371/30885 C9844/9844/62, 1 October 1942, Law, Foreign Office Memorandum.
55 Ibid.; FO 371/30917 C7839/61/18, 21 August 1942, Roberts to G. Lias, Ministry of Information.
56 FO 371/30923 C11923/61/18, 26 November 1942, conversation between Silverman, Easterman and Law.
57 *The Times*, 18 December 1942, Wiener Library, 215D, Press cuttings; FO 371/30923 C11975/61/18, 7 December 1942, Foreign Office to Washington; C12147/61/18, 8 December 1942, Telegram from Foreign Office to the Dominions; C11923/61/18, 1 December 1942, Roberts, Minutes; FO 371/30925 C12716/61/18, 16 December 1942, Deputation from the Council of Christians and Jews; Law, Minute.
58 FO 371/30923 C12147/61/18, 5 December 1942, Eden to Winant and Maisky; C11975/61/18, 7 December 1942, Foreign Office to Washington.
59 ACC 3121 C11/7/3a/2, 3 December 1942, JFC Emergency Meeting.

60 Ibid. ACC 3121 A/32, 7 December 1942, Board Executive Committee, Minutes.
61 Acc 3121 C11/2/37/2, 25 November 1942, Brotman to Stein.
62 FO 371/30925 C12711/61/18, 17 December 1942, Extract from HC Debates.
63 The Earl of Avon, *The Eden Memoirs: The Reckoning* (London 1965), p. 358.
64 FO 371/30925 C12711/61/18, 16 December 1942, Roberts, Minutes; CZA C2/308, 14 December 1942, Easterman to Law.
65 FO 371/ 36648 W121/49/48, 23 December 1942, Wyndham Deedes to Eden.
66 BOD Annual Report, 1943, p. 39.
67 *Manchester Guardian*, 18 December 1942, 'Urgency of Practical Measures', Wiener Library, 215D, Press cuttings; CZA A354/50, 18 February 1944, Hertz File, 'Speaker's Notes'.; BOD Annual Report 1942, p. 35. *Manchester Guardian*, 12 January 1943, Wiener Library, Press cuttings, 215B.
68 FO 371/30925 C12711/61/18, 17 December 1942, Extract from HC Debates, p. 2; C12748/61/18, 18 December 1942, Brodetsky to Eden.
69 Acc 3121 BOD C11/7/1/1/, 24 December 1942, Consultative Committee Meeting, Minutes.
70 BOD Annual Report 1943, p. 35.
71 *Manchester Guardian*, 18 December 1942, 'Urgency of Practical Measures', Wiener Library, Press cuttings, 215D; CZA Z4/302/26, 22 December 1942, JA, Minutes, statement by Simon Marks.
72 *J.C.*, 25 December 1942, p. 8.
73 CZA C2/295, 21 December 1942, Suggestions of Practical Steps; FO 371/36648 W415/49/48, 6 January 1943, 'Measures proposed for the Rescue of European Jewry'.
74 Acc 3121 C11/7/1/1, 24 December 1942, Emergency Consultative Committee Meeting, Minutes.
75 CZA C2/510, 28 December 1942, Barou to Brodetsky; 28 December 1942, Easterman to Brotman.
76 Acc 3121 BOD C11/7/3a/2, 18 December 1942, Brodetsky to Samuel; C11/7/3a/4, 18 December 1942, interview with Roberts.
77 FO 371/30925 C12853/61/18, 23 December 1942, Deputation to Eden; Acc 3121 C10/2/8/1, 23 December 1942, Eden to Samuel.
78 Acc 3121 C2/2/5/1, 30 December 1942, meeting with Law; C1//7/1/1, 4 January 1943, Consultative Committee Meeting, Minutes.
79 Acc 3121 C11/7/3a/2, 7 January 1943, Nazi Extermination Policy, Burlington House Meeting.
80 Ibid.; C11/7/1/5, 7 January 1943, Rathbone, 'Jewish Massacres: The Case for an Offer to Hitler'; C2/2/5/1, 19 January 1943, 'Suggested Steps for Saving Jews in Nazi Occupied Europe'.
81 Acc 3121 E1/31, 15 January 1943, Hertz to Brodetsky. Brodetsky rejected the idea. E1/31, 27 January 1943, Brodetsky to Hertz.
82 Ibid., 11 January 1943, Brodetsky to Hertz; C2/2/5/1, 12 January 1943, Brodetsky to Sir George Jones.
83 Schonfeld, 'No Alternative to Zion', *Message to Jewry*, p. 163; CZA Z4/302/26, 21 December 1942, JA, Minutes. Brodetsky insisted that

'if Palestine was not properly mentioned then he would not be a member of the delegation to Eden'.

84 Acc 3121 C2/2/5/2, 12 January 1943, Schonfeld to Brodetsky; C2/2/5/1, 15 January 1943, Sir George Jones to Brodetsky.
85 MS 183 Schonfeld 656/1 [Poll-Pz], 'Motion'; 153/1 (f.1), 12 February 1943, Schonfeld to the Editor.
86 MS 183 Schonfeld 656/1 [Poll-Pz], 11 January 1943, Brodetsky to Hertz; *J.C.*, 29 January 1943, p. 5; Acc 3121 E1/31, 3 February 1943, Brodetsky to Hertz; *J.C.*, 5 February 1943, p. 6.
87 Acc 3121 C2/2/5/1, 29 January 1943, Brotman to I. Greenberg, Editor, *J.C.*; Acc 3121 E1/31, 3 February 1943, Brodetsky to Hertz.
88 Acc 2805/6/1/17, 3 February 1943, Brodetsky to Hertz. See also Acc 3121 BOD C11/7/1/1, 25 January 1943, Consultative Committee Meeting, Minutes.
89 C2/2/5/2, 22 January 1943, Schonfeld to Brotman.
90 Acc 3121 E1/31, 9 February 1943, R. Oppenheim, Secretary, Agudat Israel, to Brotman; Acc 2805/6/1/17, 4 February 1943, Hertz to Brodetsky.
91 *J.C.*, 29 January 1943, p. 5; 5 February 1943, p. 6; 12 February 1943, p. 5; 6 June 1961, p. 13; Interview with Marcus Retter, August 1994, New York. Retter, who worked with Schonfeld, understandably supports his view.
92 FO 371/36649 W1067/49/46, 30 January 1943, Eden to Sir Austin Hudson, MP.
93 HL Debates, 23 March 1943, vol. 26, col. 827.
94 Ibid.
95 CZA C2/296, 19 January 1943, copy of Attlee's statement in House of Commons.
96 *The Times*, 28 January 1943, Wiener Library, 215 B, Press cuttings.
97 Cab 95/15, 27 January 1943, Cabinet Committee on Refugees, Minutes.
98 FO 371/36694 W416/124/48, 29 January 1943, Law, conversation with Brodetsky and Brotman.
99 Acc 3121 C11/6/4/1, 23 February 1943, Brotman to Law. For urgency of the situation, see CZA L22/149, 19 January 1943, Lichtheim Report.
100 Acc 3121 E3/536/1, 20 March 1943, National Committee to Eden, Washington.
101 Acc 3121 C11/7/1/1, 15 February 1943, Emergency Consultative Committee Meeting, Minutes.
102 Acc 3121 B5/2/4, 19 February 1943, Brotman to Brodetsky.
103 Acc 3121 C11/6/4/1, 23 February 1943, Brotman to Law; 25 February 1943, Brotman to Roberts; 16 March 1943, Roberts to Brotman.
104 Acc 3121 C11/7/3a/2, 25 February 1943, Brodetsky and Stein to Law; 15 March 1943, Randall to Brodetsky and Stein.
105 Acc 3121 E3/536/1, 20 March 1943, National Committee to Eden, Washington.
106 Foreign Relations of the United States [FRUS], 1943, vol. 1, pp. 134–47; FO 20/107, W240/351/50, Weekly Political Intelligence Summaries, January to June 1943, no. 175, p. 11; BOD Annual Report 1943, p. 40.
107 FRUS, 1943, vol. 111, pp. 38–9, Memorandum of conversation by Harry Hopkins, Special Assistant to President Roosevelt.

108 Acc 3121 E3/536/1, 8 April 1943, Mary Sibthorp, National Committee Secretary, to Brodetsky.
109 Ibid., Draft Statement for [first] Conference 16 March 1943; 6 April 1943, 'Twelve-Point Programme for Rescue Measures'; 9 March 1943, National Committee Conference, Minutes.
110 *JTA*, 28 March 1943 and *Manchester Guardian*, 5 April 1943, 'Speedy Rescue of Jews', Wiener Library, 215 A, Press cuttings.
111 FO 371/36659 W6301/49/48, 15 April 1943, Memorandum; BOD Annual Report 1943, p. 42.
112 FO 371/36658 W5684/49/48, 24 March 1943, W. Strang, Memorandum; 15 April 1943, Minutes.
113 Ibid., W5673/49/48, 9 April 1943, Rathbone to Eden; E.A. Walker, Minutes; 10 April 1943, Rathbone to Eden.
114 FO 371/ 36658 W5534/49/48, 8 April 1943, Halifax, Washington, to Foreign Office; FO 371/36659 W6301/49/48, 9 April 1943, Brodetsky to Foreign Office; 11 April 1943, Walker, Minutes; Perlzweig approached Halifax with a similar request, see W6042/49/48, 16 April 1943, Washington to Foreign Office; CZA Z4/15202, 29 April 1943, Walker to Linton.
115 FO 371/36731 W6933/6933/48, 3 May 1943, Law to Eden.
116 FO 371/36725 W6785/6711/48, 5 May 1943, Record of discussion at Bermuda, Discussion no. 2, 20 April 1943; W7106/6711/48, 10 May 1943, Report of Bermuda Refugees, Discussion.
117 FRUS, 1943, vol. 1, pp. 143–4. See pp. 136–7.
118 Acc 3121 C2/2/5/2, 31 March 1943, Emerson to Revd. W.W. Simpson; 4 April 1943, Simpson to Archbishop of Canterbury.
119 CZA Z4/302/27, *inter alia*, 19 April 1943 and 3 May 1943, JA, Minutes.
120 FO 371/36725 W6785/6711/48, 28 April 1943, Discussion no. 12.
121 National Archives, 840.48 REFUGEES/4009, 29 June 1943, Breckinridge Long, assistant Secretary of State, to Hull.
122 Feingold, *The Politics of Rescue*, p. 206.
123 FO 371/36731 W6933/6933/48, 3 May 1943, Law to Eden.
124 FO 371/36725 W7541/6711/48, 28 June 1943, UK Delegates to the Bermuda Conference to Eden.
125 BOD Annual Report 1943, p. 43.
126 FO 371/36725 W7127/6711/48, 10 May 1943, Harold Beeley, Foreign Office Research Department, to Randall.
127 Kubowitzki, *Unity in Dispersion*, p. 165.
128 Acc 3121 E3/536/1, 22 April 1943, Cazalet to *The Times*; E/536/2, December 1943, National Committee, letter.
129 *News Chronicle*, 'How not to hold a Conference on Refugees' and *The Observer*, 'Honour our Guide', cited in CZA A354/50, Joseph Hertz Papers, 18 February 1944, Speakers Notes on 'Jewish Situation in Central Europe', pp. 11–12. *J.C.*, 23 April 1943, p. 8; 7 May 1943, p. 8. *Jewish Weekly*, 30 April 1943, vol. VII, no. 370, p. 1.
130 HC Debates, Fifth Series, 1942–1943, vol. 389, cols. 1117–1204, especially pp. 1120, 1129–30, 1124.
131 Ibid., pp. 1137, 1157–58, 1184. For Rathbone's critical view of Morrison, 'whom she never forgave', see Mary D. Stocks, *Eleanor Rathbone: A Biography* (London, 1949), pp. 300–1.

132 Acc 3121 C2/2/5/1, 20 May 1943; AIWO, Report, January to June 1943, p. 5. AJAC coll. 361 A14/5, 17 May 1943, Perlzweig to Easterman.
133 Acc 3121 E3/536/2, 26 July 1944, National Committee, 'Our Purpose', points for Deputation to Foreign Secretary.
134 FO 371/36725 W9961/6711/48, 4 July 1943, Brotman to Foreign Office; BOD Annual Report, 1943, pp. 19–20.
135 Acc 3121 C11/7/1/5, 10 June 1943, interview with Randall.
136 Acc 3121 C2/2/5/1, 16 July 1943, Brodetsky to Dr. J.M. Machover, United Emergency Committee for European Jewry, Sydney.

7 Pawns in the Game of War (Summer 1943–Autumn 1944)

1 Acc 3121 B5/2/1, 25 July 1943, Board Meeting.
2 Bolchover, *British Jewry and the Holocaust*, pp. 54–7.
3 Acc 3121 E/536/1, May 1943, Cazalet, letter; 8 June 1943, National Committee, Minutes.
4 Ibid., 16 June 1943, Short Secretarial Report. By mid-June, 40,000 copies of 'Rescue the Perishing' were in circulation, and about 55,000 copies of the Twelve-Point Programme.
5 FO 371/36662, W8192/49/48, 25 May 1943, Peake to Rathbone.
6 Acc 3121 E3/536/1, 16 June 1943, Short Secretarial Report. By September 1943, the National Committee had rejected the idea of liaison with America; E3/536/2, 23 September 1943, National Committee Executive Meeting.
7 FO 371/36665 W11588/49/48, 9 August 1943, Rathbone: Note on the Position Regarding Rescue From Nazi Terror and Post-War Refugee Policy.
8 Acc 3121 E3/536/2, 9 November 1943, National Committee Meeting; 25 November 1943, Rathbone to Hall; HC Debates, Fifth Series, 2 December 1943, vol. 395, cols. 1467–71.
9 FO 371/42751 W2859/83/48, 25 February 1944, Minutes, Lady C. Cheetham and Randall.
10 Acc 3121 B5/2/7/1, 31 January 1944, Brotman to Brodetsky.
11 Acc 3121 E3/536/1, Hertz to United Synagogue (n.d., presumably April 1944); 10 May 1944, National Committee Executive Meeting, Minutes; 2 June 1944, Wilfred Israel to Brotman.
12 Acc 3121 E3/536/2, 'Continuing Terror', p. 2.
13 FO 371/36711 W3042/1315/48, 18 February 1943, Schonfeld to Millard, 2 March 1943, Millard to Schonfeld.
14 Acc 3121 C2/2/5/2, 10 November 1943, Lord Crewe to Churchill.
15 HC Debates, Fifth Series, 2 December 1943, vol. 395, col. 1471; CZA A354/50, Joseph Hertz Papers 18 February 1944, 'Jewish Situation', p. 19.
16 Acc 3121 E3/536/2, 26 November 1943, Rathbone to Hall; E3/536/1, 13 December 1943, Rathbone: Note on the Proposed Declaration.
17 FO 371/42745 W127/26/48, 29 December 1943, Randall, Minutes.
18 FO 371/42751 W543/83/48, 14 December 1943, Rathbone to Hall.

19 Ibid., 7 January 1944, Hall to Rathbone; 11 January 1944, notes on points for submission to Eden; W544/83/48, 8 January 1944, Foreign Office note on Rathbone's points for 11 January deputation; W855/83/48, 14 January 1944, Randall, Minutes and Randall to Emerson; Acc 3121 E3/536/1, 18 January 1944, National Committee Executive Meeting, Minutes.

20 FO 371/42751 W1060/83/48, 1 February 1944, interview with Brodetsky.

21 FO 371/42845 WR 346/13/48, 8 August 1944, telegram no. 235, Foreign Office to Lisbon.

22 FO 371/42811 WR 481/3/48, 28 July 1944, Cheetham, Minutes; WR 484/3/48, 5 September 1944, Paul Mason, head of Refugee Department, to Emerson; FO 371/42845 WR 346/13/48, 18 July 1944, Sir R. Campbell, Lisbon.

23 FO 371/36666 W12841/49/48, 3 September 1943, 'The Refugee Situation', Law, Memorandum.

24 Acc 3121 C2/2/5/2, 19 August 1943, Law to Crewe and *inter alia*, C11/7/3a/2, 10 August 1943, interview with Emerson; C2/2/5/2, 29 November 1943, Brodetsky to Emerson; B5/2/1, 27 June 1944, conversation with Patrick Malin, deputy Director, IGCR.

25 Acc 3121 C2/2/5/3, 11 August 1944, Board to IGCR.

26 Ibid., 15–17 August 1944, William Frankel, Report of Fourth Plenary Session of the IGCR; AJYB, vol. 47 (1945–46), p. 347.

27 FO 371/42751 W544/83/48, 8 January 1944, notes on Rathbone's points for 11 January deputation; Wasserstein, *Britain and the Jews of Europe*, p. 218.

28 BOD Annual Report, 1944, p. 41; Acc 3121 E3/536/2, 2 October 1945, WRB, Twenty Months' Humanitarian Record.

29 Acc 3121 C2/2/5/3, 14 September 1944, Brotman interview with James Mann, British representative of the WRB.

30 Acc 3121 C11/7/3a/2, 1 February 1944, interview with Hall; FO 371/42751 W1060/83/48, 3 February 1944, Randall, Minutes. Hall was referring to the Cabinet Committee on the Reception and Accommodation of Refugees.

31 Ibid.

32 FO 371/42727 W1629/16/48, 30 January 1944, Easterman to Law; W2231/16/48, 9 February 1944, Parliamentary Question Time; W3012/16/48 16 February 1944, Emanuel Cellar to Halifax. For the British press, see W2413/16/48, 12 February 1944, extract from *Manchester Guardian*; *The Times*, 10 April 1944, p. 3.

33 FO 371/42727 W3201/16/48, 22 February 1944, extract from *The Times*; Randall, Minutes.

34 *Jewish Weekly*, 10 March 1944, vol. VIII, no. 415, p. 1.

35 Acc 3121 C11/7/3a/2, 27 March 1944, interview with Randall; 28 March 1944, interview with Major Arthur Henderson; AJYB, vol. 46 (1944–45), p. 190.

36 FO 371/30917, C7870/61/18, 6 August 1942, Treatment of War Criminals; HL Debates, 1941–42, vol. 124, cols. 581–6; CZA 9775a, WJC, Report National Conference 23–24 October 1943, p. 9.

37 FO 371/30917 C7870/61/18, 6 August 1942, Treatment of War Criminals;

Fox, 'The Jewish Factor in British War Crimes Policy in 1942', *English Historical Review*, vol. XCII, no. 362 (January 1977), p. 98; Priscilla Dale Jones, 'British Policy towards German Crimes against German Jews, 1939–1945', *Leo Baeck Institute Year Book*, vol. XXXVI (1991), pp. 339–66. This became a major controversy in 1945, finally resolved in August 1945 with the establishment of a new legal category of 'Crimes Against Humanity'. See Acc 3121 C11/7/2/9, 26 April 1945, Board to A. Greenwood.

38 FO 371/36662 W8192/49/48, 4 June 1943, Randall, Minutes.

39 CZA C2/540, 6 October 1943, Jan Masaryk to Easterman; 11 October 1943, Easterman to Masaryk; FO 371/34377 C13026/31/62, 3 November 1943, Goodman to Hall; *Jewish Weekly*, 12 November 1943, no. 398, vol. VII, p. 1.

40 AIWO A-37, 3 November 1943, Goodman to Hall; 13 November 1943, G.W. Harrison, Foreign Office, to Goodman.

41 Acc 3121 C2/2/5/2, 10 November 1943, Crewe to Churchill; B5/2/4/1, 5 November 1943, Brodetsky to Brotman.

42 CZA C2/299, 8 February 1944, Proceedings of WJC; FO 371/42751 W1635/83/48, [n.d.] February 1944, Foreign Office Memorandum; Acc 3121 C2/2/5/3, 16 February 1944, J. Slawson, American Jewish Committee, to J.W. Pehle, WRB.

43 CZA C2/666, 22 February 1944, Melchett to Eden.

44 Cab 95/15, J.R. (44), 1st Meeting, 14 March 1944, Cabinet Committee on Refugees.

45 CZA C2/666, 11 March 1944, Eden to Melchett; 14 March 1944, Melchett to Easterman.

46 Acc 3121 B5/2/7/2, 22 March 1944, Dr. D. Mowshowitz to Brodetsky.

47 CZA C2/666, 24 March 1944, Easterman to Melchett; 29 March 1944, Easterman to Melchett.

48 FO 371/39258 C3849/15/21, 23 March 1944, Telegram no. 1249, Clifford Norton, Berne, to Foreign Office.

49 CZA C2/458, Chronology of Events, p. 15; AJYB, vol. 46 (1944–45), p. 156.

50 Acc 3121 C9/1/4a, 21 March 1944, FAC Emergency Meeting, Minutes.

51 Acc 3121 C11/7/3a/2, 28 March 1944, interview with A. Henderson; FO 371/42723 W4878/15/48, 10 April 1944, Foreign Office to HM's Charge d'affaires to the Yugoslav Government in Cairo; FO 371/42724 W5799/15/48, 21 April 1944, Randall to Hertz; 26 April 1944, Donald Hall, Foreign Office, to Easterman.

52 CZA C2/15, 28 March 1944, 'Special Conference'.

53 AJAC MS coll. 361 D108/18, 22 March 1944, conversation with Zinchenko; CZA C2/15, Note of action taken from 21 to 23 March 1944; 28 March 1944, 'Special Conference'.

54 AJAC MS coll. 361 D108/18, 14 June 1944, Kubowitzki to Members of the Office Committee; CZA C2/15, 28 March 1944, 'Special Conference'.

55 Acc 3121 B5/2/7/2, 18 May 1944, Brotman to Brodetsky.

56 Ibid. Nevertheless, see John Cornwell, *Hitler's Pope: The Secret History of Pius XII* (New York, 2000). Cornwell maintains that the Pope

could never bring himself to publish a clear message of condemnation of the enormous crimes against Europe's Jews and other minorities who were earmarked for physical extermination. Cornwell concludes that a forceful statement from Rome would have made a difference to the fate of European Jews. The least it would have done was to warn the Jews that deportation meant certain death, resulting in more fleeing or going into hiding. Furthermore it would have encouraged greater willingness on the part of the Catholic populations to help their Jewish neighbours.

57 FO 371/42723 W4586/15/48, 21 March 1944, Randall, Minute.
58 FO 371/42724 W5286/15/48, 4 April 1944, W.D. Allen to Miss Barker, Political Intelligence Department.
59 Ibid., W5791/15/48, 11 April 1944, message from Lichtheim and Riegner.
60 Ibid., 17 April 1944, Walker, Minute; 28 April 1944, P. Scarlet. The PWE consisted of portions of the Ministry of Information, the Special Operations Executive and the BBC. It began functioning in August 1941 and was responsible for overt and covert propaganda to enemy and enemy-occupied territory.
61 Randolph L. Braham, *The Politics of Genocide: The Holocaust in Hungary*, vol. 2 (New York, 1981), pp. 691–731; Shlomo Aronson, '"The Quadruple Trap" and the Holocaust in Hungary', David Cesarani, ed., *Genocide and Rescue: The Holocaust in Hungary* (Oxford, 1997), p. 94.
62 CZA C2/46, 1 June 1944, Easterman to E. Thurtle, Ministry of Information; 15 June 1944, Thurtle to Easterman; 16 June 1944, Easterman to Thurtle; 19 June 1944, Thurtle to Easterman.
63 Martin Gilbert, *Auschwitz and the Allies* (London, 1981), pp. 190–8, 231–9.
64 CZA C2/15, 25 June 1944, Schwarzbart, Communique; FO 371/42807 WR 75/3/48, 26 June 1944, Telegram, no. 2949 from Norton, Berne, to Foreign Office; FO 371/42809 WR 218/3/48, 4 July 1944, Hubert Ripka, acting Czech Minister of Foreign Affairs, to Philip Nichols, British representative to Czech Republic.
65 CZA C2/97, 26 June 1944, Easterman to Hall; FO 371/42807 WR 18/3/48, 5 July 1944, interview, Hall, Silverman and Easterman.
66 Acc 3121 C2/2/5/3, 18 June 1944, Board Resolution; FO 371/42809 WR 225/3/48, 12 July 1944, Brodetsky to Hall.
67 Acc 3121 C2/2/5/3, 18 July 1944, interview with I.L. Henderson; FO 371/42810 WR 329/3/48, 19 July 1944, Henderson, Minute.
68 Acc 3121 C11/7/3a/2, 28 March 1944, interview with Major A. Henderson.
69 FO 371/42807, WR 28/3/48, 29 June 1944, Easterman to Hall; 5–6 July 1944, A.R. Dew and I.L. Henderson, Minutes.
70 FO 371/42809 WR 226/3/48, 13 July 1944, Foreign Office Telegram no. 2107 to V.M. Molotov; 14 July 1944, Eden to HM Ambassador, Moscow.
71 CZA C2/46, 15 June 1944, Thurtle to Easterman; FO 371/42810, WR 302/3/48, 5 July 1944, interview, Hall, Silverman and Easterman; 12 July, Scarlett, Minutes; FO 371/42807 WR 75/3/48, 3 July 1944, Eden, Minute.

8

8

72 CZA C2/16, 1 July 1944, Melchett to Churchill; 3 July 1944, Archbishop of Canterbury to Churchill; C2/783, 11 July 1944, Easterman to Archbishop of Canterbury.
73 FO 371/42807 W95/3/48, 4 July 1944, P.D. [Pierson Dixon], Minutes.
74 FO 371/428089 WR 269/3/48, 13 July 1944, Churchill to Melchett and Archbishop of Canterbury.
75 HC Debates, Fifth Series, 5 July 1944, vol. 401, cols. 1160–62; FO 371/42808 W106/3/48, 10 July 1944, I.L. Henderson to J.M. Martin; CZA C2/16, 6 July 1944, Easterman to Melchett.
76 FO 371/42809 WR 291/3/48, 15 July 1944, Easterman to Hall; 22 July 1944, Minutes, I.L. Henderson.
77 CZA C2/17, 21 July 1944, Barou and Easterman, Hungary.
78 FO 371/42808 WR 129/3/48, 6 July 1944, Rathbone to Eden; FO 371/42809 WR 226/3/48, 13 July 1944, Telegram no. 2107, Foreign Office to Moscow; FO 371/42810 WR 363/3/48, 18 July 1944, Randall, Minute; FO 371/42815 WR 784/3/48, 17 August 1944, Molotov to Eden.
79 Acc 3121 E3/536/2, 26 July 1944, National Committee, 'Proposals'; FO 371/42811 WR 437/3/48, 22 July 1944, E. Shinwell to Eden; WR 457/3/48, 25 July 1944, Note for Eden; FO 371/42810 WR 363/3/48, 1 August 1944, Walker, Minute; W 437/3/48, 29 July 1944, Walker, Minute; FO 371/42812 WR 500/3/48, 27 July 1944, Foreign Office Memorandum.
80 FO 371/42809, WR 215/3/48, 18 July 1944, Foreign Office Telegram no. 581 and no. 2355 to Stockholm and Berne (respectively).
81 Braham, *Jewish Leadership during the Nazi Era*, pp. 1104–9; Yehuda Bauer, *Jews for Sale? Nazi–Jewish Negotiations, 1933–1945* (New Haven, 1994), pp. 172–95.
82 Gilbert, *Auschwitz and the Allies*, p. 216; Mss VG, 18 July 1944, Polish Ministry of Foreign Affairs to Goodman.
83 Acc 3121 C11/7/1/6, 27 June 1944, Schwarzbart to Mikolajczyk; 18 July 1944, interview, Brodetsky and Hall.
84 Acc 3121 B5/2/7/1, 29 August 1944, Brotman to Brodetsky.
85 WJC, 1 July 1944, Kubowitzki to John W. Pehle, WRB, cited in Gilbert, *Auschwitz and the Allies*, p. 256.
86 14 August 1944, John J. McCloy, Assistant Secretary of State, to Kubowitzki, cited in Kubowitzki, *Unity in Dispersion*, p. 167; CZA C2/458, Chronology of Events, p. 18.
87 AJAC MS col. 361 D109/1, 10 August 1944, E. Frischer to WJC.
88 Dina Porat, *The Blue and Yellow Stars of David: The Zionist Leadership in Palestine and the Holocaust, 1939–1945* (London, 1990), p. 216.
89 FO 371/42809 WR 276/3/48, 6 July 1944, conversation with Weizmann, Minute.
90 CZA Z4/15202, 11 July 1944, Note on the proposal for bombing death-camps.
91 FO 371/42809 WR 277/3/48, 15 July 1944, Sinclair to Eden.
92 FO 371/42814 WR 749/3/G, 13 August 1944, Air Commodore G.W.P. Grant, to V.F.W. Cavendish-Bentinck, Foreign Office.
93 Ibid., 16 August 1944, Linton to I.L. Henderson.

94   Ibid., 18 August 1944, I.L. Henderson; 21 August 1944, R. Allen, Minutes.
95   FO 371/42806 WR 823/1/4, 18 September 1944, Mason, Minutes.
96   FO 371/42814 WR 749/3/G, 1 September 1944, Law to Weizmann.
97   Ibid., 26 August 1944, Walker, Minutes.
98   AIWO A-37, 2 September 1944, L. Koziebrodzki, Polish Ministry of Foreign Affairs, to Goodman.
99   CZA Z4/10405, 20 September 1944, Linton to Mason.
100 FO 371/42818 WR1174/3/48, 20 September 1944, Linton to Mason; 25 September 1944, Cheetham and Mason, Minutes; Acc 3121 C11/7/1/6, 28 September 1944, Brotman, conversation with Mason.
101 Acc 3121 A/32, September 1944, FAC, Minutes, p. 243.
102 FO 371/42821 WR1596/3/48, 10 November 1944, Mason to K.E. Robinson, Colonial Office.
103 FO 371/42818 WR 1174/3/48, 25 September 1944, Cheetham, Minutes.
104 FO 371/39454 C14201/131/55, 12 October 1944, Mason, Minute.
105 FO 371/42809 WR 285/3/48, 20 July 1944, Foreign Office to Washington; Braham, *Politics of Genocide*, pp. 718, 767.
106 FO 371/42809 WR 285/3/48, 18 July 1944, telegram no. 3328, Norton, Berne, to Foreign Office.
107 Wasserstein, *Britain and the Jews of Europe*, p. 263.
108 FO 371/42810 WR 329/3/48, 19 July 1944, Minute, I.L. Henderson; WR 388/3/48, 21 July 1944, Memorandum, discussion with Shertok and Linton.
109 FO 371/42812 WR 500/3/48, 26 July 1944, National Committee deputation to Eden; FO 371/42814 WR 680/3/48, 31 July 1944, Rathbone to Eden.
110 FO 371/42808 WR 170/3/48, 1 July 1944, Morrison to Eden.
111 FO 371/42809 WR 285/3/48, 18 July 1944, Randall, Minutes; FO 371/42810 WR 315/3/48, 19 July 1944, Hankey, Minutes; 22 July 1944, Foreign Office to Washington.
112 Mss VG, 4 August 1944, Goodman to *inter alia*, the High Commissioner of Australia; 29 August 1944, American Embassy to Goodman. See pp. 184–6.
113 Acc 3121 B5/2/7/1, 9 August 1944, Frankel to Brodetsky.
114 CZA S25/1678, cited in Gilbert, *Auschwitz and the Allies*, p. 326; Wasserstein, op. cit., 243. see also Theo Tshuy, *Dangerous Diplomacy: The Story of Carl Lutz* (Cambridge, 2001), for the lesser known but equally important role played by the Swiss diplomat in wartime Budapest in securing protective papers for thousands of Jews in Hungary.
115 FO 371/42725 W8099/15/48, copy of letter dated 8 May 1944, Hertz to Churchill.
116 Acc 3121 C11/11/3/2, 28 July 1944, Eden to Hertz.
117 Acc 3121 E3/536/2, 24 July 1944, Rathbone, 'Facts and Proposals'.
118 FO 371/42809 WR 194/3/48, 11 July 1944, Eastwood to Randall; WR 275/3/48, 15 July 1944, Oliver Stanley to Sir H. MacMichael, High Commissioner for Palestine.

119 FO 371/42810 WR 320/3/48, 19 July 1944, MacMichael to Stanley.
120 FO 371/42821 WR 1634/3/48, 3 November 1944, Eastwood to Mason.
121 FO 371/42814 WR 685/3/48, 11 August 1944, interview, Hall and National Committee.
122 FO 371/42809, WR 290/10/G, 15 July 1944, J. Weytko, Polish Embassy, to Randall; 25 July 1944, I.L. Henderson, Minute.
123 Acc 3121 B5/2/7/2, 31 July 1944, Brotman to Brodetsky.
124 FO 371/42814 WR 672/3/48, 3 August 1944, Memorandum, Eden.
125 Ibid., WR 682/3/48, 8 August 1944, Memorandum, Eden; 1 August 1944, telegram no. 6773, Sir R. Campbell to Eden.
126 Ibid., WR 705/3/48, 17 August 1944, Foreign Office to Washington.
127 FO 371/42819 WR 864/3/48, 23 August 1944, conversation with Linton.
128 FO 371/42816 WR 890/3/48, 25 August 1944, Lord Moyne, Cairo, to Eden.
129 Acc 3121 C2/2/5/3, 31 August 1944, conversation with Mason; FO 371/42817 WR 993/3/48, 31 August 1944, Foreign Office Memorandum.
130 Acc 3121 B5/2/7/1, 1 September 1944, Brotman to Brodetsky.
131 FO 371/42817 WR 993/3/48, 1 September 1944, Dew, Minute; 7 September 1944, Cheetham, Minute; 8 September 1944, Mason, Minute; 13 September 1944, Mason to Brotman; 22 September 1944, Brotman to Mason.
132 FO 371/42815 WR 752/3/48, 9 August 1944, Rathbone to Eden; See Randolph L. Braham, 'The Rescue of the Jews of Hungary in Historical Perspective', *Proceedings of the Fifth Yad Vashem International Historical Conference, Jerusalem, March 1983* (Jerusalem, 1988), pp. 465–6.
133 CZA C2/458, Chronology of Events, p. 21; FO 371/42820 WR 1419/3/48, 23 October 1944, Mason to Easterman.
134 Acc 3121 B5/2/1, 18 October 1944, interview with Hall; FO 371/42820 WR 1433/3/48, 17 October 1944, Easterman to Mason; WR 1507/3/48, 18 October 1944, Foreign Office, Minute.
135 Ibid, 17 October 1944, Mason, Minute.
136 FO 371/42821 WR 1596/3/48, 10 November 1944, Mason, Minute.
137 Ibid., 24 October 1944, Cairo to Foreign Office; Acc 3121 C11/7/3a/2, 13 November 1944, conversation with Mason.
138 FO 371/42824 WR 2040/3/48, 30 November 1944, meeting between Brodetsky and Mason.
139 FO 371/42824 WR 1991/3/48, 4 January 1945, Mason to Dr. Zalmanovits, WJC.
140 AJYB, vol. 47 (1945–46), p. 425.
141 Acc 3121 C2/2/5/3, 14 September 1944, interview with J. Mann.
142 Mss VG, 9 August 1943, Goodman to J.P. Walshe, High Commissioner for Ireland.

8 Rescue Efforts: A Chronicle of Failure?

1 FO 371/36694, W416/124/48, 28 January 1943, Randall, Minutes. This document refers to the proposal to get 70,000 Jews out of Romania; CAB 95/15 J.R. (44), 2nd Meeting, 31 May 1944, 13 July 1944, War

Cabinet Committee on the Reception and Accommodation of Refugees; FO 371/42809 WR 274/3/48, 16 July 1944, Churchill, Minutes.
2 FO 371/42808 WR 170/3/48, 1 July 1944, Morrison to Eden. Morrison is referring to the Joel Brandt deal.
3 FO 371/42731 W3199/17/48, 1 March 1944, Randall to Emerson.
4 FO 371/32680 W14587/4555/48, 29 October 1942, Dingle Foot, MEW, to Law; *J.C.*, 16 July 1943, p. 5.
5 Herbert Katski, interview, August 1994, New York.
6 AR 3344.557, 28 April 1943, Report submitted by David Sulzberger to JDC Executive Committee.
7 FO 371/42857 WR 287/41/48, 15 July 1944, H.S. Gregory, Trading with the Enemy, to Randall.
8 CAB 95/15 J.R. (44) 1st Meeting, 14 March 1944, War Cabinet Committee on the Reception and Accommodation of Refugees; FO 371/42857 WR 405/41/48, 21 July 1944, C.H.M. Wilcox, Treasury, to Randall.
9 Ibid., WR 287/41/48, 15 July 1944, Gregory to Randall; WR 380/41/48, 21 July 1944, R.A.B. Mynors, Treasury, to Gregory.
10 FO 371/42752 W2128/86/48, 8 February 1944, Schonfeld to Randall; 14 February 1944, Minutes, Cheetham. For the agreement between the Federation and JDC, see AJJDC AR 3344.558, 13 September 1943, J.C. Hyman, JDC Executive Vice-Chairman, to Hertz.
11 FO 371/42752 W2128/86/48, 15 February 1944, Randall to Mynors; W2453/86/48, 16 February 1944, Foreign Office to Stockholm; W2672/86/48, 20 February 1944, Stockholm to Foreign Office; W3145/86/48, 26 February 1944, Mynors to Randall.
12 Ibid., W2673/86/48, 18 February 1944, Mynors to Randall.
13 FO 371/42777 W4062/667/48, 9 March 1944, Hertz to Eden.
14 Ibid., W4472/667/48, 20 March 1944, W.A. Camps, MEW, to I.L. Henderson.
15 FO 371/42777 W4615/667/48, 23 March 1944, Trading with the Enemy Department to G.H. Hall.
16 Ibid., W7712/667/48 12 May 1944, Camps to Randall; W9426/667/48, 4 June 1944, Hertz to Eden.
17 MS 183 Schonfeld, 427 (f.1), 4 June 1944, Hertz to Emerson; 24 September 1944, Schonfeld to Emerson; 2 October 1944, Emerson to Schonfeld; 10 November 1944, Schonfeld to J.G. Sillem, IGCR; 21 November 1944, Sillem to Schonfeld.
18 M. Marrus and R. Paxton, *Vichy France and the Jews* (New York, 1983), pp. 263–9.
19 FO 371/32680 W12687/4555/48, 21 September 1942, Randall, Minutes.
20 Cab 66/29 W.P. (42), 427, 23 September 1942, Morrison, Memorandum to War Cabinet.
21 FO 371/32680 W13107/4555/48, 28 September 1942, War Cabinet Offices, Conclusion 130 (42); MS 183 Schonfeld 290, 30 September 1942, Hertz to Sir Alexander Maxwell.
22 FO 371/32680 W13371/4555/48, 29 September 1942, conversation, Hertz and Cranborne; 7 October 1942, Randall, Minutes; 9 October 1942, Randall to J.B. Sidebotham, Colonial Office; MS 183 Schonfeld 290, 22 October 1942, Cranborne to Hertz.

23 Ibid., 30 October 1942, Hertz to Cranborne.
24 CCJR, Annual Report 1942, p. 3.
25 HC Debates, Fifth Series, 3 February 1943, vol. 386, col. 865.
26 MS 183 Schonfeld 665 [We-Weir], 28 May 1942, Schonfeld to Wedgwood.
27 S. Adler-Rudel, 'A Chronicle of Rescue Efforts', *Leo Baeck Institute Year Book*, XI, (1966), pp. 213–41.
28 N. Bentwich, *Jewish Youth Comes Home 1933–1943* (Connecticut, 1944), pp. 105–9.
29 D. Porat, *The Blue and Yellow Stars of David* (London, 1990), pp. 144–9.
30 Acc 3121 C/11/2/38, 16 March 1943, Roberts to Brotman.
31 Acc 3121 C11/6/4/1, 25 February 1943, Brotman to Roberts; 16 March 1943, Roberts to Brotman; C11/7/3a/2, 15 April 1943, Brodetsky to Eden, Memorandum; FO 371/36734 W7542/7542/48, 17 May 1943, Draft Speech for 19 May 1943 Debate.
32 Israel State Archives, P574/17, 11 June 1943, W. Fuller, Chief Secretary's Office, Jerusalem, to Executive of Jewish Agency, Jerusalem; Acc 3121 C2/2/5/1, 24 May 1943, Brotman to Hertz.
33 FO 371/42751 W3579/83/48, 1 March 1944, Randall, 'Table showing German civilians in the British Empire'; FO 371/42725 W8099/15/48, copy of letter dated 8 May 1944, Hertz to Churchill; FO 371/42808 WR 161/3/48, 1 July 1944, Sir R. Campbell, Washington, to Randall.
34 FO 371/42810 WR 320/3/48, 19 July, MacMichael to Stanley; see pp. 157–8.
35 Pamela Shatzkes, 'Kobe: A Japanese Haven for Jewish Refugees, 1940–1941', *Japan Forum* vol. 3, no. 2 (September 1991), pp. 257–73.
36 FO 371/32681 W15130/4555/48, 9 November 1942, Cranborne to Hertz; 27 November 1942, Randall to Sidebotham.
37 AIWO J. Rosenheim Collection, Box 47 Microfilm Reel 11 (hereafter 47/11), 1 April 1943, Colonial Office to Rabbi Semiaticki.
38 Ibid., 19 May 1943, Rosenheim to Goodman; 22 September 1943, Goodman to Rabbi Kalmanowitch, New York.
39 Ibid., 27 August 1943, Cable from Shanghai to Switzerland; 8 October 1943, Karol Kraczkiewicz, Polish Foreign Ministry, to Goodman.
40 MS 183 Schonfeld 654 [Fi-Foy], 10 October 1943, Hertz to Eden; AIWO, A-37, 28 November 1944, Koziebrodzki, Polish Foreign Ministry, to Springer; AIWO 47/11, 18 May 1943, Sikorski to Hertz.
41 AIWO Report, January–June 1943, p. 20 and July–December 1943, p. 7.
42 AIWO 47/11, 8 October 1943, Kraczkiewicz to Goodman; 9 December 1943, Goodman to Kraczkiewicz; extract from *JTA*, 2 December 1943; 25 April 1944, Report of Activities, January–April 1944, p. 2; 30 May 1944, Goodman to Rosenheim.
43 MS 183 Schonfeld 654 [Fi-Foy], 2 November 1943, Law to Hertz; 8 November 1943, Hertz to Law; 22 November 1943, Law to Hertz; 30 November 1943, Hertz to Hall.
44 AIWO 47/11, 3 January 1944, Rosenheim to Goodman. AIWO A-37, 28 November 1944, Koziebrodzki to Springer.
45 AIWO 47/11, 29 March 1944, Rosenheim to Goodman; MS 183 Schonfeld 654 [Fi-Foy], 3 July 1945, Schonfeld to Mason.

46 Nathan Eck, 'The Rescue of Jews with the Aid of Passports and Citizenship Papers of Latin American States', *Yad Vashem Studies*, vol. 1 (Jerusalem, 1957), pp. 125–52; Isaac Lewin, 'Attempts at Rescuing European Jews with the Help of Polish Diplomatic Missions during World War Two', *The Polish Review*, vol. XXII, no. 4 (1977), pp. 11–12. See bibliography for David Kranzler's book on George Mandel Montello.

47 Jacob Sloan, ed., Notes from the Warsaw Ghetto: The Journal of Emmanuel Ringelblum (New York, 1958), p. 267.

48 Ibid.

49 Acc 3121 C2/2/5/1, 21 June 1943, Professor Hugo Valentin, Upsala, Sweden, to Brodetsky; 7 September 1943, Brodetsky to Valentin; C11/7/3a/2, 18 July 1944, interview, Brodetsky, Hall and Henderson.

50 FO 371/42755 W3256/91/48, 29 February 1944, Emerson to Howard Bucknell Jr., American Embassy, London.

51 J. Presser, *Ashes in the Wind: The Destruction of Dutch Jewry* (London, 1968), p. 228.

52 MS 183 Schonfeld 654 [Fi-Foy], 16 December 1943, Schonfeld to Hall; FO 371/42755 W93/91/48, 30 December 1943, Schonfeld to Randall; 10 January 1944, W274/91/48, 10 January 1944, Hall to Hertz; AIWO 47/11, 29 December 1943, telegram, Goodman to Rosenheim; Acc 3121 C11/6/4/1, 24 December 1943, Professor Samson Wright to Roberts.

53 MS 183 Schonfeld 654 [Fi-Foy], 17 February 1944, Schonfeld to Randall; 6 April 1944, Randall to Schonfeld; FO 371/42755 W5499/91/48, 6 April 1944, Brotman to Randall; 14 April 1944, Randall to Brotman; MS 183 Schonfeld 427 (f.1), 16 February 1944, Schonfeld to Emerson.

54 FO 371/42755 W5499/91/48, 6 April 1944, Brotman to Randall; 14 April 1944, Randall to Brotman.

55 FO 371/42755 W9259/91/48, 3 April 1944, Sofka Skipwith to Jock Balfour; W10325/91/48, 27 June 1944, Balfour (Moscow), to Randall; Mss VG, 3 April 1944, Skipwith and Zeidman to Goodman; interview, Victor Goodman, August 1995, London.

56 Lewin, *'Attempts at Rescuing European Jews'*, pp. 11–12.

57 AIWO 47/11, 16 May 1944, J.P. Walshe to Goodman; 15 June 1944, Rosenheim to Goodman; 28 June 1944, Goodman to Kraczkiewicz; FO 371/42755 W8472/91/48, 24 May 1944, Brotman to Randall; W9409/91/48, 12 June 1944, Goodman to Randall; Goodman to Walshe.

58 Ibid., W9409/91/48, 16 June 1944, Randall to Goodman; W9897/91/48, 26 June 1944, telegram no. 781, Foreign Office to Madrid. The High Commissioner for Palestine had approved about 90 interned families for admission to Palestine. However, as they all held South American passports, Randall felt it would 'not be practicable to put their names on the Palestine exchange list'.

59 Acc 3121 C2/2/5/3, Board Report, deportation of Jews of Polish origin from the camp at Vittel (n.d.).

60 AIWO 47/11, 13 July 1944, Rosenheim to Goodman; 24 July 1944, Goodman to Rathbone.

61 AJAC MS Coll. 361 D109/6, 10 July 1944, Grant, eyewitness report;

FO 371/42872 WR 1004/120/48, 16 August 1944, Goodman to Randall; AIWO, A-37, 21 August 1944, Goodman to M. Viturro, Spanish Embassy, London; Mss VG, 6 September 1944, Goodman to Walshe; MS 183 Schonfeld 654 [Fi-Foy], 18 August 1944, Schonfeld to Walker; 25 August 1944, Walker to Schonfeld.

62 Acc 3121 C2/2/5/3, 31 August 1944, conversation with Mason; 14 September 1944, interview, William Frankel and James Mann; FO 371/42872 WR 1221/120/48, 3 October 1944, Mason to Schonfeld; WR 1541/120/48, 17 November 1944, Mason to Goodman; WR 1799/120/48, 30 November 1944, Goodman to Mason; WR 1930/120/48, 1 December 1944, Schonfeld to Mason.

63 *International Herald Tribune*, Mary Blume '1944: The Many who were not Forgotten', 11–12 June 1994, back page. Skipworth was put on a slow train to Lisbon and included in a separate exchange agreement whereby British subjects were exchanged for Germans interned in South Africa. See A.N. Oppenheim, *The Chosen People – The Story of the '222 Transport' from Bergen-Belsen to Palestine* (London, 1996), pp. 97–101. According to Oppenheim, some fifty Vittel internees, holding Palestine certificates, were included in the third Palestine exchange. See also D. Kranzler, *Thy Brother's Blood*, (New York, 1987), pp. 102–4, 172.

64 Aaron Zwergbaum, 'Exile in Mauritius', *Yad Vashem Studies*, IV (Jerusalem, 1960), pp. 191–257. See Acc 3121 C14/26/2 for negative reports from detention camp in Mauritius to London, *inter alia*.

65 CO 323/1846/2, 3 September 1942, Hertz to Cranborne; 11 September 1942, Memorandum; 29 September 1942, conversation, Cranborne and Hertz.

66 Ibid., 15 February 1943, G.H. Gater, Colonial Office to JA; FO 371/42777 W2924/667/48, 23 February 1944, P.Q., Mr. Martin and W9689/667/48, 14 June 1944, P.Q., Graham White; W4885/667/48, 30 March 1944 and 22 May 1944, Michael Wright, British Embassy, Washington, to Refugee Department; FO 371/42814, WR 685/3/48, 8 August 1944, conversation, Rathbone and Cranborne.

67 FO 371/42777 W8260/667/48, 22 May 1944, Colonial Office to Randall.

68 CO 323/1846/2, 19 September 1942, Cranborne, Minutes; 29 September 1942, conversation, Cranborne and Hertz.

69 Ibid., 15 February 1943, Minutes.

70 Ibid., 29 April 1943, Clark, Minutes; 21 May 1943, Stanley to Randall; MS 183 Schonfeld 290, 24 February 1943, Colonial Office to Schonfeld.

71 CO 323/1846/2, 5 May 1943, Schonfeld to Stanley.

72 Ibid., 21 May 1943, Colonial Office to Randall; 30 May 1943, Hertz to Stanley; 3 June 1943, Colonial Office to East Africa, Cyprus, Mauritius, and the Seychelles; 15 March 1943, Randall to Sidebotham; 18 March 1943, Stanley to Schonfeld; 13 April 1943, E. Raczynski to Sir A. Cadogan.

73 Ibid., 23 February 1943, Stanley to Schonfeld; 3 March 1943, Sidebotham, Minute; 15 March 1943, Randall to Sidebotham; 18 March 1943, Stanley to Schonfeld.

74 Ibid., 10 June 1943, East African Governors Conference to Stanley;

11 June 1943, Logan, Seychelles, to Stanley; 10 June 1943, Sir D. Mackenzie Kennedy, Mauritius, to Stanley; 18 June 1943, Stanley to Hertz; 21 June 1943, Hertz to Stanley.

75 FO 371/36735 W9463/8833/48, 13 July 1943, Randall to S.M. Campbell, Colonial Office.

76 MS 183 Schonfeld 654 [Fi-Foy], 23 July 1943 Schonfeld to Randall; FO 371/36735 W11710/8833/48, 19 August 1943, Refugee Department to The Chancery, British Embassy, Lisbon; W13532/8833/48, 9 September 1943, British Embassy, Angora to Eden.

77 CO 323/1846/2, 29 July 1943, Minutes.

78 Ibid., 20 July 1943, J. Megson, Minutes; 28 July 1943, Eastwood, Minutes.

79 FO 371/36735 W12392/8833/48, 5 August 1943, telegram no. 612, Stanley to Mauritius; W12809/8833/48, 3 September 1943, Colonial Office to Schonfeld; CO 323/1846/2, 3 September 1943, C.H. Thornley to Schonfeld; 9 September 1943, Stanley to Kennedy, Mauritius; FO 371/42777 W2617/667/48, 17 February 1944, J. Megson, Colonial Office, Minute.

80 FO 371/42777 W1869/667/48, 4 February 1944, Schonfeld to Randall; W4472/667/48, 20 March 1944, Camps to Henderson.

81 MS 183 Schonfeld 654 [Fi-Foy], 3 March 1944, Schonfeld to Randall; 25 March 1944, Randall to Schonfeld.

82 FO 371/42777 W6700/667/48, 26 April 1944, Schonfeld to Randall; W8706/667/48, 7 June 1944, Randall to Schonfeld.

83 MS 183 Schonfeld 654 [Fi-Foy], 19 April 1944, Schonfeld to Randall; 4 May 1944, Randall to Schonfeld; see note 33.

84 FO 371/42777 W8260/667/48, 4 May 1944, Hertz to Stanley; 22 May 1944, Stanley to Randall. MS 183 Schonfeld 654 [Fi-Foy], 24 July 1944, Schonfeld to Randall; FO 371/42859 WR 1502/45/48, 25 October 1944, Schonfeld to Mason.

85 FO 371/42777 W10001/667/48, 20 June 1944, telegram no. 501, Stanley to Mauritius.

86 FO 371/42858 WR 45/45/48, 29 June 1944, telegram from Mauritius to Stanley; FO 371/42859 WR 1502/45/48, 19 July 1944, Stanley to Hertz; FO 371/42858 WR 916/45/48, 28 July 1944, E. Rainer, Mauritius, to Dr. Ed, Jerusalem.

87 Ibid., WR 416/45/48, 24 July 1944, Schonfeld to Randall; MS 183 Schonfeld 654 [Fi-Foy], 12 October 1944, Mason to Schonfeld; FO 371/42859 WR 1502/45/48, 25 October 1944, Schonfeld to Mason.

88 FO 371/42859 WR 1841/45/48, 21 November 1944, Schonfeld to Mason and Eastwood; WR 1941/45/48 9 December 1944, telegram no. 3763, Foreign Office to Berne; FO 371/51146, WR 55/55/48, 5 January 1945, Henderson, Minute; WR 87/55/48, 8 January 1945, Schonfeld to Henderson.

89 FO 371/42859 WR 1972/45/48, 13 December 1944, Mason to Eastwood; MS 183 Schonfeld 654 [Fi-Foy], 10 April 1945, Henderson to Schonfeld; 15 April 1945, Schonfeld to Henderson.

90 MS 183 Schonfeld 593/1, CRREC, 1938–1948, Rescue Work.

91 Meier Sompolinsky, *The British Government and the Holocaust: The Fail-*

ure of the Anglo-Jewish Leadership? (Brighton, 1999), p. 166. I am grateful to David Kranzler who enlightened me on the Mauritius scheme, its importance and the misunderstanding found among historians.

92 Dermot Keogh, 'The Irish Free State and the Refugee Crisis, 1933–45', Paul R. Bartrop, ed., *False Havens: The British Empire and the Holocaust* (New York, 1995), pp. 211–37.

93 Mss VG, 8 April 1943, Goodman to Dulanty; 3 May 1943, Goodman to Walshe; Mss SG, 16 May 1943, 'Goodman goes to Dublin'.

94 Ibid., 5 May 1943, Goodman to Walshe.

95 Ibid., 20 May 1943, Goodman to Dulanty.

96 Acc 3121 C11/6/4/1, 10 June 1943, interview with Randall.

97 Mss VG, 7 July 1943, Points of discussion with Randall; 9 August 1943 and 24 November 1943, Goodman to Walshe.

98 Ibid., 23 July 1943, Goodman to J.A. Belton, Office of the High Commissioner for Ireland.

99 Ibid., 9 August 1943, Goodman to Walshe.

100 Ibid., 6 September 1943, Goodman to Dulanty; 7 September 1943, Dulanty to Goodman; 17 September 1943, Goodman to Dulanty; 20 October 1943, Goodman to Dulanty.

101 Mss VG, 9 November 1943, Goodman to Dulanty; 24 November 1943, Goodman to Walshe; 1 December 1943, Paschal Robinson, Papal Nuncio, to Goodman.

102 Mss VG, 29 November 1943, Walshe to Goodman; 19 December 1943, Goodman to Walshe. See in same file *J.C.* and *Jewish Weekly*, 3 November 1943; for counter report, see *JTA*, 13 November 1943.

103 FO 371/36518 W17133/4/49, 11 December 1943, Cheetham, Minute; W17685/4/49, 16 December 1943, Cranborne to Hore-Ruthven; W17783/4/49, 21 December 1943, Broomfeld, Ministry of War Transport, to Henderson.

104 Mss VG 17 March 1944, Goodman to Dulanty; 31 March 1944, Goodman to Walshe.

105 Ibid., 7 July 1944, telegram, Goodman to Walshe; 10 July 1944, telegram, Walshe to Goodman; 31 July 1944, Goodman to Dulanty.

106 FO 371/42815 WR 785/3/48, 16 August 1944, E.G.M. [Initld.], Dominions Office; 23 August 1944, Walker, Foreign Office, to Maclennan, Dominions Office.

107 Mss VG, 29 August 1944, Sidney H. Browne, American Embassy to Agudas Israel; FO 371/42817 WR 1125/3/48, 8 September 1944, Browne to Mason; 21 September 1944, Mason to Browne; 18 September 1944, Cheetham, Minutes; AIWO, A-37, 12 September 1944, Goodman to Irish Red Cross.

108 D. Wyman, *Abandonment of the Jews* (New York, 1985), pp. 276–7. Wyman maintains that only 463 Jews were involved in the three transfers. On transport problems, see Wasserstein, *Britain and the Jews of Europe*, p. 235.

109 Porat, *The Blue and Yellow Stars of David*, p. 148. For example, see Yad Vashem Archives, O48/B19-6 (69/65), 17 March 1944, Goodman to Dulanty. A letter received through the Red Cross, dated January 1944, states that some people living in Amsterdam had been saved

from deportation through visas granted by South American countries. See also Lewin, 'Attempts at Rescuing European Jews', p. 12; Nathan Eck, 'The Rescue of Jews with the Aid of Passports and Citizenship Papers of Latin American States', *Yad Vashem Studies*, vol. I (1957), pp. 151–2.

9   Relief Efforts: A Chronicle of Success?

1   Brodetsky, *Memoirs*, p. 208.
2   CZA C2/409, August 1942, British Section, 'Help for the Ghettos'.
3   FO 837/1214, 15 February 1943, MEW, 'Summary of the Main Reasons for Continuation of the Food Blockade' ('Summary').
4   HC Debates, Fifth Series, 1939–1940, vol. 364, col.1161; FO 837/1214 T550/G/Z, 24 February 1943, MEW, Note on Blockade Policy Respecting Relief (Blockade Policy), p. 1.
5   FO 371/36725 W6785/677/48, 20 April 1943, Discussion no. 2.
6   FO 371/36518 W17877/4/49, 25 December 1943, MEW to W. Reifler, American Embassy, London.
7   FO 837/1214, 15 February 1943, MEW 'Summary'. There were political and strategic reasons for feeding the starving population of Greece. See Procopis Papastratis, *British Policy towards Greece during the Second World War, 1941–1944* (Cambridge, 1984), pp. 114–18.
8   FO 837/1214, T550/G/Z, 24 February 1943, 'Blockade Policy', p. 2.
9   FO 837/1223, 17 March 1942, W.A. Camps, MEW, Minutes.
10 FO 837/1214, 15 February 1942, MEW, 'Summary'; FO 371/36518 W17877/4/49, 25 December 1943, MEW to Reifler.
11 FO 371/36665 W12089/49/48, 18 August 1943, Easterman to Law; Acc 3121 C11/12/94, 6 February 1942, B. Margulies, Council of Polish Jews in Britain; AJJDC AR 3345.536 [n.d.] efforts by the Federation of Czech Jews; June 1942, Rhys Davis MP raised the question in the Commons.
12 AJAC MS 361 D2/5, 22 April 1941, E.F. Henriques, Trading With The Enemy Department, to British Section and 'Relief Activities of the WJC'; 22 August 1941, Congress Weekly: 'A Painful Controversy'; 30 June 1941, Perlzweig to Easterman; FO 371/32681 W14681/4555/48, 3 November 1942, Postal and Telegraph Censorship, Report on Jewry.
13 MS 183 Schonfeld 673 [AG-AL], August 1942, AIWO.
14 AJAC MS coll. 361, D2/5, 24 October 1941, S. Wise to Halifax; 22 October 1942, I.M. Minkoff to Perlzweig.
15 FO 371/42731 W2640/17/48, 12 February 1944, H. Bucknell, Jr., US Embassy, London, to Emerson; 17 February 1944, British Embassy, Washington, to Foreign Office; February 1944, Eden to Winterton; W3199/17/48, 28 February 1944, Bliss, MEW, to Randall.
16 FO 837/1214 T550/G/Z, 24 February 1943, 'Blockade Policy', pp. 2–3; 13 April 1943, Selborne to Eden, pp. 6–7.
17 FO 837/1223 T550/129, 20 January 1942, Camps to G.G. Markbreiter, Home Office.

18 FO 837/1214, T550/G/Z, 24 February 1943, 'Blockade Policy', p. 10; FO 371/42731 W303/17/48, 22 December 1943, Randall to Emerson.
19 FO 837/1223 T550/129, 20 January 1942, Camps to Markbreiter.
20 Acc 3121 B5/2/2/3, 5 February 1942, Brotman to Brodetsky.
21 Acc 3121 C11/12/94, 4 February 1942, Goodman to Brotman; MS 183 Schonfeld 673 [AG-AL], August 1942, AIWO.
22 Acc 3121 C11/12/91, 29 June 1942, Lionel L. Cohen, MEW, to Brotman.
23 Ibid., 23 July 1942, Conference, Relief of Jews in the Ghettos; 10 July 1942, interview with Stanczyk.
24 Ibid., 30 July 1942, 'Postal Packets to the Ghettos'; 15 September 1942, copy of letter from A.S. Tolhurst, Trading with the Enemy Department.
25 CZA C2/416, 7 August 1942, Easterman to Brotman.
26 Acc 3121 C11/12/91, 30 July 1942, 'Postal Packets to the Ghettos'; 15 September 1942, Tolhurst to Brotman; 12 October 1942, Zygielbaum to Brotman.
27 CCJR, 27 July 1942, Executive Committee Meeting, Minutes, p. 2 and 23 September 1942, p. 3; Acc 3121 C11/12/91, 31 July 1942; 24 August 1942, Brodetsky to Simon Marks.
28 Ibid., 17 November 1942, Goodman to Brotman.
29 Ibid., 24 November 1942, Easterman to Brotman; 24 December 1942, Brotman to Camps.
30 Ibid., 23 July 1942, Conference, Relief of Jews in the Ghettos; 30 July 1942, 'Postal Packets to the Ghettos', p. 2; 24 December 1942, Brotman to Camps; 30 December 1942, Brotman to A. Schoyer; 14 January 1943, Brotman to Dr. Grosfeld.
31 Ibid., 27 November 1942, Brotman to Schwartz.
32 Ibid., 25 November 1942, Brotman to Marks; 26 November 1942, Camps to Brotman; 13 December 1942, L.M. Montefiore to Brotman; 14 December 1942, Brotman to M. Stephany.
33 Acc 3121 C11/12/92/3, 2 April 1943, Herbert Katski, JDC, Lisbon, to Brotman; 22 April 1943, Brotman to Katski.
34 AJJDC AR 3344.801, 2 July 1943, Katski to Brotman; Katski, interview, August 1994, New York.
35 Acc 3121 C11/12/92/3, 28 May 1943, Brotman to Edith Pye, Famine Relief Committee; AJJDC AR 3344.801, *inter alia*, 6 March 1943, Katski to JDC, New York.
36 Ibid., 26 June 1943, Report from Caldas da Rainha, Lisbon, to the JDC, New York.
37 Acc 3121 C11/12/92/2, 23 August 1943, Schimitzek, Lisbon, to Stanczyk; 16 August 1943, Katski to Brotman.
38 Ibid., 11 August 1943, Postal Packets Scheme.
39 Ibid., 30 October 1943, Schimitzek to Stanczyk.
40 Michael Weichert, *Yidishe Aleinhilf* cites Memorandum, Order of 18 November 1942, p. 377; Epilogue, pp. 356–7.
41 Acc 3121 C11/12/92/2, 22 May 1943, notification that JUS had re-opened; AJJDC AR 3344.801, 2 July 1943, Katski to Brotman; Weichert, pp. 156, 158, 169, 348, 352, 385.
42 AJJDC AR 3344.801, 15 and 29 July 1943, Weichert to the Committee

for the Assistance of the War Stricken Jewish Population, Geneva. For a positive opinion of Weichert, see Malvina Graf, *The Krakow Ghetto and the Plaszow Camp Remembered* (Florida, 1989), pp. 81–2, 129.

43   AJJDC AR 3344.802, 2 September 1943, Katski to JDC, New York; Acc 3121 C11/12/92/5, 24 September 1943, *South African Times* report that all parcels were being confiscated. For contradictory reports that the JUS was receiving parcels, see C11/12/92/3, 30 October 1943, Schimitzek to Board.

44   Acc 3121 C11/12/92/2, 5 November 1943, conversation, Brotman and Schwartz; 26 November 1943, Brotman to Schwarzbart.

45   Acc 3121 C11/12/92/5, 22 March 1944, Brotman to Camps. For a positive report on the amounts received by the JUS, see 11 May 1944, Schimitzek to Stanczyk; 22 March 1944, Schwartz to Brotman; 9 May 1944, JDC, Lisbon, to Schimitzek.

46   Ibid., 30 May 1944, confidential, Stanczyk to Brotman; 1 June 1944, Brotman to Stanczyk; AJJDC AR 3344.802, 24 May 1944, Report of Jewish National Committee in Poland.

47   Ibid., 30 May 1944, Stanczyk to Brotman; 1 June 1944, Brotman to Schwarzbart.

48   Ibid., 14 June 1944, Hurwitz to Brotman; 11 July 1944, Hurwitz to Stanczyk; 14 July 1944, Stanczyk to Brotman.

49   Ibid., 21 July 1944, interview with Stanczyk.

50   Weichert, *Yidishe Afeinhilf*, pp. 173, 355, 363. Weichert claims that Joseph Horn, Tadeusz Pankiewicz and others commented on how invaluable was the help from the JUS. See Tadeusz Pankiewicz, *The Crakow Ghetto Pharmacy* (New York, 1987).

51   Acc 3121 C11/12/91, 23 December 1942, Frischer to Brotman.

52   Acc 3121 C11/12/92/3, 5 March 1943, Frischer to Brotman; FO 371/42731 W303/17/48, 14 November 1943, 'Help to Groups of Refugees in Europe'; Mss VG, Memorandum, Parcels to Camps in Czechoslovakia and other parts of Europe [n.d. probably 1944].

53   Acc 3121 C11/12/92/5, 17 November 1943, British Red Cross to Brotman; 6 May 1944, Frischer to Brodetsky. For 'confirmation from the addresses that the parcels and their contents were received in good order', see Mss VG, Memorandum, ff. 52.

54   Ronald W. Zweig, 'Feeding the Camps: Allied Blockade Policy and the Relief of Concentration Camps in Germany, 1944–1945', *Historical Journal* (September 1998).

55   Acc 3121 C11/12/92/2, 21 August 1943, Frischer to Brodetsky; 28 August 1943, Frischer to Brodetsky; 17 September 1943, Frischer to Brotman; 21 September 1943, Brotman to Camps; 25 September 1943, Camps to Brotman; 16 November 1943, Frischer to Stephany. Meanwhile. the JDC, in May 1943, was authorized by the US Treasury to transfer $12,000 a month to its Lisbon office for the shipment of individual food parcels to non-Czech inmates at Teresienstadt. In May 1944, the JDC increased the monthly allocation to $14,000 and in August to $16,000. See files AJJDC AR 3344.542-544.

56   FO 371/42731 W1133/17/48, 29 January 1944, Randall to Camps; W1808/17/48, 2 February 1944, Camps to H.O. Fiser, Czech Ministry

of Social Welfare; Acc 3121 C11/12/92/5, 2 February 1944, Camps to Brotman.

57 Ibid., 6 May 1944, Frischer to Brodetsky; 8 May 1944, Brodetsky to Stephany.

58 Ibid., 24 May 1944, Brotman to Hertz; 31 May 1944, Frischer to Brodetsky. The ICA had already given £13,000, but this came from Baron Hirsch's fund, which was not British.

59 Ibid., 8 May 1944, Brodetsky to Stephany; 13 June 1944, Brodetsky to Frischer.

60 Ibid., 21 May 1944, Hertz to Brotman; 24 May 1944, Brotman to Hertz; 1 June 1944, A.G. Wrightson, MEW, to Brotman.

61 Ibid., 18 July 1944, Wrightson to Brotman; 7 August 1944, M.A. Urbanski, Polish Ministry of Social Welfare, to Wrightson; 11 August 1944, Rith Quennell, MEW to Urbanski; 28 August 1944, Brotman to Urbanski.

62 Ibid., 7 August 1944, Schimitzek to Brotman; 28 September 1944, Brotman to Samuel; Acc 3121 C2/2/5/3, 18 July 1944, interview with Hall.

63 Acc 3121 C11/12/92/5, 21 July 1944, interview with Stanczyk; C9/1/92/4, 18 August 1944, cable from Lichtheim to Linton.

64 Acc 3121 C11/12/92/5, 10 November 1944, J.L. Teicher, Polish National Council, to Brotman.

65 Katski, interview, August 1994. Katski maintains that a certain number of relief packages did get through, although he cannot quantify numbers. Acc 3121 C11/12/92/5, 28 November 1945, Brotman to Schwarzbart, enquiring if the latter had any definite information about the receipt of parcels.

66 Ibid., 22 November 1945, J.M. Rich, Secretary, South African Board of Deputies, to Brotman. Rich had enquired about these 'clandestine' relief efforts, see 28 November 1945, Brotman to Rich.

67 FO 371/36694 W124/124/48, 31 December 1942, H.E. Caustin, Allied Post-War Requirements Bureau.

68 FO 371/35220 U5342/3646/74, 28 October 1943, Foreign Office, Minute.

69 FO 371/40521 U602/41/73, 20 January 1944, War Cabinet Conclusions (Extract) 9 (44). The UK made a contribution of £80 million to UNRRA in January 1944.

70 Zorach Warhaftig, *Relief and Rehabilitation* (New York, 1944), p. 34.

71 WJC Memorandum on Post War Relief and Rehabilitation of European Jewry, submitted to UNRRA, 11 November 1943, cited in Warhaftig, 'Relief and Rehabilitation', pp. 16–19.

72 FO 371/36694 W124/124/48, 28 December 1942, CRREC proposals; W416/124/48, 30 December 1942, Brodetsky, meeting with Law; Acc 3121 B5/2/1, 15 April 1943, Brodetsky, interview with Governor Herbert H. Lehman, Director of UNRRA; FO 371/35298 U5661/933/73, 10 November 1943, G. Pinsent, Relief Department, Foreign Office, to Schonfeld; 12 November 1943, Schonfeld to Pinsent.

73 AJAC MS Coll. 361, D4/13, 11 April 1944, WJC Relief Committee, Minutes, p. 3; FO 371/40527 U1992/41/73, 6 March 1944, interview with Sir G. Rendel, Foreign Office; FO 371/40533 U2420/202/73, 17

March 1944, Goodman to Rendel; FO 371/41129 UR 49/15/850, 26
June 1944, Sir Frederick Leith-Ross, Chairman of the Inter-Allied Com-
mittee on Post-War Requirements Bureau, to E.L. Hall-Patch, Relief
Department, Foreign Office.

74 Acc 3121 C11/7/3a/2, 1 October 1942, interview with Law; C11/64/2,
18 December 1942, Brodetsky to Law; 18 December 1942, Brodetsky
to Wise; CBFRR, 28 May 1945, Minutes, p. 5.

75 Acc 3121 C11/7/3a/2, 1 October 1942, interview with Law; B5/2/2/3,
10 December 1942, Brotman to Brodetsky; CZA A255/491, 1 January
1943, Brotman to I. Sowerby, Allied Post-War Requirements Bureau.

76 FO 371/36694 W416/124/48, 30 December 1942, Notes for Law's meeting
with Brodetsky; Acc 3121 C11/7/3a/2, 28 January 1943, Brodetsky,
interview with Law.

77 The Committee for Jews in Germany, established in 1945 by the
Board, dealt with these issues. See Statements, one on post-war policy
in general and the other on Palestine in particular, in 'The Jews in
Europe – their Martyrdom and their Future' (Board of Deputies,
1945). These issues are not addressed here.

78 FO 371/41285 UR 313/313/854, 19 September 1944, informal interview with representatives of the JCRA and Board.

79 Acc 3121 B5/2/4, 21 January 1943, Brotman to Brodetsky; CZA A255/
491, 13 June 1945, JCRA.

80 CZA A255/491, 21 February 1944 and 4 April 1944, JCRA Volunteer
Committee Meeting; Bentwich, *They Found Refuge*, p. 136.

81 FO 371/35298 U933/933/73, 25 February 1943, Gorvin to N.B. Ronald,
Foreign Office; FO 371/36694 W5081/124/48, 25 March 1943, W.D.
Hogarth to Gorvin; FO 371/40555 U5951/202/73, 4 July 1944, Enrol-
ment of Foreign Doctors in COBSRA Teams; CZA C2/111, 4 February
1943, Executive Committee, Immediate Relief in Europe; CZA A255/
491, 8 September 1944, JCRA to Harry Kassel, French North Africa;
CBF, 10 May 1945, Minutes, p. 3.

82 FO 371/40537 U3586/41/73, 25 April 1944, telegram from Lord Moyne,
Cairo, to Foreign Office; U3614/41/73 17 May 1944, Leith-Ross to
Hall-Patch.

83 CBF Microfilm reel 23, file 123/47, 4 February 1945, JCRA 1943–
1944, Survey of Past and Suggestions for Future.

84 FO 371/36694 W124/124/48, 28 December 1942, CRREC, Immediate
Problems and Proposals for Religious Reconstruction of Continental
Jewry.

85 Ibid., 31 December 1942, Caustin to Ronald; FO 371/35298 U5688/
933/73, 27 January 1944, Comments on CRREC Memorandum; FO
371/35298 U5019/933/73, 16 October 1943, Hall-Patch to G. Morgan,
War Office.

86 FO 371/35298 U4259/933/73 13 September 1943, R. Ashton, Minute.

87 Ibid., 1 September 1943 G.H.C. Amos, Ministry of Food, to Sir Robert
Waley-Cohen.

88 *J.C.*, 6 August 1943, p. 5; MS 183 Schonfeld, 593/1, CRREC Report
for period ending 1 November 1945, pp. 2–3.

89 FO 371/35298 U5019/933/73, 11 October 1943, Morgan to Huxley,

Relief Department; FO 371/49103 Z2135/103/17, 21 February 1945, Camps, Minute; FO 371/51355 UR 524/47/850, 9 February 1945, Ministry of Food, Memorandum.

90 FO 371/41285 UR 607/313/854, 1 August 1944, Schonfeld to War Office; MS 183 Schonfeld, 593/1, Report for period ending November 1945, p. 5; AIWO F-21, Rosenheim Correspondence, CRREC, December 1943; 25 May 1945, Schonfeld to W.J. Worth, War Office.

91 CZA A255/491, 1 December 1944, Notes of the work of the JCRA.

92 FO 371/36694 W6194/124/48, 13 April 1943, Schonfeld to Leith-Ross; Schonfeld, *Message to Jewry*, p. 154.

93 Chaim Bermant, 'One of God's Cossacks', *J.C.*, 19 February 1982, p. 22.

94 CZA C2/782, 15 December 1944, Brodetsky to Anthony de Rothschild.

95 CBFRR, 14 August 1945, Minutes, p. 1.

96 FO 371/51355 UR 993/47/850, 28 March 1945, Brooks (Treasury) to Hall-Patch.

97 Ibid., UR 632/47/850, 22 February 1945, Reading to Law.

98 CBFRR, 13 March 1945, Emergency Committee Meeting.

99 CBFRR, Annual Report, 1943–1944, p. 8 and 1945, p. 5.

100 Albert M. Hyamson, 'British Jewry in Wartime', *Contemporary Jewish Record*, vol. VI, no. 1 (February 1943), pp. 14–22.

101 CBF, Microfilm Reel 21, File 111, Leonard G. Montefiore, Fund Raising Appeal; CBFRR, 22 August 1945, Minutes, p. 3.

102 AJYB, vol. 42, 5701 (1941–1942), p. 132. The sluggish response of Anglo-Jewry to its own Essential Services Appeal during the evacuation period in 1941 was noted: 'The fact that an appeal issued contemporaneously by the Jewish National Fund (1941) raised no less than £64,950 within three months suggests, perhaps, that Jewish interests shifted ... and that the prospect of securing a permanent future for oppressed Jewries in Palestine attracted greater support than the temporary alleviation of a local plight'; AJYB, vol. 47, 5705 (1945–1946), p. 350.

103 CBFRR, 13 March 1945, Emergency Committee Meeting, Minutes; 4 June 1945, Report by Leonard Cohen.

104 CBFRR, 8 October 1945, Minutes, pp. 2–3; 13 November 1945, Minutes. The Treasury did, however, agree to grant pound for pound to the voluntary bodies for relief and rehabilitation in Europe and the JCRA was consequently able to recover half its principal expenditure. CBFRR, Annual Report, 1945, p. 6.

105 FO 371/40555 U5726/202/73, 9 June 1944, K.J. Gabbett, Relief Department, Foreign Office; Interview Henry Lunzer, a member of the JRU, June 1994, London; AR 3344.558, 19 October 1944, Recent Developments in the Work of the JCRA.

106 CZA A255/491 19 March 1945, N. Bentwich, 'Jewish Relief Units'; 30 October 1944, Leonard Cohen, 'Note on Jewish Relief and Rehabilitation'. See also Bentwich, *They Found Refuge*, p. 134; Isaac Levy, *Witness to Evil: Bergen Belsen 1945* (London, 1995), pp. 27–8.

107 FO 371/41285 UR 313/313/854, 12 September 1944, interview at the Foreign Office.

108 CZA C2/782, 15 December 1944, Brodetsky to Anthony de Rothschild.
109 CBF Microfilm reel 23, file 123/47, 4 February 1945, JCRA 1943–1944, Survey of Past and Suggestions for Future.

Conclusion: Lack of Will or Lack of Skill?

1   Shabtai Rowson, cited in AJYB 5704 (1944–45), vol. 46, p. 187.
2   Acc 3121 A/29, 21 March 1938, Board Minutes.
3   See p. 107.
4   Neville Laski, December 1939, Retirement Speech, p. 8.
5   Ibid., p. 2.
6   Sonia Orwell and Ian Angus, *The Collected Essays*, vol. III, pp. 332–3.
7   *J.C.*, 1 April 1960, 'A President Looks Back'.
8   Alderman, *Modern British Jewry*, p. 278.
9   *J.C.*, 2 May 1975.
10 Brodetsky, *Memoirs*, p. 195.
11 Israel Finestein, 'Selig Brodetsky 1888–1954: The Prodigy from Fashion Street', Aubrey Newman, ed., *The Jewish East End 1840–1939* (JHS, 1981), p. 107.
12 *Birmingham Mail*, 8 June 1944, cited in Acc 3121 B5/2/7/2.
13 Brodetsky, *Memoirs*, p. 223.
14 Finestein, 'Selig Brodetsky 1888–1954', op. cit., p. 104.
15 RA XI/35/61, 16 October 1941, Anthony de Rothschild, 'Memorandum of Interview with Lord Moyne', cited in London, *Whitehall and the Jews*, p. 41.
16 *J.C.*, archive, 'Selig Brodetsky' (no date).
17 Chaim Weizmann, *Trial and Error* (1949), pp. 494–6.
18 *J.C.*, 20 February 1970.
19 See, for example, pp. 167–8.
20 Isidore Epstein, ed., *Joseph Herman Hertz, 1872–1946, In Memoriam* (London, 1947), p. 31.
21 See p. 120.
22 Epstein, *Joseph Herman Hertz*, p. 12.
23 See pp. 52, 172; Acc 3121 C11/7/1/6, 31 May 1943, Hertz address, Reception for prominent Jewish personalities of Allied Countries at the Dorchester Hotel.
24 CZA A255/491, JCRA and CRREC, hand-written note by N. Bentwich (n.d., probably 1943–44).
25 *J.C.*, 26 April 1996, p. 27; interview, Lord Jakobovits, January 1994; Chaim Bermant, *Lord Jakobovits, The Authorized Biography of the Chief Rabbi* (London, 1990), p. 19: 'If I am alive today, it is entirely due to the efforts of that man [Schonfeld] and the same can be said for countless others.' See Ms 183 Schonfeld 593/1, CRREC 1938–1948, p. 1. According to this report, from 1938 until the outbreak of war, Schonfeld rescued 1,300 individuals.
26 Rudolf Mandelbaum, 'My Perspective of the Holocaust', 18 April 2001, unpublished manuscript.
27 Conversation with Jonathan Schonfeld, April 1994.

28 *J.C.*, October 1961, cited in Mss VG files.
29 Ibid.
30 Walter Laqueur, 'Jewish Denial and the Holocaust', *Commentary*, vol. 68 (July–December 1979), p. 45.
31 Eva Reading, *For the Record: The Memoirs of Eva, Marchioness of Reading* (London, 1973), p. 176.
32 Laqueur, 'Jewish Denial', p. 45.
33 Acc 3121 E3/536/2, 29 March 1946, National Committee, circular letter, no. VIII.
34 Brodetsky, *Memoirs*, p. 221.
35 FO 371/36694 W416/124/48, 29 January 1943, Law, Minutes; See pp. 117, 131.
36 Brodetsky, *Memoirs*, p. 218.
37 Bank of England: £1 in 1939 was equivalent to £27.19 at February 1997 rates.
38 Zorach Warhaftig, *Refugees and Survivors: Rescue Efforts during the Holocaust* (Jerusalem, 1988), pp. 324–5. interview, Warhaftig, July 1994: 'I have a bitter heart.'
39 FO 371/30925 C12716/61/18, 16 December 1942, Law, Minute.
40 FO 371/36694 W 416/124/48, 29 January 1943, Law, Minute.
41 Ibid., 28 January 1943, Walker, Minute; 28 January 1943, Randall, Minute.
42 See pp. 137.
43 For negotiating skills see Roger Fisher and William Ury, *Getting to Yes: Negotiating Agreement Without Giving In* (London, 1996).
44 See p. 84.
45 Wasserstein, 'Patterns of Jewish Leadership in Great Britain during the Nazi Era', p. 36.
46 Weizmann, *Trial and Error* (London, 1949), p. 243.
47 Isaiah Berlin, 'The Biographical Facts', in M.W. Weisgal and J. Carmichal, eds., *Chaim Weizmann, A Biography by Several Hands* (London, 1962), pp. 31–6. On the motives for the Balfour Declaration, see Leonard Stein, *The Balfour Declaration*.
48 Brodetsky, *Memoirs*, p. 192.
49 See pp. 132, 191.
50 James N. Rosenau, *Turbulence in World Politics: A Theory of Change and Continuity* (1990), pp. 438, 448. See also Leo Mates, 'The Holocaust and International Relations', Lyman H. Legters, ed., *Western Society after the Holocaust* (Boulder, Colorado, 1975), pp. 131–47.
51 CO 323/1846/2, 2 July 1943, Colonial Office to Foreign Office: 'I am afraid that we never understood that you would attempt to bring as many as 100 Rabbis within this special scheme.'
52 Brodetsky, *Memoirs*, p. 223.
53 FO 371/24100 W 13311/3231/98, 8 September 1939, Parliamentary Questions, Colonel Wedgwood to Sir John Anderson.
54 See p. 115.
55 Geoffrey Alderman, 'British Jewry: Religious Community or Ethnic Minority?', Jonathan Webber, ed., *Jewish Identities in the New Europe* (London, 1994), pp. 189–92. Alderman points out that the Board of

Deputies has 'consistently opposed the inclusion of a Jewish category in the question on ethnic origins in the decennial census'. Marlene Schmool confirms that certainly until the 1991 census there was a reluctance for Jews to be considered as an ethnic rather than a religious group; however, this is now changing although the Board has not yet reconsidered the ethnic question at the plenary level.

56 HC Debates, 19 May 1943, col. 1141.
57 Acc 3121 E3/536/1, January 1944, 'Continuing Terror: How to Rescue Hitler's Victims', pp. 8–9.
58 See p. 130.
59 Acc 3121 E3/536/1, 31 May 1943, National Committee, Resolutions of various organisations. See p. 118.
60 Acc 3121 E3/536/1, January 1944, 'Continuing Terror', p. 9; Michael Balfour, *Propaganda in War 1939–1945: Organisations, Policies and Publics in Britain and Germany* (London, 1979), p. 303.
61 A. Leon Kubowitzki, 'Address on the Rescue Attempts of the World Jewish Congress', WJC (British Section), War Emergency Conference of the WJC, November 1944, p. 22.
62 Henry R. Huttenbach, 'Comment: Human Rights and the Memory of the Holocaust – Is there a Connection?', Legters, ed., *Western Society after the Holocaust*, p. 149.
63 See, for example, FO 371/32680 W12853/4555/48, 25 September 1942, Frank K. Roberts, Minutes; Frank Roberts, *Dealing with Dictators: The Destruction and Revival of Europe, 1930–1970* (London, 1991), p. 46.
64 Earl of Avon (Sir Anthony Eden), *The Eden Memoirs: The Reckoning* (London, 1965); Herbert Morrison (Lord Morrison of Lambeth), *Herbert Morrison: An Autobiography* (London, 1960); Roberts, *Dealing with Dictators*.
65 Quoted in Gilbert, *Auschwitz and the Allies*, p. 341. Gilbert paints a positive view of Churchill: 'In making Allied policy, however, Churchill was not always the final arbiter'.
66 For a more critical view of Churchill, see Michael Cohen, *Churchill and the Jews* (London, 1985).
67 Yehuda Bauer, 'Rescue by Negotiations? Jewish Attempts to Negotiate with the Nazis', in M. Marrus, ed., *The Nazi Holocaust*, vol. 9 (London, 1989), p. 20.
68 See pp. 159, 160.
69 Wasserstein, *Britain and the Jews of Europe*, p. 352.
70 See, for example, Brodetsky, *Memoirs*; Bentwich, *My Seventy-Seven Years*; and Bernard Homa, *Footprints on the Sands of Time* (Gloucester, 1990).

Bibliography

Primary Material

Unpublished
Organisation and Private Papers
Agudat Israel World Organisation, New York (AIWO)
Annual Reports 1938–1945

A-37   Correspondence: Harry Goodman file 1944–1945.
E-31   Rosenheim Correspondence: CRREC 1941–1944.
F-21   Rosenheim Correspondence: Great Britain – Board of Deputies 1944.
Box 47   Reel 11 – J. Rosenheim Collection.

American Jewish Joint Distribution Committee, 1933–1944, New York (AJJDC)

AR   3344
256   IGCR Evian Conference.
445   Austria.
536   Federation of Czech Jews.
541   Refugees.
557   England: General.
558   England: CRREC.
575   England: Council for German Jewry; Central Council for Refugees 1938–39.
589   Refugee Children's Movement, London.
801   Poland: Board of Deputies – Food Package scheme (September) 1942–43.
802   Poland: Board of Deputies – Food Package scheme 1944.

American Jewish Archives, Cincinnati (AJAC)
MS coll. 361   World Jewish Congress

Series A. Central Files, 1919–1975.

A13   Correspondence: Britain 1936–1941.
A14   Correspondence: Britain 1937–1943.

Series D. Relief and Rescue Departments, 1938–1969.

D2   General Files 1941–1947.
D4   Correspondence and misc., 1941–1959.

D108   Rescue Plans and activities in various countries 1940–1945.
D109   Miscellaneous activities (exchange, food, protective papers)
         1942–1947.

Anglo-Jewish Archives, Parkes Library, Southampton University
MS 183 Papers of Rabbi Solomon Schonfeld.
Section F Chief Rabbi's Religious Emergency Council.
Correspondence: Alphabetical

          673 AG-AL; 668 EM-EZ; 636 FAU-FEU; 655 FL-FOY; 638 GA-
          GE; 427 I-J; 640 MAR-MZ; 656/1 POLL-PZ; 297/1 R (Reports);
          676 SA-SAW; 652 Sch-Schl; 662 WA-WAZ; 665 WEB-WEIR;
          663/2 U-Z.

Correspondence: General

117/8   Austrian and German Jewry 1938–1941.
228/1   Correspondence, papers, internees and POWS 1940.
290   Correspondence: government ministries, including Ministry of
         Food and the Home Office 1939–1942.
384   Central British Fund/Central Council for Jewish refugees: cor-
         respondence, papers 1938–1942.
593/1   Report on work of CRREC, report by Solomon Schonfeld on
         visit to internment camps on the Isle of Man, 1940–1948.
617/2   Child Refugees 1933–1939.

Schonfeld Papers (UCL), previously held by Mocatta Library, University
   College, London. Papers made available by Joseph Munk.

Central Zionist Archives, Jerusalem (CZA)
Institutional Records

C2   Offices of the World Jewish Congress, London 1936–1968.
L22   Jewish Agency for Palestine, Geneva Office 1925–1948.
S25   Jewish Agency for Palestine, Jerusalem, Political Department
         1921–1948.
Z4   Jewish Agency for Palestine, Central Office, London 1917–1955.

Private Papers

A255   Norman Bentwich 1883–1971.
A82   Selig Brodetsky 1888–1954.
A173   Josef L. Cohen ?–1940.
A354   Joseph Herman Hertz 1872–1946.
A289   Harry Sacher.

Central British Fund

Papers of the Central British Fund and the Jewish Refugees Committee were made available by Dr.Amy Gottlieb. These include:
Minute Books 1938–1945, Agenda Files and Annual Reports for Central British Fund (CBF) and later known as Central Council for Jewish Refugees (CCJR) and then Central British Fund for Jewish Relief and Rescue (CBFRR); Jewish Refugees Committee (JFC) and German Jewish Aid Committee (GJAC) 1938–1945.

Harry Goodman (Private Collection)

These papers were made available by his sons Victor Goodman (Mss VG) and Simon Goodman (Mss SG).

Institute of Contemporary History and Wiener Library, London
Central British Fund [Microfilm]

Reel 21 file 111   Leonard G. Montefiore.
Reel 23 file 123   Jewish Committee for Relief Abroad.
Reel 23 file 75   Jewish Refugees Committee (German Jewish Aid Committee) Executive Board Minutes

Israel State Archives, Jerusalem
GL 8586   Papers of Zorach Warhaftig.
P 574   Leo Kahn.

Lambeth Palace, London
Volume 29: George Bell, Bishop of Chichester.

London Metropolitan Archives
Acc 3121 – Board of Deputies of British Jews (archives previously held at Woburn House, London, until 1995).
Annual Reports 1938–1945.
A/26-A/32 Minute Books 1932–1945.

B   President and Secretaries:
B4   Coded Series (alphabetical).
B5   Brotman/Laski/Brodetsky Papers.
C   Committee and Departmental Papers:
C2   Aliens Committee.
C9   Evacuations and Related Wartime Activity.
C10   Executive Committee.
C11   Foreign Affairs.
E   General Correspondence:
E1   Subject Files (alphabetical).
E2   Subject files, clerk/administrative secretary's papers.
E3   Numbered box series.

Acc 2805 – Chief Rabbi Dr. Joseph Hertz.

Rothschild Archives, London
XI/35   Papers of Anthony de Rothschild.

Wiener Library, Tel Aviv
215B   Press Cutting, British Press.
215D   Press Cutting, British Press.

Yad Vashem, Jerusalem
048/19   Britain: Agudat Israel (O48/B19 Harry Goodman's work in Eire).

Official Documents
Public Record Office, Kew, London
Foreign Office
FO 20/107 Foreign Office: Weekly Political Intelligence Summaries
FO 371   Foreign Office: Political Departments: General Correspondence 1906–1966.
FO 372   Foreign Office: Treaty Department and Successors: General Correspondence, 1906–1965.
FO 837   Ministry of Economic Warfare, 1931–1951.

Cabinet Office
CAB 23   War Cabinet and Cabinet Minutes, 1916–1939.
CAB 24   War Cabinet and Cabinet: Memoranda (GT, CP, G War Series), 1915–1939.
CAB 27   War Cabinet and Cabinet: Miscellaneous Committees: Records (General Series), 1915–1939.
CAB 65   War Cabinet and Cabinet: Minutes (WM and CM Series), 1939–1945.
CAB 66   War Cabinet and Cabinet: Memoranda (WP and CP Series), 1939–1945.
CAB 95   War Committees and Cabinet: Committees on the Middle East and Africa (ME, A and other Series), 1939–1945.

Colonial Office
CO 323   Colonies, General: Original Correspondence, 1689–1952.
CO 733   Palestine Original Correspondence, 1921–1949.

Home Office
HO 213   Home Office: Aliens Department: General (GEN) Files and Aliens' Naturalisation and Nationality (ALN and NTY Symbol Series) Files, 1914–1948.
HO 214   Internees: Personal Files, 1940–1949.
HO 215   Internment: General Files, 1940–1951.
HO 294   Czech Refugee Trust: Records.

United States National Archives, Washington D.C. (Microfilm Series)
840.48   Refugees.

Interviews and Oral Histories
Interviews
Chaim Bermant, May 1996, London.
Judge Israel Finestein (President of the Board of Deputies 1991–1994), September 1997, London.
Rosie Goldfield, July 1994, Jerusalem.
Victor Goodman, August 1995, London.
Aryeh Handler, May 1994, London.
Immanuel, Lord Jakobovits, (Chief Rabbi 1967–1991), January 1994, London.
Herbert Katski, August 1994, New York.
Henry Lunzer, June 1994, London.
Phineas May, November 1994, London.
Marcus Retter, August 1994, New York.
Jonathan Schonfeld, April 1994, London.
Moses Schonfeld, New York 1991, New York.
Felice Selton, June 1994, London.
Joan Stiebel, London, March 1994.
Zorach Warhaftig, July 1994, Jerusalem.

Oral Histories
Salomon Adler-Rudel, recorded 24 June 1965, Institute of Contemporary Jewry, Jerusalem, Oral History Department, 27 (17), pp. 1–24.
Hans Gal, Imperial War Museum, Department of Sound Records, no. 004304/4, Reel 03.
Aryeh Handler, recorded 20 April 1993, Institute of Contemporary Jewry, Jerusalem, Oral History Department, 14 (156), part II, pp. 1–12.
Julius Layton, Imperial War Museum, Department of Sound Records, no. 004382/03.
Mandelbaum, Rudolf, 18 April 2001, 'My Perspective of the Holocaust' (unpublished).
Henry Pels, recorded 18 April 1966, Institute of Contemporary Jewry, Jerusalem, Oral History Department, 27 (35), pp. 1–13.
Chaim Raphael, Imperial War Museum, Department of Sound Records, no. 004289/2.

PhD Theses
Louise London, 'British Immigration Control Procedures and the Jewish Refugees 1933–1942' (London University, 1992).
Meier Sompolinsky, 'Ha-Hanhagah Ha-Anglo Yehudit, Memshelet Britaniah ve-ha-Sho'ah' (Bar Ilan University, Israel, 1977).

Published Material

Official Publications

Hansard Parliamentary Debates, Fifth Series, House of Commons (HC), 1939–1945. (vols. 275, 341, 364, 389); House of Lords (HL), 1943 (vol. 26).

Foreign Relations of the United States, vol. 1 (1938) Political Refugees; vol. 1 (1943) Bermuda Conference. (FRUS)

Newspapers and Journals

American Jewish Year Book (1941–1946).
Jewish Chronicle.
Jewish Telegraphic Agency.
Jewish Weekly.
The Times.
The Daily Telegraph.
The Jewish Year Book (1940, 1945–1946).

Memoirs and Biographies

Alberti, Johanna, 'Woman of Ideas, Eleanor Rathbone (London, 1996).
Avon, Earl of (Sir Anthony Eden), The Eden Memoirs: The Reckoning (London, 1965).
Bentwich, Norman, My Seventy-Seven Years: An Account of My Life and Times 1883–1960 (London, 1962).
Bermant, Chaim, Lord Jakobovits: The Authorized Biography of the Chief Rabbi (London, 1990).
Blond, Elaine, Marks of Distinction: The Memoirs of Elaine Blond (London, 1988).
Brodetsky, Selig, Memoirs: From Ghetto to Israel (London, 1960).
Henriques, R., Sir Robert Waley-Cohen (London, 1966).
Homa, Bernard, Footprints on the Sands of Time (Wiltshire, 1990).
Jasper, Ronald C.D., George Bell, Bishop of Chichester (London, 1967).
Kranzler, D. and Hirschler, G., Solomon Schonfeld: His Page in History (New York, 1982).
Morrison, Herbert (Lord Morrison of Lambeth), Herbert Morrison: An Autobiography (London, 1960).
Reading, Eva, For the Record; The Memoirs of Eva, Marchioness of Reading (London, 1973).
Roberts, Frank, Dealing with Dictators: The Destruction and Revival of Europe 1930–70 (London, 1991).
Rose, Norman, Lewis Namier and Zionism (Oxford, 1980).
Samuel, Viscount H., Memoirs (London, 1945).
Shepherd, Naomi, Wilfred Israel: German Jewry's Secret Ambassador (London, 1984).
Shinwell, E., Lead with the Left: My first 96 Years (London, 1981).
Stocks, Mary. Eleanor Rathbone: A Biography (London, 1949).
Templewood, First Viscount (Sir Samuel Hoare), Nine Troubled Years (London, 1954).

Wedgwood, C.V. *The Last of the Radicals, Josiah Wedgwood* (1951).
Wedgwood, Josiah C., *Memoirs of a Fighting Life* (London, 1941).
Weichert, Michael, *Yidishe Aleinhilf* (Tel Aviv, 1963), trans. Esther Held, London, 1994.
Weizmann, Chaim, *Trial and Error* (London, 1949).
Wiesel, Elie, *All Rivers Run to the Sea* (London, 1996).

Secondary Sources

Books

Abella, Irving and Troper, Harold, *None is Too Many. Canada and the Jews of Europe* (Ontario, 1986).
Alderman, Geoffrey, *Federation of Synagogues* (London 1987).
—— *London Jewry and London Politics 1889–1986* (London 1988).
—— *Modern British Jewry* (Oxford 1992).
Angell, Norman and Buxton, Dorothy Frances, *You and the Refugee: The Morals and Economics of the Problem* (London, 1939).
Archives of the Holocaust, An International Collection of Selected Documents, Jonathan Helfand, ed., vol. 18, Yeshiva University (London, 1991).
Balfour, Michael, *Propaganda in War 1939–1945: Organisations, Policies and Publics in Britain and Germany* (London, 1979).
Barkai, A., *Boycott to Annihilation: The Economic Struggle of German Jews, 1933–1943* (London, 1989).
Bauer, Yehuda, *American Jewry and the Holocaust: The American Jewish Joint Distribution Committee, 1939–1945* (Detroit, 1981).
—— *Jewish Reactions to the Holocaust* (Jerusalem, 1989).
—— *Jews for Sale? Nazi-Jewish Negotiations, 1933–1945* (New Haven, 1994)
Behrens, C.B.A., *Merchant Shipping and the Demands of War* (London, 1955)
Bentwich, Norman, *They Found Refuge* (London, 1956).
—— *Wanderers in the War 1939–1945* (London, 1946).
—— *Wanderer between Two Worlds* (London, 1941).
—— *Jewish Youth Comes Home 1933–1943* (Connecticut, 1944).
Berghahn, Marion, *Continental Britons: German-Jewish Refugees from Nazi Germany* (Oxford, 1988).
Bermant, Chaim, *The Cousinhood: The Anglo-Jewish Gentry* (London, 1971).
—— *Troubled Eden: An Anatomy of British Jewry* (London, 1969).
Black, Eugene C., *The Social Politics of Anglo-Jewry 1880–1920* (Oxford, 1988).
Blakeney, Michael, *Australia and the Jewish Refugees 1933–1948* (Sydney, 1985).
Bolchover, Richard, *British Jewry and the Holocaust* (Cambridge, 1993).
Braham, Randolph L., ed., *Jewish Leadership during the Nazi Era: Patterns of Behavior in the Free World* (New York, 1985).
—— *The Politics of Genocide: The Holocaust in Hungary*, vol. 2 (New York, 1981).
Brecher, Frank, *Reluctant Ally: United States Policy Toward the Jews from Wilson to Roosevelt* (New Haven, 1992).
Breitman, Richard and Kraut, Alan M., *American Refugee Policy and European Jewry, 1933–1945* (Bloomington, 1987).

Burleigh, M. and Wippermann, W., *The Racial State: Germany 1933–1945* (Cambridge, 1991).
Butler, David and Stokes, Donald, *Political Change in Britain: Forces Shaping Electoral Choice* (London, 1969).
Butler, J.R.M., *History of the Second World War: Grand Strategy*, vol. III, part II (1964).
Butterfield, Herbert, *History and Human Relations* (London, 1951).
Cesarani, David, *The Jewish Chronicle and Anglo-Jewry 1841–1991* (Cambridge, 1994).
Cesarani, David, ed., *The Making of Modern Anglo-Jewry* (Oxford, 1990).
—— *The Final Solution: Origins and Implementation* (London, 1994).
—— *The Jewish Chronicle and Anglo-Jewry, 1841–1991* (Cambridge, 1994).
Cohen, Michael J., *Churchill and the Jews* (London, 1985).
Cohen, Stuart, *English Zionists and British Jews* (Princeton, 1982).
Cooper, Howard and Morrison, Paul, *A Sense of Belonging: Dilemmas of British Jewish Identity* (London, 1991).
Cornwell, John, *Hitler's Pope: The Secret History of Pius XII* (New York, 2000).
Darton, Lawrence, *An Account of the Work of the Friends Committee for Refugees and Aliens* (London, 1954).
Dawidowicz, L. *The War Against the Jews 1933–1945* (London, 1975).
Ehrman, J., *Grand Strategy*, vol. V (London, 1956).
Emden, Paul H., *Jews in Britain: A Series of Biographies* (London, 1944).
Endelman, Todd, *Radical Assimilation In English Jewish History, 1656–1945* (Bloomington, 1990).
Engel, David, *In the Shadow of Auschwitz: The Polish Government-in-Exile and the Jews, 1939–1942* (London, 1987).
—— *Facing the Holocaust: The Polish Government-in-Exile and the Jews, 1943–1945* (London, 1993).
Feldman, David, *Englishmen and Jews* (London, 1994).
Feingold, Henry, L., *Politics of Rescue: The Roosevelt Administration and the Holocaust 1938–1945* (New Brunswick, 1970).
Finger, Seymour Maxwell, ed., *The Goldenberg Report, American Jewry During The Holocaust* (New York, 1984).
Fisher, Roger and Ury, William, *Getting to Yes: Negotiating an Agreement without Giving in* (London, 1982, 1996).
Friedman, Isaiah, *The Question of Palestine, 1914–1918: British-Jewish-Arab Relations* (London, 1973).
Forster, E.M., *Two Cheers for Democracy* (London, 1951).
Fraenkel, Josef, *The History of the British Section of the World Jewish Congress* (London, 1976).
Friedman, Saul S., *No Haven for the Oppressed: United States Policy toward Jewish Refugees, 1938–1945* (Detroit, 1973).
Fuchs, Abraham, *The Unheeded Cry* (New York, 1984).
Gainer, Bernard, *The Alien Invasion: The Origins of the Aliens Act of 1905* (London, 1972).
Gannon, Franklin R., *The British Press and Nazi Germany 1936–1939* (Oxford, 1971).
Gartner, Lloyd P., *The Jewish Immigrant in England 1870–1914* (London, 1973).

Gershon, Karen, ed., *We Came as Children: A Collective Autobiography* (London, 1966, 1989).

Gilbert, Martin, *Auschwitz and the Allies* (London, 1981).

—— *Second World War* (London, 1999)

Gillman, P. and Gillman, L., *'Collar The Lot'. How Britain Interned and Deported its Wartime Refugees* (London, 1980).

Gollancz, Victor, *Let My People Go* (London, 1942).

Gottlieb Zahl, Amy, *Men of Vision: Anglo-Jewry's Aid to the Victims of the Nazi Regime 1933–1945* (London, 1998).

Gould, Julius and Esh, Shaul, *Jewish Life in Modern Britain* (London, 1964).

Graf, Malvina, *The Krakow Ghetto and the Plaszow Camp Remembered* (Florida, 1989).

Hertz, Joseph H., *Readings from Holy Scriptures (annotated) – for the Jewish Members of His Majesty's Forces* (London, 1942, 1944).

Hilberg, Raul, *The Destruction of the European Jews* (Great Britain, 1985).

—— *Perpetrators Victims Bystanders: The Jewish Catastrophe 1933–1945* (New York, 1992).

Hirschfeld, Gerhard, *Exile in Great Britain: Refugees from Hitler's Germany* (London, 1984).

Holmes, Colin, *Anti-Semitism in British Society, 1879–1939* (London, 1979).

—— *John Bull's Island: Immigration and British Society 1871–1971* (London, 1988).

Homa, Bernard, *Orthodoxy in Anglo-Jewry 1880–1940* (London, 1969).

—— *A Fortress in Anglo-Jewry: The Story of Machzike Adath* (London, 1952).

Howard, M., *History of the Second World War: Grand Strategy*, vol. IV (London, 1972).

Jakobovits, Immanuel, *'If Only My People . . .': Zionism in My Life* (London, 1984).

Josephs, Zoe, *Survivors: Jewish Refugees in Birmingham 1933–1945* (Exeter, 1988).

Kranzler, David, *Thy Brother's Blood: The Orthodox Jewish Response during the Holocaust* (New York, 1987).

—— *The Man who Stopped the Trains to Auschwitz: George Montello, El Salvador and Switzerland's Finest Hour* (Syracuse, 2000).

Kubowitzki, Leon A., *Unity in Dispersion: A History of the World Jewish Congress* (New York, 1948).

Kushner, Tony, *The Holocaust and the Liberal Imagination: A Social and Cultural History* (Oxford, 1994).

—— *Persistence of Prejudice: Antisemitism in British Society During the Second World War* (Manchester, 1988).

Lafitte, François, *The Internment of Aliens* (London, 1988).

Laqueur, Walter, *The Terrible Secret: An Investigation into the Suppression of Information about Hitler's 'Final Solution'* (London, 1980).

Laski, Neville, *Jewish Rights and Jewish Wrongs* (London, 1939).

Lebzelter, G.C., *Political Anti-Semitism in England, 1918–1939* (London, 1978).

Legters, Lyman H., ed., *Western Society after the Holocaust* (Boulder, Colorado, 1983).

Levin, S.S., ed., *A Century of Anglo-Jewish Life: Lectures to Commemorate the Century of the United Synagogue* (London, 1970).

Leverton, B. and Lowensohn, S., *I Came Alone: The Stories of the Kindertransports* (Sussex, 1990).
Levy, Isaac, *Witness to Evil: Bergen Belsen 1945* (London, 1995).
Lipman, V.D., *A History of the Jews in Britain since 1858* (Leicester, 1990).
Lipman, V.D., ed., *Three Centuries of Anglo-Jewish History* (Cambridge, 1961).
London, L., *Whitehall and the Jews 1933–1948: British Immigration Policy and the Holocaust* (Cambridge, 2000).
Lookstein, H., *Were We Our Brother's Keepers? The Public Response of American Jewry to the Holocaust, 1938–1944* (New York, 1985).
Mackenzie, Robert T. and Silver, Allan, *Angels in Marble, Working Class Conservatives in Urban England* (London, 1968).
Mamatey, Victor S. and Luza, Radomir, *A History of the Czechoslovak Republic, 1918–1948* (Princeton, 1973).
Marrus, Michael R., *The Holocaust in History* (London, 1987).
—— *The Unwanted, European Refugees in the Twentieth Century* (Oxford, 1985).
Marrus, Michael R. and Bramwell, Anna C., eds., *Refugees in the Age of Total War.* (London, 1988).
Marrus, Michael R and Paxton, Robert O., *Vichy France and the Jews* (New York, 1983).
Mckibbin, Ross, *Classes and Cultures: England, 1918–1951* (Oxford, 1998).
Medlicott, W.N., *The Economic Blockade*, 2 vols. (London, 1952, 1959).
Medoff, R., *The Deafening Silence: American Jewish Leaders and the Holocaust* (New York, 1987).
Mill, John Stuart, *On Liberty* (London, 1859, 1974).
Morse, Arthur D., *While Six Million Died* (London, 1968).
Mosse, Werner E., *Second Chance, Two Centuries of German-Speaking Jews in the United Kingdom* (Tubingen, 1991).
Newman, A., *The United Synagogue* (London, 1976).
Oppenheim, A.N., *The Chosen People: The Story of the '222 Transport' from Bergen-Belsen to Palestine* (London, 1996).
Orwell, Sonia, and Angus, Ian, eds., *The Collected Essays, Journalism and Letters of George Orwell* (London, 1968), Volumes II and III (1940–1945).
Overy, Richard J., *Why the Allies Won* (London, 1995).
Pankiewicz, Tadeusz, *The Crakow Ghetto Pharmacy* (New York, 1987).
Papastratis, Procopis, *British Policy towards Greece during the Second World War, 1941–1944* (Cambridge, 1984).
Patkin, Benzion, *The Dunera Internees* (Sydney, 1972).
Pehle, Walter H., ed., *November 1938: From 'Reichskristallnacht' to Genocide* (Oxford, 1991).
Penkower, M., *The Jews Were Expendable: Free World Diplomacy and the Holocaust* (Illinois, 1983).
Perl, William R., *The Holocaust Conspiracy: An International Policy of Genocide* (New York, 1989).
Pollins, Harold, *Economic History of the Jews in England* (London, 1982).
Porat, Dina, *The Blue and Yellow Stars of David: The Zionist Leadership in Palestine and the Holocaust, 1939–1945* (London, 1990).
Presland, J., *A Great Adventure: The Story of the Refugee Children's Movement* (London, 1944).

Presser, J., *Ashes in the Wind: The Destruction of Dutch Jewry* (London, 1968).

Proudfoot, Malcolm. *European Refugees: A Study in Forced Population Movement 1939–52* (London, 1957).

Rathbone, Eleanor, *Rescue the Perishing* (London, 1943).

Rose, Norman, *Chaim Weizmann; A Biography* (London, 1986).

Rosenau, James N., *Turbulence in World Politics: A Theory of Change and Continuity* (London, 1990).

Rubinstein, William D., *A History of the Jews in the English-Speaking World: Great Britain* (London, 1996).

——— *The Myth of Rescue: Why the Democracies Could not have Saved More Jews from the Nazis* (London, 1997).

Schleunes, Karl A., *Twisted Road to Auschwitz: Nazi Policy toward German Jews 1933–1939* (Chicago, 1970).

Schonfeld, Rabbi Dr. Solomon, *Message to Jewry* (London, 1959).

Sharf, Andrew, *The British Press and Jews Under Nazi Rule* (Oxford, 1964).

Sherman, A.J., *Island Refuge, Britain and Refugees from the Third Reich 1933–1939* (London, 1973, 1994).

Simpson, Sir John Hope, *Refugees, Preliminary Survey of a Survey* (London, July 1938).

——— *The Refugee Problem: Report of a Survey* (Oxford, January 1939).

——— *Refugees: A Review of the Situation since September 1938* (London, August 1939).

Sloan, J., *Notes from the Warsaw Ghetto:The Journal of Emmanuel Ringelblum* (New York, 1958).

Sompolinsky, Meier, *Britain and the Holocaust: The Failure of Anglo-Jewish Leadership?* (Brighton, 1999).

Stein, Leonard, *The Balfour Declaration* (London, 1961).

Stent, Ronald, *A Bespattered Page? The Internment of His Majesty's 'Most Loyal Enemy Aliens'* (London, 1980).

Stevens, Austin, *The Dispossessed, German Refugees in Britain* (London, 1975).

Tartakower, Aryeh, and Grossman, Kurt R., *The Jewish Refugee* (New York, 1944).

Troen, Selwyn Ilan and Pinkus, Benjamin, eds., *Organizing Rescue: Jewish National Solidarity in the Modern Period* (London, 1992).

Turner, Barry, *And the Policeman Smiled ... 10,000 Children Escape from Nazi Germany* (London, 1991).

Tschuy, Theo, *Dangerous Diplomacy: The Story of Carl Lutz* (Cambridge, 2001).

Warhaftig, Zorach, *Refugee and Survivor: Rescue Efforts during the Holocaust* (Jerusalem, 1988).

Wasserstein, Bernard, *Britain and the Jews of Europe, 1939–1945* (Oxford, 1979 and Leicester, 1999).

Wischnitzer, Mark, *To Dwell in Safety: The Story of Jewish Migration since 1800* (Philadelphia, 1949).

Wyman, David S., *Paper Walls: America and The Refugee Crisis 1938–41* (Amherst, Mass. 1968).

——— *The Abandonment of The Jews* (New York, 1984).

Yahil, Leni, *The Holocaust: The Fate of European Jewry, 1932–1945* (Oxford, 1990).

Zweig, Ronald W., *Britain and Palestine during the Second World War* (London, 1986).

Articles

Adler-Rudel, S., 'A Chronicle of Rescue Efforts', *Leo Baeck Institute Year Book*, XI (1966), pp. 213–41.
—— 'The Evian Conference on the Refugee Question', *Leo Baeck Institute Year Book*, XIII (1968), pp. 235–73.
Alderman, Geoffrey, 'British Jewry: Religious Community or Ethnic Minority?', in Jonathan Webber, ed., *Jewish Identities in the New Europe* (London, 1994).
Aronson, Shlomo, 'The "Quadruple Trap" and the Holocaust in Hungary', in D. Cesarani, ed., *Genocide and Rescue: The Holocaust in Hungary 1944* (Oxford, 1997), pp. 93–121.
Bauer, Yehuda, 'When did they Know?', *Midstream*, vol. 14 (April 1968), pp. 51–8.
—— 'Jewish Foreign Policy during the Holocaust', *Midstream*, 30, no. 10 (1984), pp. 22–5.
—— 'Rescue by Negotiations? Jewish Attempts to Negotiate with the Nazis', in M. Marrus, ed., *The Nazi Holocaust*, vol. 9 (London, 1989).
Blidstein, Ya'akov, 'The Redemption of Captives in Halakhic Tradition: Problems and Policy', in Selwyn Ilan Troen and Benjamin Pinkus, eds., *Organizing Rescue: Jewish National Solidarity in the Modern Period* (London, 1992), pp. 20–30.
Board of Deputies of British Jews, 'The Jews in Europe: Their Martyrdom and their Future' (London, 1945).
Braham, Randolph L., 'The Rescue of the Jews of Hungary in Holocaust Perspective', *The Historiography of the Holocaust: Proceedings of the Fifth Yad Vashem International Historical Conference Jerusalem, March 1983*, (Jerusalem, 1988) pp. 447–66.
Breitman, Richard, 'The Allied War Effort and the Jews, 1942–43', *Journal of Contemporary History*, vol. 20, no. 1 (1985), pp. 135–55.
Brotman, A.G., 'Jewish Communal Organisations', in Julius Gould and Shaul Esh, eds., *Jewish Life in Modern Britain* (London, 1964), pp. 1–17.
Carlebach, J., 'The Impact of German Jews on Anglo-Jewish Orthodoxy', in *Second Chance, Two Centuries of German-Speaking Jews in the United Kingdom*, co-ed., W.E. Mosse (Tubingen, 1991), pp. 405–25.
Cesarani, David, 'The Transformation of Communal Authority in Anglo-Jewry, 1914–1940', in Cesarani, D., ed., *The Making of Modern Anglo-Jewry* (Oxford, 1990), pp. 115–40.
—— 'An Embattled Minority: The Jews in Britain During the First World War', in T. Kushner and K. Lunn, eds., *Politics of Marginality: Race, the Radical Right and Minorities in Twentieth Century Britain* (London, 1990), pp. 61–81.
Cohen, Stuart, A., 'Selig Brodetsky and the Ascendancy of Zionism in Anglo-Jewry: Another View of His Role and Achievements', *Jewish Journal of Sociology* vols. 23–24 (1981–82), pp. 25–38.
—— 'Same Places, Different Faces; A Comparison of Anglo-Jewish Conflicts over Zionism During World War I and World War II', S.A. Cohen

and E. Don-Yehiya, eds., *Comparative Jewish Politics Volume II: Conflicts and Consensus in Jewish Political Life* (Tel-Aviv, 1986), pp. 61–78.

—— 'Sources in Israel for the Study of Anglo-Jewish History – An Interim Report', *The Jewish Historical Society of England Transactions*, vol. XXVII, Miscellaneous Part XII (1978–1980), pp. 129–47.

Eck, Nathan, 'The Rescue of Jews with the Aid of Passports and Citizenship Papers of Latin American States', *Yad Vashem Studies*, 1 (Jerusalem, 1957), pp. 125–52.

Endelman, Todd M., 'English Jewish History', *Modern Judaism*, 11 (Johns Hopkins University Press 1991), pp. 91–109.

—— 'Native Jews and Foreign Jews in London, 1870–1914', David Berger, ed., *The Legacy of Jewish Migration: 1881 and its Impact* (New York, 1983), pp. 109–129.

Engel, David, 'The Western Allies and the Holocaust', *Polin*, 1 (1986), pp. 300–15.

Eppler, Elizabeth E., 'The Rescue Work of the World Jewish Congress During the Nazi Period', *Rescue Attempts during the Holocaust: Proceedings of the Second Yad Vashem International Historical Conference Jerusalem, April 1974* (Jerusalem, 1977), pp. 47–69.

Epstein, Isidore, ed., *Joseph Herman Hertz, 1872–1946, In Memoriam* (London, 1947).

Feingold, Henry, 'Roosevelt and the Settlement Question', Michael Marrus, ed., *Bystanders to the Holocaust: The Nazi Holocaust*, vol. 8 (London, 1989), pp. 271–329.

Finestein, Israel, 'Selig Brodetsky 1888–1954: The Prodigy From Fashion Street', *The Jewish East End 1840–1939, Proceedings of the Conference held on 22 October jointly by the Jewish Historical Society of England and the Jewish East End Project of the Association for Jewish Youth* (London, 1981), pp. 99–107.

Ford, Mary, 'Child Refugees in Britain', *Immigrants and Minorities* (1985), pp. 135–51.

Fox, John P., 'Great Britain and the German Jews 1933', *Wiener Library Bulletin*, vol. 36 no. 26/7 (1972), pp. 40–6.

—— 'The Jewish Factor in British War Crimes Policy in 1942', *English Historical Review*, vol. XC11, no. 362 (January 1977), pp. 82–106.

Friedman, Menachem, 'The Haredim and the Holocaust', *The Jerusalem Quarterly*, no. 53 (Winter 1990), pp. 86–114.

Gartner, Lloyd P., 'A Quarter of a Century of Anglo/Jewish Historiography', *Jewish Social Studies* (Spring 1986), pp. 105–26.

Gewirtz, Sharon, 'Anglo-Jewish Responses to Nazi Germany 1933–39: The Anti-Nazi Boycott and the Board of Deputies of British Jews', *Journal of Contemporary History*, vol. 26 (1991), pp. 255–76.

Gilbert, Martin, 'British Government Policy towards Jewish Refugees (November 1937–September 1939)', *Yad Vashem Studies*, vol. X111 (1979), pp. 127–67.

Greenberg, Gershon, '"Faith, Ethics and the Holocaust": Orthodox Theological Responses to *Kristallnacht*: Chayyim Ozer Grodzensky ('Achiezer') and Elchonon Wassermann', *Holocaust and Genocide Studies*, vol. 3, no. 4 (1988), pp. 431–41.

—— 'Sovereignty as Catastrophe: Jakob Rosenheim's *Hurban Weltanschauung'*, *Holocaust and Genocide Studies*, vol. 8, no. 2 (Fall 1994), pp. 202–24.

Hirschfeld, Gerhard, '"A High Tradition of Eagerness..." British Non-Jewish Organisations in Support of Refugees', in W.E. Mosse, ed., *Second Chance, Two Centuries of German-Speaking Jews in the United Kingdom* (Tubingen, 1991), pp. 599–610.

Hoch, P.K., Gaoling the Victim', *Immigrants and Minorities*, vol. 4, no. 1 (March 1985), pp. 79–83.

Hyamson, A.M., 'British Jewry in Wartime', *Contemporary Jewish Record*, vol. VI, no. 1 (February 1943), pp. 14–22.

Jones, Priscilla Dale, 'British Policy towards German Crimes against Jews, 1939–1945', *Leo Baeck Institute Year Book*, vol. XXXIV (1991), pp. 339–66.

Katzburg, Nathaniel, 'British Policy on Immigration to Palestine During World War II', *Rescue Attempts during the Holocaust, Proceedings of the Second Yad Vashem International Historical Conference–April 1974* (Jerusalem, 1977), pp. 183–205.

Keogh, Dermot, 'The Irish Free State and the Refugee Crisis, 1933–45', in Paul R. Bartrop, ed., *False Havens: The British Empire and the Holocaust* (London, 1995), pp. 211–37.

Krikler, B., 'Anglo-Jewish Attitudes to the Rise of Nazism' (unpublished, probably 1960s, Wiener Library, London).

Kushner, Tony, 'The Impact of British Anti-semitism, 1918–1945', in D. Cesarani, ed., *The Making of Modern Anglo-Jewry* (Oxford, 1990), pp. 191–208.

Laqueur, Walter, 'Jewish Denial and the Holocaust', *Commentary*, vol. 68, no. 6 (July–December 1979), pp. 44–55.

Lewin, Isaac, 'Attempts at Rescuing European Jews with the Help of the Polish Diplomatic Missions during World War Two', *The Polish Review*, vol. XXII, no. 4 (1977), pp. 3–23.

Lipman, V. D., 'Anglo-Jewish Attitudes to the Refugees from Central Europe 1933–1939', in W.E. Mosse, co-ed., *Second Chance, Two Centuries of German-Speaking Jews in the United Kingdom* (Tubingen 1991), pp. 519–32.

London, Louise, 'British Immigration Control Procedures and Jewish Refugees 1933–1939', in W.E. Mosse, co-ed., *Second Chance. Two Centuries of German Speaking Jews in the United Kingdom* (Tubingen 1991), pp. 485–517.

—— 'British Government Policy and Jewish Refugees 1933–1945', *Patterns of Prejudice*, 23 (1989–90), pp. 26–43.

—— 'Jewish Refugees and British Government Policy, 1930–1940', in D. Cesarani, ed., *The Making of Modern Anglo-Jewry* (Oxford 1990), pp. 163–90.

Mates, Leo, 'The Holocaust and International Relations', in Lyman H. Legters, ed., *Western Society after the Holocaust* (Boulder, Colorado, 1983), pp. 113–47.

Mendelson, E., 'The Politics of Agudas Yisroel in the Inter-War Period', *Soviet Jewish Affairs*, vol. 2, no. 2 (1972).

Milton, S., 'The Expulsion of Polish Jews from Germany: October 1938–July 1939: Documentation', *Leo Baeck Institute Year Book*, 29 (1984), pp. 169–99.

Prendergast, Dame Simone, 'The Jewish Refugees Committee 1933–1987', *Association of Jewish Refugees* (February 1988), p. 2.

Rosenstock, Werner, 'Exodus 1933–1939. A Survey of Jewish Emigration from Germany', *Leo Baeck Institute Year Book* 1 (1956), pp. 373–90.

Seyfert, Michael, 'His Majesty's Most Loyal Internees', in Gerhard, Hirshfeld, ed., *Exile in Great Britain* (Oxford, 1984), pp. 163–93.

Shatzkes, Pamela, 'Kobe, A Japanese Haven for Jewish Refugees, 1940–1941', *Japan Forum*, vol. 3, no. 2 (September 1991), pp. 257–73.

Shimoni, Gideon, 'From Anti-Zionism to Non-Zionism in Anglo-Jewry, 1917–1937', *Jewish Journal of Sociology*, 28:1 (1986), pp. 19–47.

—— 'The Non-Zionists in Anglo-Jewry, 1937–48', *Jewish Journal of Sociology*, 28:2 (1986), pp. 89–115.

—— 'Selig Brodetsky and the Ascendancy of Zionism in Anglo-Jewry 1939–1945', *Jewish Journal of Sociology*, 22:2 (1980), pp. 125–61.

Silberklang, David, 'Jewish Politics and Rescue: The Founding of the Council for German Jewry', *Holocaust and Genocide Studies*, vol. 7, no. 3 (Winter 1993), pp. 333–71.

Sompolinsky, Meir, 'Anglo-Jewish Leadership and the British Government, Attempts at Rescue 1944–1945', *Yad Vashem Studies*, vol. 13 (1979), pp. 211–47.

—— 'Jewish Institutions in the World and the Yishuv as Reflected in the Holocaust Historiography of the Ultra-Orthodox', *The Historiography of the Holocaust: Proceedings of the Fifth Yad Vashem International Historical Conference Jerusalem, March 1983*(Jerusalem 1988), pp. 609–30.

Stiebel, Joan, 'The Central British Fund for World Jewish Relief', *Transactions of the Jewish Historical Society of England*, Sessions 1978–1980 vol. 27 and Miscellaneous Part XII (1982), pp. 51–60.

Stent, Ronald, 'Jewish Refugee Organisations', in W.E. Mosse, co-ed., *Second Chance, Two Centuries of German-Speaking Jews in the United Kingdom* (Tubingen, 1991), pp. 579–98.

Strauss, Herbert A., 'Jewish Emigration from Germany: Nazi Policies and Jewish Responses' (1), *Leo Beck Institute Year Book*, XXV (1980), pp. 313–61.

—— 'Jewish Emigration from Germany: Nazi Policies and Jewish Responses' (2), *Leo Beck Institute Year Book*, XXVI (1981), pp. 344–409.

Union of Orthodox Hebrew Congregations, 'The Child Estranging Movement' (London, January 1944).

Vago, Bela, 'The British Government and the Fate of Hungarian Jewry in 1944', *Rescue Attempts during the Holocaust: Proceedings of the Second Yad Vashem International Historical Conference Jerusalem, April 1974* (Jerusalem, 1977), pp. 205–24.

Warhaftig, Zorach, 'Relief and Rehabilitation', *Institute of Jewish Affairs* (New York, 1944).

Wasserstein, Bernard, 'The British Government and the German Immigration 1939–1945', in G. Hirschfeld, ed., *Exile in Great Britain* (London, 1984), pp. 63–82.

—— 'Patterns of Jewish Leadership in Great Britain during the Nazi Era', in Randolph Braham, ed., *Jewish Leadership during the Nazi Era: Patterns of Behaviour in the Free World* (New York, 1985), pp. 29–45.

—— 'The Myth of "Jewish Silence"', *Midstream* (August–September 1980), pp. 10–16.

—— 'The Tyranny of Conventional Assumption: The Jewish Refugee Issue in Britain 1939–1945', *CBF Conference on Jewish Refugees and Refugee Work 1933–1993* (unpublished, London, March 1993).

Williams, Bill, 'The Anti-semitism of Tolerance: Middle Class Manchester and the Jews 1870–1900', in A.J. Kidd and K.W. Roberts, co-eds., *City, Class and Culture: Studies of Social Policy and Cultural Production in Victorian Manchester* (Manchester, 1985), pp. 74–102.

Yahil, Leni, 'The Historiography of the Refugee Problem and of Rescue Efforts in the Neutral Countries', *The Historiography of the Holocaust: Proceedings of the Fifth Yad Vashem International Historical Conference Jerusalem, March 1983* (Jerusalem 1988), pp. 513–33.

Zwergbaum, Aaron, 'Exile in Mauritius', *Yad Vashem Studies*, IV (Jerusalem 1960), pp. 191–257.

Zweig, Ronald W., 'Feeding the Camps: Allied Blockade and the Relief of Concentration Camps in Germany, 1944–1945', *Historical Journal* (September 1998).

Index

Note: Bold page numbers refer to illustrations

Britons, The, nationalist
  group 30
Brodetsky, Professor Selig 10,
  14–15, **111**, 188
  appeal to Archbishop of
    Canterbury 115
  assessment of 6, 220–2, 227, 228
  and British Section 41
  and call to bomb
    Auschwitz 151, 155
  and Consultative Committee 39
  and food parcel schemes 192,
    193, 198, 199
  and fund-raising 212
  and guarantees to neutrals 137,
    234
  and Hungarian crisis 144, 147,
    161
  and IGCR 138
  importance of Palestine to 109,
    114, 125
  lack of political flair 221–2,
    230, 231, 234, 235 6
  opposition to Schonfeld's
    initiatives 122–3
  and relief teams in USSR
    214–15
  rescue proposals 119, 139, 140,
    173
  'Suggested Steps for Saving
    Jews. . .' 120
  view of internment 87, 90–1,
    93, 94
  view of Jewish persecution 101
  Zionism of 6, 15, 22–3, 43, 220
Brotman, A.G. 15, 43, **113**
  appeal for shipping 133
  assessment of 223–4, 227, 228,
    230
  and call to bomb
    Auschwitz 151, 154
  and exchange schemes 169
  and food parcel scheme 194,
    196, 199–200, 201
  and Hungarian crisis 144, 155,
    159
  on internment 91
  on news of Final Solution 112,
    116–17

opposition to Schonfeld's
  initiatives 123
relations with Foreign
  Office 125, 159
urges Jewish exceptionalism 115
Budapest 63, 155, 160
Bulgaria 126, 159, 178
  Jewish children 107, 168, 178–9
  Jewish Relief Unit in 214

Cabinet Committees
  on Alien Restrictions (1933) 26
  on Reception and
    Accommodation of
    Refugees 118
Cable Street, Battle of (1936) 32
Camps, W.A. 192, 198
Canada 60, 85, 91, 97, 98
Canterbury, Archbishop of (Cosmo
  Gordon Lang), and
  Schonfeld 37, 115
Canterbury, Archbishop of
  (William Temple) 118, 123–4,
  149
  and Schonfeld 122, 123
Casablanca Conference
  (1943) 163
Cazalet, Col. Victor 131, 132,
  247n
Central British Fund 2, 26–7, 168
Central British Fund for Jewish
  Relief and Rehabilitation 203,
  209, 211
Central Committee for
  Internees 94, 95, 97
Central Council for Jewish
  Refugees 83–4, 168, 196
  fund-raising 84, 193, 196, 257n,
    260n
  and internment 87, 92
  see also Council for German
    Jewry
Central Office of Refugees 92
Chamberlain, Houston Stewart 19
Chamberlain, Neville 67, 233
Cheetham, Cynthia, Lady 154,
  159, 239
Chelmno, extermination
  camp 110